WITHDRAWN

The
Partition
of
Palestine

SUNY Series in Israeli Studies

Russell Stone, Editor

The Partition of Palestine

Decision Crossroads in the Zionist Movement

Itzhak Galnoor

STATE UNIVERSITY OF NEW YORK PRESS

Cover map: Partition plan of 1937

Production by Ruth Fisher
Marketing by Dana E. Yanulavich

Published by
State University of New York Press, Albany

For information, address the State University of New York Press,
State University Plaza, Albany, NY 12246

Library of Congress Cataloging-in-Publication Data
Galnoor, Itzhak.
    The partition of Palestine :   decision crossroads in the Zionist
movement / Itzhak Galnoor.
        p.   cm.
    Includes bibliographical references and index.
    ISBN 0-7914-2193-7 (alk. paper). —   ISBN 0-7914-2194-5 (pbk. :
alk. paper)
    1. Palestine—History—Proposed partition, 1937. 2. Zionism—
History. I. Title.
DS126.G32   1995
956.94'04—dc20   93-51016
                                                                          CIP

10 9 8 7 6 5 4 3 2 1

Dedicated to the memory of
Dan (Dindush) Horowitz

Contents

Illustrations

Figures

Maps

Tables

Acknowledgments

This book is part of a more comprehensive study by the author about "state, territory, and boundaries." The research was supported by grants from the Israel Foundations Trustees (1986–1989) and the Basic Research Foundation of the Israeli Academy of Sciences and Humanities. I began the research in 1986, during a sabbatical year at the Ben-Gurion Research Center, at Sde Boqer. I would like to thank all people in the center and the Ben-Gurion Archives for their assistance and valuable contribution. In the final stage of preparing the book, I was assisted by research grants from the Faculty of Social Sciences and the Shaine Center, both at the Hebrew University. Three of my best graduate students in the Political Science Department of the Hebrew University participated in the research: Danna Arieli-Horowitz, Avner de-Shalit, and Yosef Hetz. I am greatly indebted to them, and to my friend Gila Svirsky, who edited this manuscript, for their contributions to this study. Special thanks to my colleagues for their extremely useful comments at various stages of the writing: Michael Brecher, Yosef Gorni, Yosef Heller, Baruch Kimmerling, Charles Liebman, Eli Shaltiel, and Stanley Waterman. I would also like to thank Lisa Gann-Perkal, who translated the manuscript into English.

I dedicated this book to the memory of my friend Dan Horowitz, who accompanied this study from its inception and did not spare his razor sharp criticism from the chapters in the first draft that he had a chance to read. I missed his incisive thought and his intellectual chiding as the book progressed, and I miss his friendship now.

Introduction

> The desire to acquire territorial possessions is a very natural and ordinary thing, and when those men do it who can do so successfully, they are always praised and not blamed, but when they cannot and want to do so at all costs, they make a mistake deserving of great blame.
>
> —N. Machiavelli, *The Prince*[1]

Some seventy years since the boundaries of the British Mandate for Palestine (E.I.)[2] were set, the state of Israel still lacks a defined territory and agreed-upon borders, other than the Mediterranean Sea and the border with Egypt. This unusual situation, as well as the ongoing internal debate within Israeli society about the future of the territories conquered in 1967, influenced my decision to study the perceptions of territory and boundaries within the Zionist movement.

I took a first step in this direction with my colleague Abraham Diskin in a content analysis of the positions presented in the Israeli Knesset (parliament) during the debates on the peace agreements with Egypt.[3] An additional catalyst was the Lebanon War in June 1982, and the Israeli government's declaration at its outset that it has no territorial claims in Lebanon.[4] The declaration surprised me enough to warrant a reexamination of the biblical sources, to confirm that southern Lebanon is part of the Promised Land—the historic Eretz Israel. It was included in the promise made to the Israelites when they came out of Egypt, assigned to the tribe of Asher (Joshua 19:28), and certainly part of the kingdom of David and Solomon. Furthermore, in 1919 the Zionist Organization claimed an area in south Lebanon ("the northern Galilee") as part of the "national home" at the Versailles Peace Conference.[5] Why, I asked myself, is there such a sharp distinction between southern Lebanon and other parts of Eretz Israel, parts considered holy and nonnegotiable by many Israelis?

1

Next I returned to Machiavelli, where I found unequivocal support for the "realpolitik" of territorial conquest. But this raised other questions: What is this "natural and ordinary desire" to acquire territories? Does territory bear absolute or relative importance in collective human behavior? Is this how nations actually conduct their territorial politics? Is Napoleon's famous dictum— "La Politique de toutes les puissances est dans leur geographie" ["The politics of all great powers is inherent in their geography"]— debatable?

In conversations with the late Professor Albert Hourani of St. Antony's College in Oxford, we discussed Arab and Jewish attitudes toward territory and boundaries in the Middle East. I learned from him that this subject had not been researched in the wideranging literature on Arab and Palestinian nationalism. Later I discovered that there was also no such focused research in the many studies on the Zionist movement, the state of Israel, or the Arab-Israeli conflict.

Hence, the subject of this book, crystallized in this round-about way, exceeds the specific case of the local conflict. The general question, simply stated, is this: Which has the upper hand in territorial decisions—politics or geography? Therefore the book opens and closes with a general theoretical discussion of state, territory, and boundaries. The more limited purpose of this book, however, is to analyze the main internal decisions of the pre-1948 Zionist movement on the question of territory and boundaries and the arguments and positions underlying these decisions. To do this, I examine in detail the most important *internal* decision leading up to the establishment of the state of Israel—the Zionist movement's 1937 decision in response to the report issued by the British Royal Commission headed by Lord Peel.

My initial intention was to use the 1937 decision as a pilot study for an examination of the theoretical and methodological framework. I decided to see it published separately when I realized that the partition *pulmus*[6] of 1937 encompasses the territorial dilemmas that have attended the Zionist movement and the state of Israel (and perhaps also the Palestinian movement) ever since, despite profound changes of circumstance and historical context. The reader should know, therefore, that in writing this book, I became increasingly convinced that the pre-1948 decisions are very relevant to the understanding of the broader dimensions of the current Arab-Palestinian–Israeli conflict. In Chapter Eleven, I discuss this issue explicitly.

Most of the book is devoted to analysis and comparison of the various positions regarding territory and boundaries leading up to the 1937 decision. I then examine the decision-making process, the content of the decision, its significance for the Zionist movement, and the meaning of this decision in terms of the theoretical issues raised in Chapter One. The final chapter stands back from the 1937 decision, placing it in the wider context of the territorial decisions made before the establishment of the state of Israel.

The key question in this book is whether the Zionist movement, in its decisions before 1948, was willing to consider a trade-off between territory and other values. With this question before us, and keeping in mind the more general aims of this book, a number of limitations have been imposed on this study, which should be noted:

- This book does not provide a chronology of events, except for purposes of background. Accordingly, no attempt is made to systematically present the developments in the Jewish world, the Zionist movement, or the Jewish community in Palestine (the *Yishuv*) during this critical period on the eve of World War II.

- The focus here is on the decisions adopted within the Zionist movement—its institutions and leadership—following publication of the Royal Commission report. All other important factors—the British government, the League of Nations, the Palestinian Arabs, and the Arab states— constitute the "environment" for our analysis of the internal debate and decisions. These external factors come up as constraints that influenced the participants' political behavior, for example, the feeling among most of those in the Zionist movement that a decision could be avoided; and, second, as background material that fed the participants' speculations concerning future events and thus influenced their arguments and positions, as well as the decision itself.

- The sources for this study are mainly what was said by participants in the various party, movement, and public forums. Do these pronouncements really reflect their true opinions? For purposes of this study, the inner thoughts of the individuals involved are immaterial. We are interested only in their political positions as presented in closed meetings or publicly. When a disparity between their positions in the debate and their subsequent votes was discovered, it is important to our subject and examined closely.

• The 1937 debate is discussed in the language of the time, hence the need to quote extensively from the available material. Occasionally, however, I could not resist the temptation to formulate the issue in the language of the contemporary discourse. For example, I labeled the disagreement concerning the need for a Jewish majority in the partitioned state as a *demographic* issue. Indeed, the more I read the arguments presented in 1937, the more I realized how little has changed over the past fifty years in the fundamental debate on territory and boundaries. Not a single argument raised today on these issues by both Israelis and Palestinians was not expressed back then by the participants in the debate.

• The theoretical framework used here forces the arguments and choices into categories that do not exist as such in political reality. The debaters themselves might well have refused to locate themselves on the continuum of positions as given in Chapter Four, objecting that their arguments were more varied and nuanced than represented here. That is quite possible. But to clarify the main positions, it was necessary to distill the central arguments and treat them comparatively. Sharpening our observations on a specific object is a tool for illuminating a complex reality, as long as the purpose and the object (in this case, territorial attitudes are well-defined.

• Finally, the purpose of this study is not to reveal new historical facts or to bring new material to light. It processes mainly known material from a different angle and for different research requirements.

I have allowed myself one small departure from the rather strict approach of this study, a visit to the Tonhalle auditorium in Zurich where the Twentieth Zionist Congress met in 1937. I brought along a photograph of the festive opening session of the congress, and was amazed to see that the room had barely changed. I sat in the empty hall and imagined the delegates filling up the rows and the balconies on either side, Weizmann and Ussishkin at the center of the dais, before them a black-bordered inscription, "Nahum

Sokolow, of blessed memory," and behind them a looming portrait of Herzl. In two corners of the hall stood the flags that, in a decade, would become the flag of the state of Israel; and for one brief moment, I could feel the burden of responsibility weighing on the congress delegates in the fateful decision of 1937.

1 State, Territory, and Boundaries: A General Discussion

> The land should be large enough to support a certain
> number of people living moderately and no more.
>
> *The Laws of Plato*, Book V, § 737

The ability to link a particular territory to one particular group is essential to the definition of the modern nation-state. Does this mean that a particular territory associated with one national group will have clear and precise boundaries? This question raises the complexity of the relationships among "nation-state," "territory," and "boundaries." Other characteristics of the nation-state—a common heritage or a common language, for example—often breed territorial fluidity and indistinct boundaries between states and peoples. The territorial identity of the nation-state is such a new phenomenon that, according to recent research, even France— perhaps the model of a territorial nation-state—became one only in the middle of the nineteenth century and not in the revolution of 1789.[1] A deeper complication is the question of the territorial motivation of individuals and communities. Is the territorial behavior of people analogous to that of animals, that is, essentially instinctive? What indeed is the function of territory?

Territorial Behavior

The territorial instinct of certain animals, including the need to set boundaries, is one of the main research interests of ethology, the study of the biology of behavior, particularly the comparative study of animal behavior.[2] Human ethology examines these behavioral patterns among humans. Although the subject is fascinating, findings are not conclusive about the motivations or patterns of human

7

territorial activity. There is consensus among ethologists that territoriality among some animals is inherited and instinctive, but generalizations about territoriality are not clear for animals at a higher level of development. "Pure" territoriality exists, for example, among lower primates, while those that are more developed—such as chimpanzees and baboons—have no group-protected territory.[3]

Empirical studies about the territorial behavior of humans as individuals and in groups are still few and relatively new. Some literature speculates that human territorialism is instinctive, and expressed in violence and belligerence, which is intended to ensure identity and defense.[4] But applying research conclusions about animal behavior to the behavior of humans is not possible, also because we still lack evidence and a clear understanding of human territorial behavior.[5] In general, the existence of an inherited "territorial imperative" among humans that is rooted in their evolutionary past and that dictates their drive to control or defend territory has not yet been proven.

Critics of the popular approach point out the lack of evidence that human territorial behavior is homologous to that of animals.[6] Most ethologists maintain that despite the superficial similarity, the needs that human territoriality is intended to satisfy are on an entirely different evolutionary plane (and not just "higher"), such as self-identity, prestige and status, and the desire for accomplishment and reward.[7] In collective human behavior, the analogy to animals is almost entirely obscured by the fact that communities and nations compete mainly for power, of which territorial control is just one component, and occasionally only instrumental at that. For example, human communities have proven that they are capable of relinquishing territory not only to survive, but also to attain other common goals such as social homogeneity or economic advantage.[8] Moreover, the individualism of the modern human being is clearly a "deviation" from territorial determinism.

This short discussion about human territorial behavior raises the question of causal relations in the role of territory. Let us set aside this question at the level of the individual, and begin to focus on the various approaches concerning peoples and states.

The Roles of Territory

"Geography does not argue, it simply is," noted Spykman to emphasize the influence of geography on the state.[9] This approach may lead to "geographical determinism," according to which human events, or at least political events between states, are no more than an accumulation of geographical facts. A particular territory forms a particular community, and this relationship is therefore the primary explanation for what transpires inside the community and in its external behavior. Interestingly, some determinists actually invert the order of the causal explanation. Fichte, for example, argued that "it is not because men dwell between certain mountains and rivers that they are a people, but on the contrary, men dwell together . . . because they were a people already by a law of nature which is much higher."[10]

In the same way, the claim that boundaries between states must coincide with linguistic maps turns common language, and not necessarily common territory, into the main factor behind the formation of the nation-state. All these approaches strive for an objective standard, or a natural law, to explain how the relationship develops between a human community and territory. The other approach is entirely opposite: "The territory is a physical manifestation of the state's authority, and yet allegiance to territory or homeland makes territory appear as a source of authority."[11]

Here, territory is entirely passive, and it becomes a motivating and activating factor only through human beliefs and actions. Therefore, territory in the modern state has a specific function: the expression of political power, the control of access to distinguish between the included and the excluded, the determination of social relations defined as citizenship, and the conduct of international relations according to territorial partitions between states. This approach bestows on territory a central role in collective behavior while eliminating most of its emotional content. Land becomes a natural endowment, a resource like any other, and not the homeland, fatherland, or motherland.

But what about the well-known subjective element in the territorial behavior of peoples and states? Can it be viewed simply as the legitimization of other needs, as a means for attaining other goals? We know that peoples identify with a particular territory and even imbue it with their national and cultural essence, past and future.[12] For this reason, this book separates the collective roles of territory into two categories. This first is the emotional attachment of people who relate to territory as an inseparable part of their individual and collective identity and therefore also of the nation. The second is the functional orientation of people who relate to territory as a means of satisfying defined needs rooted in culture, society, and politics. The first approach, when distilled, is reminiscent of the "territorial imperative" argument, whereas the second approach, when it views territory solely as a device for advancing other needs, ignores its symbolic and emotional significance, thus exaggerating its functionalism.[13]

The approach adopted in this book is based on Gottmann, who refused to create iron-clad rules of motivation, but recognized the duality in the attachment to territory "as a geographical expression both of a social function and of an institution rooted in the psychology of people."[14] It stems from this that emotional needs and functional needs abide together. We cannot ignore them—nor the internal tension between them—when analyzing territorial decisions. This dualism can be found in the arguments expressed as well as in concrete positions adopted in territorial decision making.

Gottmann also points out the varied meanings attributed by various disciplines to *territory*.[15] Politicians view territory mainly in terms of population and resources; the military, as topography dictating tactical and strategic considerations; jurists, as a matter of legal jurisdiction; experts in international law, as an expression of sovereignty and its spatial enforcement; whereas to geographers, territory is part of an expanse defined by boundaries for specific purposes. All these meanings are relevant for the analysis of political decisions in territorial matters. We will disregard the question of individual motivations in territorial behavior and focus solely on the collective aspect of the territorial problem, an issue that also encompasses the role of territory in defining the meaning of the state.

Territory and the State

The state, like territory, is simultaneously tangible (passport control at borders) and intangible (a symbol and an object of identification).[16] We will posit, therefore, that a state's claim to sovereignty over a particular territory reflects these two components: an expressive manifestation and an instrumental manifestation of the needs of a particular collective.

In most definitions, the existence of the state depends on government, population, and territory; that is, on the state's ability to maintain social order within a community designated by territorial boundaries. MacIver's four theories of the state will serve as the basis for our examination of the territorial implications of each definition:[17]

1. *The state as a power system.* State power means principally the monopolistic use of coercive force to ensure social order.

2. *The state as a social contract.* The contract is based on natural rights and the free will of individuals in society. Hence the state is a result of an agreement based on the will of the people to pursue common goals.

3. *The state as a unity.* The state is analogous to a living organism with its own laws of survival, distinct "personality," self-consciousness, and even separate will. When this unity appears in a particular community, an internal bond is created between the state and the nation.

4. *The state as an "association."* The state is a normative arrangement that establishes a legal entity for specific purposes of the civil society. It is therefore an artificial organization (not found in nature), practically a fiction endowed with well-defined powers, such as the monopoly on coercive force, to attain particular goals.[18]

Table 1.1. Theories of the State and Territorial Concepts

STATE DEFINITION	TERRITORIAL CONCEPTS
Power system	The control of territory is a result of force and balance of power. The boundaries of sovereignty are determined by the power of the rulers and governments.
Social contract	The contract is enforceable on the territory of the parties to the agreement. The right to self-determination is therefore delineated by the territory of the participating members sharing common goals. If the agreement is irrevocable, it is also impossible to change its area of enforcement.
Unity	The territory is determined by the natural borders of the organism; "the homeland" is the geographic imprint made by history in realizing the characteristics of the community-people-nation.
Association	The territory is a legally defined area of jurisdiction upon which the state "association" has special rights (such as sovereignty) for attaining particular goals (such as maintenance of social order).

Although MacIver does not discuss the territorial aspects of these four state theories, Table 1.1 attempts to outline some of the territorial implications inherent in them.

In sixteenth-century Europe, the state was considered essentially a power system, hence the theories of Jean Boudein on absolute monarchic sovereignty. The view of the state as social contract, whether according to Hobbes, Locke, or Rousseau, discarded most of the mysticism attached to the state and replaced it with the natural right of free individuals who join together to achieve common goals. This approach somewhat obscured the distinction between society and state, says MacIver, which is perhaps why others began to look for the organic roots of the state in response to its demystification and the emphasis on individual rights. There was a new emphasis on the "personality" of the state that, according to Fichte, is more pure and rational than the particularistic desires of individual members. And so a certain cycle was closed: The social contract became holy, with its own irreversible will. Later, it would become easy to infuse cultural, religious and other elements into this concept and to maintain that the state as a unity also expresses the spirit of the nation. Thus, a three-way link was created between the modern state, nationality, and territory. In contrast, the state as an "association" returns to the foundations of the social contract, adding a normative basis to the agreement among its participants. This approach regards the state as an extension of society. It can neither grow nor atrophy, but only serve (or fail to serve) the goals of its members. In this state, territory is a functional and rather "fluid" component because association members (the citizens) have the right to enter or exit according to their own perception of the costs and benefits.

The last two concepts in Table 1.1 contain the components we related to territorial arguments. When the state is a unity, the dominant component is expressive—axiomatic identification with the organic state or the national homeland. When the state is an association, the dominant component is instrumental—a continuous assessment of the advantages over the disadvantages of belonging. There is a specific kind of "geographic determinism" within the concept of the state as a unity: The will to have the nation's borders, state's sovereignty, and territorial area coincide. For instance, the territory is the body of the national organism and the language is the soul.[19] For the state as an association, geography is a dependent variable: It can be based on national identity as well as on other interests—economic, for example. Hence, the territorial extent of the association is the result of specific social needs. In theory, self-determination need not necessarily be based on national identity.

Territory and the Nation-State

We will not delve into the many questions related to defining nationalism and the nation-state. Whether the emphasis is on common language, religion, heritage, or unity in the face of an external threat, the concept of nationhood is tangibly and symbolically linked to a particular piece of land.[20] However, since nationalism also develops in territories where dissimilar groups have undergone a process of convergence, the question of which came first, common territory or national consciousness, must remain open. The territorial nation-state developed first in Europe as a replacement for the former feudal system and a continuation of the concept of territorial sovereignty.[21] When the aspiration for self-determination and the ambition to achieve statehood became congruent, a major complication arose in determining the "correct" territorial boundaries between states.

The situation was relatively simple, if not "just" in the eyes of many communities, as long as military occupation or traditional sovereignty on a particular territory served as the de facto basis for determining boundaries. But when the search began for an objective criterion to define the geographic legitimacy of nation-states, it could not easily be found, and it was impossible to agree on its implementation. Most of the groups that sought and are still seeking territorial self-determination did not and probably will not achieve their goal. According to Murdock's "Ethnographic Atlas," in the 1960s, in addition to existing states, there were no fewer than 862 ethnically distinct societies that could seemingly claim self-determination within a territorial state.[22] As Taylor notes, "There may well be only one deity, but he or she has certainly been generous in designating 'chosen people'."[23]

In the late twentieth century, the world is divided into about 200 states. The process of determining sovereign geographical units has been more or less completed, with the possibility of some upheavals and additions resulting from recent changes in the former Soviet Union, Eastern Europe, and the Balkans. It can be predicted that the issue of establishing national territorial states will not engage us to the same extent in the twenty-first century. The principle of "self-determination" that illuminated the "Spring of Nations" in nineteenth-century Europe encountered great difficulties when the victorious powers tried to apply it at the Versailles Peace Conference after World War I. President Woodrow Wilson agreed with Robert Frost that "good fences make good neighbors" and searched for "an evident principle" for establishing reasonable political boundaries between the nations that would inherit the

Hapsburg and Ottoman Empires. Yet, as a former professor of political science, Wilson was aware of the difficulties and practical
obstacles to acting according to the principle of self-determination:
"All properly defined national aspirations must be satisfied in order
that the matter will not make existing differences and disagreements permanent or raise new ones."[24]

Delegations of peoples demanding self-determination appeared
before the Versailles Conference, including representatives of the
Zionist organization, headed by Weizmann, and of the Arab delegation, headed by the Emir Faisal. Most of them left empty-handed.
The territorial partition of the Middle East and the mandatory
system of the League of Nations were ultimately determined by the
interests of the colonial powers. The results in Europe and elsewhere are well known, leading Kedourie to write that "in the confusion of the peace conference, liberty was mistaken for the twin of
nationality."[25]

Nationalism is a sense of community that, under particular
historic conditions, seeks expression through the unity of a state.[26]
Indeed, this very powerful motivation found a natural ally, yet one
full of internal contradictions, in the state. Hence the conflict between the state as a faithful reflection of primordial loyalties and
the state as a political and civil entity.[27] On the one hand, the
assumption is that the nation as a collective entity exists before or
regardless of the state. On the other hand, the nation is a political
concept that springs to life in the context of a nation-state.[28]

A nation-state whose ethnic-territorial composition coincides
with the political framework is less problematic and generally has
fewer territorial demands. Yet there are few such monoethnic states,
and they are also occasionally involved in territorial disputes.[29]
Moreover, social differences, strong internal tensions, and even sepa-
ratist demands can develop within monoethnic states. Most states
are polyethnic. Thus, the nation-state, which one would assume
creates a clear and agreed-upon criterion for distinguishing between communities, did not solve the problem of territorial borders. In the twentieth century, most international conflicts revolved
around the contradictory demands of peoples and states to a particular territory. In many, the demand to create a symmetry between the nation and its sovereign boundaries was only an excuse
to justify territorial expansionism. Either way, territorial demands
aimed at protecting the national "cradle" or the "historical homeland" are quite widespread.

Concerning "homeland" as the basis for determining the
national territory, Deutsch writes that the actual place where a

person is born "has the size of a bed or a room, not the size of a country."[30] He maintains that the development of national consciousness results from processes of communication among individuals and groups and that the erection of social or territorial barriers essentially indicates changes in communication patterns. The more active the internal communications network becomes, the greater the tendency to separate from other excluded groups. At a later stage, this process will crystallize into national consciousness, national will, and symbols expressing the uniqueness of the community.[31] Deutsch developed this approach later, when he defined organizations and autonomous communities in terms of a communication differential: Among members there is more rapid and effective communication than with outsiders.[32] This is a completely different approach to the process of boundary formation between communities, peoples, and states. Comparing this conception to MacIver's model of the state as association, we find a common emphasis on the territorial state as a normative arrangement of humans engaged in pursuing common goals. We also find a sharp antithesis to the theories emphasizing latent forces or seeking out natural laws and organic explanations for the rise of the nation-state. In 1953, Deutsch had already proposed an alternative explanation for the phenomenon of nationalism, emphasizing the social and economic processes of nineteenth century Europe. Others linked it directly to the process of modernization and stressed that nationalism is not only an ideology, but also a particular orientation intended to cement a growing and developing mass society.[33]

Gellner reversed the order in explaining the growth of nationalism.[34] A feeling of kinship is generally considered the basis for nationalism. In Gellner's opinion, however, the sweeping changes in education and communication of the industrial revolution created the need for a common "political roof"—the modern nation-state. Therefore, the mystical elements in nationalism are an artificial appendage because nationalism is not a "natural order" but an expression of the modern era. The cultural and historical "raw materials" from the prenational period are used to justify the need for a separate framework. Gellner admits that his definition is tautological: Particular conditions cause the appearance of national units, within whose framework nations are created. In any event, nationalism can be identified only after the fact. Also, there is no certainty that the presently strong identification of the political unit (the state) with the social-cultural unit (the nation) will continue in the future.

Accordingly, the present territorial partitions between nation-states will not last just because they exist or because of current definitions of sovereignty in international law. Boundaries in the modern era are becoming perforated because of global economics, communication, or the dangers to the environment.[35] At the same time, local, communal, and religious loyalties within the nation-state tend to increase. Note that those who predict that the nation-state will wither away also tend to emphasize the instrumental component in the territorial nation-state and consider expressive identification to be transient. They therefore reject any deterministic explanation of the rise of the nation-state and its territorial dimensions. Yet one cannot ignore the fact that the territorial nation-state still represents one of the strongest loyalties around the globe. It has been called the *new tribalism* due to the rise of nationalism in the former Soviet bloc and almost a return to the situation after World War I.[36] The long-term suspension of these separate loyalties within the former Soviet Union or within one state such as Yugoslavia has not reduced their intensity, despite the reverse trend in western Europe.

In sum, the internal tension among conflicting loyalties in the nation-state and beyond, including the territorial significance of this conflict, are not a thing of the past. In each case, the question is the stage of development and the degree of intensity: In other words, does the national loyalty, including the territorial element, predominate. Our approach fully admits that various and conflicting loyalties may be competing for primacy. For example, patriotic loyalty to the national homeland may be placed above personal interests and may compete with other loyalties—one's professional, communal, or cultural identity or values that transcend the boundaries of the national territory.[37] The approach here reflects the duality noted in our discussion of the territorial motivations of human behavior. Conversely, awarding primacy to the nation-state turns it into the sole player in the international arena, as we shall see below.

Geopolitics and International Relations

The discussion of boundaries requires a long introduction, which is beyond the scope of this chapter on the interrelationship of politics and geography, but a few pertinent historical facts should be noted.[38] Geopolitics, as it is now called, has roots in the European school of "environmental determinism" of the late nineteenth century, which asserted that social and political phenomena can be explained through the physical and geographical environment.[39] This theory was extended by Friedrich Ratzel (1844–1904), who claimed that human societies are subject to natural laws of growth, development, and decay and that states are organic entities which act according to these laws.[40] Ratzel was the first to use the term "living space" (*lebensräum*) to describe the expansion of states, even though he never recommended policies aimed at its realization. Next the Swedish political scientist Kjellén (1864–1922) used the term *geopolitik* to refer to a comprehensive theory of the modern state and of power relations among states.[41] Geopolitics then acquired a deterministic bias—as the concrete expression of geographic facts that politics could not (and therefore should not) ignore. For instance, the American geographer Van-Valkenburg went further than Kjellén when he mapped the world according to the cyclical presence of youthful, adolescent, mature, and old-age stages of statehood.[42]

Geopolitics became an ideology in Nazi Germany. Ethnocentricity distinguishes clearly between the writings of Ratzel and Kjellén and those of later German geopoliticists. The former strove to develop a universal science of political geography. Although the latter claimed universalism and adopted Ratzel and Kjellén as their spiritual leaders, this was only a cover for their preoccupation with Germany alone. Their geopolitics began and ended with the fate of Germany in Central Europe (*Mittlerupa*) and, over time, Europe-Asia-Africa and the entire world. What began as scientific pretension under the heading *geopolitik* and the influence of Ratzel, Kjellén, and Mackinder (see later) evolved into "geostrategy" and the racial theory of territory and space serving Nazi ideology and policies. The key figure for understanding these acrobatics was General Karl Haushofer (1869–1946).

Haushofer and his colleagues endeavored to make geopolitics the "national science of the state" (*die nationale staatwissenschaft*), a suprascience based on the nation-state and encompassing economics, sociology, anthropology, history, and law.[43] Haushofer preached simultaneously that geopolitics must become the "geographical conscience of the state."[44] This seemingly minor contradiction between *science* and *conscience* reveals the oversimplification and shallowness of a theory that reduced all human needs to concepts of space and boundaries represented by geographic maps. According to the geopolitical prescription for what Haushofer called *applied science*, states are measured by only two standards: power and territory.[45] The terms *living space, boundaries,* and *border areas* and the role of geopolitical maps in this context were extensively discussed in the publication Haushofer edited in Munich from 1924 to 1944, *Zeitschrift für Geopolitik*. However, it is difficult to present precise definitions due to their propagandistic nature as well as their internal contradictions.

Haushofer and his colleagues were geographical determinists, as evidenced by their intense preoccupation with "space" (*räum*) as the basis for understanding human, particularly political, behavior. Accordingly, the needs of the organic state are actually dictated by territorial imperatives, justifying the use of political power. Yet space is also seen as a flexible component that can change, for example, to create symmetry between the political definition of the "German State" (*Deutsches Reich*) and the linguistic definition of the "German Land" (*Deutschland*). Theoretically, therefore, certain areas that are outside the relevant space can still somehow be related to it, because of their German-speaking populations. Fine distinctions like these do not change the basic fact that territory fulfills a primary function in this approach that strives for the unity of "one land, one people and one geopolitical unit."[46]

Living space, a term Haushofer borrowed from Ratzel, includes very tenuously bonded components. Following Mackinder, Haushofer developed a series of strategic arguments, the central one being Germany's need to expand to control the essential heartland of Europe and later also of Africa.[47] Why must Germany expand? In Haushofer's writings, the arguments are still instrumental: the need to create security zones and control natural resources, routes of transportation, and communication. But later this kind of justification was quickly abandoned in favor of statements that the nation's combined "needs" determine the living space. The nuanced language is eliminated in Nazi ideology. Courses for S. S. officers included the explicit declaration that conquest of living space and settlement of Eastern European territories by Germans are not based on economic interests.[48]

The original concept of "living space" encompassed mystical foundations, but was not racist. Yet the leap in Nazi ideology to a term used in racist argumentation, *biological living space*, was not convoluted but rather an extension of the link between space and German "needs." Thus, for example, the Nazis argued that this space included areas in which "germanism" historically developed a high level of racial purity, which was particularly preserved by the pure German peasant family. So the cycle was complete, creating the link between race and territory, blood and land (*blut un boden*). Familiar romantic associations were added: space as a symbol of ancient and untamed nature, the unmediated bond with the virgin land awaiting redemption. Religious redemption was combined with national and racial pride and the supremacy of the state.[49] Nazi propaganda stated clearly and simply: "The laws of blood and land" determine German living space. Geopolitics and Nazism were thus coupled to serve the dream of a greater Germany.

The conception of boundaries was derived from the theory of living space. Consequently, Haushofer and his colleagues could not be satisfied with distinguishing between natural and artificial borders and thus inadvertently helped shatter many geographic beliefs in "natural boundaries." Ratzel regarded boundaries as dynamic and temporary, something that changes in accordance with the laws of growth and the demise of states. A borderline has no significance, only border areas or frontiers. This allowed Haushofer to conduct a systematic propaganda campaign to raise the "frontier consciousness" of the German people: after all, territorial laws dictate that a growing nation must expand its living space. In his first book, Haushofer distinguished between boundaries borrowed from nature (rivers, oceans) or natural barriers (mountain ranges, swamps, deserts) and artificial boundaries based on strategic military, economic or political interests. The latter most interested German geopoliticists. They invented the ambiguous term *organic frontiers* in an attempt to combine ideological, historical, and national justifications with practical arguments such as the need for economic depth, strategic buffer zones, and control of communication channels into one geographic definition. In the final analysis, says Bowman, *geopolitik* in Nazi Germany served simply as an apology for theft.[50]

Analysis of the significance of territory and its place in international relations greatly predated German geopolitics, especially concerning the strategic position of states. A name already mentioned is that of the British geographer Halford Mackinder (1861–1947), who decisively influenced the development of this field in the early twentieth century. Mackinder analyzed relations among the world powers and theorized that the central struggle for global control is between continental and maritime states. In his book, published on the eve of World War I, Mackinder stated that the struggle would be won by whoever controlled the central "heartland" stretching from Siberia to Persia. Whether we regard his rules as a warning against the German danger looming over Western democracies[51] or as an impartial analysis of global trends, Mackinder belongs to the determinist school. He believed that by assembling the pieces of the geographic puzzle, one inevitably understands the deployment—and even the intentions—of the world's strategic forces. Mackinder directly influenced the statesmen at the Versailles Peace Conference who redrew the map of Europe.

Mackinder also influenced American geographer Nicholas Spykman, particularly when he offered strategic policy recommendations for the United States.[52] Spykman's geographic determinism is moderate by comparison with geopoliticists like Renner, who preached American power politics along the lines of the German geopoliticists.[53] Spykman recognized that political geography examines geographic considerations together with dynamic changes in centers of power.[54] He attacked Haushofer head on, accusing him of using the concept of the state as a living organism with hidden needs to conceal and justify a policy of force and expansionism. Nevertheless, Spykman's basic approach remained very similar to an article he had written in 1938, which caused some to call him—unjustly—the *American Haushofer*.[55]

Those who use the term *political geography*, as opposed to *geopolitics*, have sought to indicate an area of study concerned with the interrelationship between politics and geography.[56] In Hartshorne's opinion, political geography is the study of "politically organized areas," and these areas in our times are states. Accordingly, his analysis of boundaries between states addresses questions of whether the neighboring states agree to their boundaries and whether the boundary is a closed buffer or open and accessible.[57]

The reaction of geographers like Hartshorne to the pseudo-science of geopolitics is understandable. But there is no need to ignore territorial questions or negate their importance in international relations, as expressed in border conflicts between states or in the link between internal and external disputes.[58] In two articles published after World War II, Gottmann drew conclusions from the failure to uncover principles of political behavior stemming from geography, as well as from the failed attempt to develop a global theory of territorial strategy and a comparative theory of border conflicts. In his opinion, intangible variables such as national loyalties are more significant than geographic variables in international relations. Moreover, political behavior revealed these variables to be as rigid as the physical facts.[59] Thus, the importance of geography in the study of international relations is primarily in recognizing the multiplicity of regional life-styles—the national iconography—because "the people and not the area determine the pattern of external relations."[60]

Reticence at using the term *geopolitics* has diminished in recent years. But neither outmoded geopolitical concepts nor the hope of constructing a grand theory of global strategy resting on "solid geographic facts" has disappeared. For example, a book published in 1988 recommended a strategy for U.S. foreign policy in accordance with Mackinder's theories. The author maintained that the strength of the Soviet Union derived from its control of the "continental heartland," hence the now embarrassing conclusions: "For as far into the future as can be claimed contemporarily relevant, the Soviet Union is going to remain the source of danger—narrowly to American national security, more broadly (and quite literally) to the exercise of values of Western civilization."[61]

With the unfolding events in the Soviet Union, it became clear already in 1989 that the "relevant future" in this prediction would not last even one year. This book is just one contemporary, characteristic example—albeit a minor one—of what is presented as "solid geopolitical facts" under geographic determinism. As to the importance of territory and boundaries in the modern, technological age, Jones wrote as early as 1945: "All boundaries that were once considered strategic have now become tactical."[62] Prescott devoted an entire chapter to analyzing various types of boundary disputes to present questions intended to create an empirical basis for such research.[63] These included the following: What is the cause of the dispute? Why did it develop at a certain time? What are the aims of the involved governments? How do they justify their positions? The new political geography thus deals less with mapping physical phenomena and more with analysis of spatial political results of political behavior.[64]

Boundaries

The Versailles Peace Conference of 1919 was the last international attempt to arrange boundaries on the basis of principles of national self-determination. At the time, many believed that this was possible, and some geographers also thought that advancing geographic knowledge would minimize the danger of postwar international disputes.[65] They also repeated, after more than 100 years, Napoleon's dictum that the boundaries of France were outlined by nature.[66]

Europe between the wars shattered these beliefs, and many geographers began to reexamine the question of boundaries after World War II. Among those who discredited the concept of "natural boundaries" between states, even as a basis for empirical research, Jones was the most outspoken when he absolutely rejected any possibility of discovering general laws for the determination of boundaries: "Every border is practically unique and therefore most generalizations are of doubtful validity."[67] Tenner was aware of the continuing search for boundaries to mark once and for all the "true" differences between societies. He therefore outlined the "ideal boundary" with some irony, suggesting the gap with reality: "[It] follows a clearly defined physical feature; encloses a homogeneous population; excludes none of the same racial stock; does not cut across economic regions or religious units; and does not interfere with well-established historical relationships."[68]

For Tenner, the best boundary depended upon prevailing conditions in the adjoining states and upon their mutual relations. Indeed, empirical studies show vast fluctuations in international European boundaries over the last 500 years (excluding Portugal, Spain, and Switzerland).[69] Muir reinforced these findings when he presented various typologies for boundary classification and disdained the arithmetical formulas intended to determine whether a certain boundary is "alive" or "dead."[70] For him, boundaries result from political realities, that do not change even if the political boundaries coincide with natural contours, because boundaries represent agreements and the results of conflicts between states. Accordingly, territorial boundaries and the conflicts surrounding them are rooted in the sense of difference and the need for segregation of communities and nations, what Deutsch termed the *internal intensity of communications*. Thus a different concept began to emerge, emphasizing the communal, national, and political aspects of geographic boundaries: "Aspiring to be unique, groups of people organize themselves within politically ordered societies and associations thereof. These societies are territorially framed. The edges of the frame are political boundaries."[71]

Boundaries, in this definition, are first of all political—a possible product of human aspirations and social organization. They have no determinist foundation and contradict the image of boundaries as the external shell of a whole and well-defined "unity" with a life of its own. This definition is also commensurate with MacIver's concept of the state as "association," including the fact that in the twentieth century, the nation-states have become the most important "associations."

This book adopts the position that the search for natural, clear, and "correct" boundaries will never be crowned with success, because the dividing lines between states are the outcome of political processes, that is, human decisions. This approach is also based on Douglas's anthropological analysis of the role of external boundaries in human behavior. One of her far-reaching conclusions is that boundaries represent an attempt to impose order and system on what is inherently an untidy human experience.[72]

Natural Boundaries

Sempel's study (1911) of the historical role of geographic factors is based on the environmental theories of Ratzel. It draws a lesson from the fact that human development has geographic points of reference to exaggerate the influence of natural barriers, such as mountain ranges and deserts, on modern civilization.[73] Sempel's conclusions on geographic boundaries, however, again duplicate Ratzel's equivocation: Nature dislikes rigid lines; even rivers and beaches change with time. Racial and state boundaries are also subject to change, especially where expansive cycles of different peoples collide.[74] Accordingly, Sempel, in a typical mixture of organic and political concepts, observes: "All natural features of the earth's surface which serve to check, retard or weaken the expansion of peoples, and therefore hold them apart, tend to become racial or political boundaries."[75]

Where does the doctrine of "natural boundaries" originate? Some believe that the need for clear and permanent boundaries between European states was already widespread in the seventeenth and eighteenth centuries. Others argue that the previous historic experience of the expansion waves of tribes and peoples (and even animals) influenced the creation of European political frameworks.[76] Either way, the hope was to bestow natural meaning on the new phenomena of sovereign states bordering one another. Hence the search for seas, rivers, lakes, mountains, and deserts to form natural barriers for defense or prevention of population movements. Where this was impossible, human-made alternatives were built, such as towers, dirt ramparts, or the chain of fortified positions in the style of the Roman Limes or the Great Wall of China.

There was a contradiction in German geopolitics between the growing organic state, whose boundaries are flexible, and the belief that stability is created when natural and political boundaries coincide. An attempt to solve this contradiction is the idea that the "growing state" expands to the next natural boundary. Concepts about the organic state and natural boundaries therefore belong to the same category: both are nourished by ideological aspirations and myths, not by empirical observation.[77] Either way, the idea of the natural boundary has lost all meaning. Boggs phrased it with sarcasm: "All borders are artificial. Some less than others."[78]

When the futile search for principles in the determination of political boundaries was abandoned, researchers began to focus on the functions of boundaries as they arose and changed over time. For example: developmental stages of boundaries, the relationship between a boundary and its environment, and the distinction between boundaries of separation and boundaries of contact.[79] In addition, international law stipulates that a boundary defines the area upon which a state's sovereignty is in effect and formulates specific rules for the acquisition of territory and the resolution of border disputes.[80] The Charter of the United Nations recognized the territorial integrity of sovereign nations: "All Members shall refrain in their international relations from the threat or use of force against the territorial integrity or political independence of any state . . . "[81]

The prevailing definition of boundaries in contemporary literature is closer to international political reality and distant from the attempt to formulate binding "laws." It also recognizes the interrelationship between boundaries and the historical development of societies and states. For example, when a boundary is determined by political dictate—even if it is a geometric line across natural areas and homogeneous population centers—it will result in human development being different on its two sides. In the long run, these differences may be expressed not only in economic relations and routes of transportation, but also in variation of language, religion, and culture.[82] Moreover, stable and recognized boundaries, even if they are artificial, contribute to the legitimacy of the state, hence, for example, the Organization of African Unity's 1963 decision to recognize the colonially derived boundaries as permanent international borders.[83] And, finally, the longing for natural boundaries deserves the following useful comment: "It must be noted that 'natural boundaries' are always the limits to which a state wishes to expand. There is no recorded case of a state wishing to withdraw to 'natural boundaries.' "[84]

Frontiers

Boundaries or borders mark defined lines in the terrain. A frontier is an undefined area that is usually not densely populated (settlement frontier) or an area whose political status is ambiguous (political frontier). In this sense, there were practically no frontiers in Europe by the nineteenth century, although there were still many areas "open" to settlement or claims of sovereignty on other continents. Hence the strong connection between the term *frontiers* and the westward movement of the U.S. line of settlement.[85]

The distinction between an area and a line is central here, because the term *frontier* is centrifugal and outwardly oriented whereas the term *boundary* is centripidal and inwardly oriented.[86] "Boundaries" and the needs associated with them may also indicate readiness to recognize limitations and to establish restrictions on the realization of personal or collective goals. By contrast, the image of the frontier always has an incomplete, open, and dynamic aspect.[87] A society or a state whose self-definition (including the territorial) is saturated with frontier images is still in the formative stage because open areas exist somewhere along its "front line" for settlement, development, or even redemption. Conversely, collective internalization of the presence of limiting boundaries reflects a political community that has reached a relatively high level of self-determination, stability, and internal cohesion.[88]

Kimmerling studied the process of settlement in immigrant countries as background to an analysis of the territorialism of Zionism and developed new concepts concerning the relationship between the frontier areas and state control over the territory.[89] He examines three types of territorial control:

1. *Presence.* Existence of missionaries, merchants, explorers, and potential settlers for purposes of laying claim to the property or as a stage in later military conquest.

2. *Ownership.* Use of legal or semilegal means to establish rights—private or public—over the land. Such rights could be an alternative to sovereignty.

3. *Sovereignty.* Establishing state authority in the territory.

These forms of control and the various combinations among them determine the status or the lack of status of the state in the frontier areas, if such exist. For instance, the existence of active "frontiers" in the American sense of the term indicates less control of the state regarding social changes, including control of the territorial location of these changes.[90]

In the second half of the twentieth century, few territories could be defined as frontiers. The "frontier spirit" motivating peoples and states to take control of new areas has also been much less intense.[91] Nevertheless, it would be an exaggeration to say that "there are no longer any frontiers—they are now a phenomenon of history."[92] In the Middle East alone, many examples refute such a conclusion. If we exclude competition for the exploitation of the ocean depths, polar regions, and outer space, what is disappearing is the frontier as a synonym for freely available resources. Frontiers do, however, exist in the political and subjective sense—as areas of undefined status or territories where states try to establish rights of presence, ownership, and sovereignty.

The issue of geographic or social frontiers is important for understanding the positions and decisions of the Zionist movement and the state of Israel. Kimmerling maintains that the case of Palestine/Land of Israel differed from frontiers elsewhere because, in effect, these territories were not "freely available" in terms of population or untapped natural resources.[93] Nevertheless, some of the perceptions and positions to be discussed in this book reflect the attempts to implement Kimmerling's types of territorial control, as well as "the frontier spirit" in the sense noted previously.

Size and Compactness

The size of the territory proportionate to the number of inhabitants was a subject of great concern to the German geopoliticists, whereas the state's geographic location interested strategic and international relations experts. Both touched upon another related question—the physical shape of the state, which results from the features and length of the boundaries. This research generally emphasizes the security aspect: the existence of defensible borders or strategic depth for deterring attacks and defending population centers and other essential targets.

The prevailing assumption is that the state's ideal shape is a circle, with its capital at the center. This form has obvious advantages: shortening the lines of transport and communications, reducing the range required for central government control, and minimizing the length of boundaries, which abet security against external threats and internal separatism.[94] A number of shape indices were developed to analyze and compare the "compactness" of states. One measures the deviation of the state's actual boundary length from that of the ideal circular circumference, which represents the shortest boundary for that area. In this simple index, this is the difference between the shortest possible land boundaries of the state's area and the actual land boundaries in the state's existing shape. The ideal state has a compactness index of 1.00. Accordingly, the most "compact states"—those whose territorial shape most closely approximates a perfect circle—are Uruguay (1.05), Nigeria (1.13), Rumania (1.37), France (1.42), and Hungary (1.47). Conversely, the least compact states—those with the most "irregular" shapes—are Chile (3.1), Thailand (2.82), and Mexico (2.58).[95] Table 1.2 calculates "compactness" of Palestine/Israel under various boundaries until 1949.

Table 1.2. Compactness Indices for Various Areas and Boundaries

	LAND AREA (KM²)[a]	LENGTH OF LAND BOUNDARIES (KM)[b]	LENGTH OF CIRCULAR BOUNDARIES (KM)[c]	INDEX OF COMPACTNESS[d]	KM OF BORDER PER 1000 KM²[e]
Mandatory Palestine (E. I.) (1922)					
	26,305	867	575	1.51	33
The Jewish State Partition Plan (1937)[f]					
	5,000	450	250	1.80	90
The Jewish State Partition Plan (1947)[f]					
	14,000	1,500	450	3.30	107
State of Israel Armistice Lines (1949)					
	20,325	1,053	505	2.09	52

[a] Not including lake areas.
[b] Not including the Mediterranean and Red Sea boundaries; including the curves in the Jordan River, which greatly extend the eastern boundary.
[c] A circle whose circumference represents the shortest boundaries for the state's land territory.
[d] $\dfrac{b}{c} = \dfrac{\text{(length of actual land boundaries)}}{\text{(length of hypothetical circular boundaries)}}$
[e] An additional index of the ratio between territory and actual boundary length.
[f] Approximations.

An exercise like that in Table 1.2 illustrates both the real and the false dilemmas faced by decision makers if they want to use such indices. In both the partition plans of 1937 and 1947, the proposed Jewish state entailed limited territory and very long boundaries: almost 1 km of border for every 10 km² of territory. But the degree of compactness in and of itself proves nothing. For instance, the militarily indefensible state proposed to the Jews in 1937 was relatively more compact—due to its tiny area—than the four times larger state of Israel within the 1949 armistice lines. Similarly, the relatively high compactness of mandatory Palestine (E.I.) did not ease severe British problems of internal control because of the struggle between Arabs and Jews. Thus, the British even became willing to forego the "geographic logic" of maintaining the unity of Palestine to solve the political problem. The United Nations Partition Plan of 1947 went even further, proposing the establishment of two states in the 26,300 km² of Palestine, which would have created two of the least compact states in the world.

In short, we know the difficulties of noncompact states like Chile and Norway even without the index; while the compactness of France, with Paris at its center, did not greatly assist its defense through two world wars. Many supplementary factors must be taken into account even if the only subject of concern is defense requirements. However, shape is also related to the citizens' image of their country as it appears on the map. Large territory, natural boundaries and compactness that shortens the length of the land boundaries all have a positive image nourished by those geopolitical and strategic concepts from the beginning of this century. These concepts and images seemed to have changed little in the modern age, despite serious doubts as to the intrinsic defensive protection provided by large territory and "natural" boundaries.[96]

Boundaries and Security

Studies of human territorial behavior stress the importance of the security motive in the drawing of boundaries. Gottmann emphasized the need for shelter and protective defense as one of the main functions of human territorialism.[97] We pointed out the role of territory in enhancing common identity derived from the ability of a certain community to declare, "This place is ours."[98] We have also noted that the desire for a territory with defensible boundaries can be based on expressive or instrumental reasoning. Communities and nations strive for "natural" boundaries because they represent a certain wholeness that they believe creates a "correct" and easily discernible national-territorial entity. Hence also the desire for "compactness," whether or not bordering states present a real security threat. The instrumental claim rests mainly on military and strategic grounds and seeks dominating heights, fortification lines, buffer zones, and "defensible borders." The German geographers were apparently first to use the term *security boundary (whergrenze)*.[99] The extensive literature on these matters started from the assumption that international relations are a struggle for power. The importance of boundaries in this context stems from the fact that these struggles have a military-territorial component.[100]

One significant change in the literature on boundaries and security is the retreat from territorial problems as an independent issue and the extension of the term *buffer* to other fields. According to Boulding, for example, the term *critical boundaries* relates not only to the military aspect but also to political and ideological factors.[101] Such "criticality" could be assigned to defense against the incursion of foreign influences or preservation of the community's identity. Another example is Wright's analysis of the economic influence of political boundaries.[102] He proposes a theory of bargaining to explain the phenomena of boundary determination, because the construction of barriers is intended to organize the flow of people, merchandise, capital, and information across both sides of the boundary. The following quotation summarizes the new literature on the "barrier effects" of boundaries: "Boundaries act as barriers to social and economic processes which would otherwise transgress them without interference. . . . Boundaries contain regions of political and social integration, and restrict the flow of communication and the formation of social and psychological associations with areas and populations lying beyond the boundary."[103]

These approaches abandoned the limited military aspect of boundaries as defensive or offensive positions and also distanced themselves from the earlier definitions of "strategic boundaries" as "time and space" formulas for analyzing international power struggles. This new literature is therefore conscious of the fact that in the modern era, boundaries do not provide the previous military advantages. Because this book deals with a decision made in 1937, it should be noted that the gradual change in military doctrines began with the development of the airplane and modern artillery and gained momentum after World War II. Already in 1945, some geographers pointed out that defensive depth is strategically more effective than a strong boundary relying on seemingly impassable barriers.[104] Territory still fulfills a singularly important role in military strategy, but modern technology has raised major questions as to the importance of borders as military barriers. Some observers even go so far as to suggest that non-conventional weapons undermine the existence of the territorial state. They wonder whether the state can continue to fulfill its central function—providing security for its residents—in the new era. Will its fate be similar to that of the fortified castle in the Middle Ages, which lost its ascendancy when artillery appeared?[105]

Almost five decades in the shadow of the bomb taught us that nuclear deterrence does not prevent—and perhaps even encourages—conventional wars. The Middle East, in particular, has become a permanent arena for this type of war; and questions of territorial importance, strategic depth, and protected boundaries continue to serve as a focus of concern as well as debate.[106]

Territorial Decisions

This book discusses the territorial decision adopted by the Zionist movement in 1937, its significance and implications, and the decision-making process itself. A central issue in the literature on decision making is the extent of rationality—empirical and normative—that exists or should exist in the decision-making process. Simon's definition is adequate for this purpose: individual and group decisions are made under conditions of "bounded rationality."[107] Accordingly, a presentation of the arguments and concrete positions adopted when the choice was required will suffice. Our analysis is concerned with the decision makers' actual willingness to consider territory and boundaries in trade for other values. The question will be whether territory is understood as an end in itself or, conversely, whether there is a willingness to weigh its expected benefits against other values such as sovereignty or security needs. In this context, we shall also examine the interrelationship between external and internal considerations.[108]

This book will therefore deal mainly with the choices as understood by participants to the internal argument. We will then analyze the decision by the same parameters used to analyze the arguments raised by the participants. We will categorize the arguments according to Parsons' distinction between expressive and instrumental orientations[109] and apply this distinction to the territorial questions.[110]

Orientation toward a particular territory requires that this territory first be part of the "cognitive map" of the collective under discussion. Kimmerling stresses that this type of orientation is also created *after the fact*; when the community established a certain bond with the territory through presence, ownership, or sovereignty.[111] In 1937, the Jewish presence in Eretz Israel was still miniscule: only a small portion of the land had been purchased, forceful conquest was impossible, and the question of sovereignty was part of the pending decision. In other words, we will examine these two orientations largely *before the fact*. From this perspective, the difference between them is even more pronounced, because the decision process within the Zionist movement was suffused with future aspirations. We will also use the terms *arguments* and *reasoning*, instead of *orientations*, to highlight the difference between the two territorial approaches, and the term *positions* to emphasize that this was a political decision.

Territorial Expressivism

Expressive arguments for control of a particular territory reflect axiomatic values that need not be proven. They can be primordial (blood ties) or symbolic (holiness), but are generally based on beliefs, ideologies, and emotional ties that reflect but do not explain why a particular territory "belongs" to a community, people, nation, or state. Mere readiness to argue about territorial belonging or its intensity may be perceived as heresy. Nevertheless, when these sentiments must be clarified, particularly to justify them to the opposition, various arguments based on natural law, historical rights, common language, race, religion, and culture are raised. In many languages, "homeland" or terms indicating kinship (fatherland) and religious ties (holy land) describe this expressive bond between a particular collective and a specific land.

There exists, therefore, a strong determinist element in expressive arguments aimed at proving that the bond to the land is controlled by indisputable laws anchored in uncontrollable supraprocesses: religion, history, nature. As we have seen, this type of conception leads to geographic determinism, to a search for natural boundaries, and even to the perception of the state as a living organism subject to its own laws of growth and decay. When the starting point is expressive, the territory and boundaries must express these precepts and cannot be subject to "technical" tests of anticipated benefits. According to this approach, political decisions that ignore this axiomatic dimension are illegitimate and, hence, self-eliminating. Territorial expressivism has a strongly self-contained inward orientation because it relies on the community's "collective subconscious."[112] A particular piece of land thus becomes the tangible expression ("homeland") of collective sentiments and memories. Deutsch used the term *collective memory* to describe this common denominator for the internalities within a group defining itself as a nation.[113]

Territorial Instrumentalism

Instrumental arguments for the need to possess a particular territory are conditional.[114] Land is a resource or a source of other resources, so its anticipated benefits should be examined in light of economic, defense, transport, and other considerations. There must be some preliminary bond that determines why a particular collective is present in a certain piece of land, and wishes to possess it. But beyond this, the breadth of the territory can be debated and its advantages must be justified. In this concept, the location of boundaries must ensure optimal utilization of the territory for communal, national, and state needs. The approach is functional and the extent of the territory and its boundaries are compared to values, interests, and other collective benefits. Instrumental arguments generally stress "needs" such as defensive lines, settlement areas, economic indispensability, water sources, social development, and sea access to prove the necessity of a particular territory.

This concept may lead to definition of the state as an "association" and of territorial sovereignty as a contract between the state and its citizenry for attaining defined needs. Political arrangements such as a federal system or an economic community indicate an instrumental approach in which territorial partitions are relaxed to attain other collective goals. Expressive sentiments draw their strength from the past, while territorial instrumentalism is decidedly more future oriented, emphasizing opportunities in decision making rather than historic rights.

Thus far, we have schematically presented two types of reasoning that are very difficult to differentiate in reality. Human sentiment and the arguments it presents are not designed to assist the researcher. Thus, a study of border conflicts shows great use of legal arguments to prove territorial possession, employed in tandem with historic, geographic, security, and economic reasoning.[115] In reality, all types of arguments are used on a per case basis, and it is doubtful whether one can distinguish between the expressive and the instrumental components in the general orientation of a community or its leaders. Kimmerling suggested a solution to this problem:

One can assume that there is no "pure" orientation toward territory, and thus orientations are likely to be mixtures of instrumental, sentimental, etc. The significance of the orientation is determined by the degree of its expression in the system. An internal order governs these orientations and constitutes a sequence that extends from the instrumental pole (the technical sub-orientation) to the most expressive one—the moral or religious sub-orientation.[116]

Accordingly, we will trace the prominence of each type of argument and subject them to a practical test: readiness to forego territory for the sake of other values and interests. This book discusses a case in which the choice was quite concrete: whether to support territorial partition of Palestine (E.I.) in return for the establishment of a sovereign Jewish state. In making this decision, expressive beliefs also had to be translated into political positions and a negative response would have to be explained. On the other hand, the need to decide also forced the instrumentalists to abandon the convenient cover of tactical considerations and to adopt a position: What do they expect for their willingness, in principle, to forego territory? The differences between these two types of arguments is clear at the extreme ends, but the mixture makes it often difficult to categorize. For example, is the reasoning behind the need for a specific territorial minimum—say, a "compact" state—an "expressive" argument on the geopolitical fate of the nation-state or an "instrumental" argument for political or economic viability of the state?

We shall take into account these subtle nuances in addressing the central question in this book: When faced with a rather concrete decision, was the Zionist movement willing to consider territorial compromises to achieve other goals?

2   The Background

Palestine is a much-promised land.

(Weizmann, testimony before the Royal Commission)[1]

Inadvertently, the "Arab Revolt" in Palestine, which began in April 1936, openly placed the possibility of establishing a Jewish state on the political agenda.[2] This "secret"—the aspiration to establish a state—was axiomatic within the Zionist movement. This is what everyone understood when Herzl said in Basel in 1897 that the First Zionist Congress was intended to "lay the cornerstone for a home in which the future Jewish nation can dwell." This was also the Zionist interpretation of the term *Jewish national home*, in the Balfour Declaration of 1917.

But beyond the hope was the question of international legitimacy of a Jewish state. The Zionist movement attached immense importance to the League of Nations' mandate for Palestine, which recognized "the historical connection of the Jewish people with Palestine and the grounds for reconstituting their national home in that country" (Preamble); as well as to the task of the British government: "The Mandatory shall be responsible for placing the country under such political, administrative and economic conditions as will secure the establishment of the Jewish national home ... and the development of self-governing institutions" (Article 2).

The British commitment to assist the Jews attain self-government became a permanent bone of contention from 1921, when Herbert Samuel, the first high commissioner, determined the policy of fixing Jewish immigration in accordance with Palestine's "economic absorptive capacity" and the interests of the local population.[3] The dispute intensified after the Arab attacks on Jews in 1929, when the British government recognized its "dual obligation" to Jews and Arabs of Palestine (E.I.)[4] and tried to restrict Jewish land purchase and immigration.[5] It marked the beginning of a convoluted British policy that, in retrospect, failed to meet the demands of both sides. For the local Arab population in Palestine, it still favored the Jewish national home and did not recognize their separate claims for self-determination. For the Zionists, this policy contradicted their aspirations, according to which the "national home" was a transitional phase intended to facilitate Jewish immigration and consolidation in Eretz Israel, en route to an independent political entity. In any event, until the mid-1930s the Zionist argument with the British government was over practical means, because the date for realizing the goal of independence still seemed quite distant.

The year 1937 marks a turning point in this process. For the first time the possibility of establishing a Jewish state was discussed not only among Jews and not only under the pseudonym of a "national home." This time the proposal was raised by the ruling power in Palestine (E.I.) and the Middle East, and it became clear for the first time that the Zionist movement and the Yishuv (Jewish community in Palestine) faced a real decision concerning statehood and its territorial dimension. Such a decision implied not abstract consent, but the need to make choices under conditions of extreme uncertainty. Practically, they faced the choice of relinquishing territorial aspirations for the possibility of a sovereign state.

Boundaries of Palestine (E.I.)

What is the territory under consideration? During Ottoman rule, Palestine was not a separate administrative unit.[6] The first political-geographical division of the country was delineated by diplomats in the Sykes-Picot Agreement of 1916. According to this agreement, the territory of the future British mandate for Palestine would be divided up among the parties to the agreement: Britain, France, Czarist Russia, and Italy. There was no mention of the Jews in Palestine or the Zionist movement in these secret agreements.[7] Nor did the Balfour Declaration relate to the boundaries of the "Jewish national home in Palestine," which the British pledged to help establish in an area not yet under their control. Palestine was also not mentioned in the exchange of letters between McMahon, the British high commissioner in Egypt, and Hussein, the Sherif of Mecca (July 1915–March 1916), which pledged to award "independence to the Arabs."[8] It was no simple task for the Jews and Arabs to formulate their demands for self-determination after World War I. They had no basis in political and geographic precedents, and the other accepted criteria (linguistic, religious, ethnic, cultural, etc.) mentioned in Chapter One were indistinct and certainly not agreed upon. The Zionist movement's mission was particularly complex because it was attempting to justify a future state of affairs: turning Eretz Israel into the home of the Jewish people under the auspices of the British mandate.

The fate of the Middle East, ultimately determined in direct negotiations between Britain and France, is beyond the scope of our discussion of the decisions within the Zionist movement.[9] It is important to note, however, that at the Versailles Peace Conference the Zionist movement was asked for the first time to define the area it desired for the Jewish "national home." A memorandum submitted in February 1919 by the Zionist Organization's delegation, headed by Weizmann, presented aspirations, principles, and arguments. It also took into account the need to weigh the territorial aspirations against other goals, such as attaining support from the Arab national movement, headed by Emir Faisal.

The main arguments in the memorandum—those intended to convince the powers "to reestablish the Jewish national home in Eretz Israel"—would reappear in the partition debate of 1937. They can be divided into two categories:[10] first, those emphasizing the historic right of the Jewish people to Eretz Israel, including the link to the fertile plains east of the Jordan River;[11] second, the need for an area sizable enough for large-scale settlement, for creating a viable economic foundation, for control of water sources and rivers, and for free access to the Red Sea and regional lines of transportation. The memorandum emphasized the need to develop political, administrative, and economic conditions that would ensure the growth of the national home and eventually lead to the establishment of an "autonomous commonwealth." Accordingly, the desired boundaries of Eretz Israel were outlined (see Map 1.1) as follows[12]:

- *In the north.* A line from the Mediterranean Sea south of Sidon to Beit Jann, including the Litani River and all sources of the Jordan River.

- *In the east.* The northern border turns southeast after it crosses the Litani River and approaches the Hijaz railway, approximately 30 km. south of Damascus. The line then runs south along the railroad track (without including it) to Ma'an and the Gulf of Aqaba.

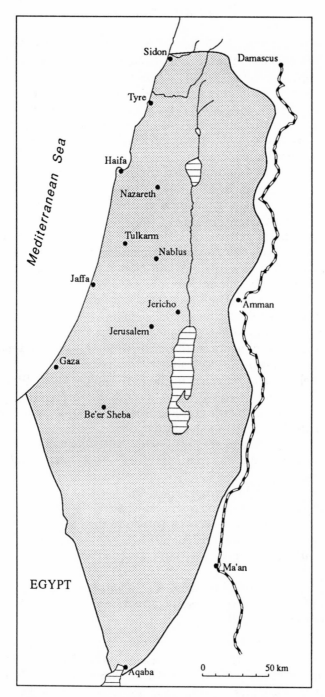

Map 1.1. The Zionist Movement's Territorial
Proposals in 1919

- *In the south.* A border to be determined with the Egyptian government.

- *In the west.* The Mediterranean Sea.

The territory within these boundaries totals some 45,000–50,000 km^2 covering what is today southern Lebanon, the Golan Heights, the Gil'ad mountains, and an area of approximately 18,000 km^2 across the Jordan River. These boundaries were the most "geographic" claimed by the Zionist movement during the pre-state period. They reflect the territorial concepts about natural boundaries that prevailed at that time, specifying the geographical requirements necessary to create a political entity that could stand on its own.[13] The 1919 memorandum emphasizes mainly natural boundaries, control of water sources, and agricultural land required for subsistence. These proposed boundaries are quite similar to the physical-natural boundaries of Eretz Israel that appear in a book published a year earlier (1918), written by Ben-Gurion and Ben-Zvi.[14] However, the territory in the Zionist Organization's memorandum is slightly more limited, already reflecting the political constraints and certain compromises (described later) with the British Foreign Office.[15]

The first problem was that the northern border was not just local, but a division between French and British interests (and future mandatory areas) in the Middle East, as well as their global concerns. The early Zionist Organization's proposal of November 1918 included most of the Litani River within the Jewish national home, but only as far as the 33'45" latitude. In the memorandum submitted to the Peace Conference the line was moved farther northward to Sidon. The idea was probably to help the British in their negotiations with the French. The British subsequently supported this proposal, but not adamantly. Other considerations in their relations with the French took precedence.

Second, Ben-Gurion and Ben-Zvi wrote that the eastern border of Eretz Israel is in the "Syrian desert" and cannot be precisely determined because, "as more desert land will be prepared for development, the eastern border of Eretz Israel will be adjusted eastward and Eretz Israel will grow."[16] But the Zionist leaders knew that they could not ask to include the entire area of Transjordan in the Jewish national home due to Faisal's demands and British plans for this area and Iraq. They also knew that the maximum they could hope for in the east would be a border running along the Hijaz railway and that even this was a doubtful possibility.

Third, the Zionists' first proposal set a southern border along the El Arish-Aqaba line, to include part of the Sinai desert. The 1919 memorandum left the matter open for negotiation with the Egyptian government. Here, too, the problem was internally British, as the border had to separate two territories under British control: the mandate for Palestine and the British protectorate in Egypt. The Rafah-Taba line, which since 1906 had served as an administrative border between Egypt and the Ottoman Empire, ultimately proved its survival ability, especially because it was already marked on the ground.

In 1919 for the first time the Zionist movement actually drew a map of Eretz Israel and thus presented a political position on its territorial aspirations. The map was based on the assumption that this position could influence the decisions of the peace conference, the powers involved, and the League of Nations. Indeed, the coordinated British-Zionist position on the northern border did influence the negotiations with France. The French starting point was that mandatory boundaries between the two powers would be determined in accordance with the Sykes-Picot Agreement. The eventual northern border represented a compromise between this position and the Zionist proposal.[17] At the end of a lengthy process, the boundaries of the British mandate for Palestine were determined by the interests of the involved powers (northern border) and internal considerations of the British government (eastern and southern borders). The Zionist movement had only a slight influence on these decisions, and we present them here quite briefly.

The negotiations between Britain and France concluded with the San Remo Agreement of April 1920, which paved the way for the League of Nations to allot the mandates to France and Britain. The northern and northeastern borders were settled only in December 1920, and it took another two years and many revisions to mark the boundary on the ground. This is the line that today serves as the border between Israel and Lebanon and that outlined the armistice line between Israel and Syria until 1967.[18] The Zionist movement saw British concessions to the French on the northern border as a breach of the commitments undertaken in the Balfour Declaration and subsequent understandings.[19]

The eastern border of the national home underwent many changes between 1920 and 1922, the main question being how Britain would fulfill its promises to the Hussein family.[20] At the Cairo Conference of March 1921, Churchill, the new secretary for the colonies, confirmed Emir Abdullah's control of Transjordan and the de facto administrative separation from Palestine (E.I.). The League of Nations authorized the British mandate in July 1922, and Article 25 of the mandate allowed Britain not to apply the provisions relating to the Jewish national home on Transjordan. A year later, Emir Abdullah was appointed ruler of Transjordan under the aegis of the British high commissioner stationed in Jerusalem. The border between Palestine (E.I.) and Transjordan was finally determined and marked only in 1927.[21] The territory east of the Jordan River was thus separated from the area of the national home.

The Zionist movement's opposition to the separation of Transjordan was expressed at the Twelfth Zionist Congress, held in Carlsbad in 1921.[22] One of the congress resolutions expressed satisfaction that "Transjordan, which was always an integral part of the Land of Israel in the eyes of the people, was again attached to the British mandate over Eretz Israel."[23] At this time, there was still hope that the arrangement in Transjordan would prove temporary, and its detachment subsequently became a divisive issue within the Zionist movement. The Revisionist Party, established in 1925 under Jabotinsky's leadership, considered this the first partition of Eretz Israel. Officially, the Zionist movement has never agreed with British exclusion of Transjordan from the Jewish national home, but in fact had no choice but to make peace with this decision.[24] The issue would be raised in the testimony of Jewish representatives before the Royal Commission, but the commission's report rejected Jewish requests to settle in Transjordan.[25] There were also repeated Jewish attempts to purchase or lease lands in Transjordan. But most efforts from the 1920s onward were directed toward the western part of Eretz Israel.[26]

Determination of the southern border between Palestine (E.I.) and Egypt was an internal matter within the British administration. One of the many proposals would have removed the "Negev Triangle" from the mandate area.[27] Hence, the outlet to the Red Sea should be seen as something of an achievement for the Zionist movement, even though its original request for an El Arish-Aqaba line was rejected.

To summarize, from the mid-1920s, Palestine (E.I.) referred to the area of some 28,000 km² west of the Jordan River, or approximately 60 percent of the area claimed by the Zionist movement in its official memorandum of 1919. Weizmann would later express his bitterness regarding British fulfillment of their commitments: "If today I were conducting negotiations as in 1917, I would insistently demand setting aside a separate territory for the Jews in Eretz Israel and in Trans-Jordan, even as reserve."[28]

The decisions of the Zionist movement at this first territorial crossroad (1919–1922), which determined the borders of mandatory Palestine, greatly differ from those that would be made at future crossroads (1937 and after). In addition to objective differences between the periods, the Zionist movement's political options were very limited at the beginning of the mandate because, among other reasons, there were only some 80,000 Jews in Palestine in 1922. Coordination with the British government of the positions appearing in the 1919 memorandum did influence award of the mandate to Britain and the determinations of the northern border. By contrast, when the territorial argument was internal, that is, with the British, or when attempts were made to reach an understanding with the Arab national movement, the Zionist movement's maneuvering room was most limited. As we shall see, the territorial arguments of 1919–1922 resemble those raised in the debate of 1937. But in 1937, the Zionist movement did face a real test of decision making, with sharper choices regarding the importance of territory weighed against the chance for sovereignty. In the 1920s, the "reduction" of the national home in the north posed a diplomatic challenge to the Zionist movement, but it could not exert real pressure on France, or alternately threaten to withdraw its support from entrusting Britain with the mandate for Palestine. At the same time, the concerns of the Arabs in Palestine that their land might be given to the Jews were ignored at this junction, despite British statements that the "national home" did not necessarily mean a Jewish state.[29] In retrospect, it seems that the territorial basis established for the national home in 1919–1922 was the largest that the Zionist movement could have achieved under the circumstances. Its subsequent problem was how to retain this area and not how to expand it.

Establishment of the Royal Commission: External Events

British policy, as determined in Churchill's White Paper of June 1922, was under constant pressure because of the internal conflict. The 1929 riots led to a reevaluation of British policy in Palestine (E.I.) and generated a series of enquiries, reports, and documents (published in 1930) that expressed the British government's readiness to accept some Arab demands and to limit Jewish immigration, land purchase, and settlement.[30] The Jews considered this new policy a flagrant denial of British commitments under its mandatory obligations. By contrast, the Arabs viewed British reaction to the riots, and particularly Prime Minister MacDonald's letter to Weizmann of February 13, 1931, delaying implementation of the 1930 White Paper,[31] as proof that the British government was continuing to aid the establishment of a Jewish state in Palestine, while ignoring the Arab majority.

Increased Jewish immigration in the 1930s aggravated Palestinian Arab opposition to Zionist aspirations. The number of Jews in the country doubled between 1931 and 1936, reaching approximately 400,000. It was accompanied by import of capital, accelerated purchase of land, and expansion of settlements. There was a sense that the Jewish national home was being realized, as the urgency to increase the pace was compounded by the distress of European Jewry. The British found themselves on the horns of this dilemma when the "Arab Revolt" broke out in April 1936. The Royal Commission's report lists a number of causes for the revolt:

- The decrease in the proportion of the Arab population of Palestine from about 90 percent in 1922 to 70 percent in 1936;

- The desire to end the mandate and establish an independent Palestinian Arab state on the model of Iraq, Transjordan, Syria, and Lebanon, which were given various levels of independence during those years;

- Uncertainty as to British intentions in the Middle East and Palestine, in light of European events and Italian and German policy in the region.[32]

The first phase of the disturbances lasted from April to November 1936, when the Royal Commission departed for Palestine (E.I.). They were renewed in September 1937 and continued intermittently until May 1939. Appointment of a high-level commission was considered in the British House of Commons as early as March 1936, before the disturbances began, in the context of establishing a legislative council.[33] High Commissioner Wauchope officially recommended the establishment of a Commission of Enquiry, and the British cabinet resolved to do it on May 18. The royal warrants granted the commission's terms of reference as follows:

To ascertain the underlying causes of the disturbances which broke out in Palestine in the middle of April; to enquire into the manner in which the Mandate for Palestine is being implemented in relation to Our obligations as Mandatory to the

Arabs and the Jews respectively; and to ascertain whether, upon a proper construction of the terms of the Mandate, either the Arabs or the Jews have any legitimate grievances upon account of the way in which the Mandate has been or is being implemented; and if the Commission is satisfied that any such grievances are well founded, to make recommendations for their removal and for the prevention of their recurrence.[34]

The commission arrived in Palestine (E.I.) in November 1936 and began to hear evidence in public and private sessions. The negative results of previous investigations caused the Jewish Agency to oppose the appointment of the commission. But once the commission was established, Jewish representatives cooperated with it fully. The Arab Higher Committee, the representative body of Palestinian Arabs, also opposed the establishment of the commission and continued to boycott it. They changed their position and appeared before the commission only toward the end of its work in the region in January 1937.

To summarize, Palestinian Arab opposition to the establishment of a Jewish national home greatly intensified in the 1930s, forcing the British government and the mandatory administration in Palestine (E.I.) to reexamine a number of policy issues:

How will Britain benefit from continuing the mandate for Palestine (E.I.), when it entails a struggle between two local communities, a high investment of military and financial resources, and continuous international pressure?

How can the gap be bridged between what the British termed *the dual obligation* to the Jews and Arabs.

Can solutions be found that will protect British interests, be supported by the two communities, and remove the Palestine (E.I.) problem from the agenda of the British government and international public opinion?

The British answered the first question positively: On the eve of World War II, the British had a growing interest in continuing to hold Palestine. British attempts to address the second and third questions started the process that eventually forced the Jews and Arabs to turn their aspirations into practical decisions regarding state, territory, and boundaries. This was a major turning point from the Zionist movement's point of view. Ever since the mandate boundaries were determined in the early 1920s, the Jews had argued with the British government over the content of the national home and the means for its realization. Now, a prestigious royal commission had proposed Jewish sovereignty in exchange for agreement to partition western Palestine.

Establishment of the Royal Commission:
Internal Events

Even though the question of territorial partition was placed on the political agenda of the Zionist movement only in 1937, proposals for "cantonization" were discussed much earlier. *Cantonization* meant geographical division into regions with some autonomous status, thus expressing the differentiated needs of the Arabs and Jews. The formation of cantons also meant that the country would remain an undivided territorial unit under one central government: British, Arab-Jewish, or joint. Arthur Ruppin, Itamar Ben-Avi, Paltiel Dickenstein, and Victor Jacobson are considered the theoretical fathers of cantonization among the Jews; Archer Cust, Douglas Duff, and Stafford Kripps among the British; and Mussa El-Alami and Ahmad El-Khlidi among the Arabs.

The ideas summarized in Table 2.1 indicate that "cantonization" meant division into autonomous areas by population features and alternatively the creation of a federated structure under British auspices.[35] Some thought in terms of the Swiss model, whereas others proposed "cantons" but actually meant separate states somehow connected to each other. What these proposals shared was the use of regional geographic partition to solve the Arab-Jewish conflict. Members of the royal commission knew of these proposals, particularly the British ones, and their impact is evident in the final report.[36]

Did Jewish leaders share these ideas? Some scholars who studied this question outlined a conspiracy between Weizmann and Colonial Secretary Ormsby-Gore for advancing the idea of partition, with Commission Chairman Lord Peel and particularly Commission Member Professor Coupland as secondary players.[37] This speculation revolves around a meeting between Weizmann and Cust on June 26, 1936. In subsequent correspondence, Weizmann rejected the creation of a Jewish canton with boundaries proposed by Cust, maintaining that "this partition is unacceptable for historic reasons and due to fundamental financial and

Table 2.1. Various Sources of the Concept of Cantons

AUTHOR	DATE	THE CANTONS	BORDERS OF THE JEWISH CANTONS	COMMENTS
Arthur Ruppin	1907[a]	Autonomous Jewish administrative areas	Unclear, mainly in the coastal region, the Carmel and Hula Valleys	
Itamar Ben-Avi	1920[b] 1930[c] 1932[d]	Two: Hebrew with Jewish representation and Arab with Arab majority	The Jewish canton would encompass two-fifths of the area of E.I.: Jerusalem-Jaffa, Rehovot-Akko-Safed-Tiberias-Metulla	Federation of the states in Palestine in the 1920 proposal. The 1932 proposal discussed the Swiss model and partition into three cantons: Jewish, Moslem, and Christian
Paltiel Dickenstein	1930[e]	Cantons with a 75% majority of Jews or Arabs	The cantons would change with population growth	The Jewish cantons would grow with immigration
Victor (Avigdor) Jacobson	1931[f]	Two cantons or states: Jewish Land of Israel and an Arab Palestine	The entire coastal area plus the Jezreel valley and Tiberias region	Related to the idea of a binational state

Ahmad El-Halidi	1933[g]	Two: Jewish and Arab to be called *Southern Syria*, by population centers. Jerusalem, Hebron, Bethlehem, Nazareth, Safed are free cities	Tel Aviv-Haifa coastal plain, Haifa-Beit Shean-Tiberias-Hula	The cantons would have joint government under British aegis
Mussa El-Alami	1933[h]	Independent Jewish canton in the coastal area and Palestinian Arab state in the remaining area	Tel Aviv-Atlit	Joint legislative council with proportional representation under the aegis of the British Mandate
L. Archer Cust	1936[i]	Two: Jewish and Arab with a mandate area in Jerusalem and Haifa. A federation headed by the mandatory government	Coastal region from Gaza to Akko plus the Jezreel and Hula valleys	The Arab canton would be united with Transjordan. Mentions the possibility of territorial partition of Eretz Israel
Stafford Kripps	1936[j]	Two federated states under British aegis	Coastal area plus the valleys	British member of parliament who made his proposal in March 1936

Table 2.1. Various Sources of the Concept of Cantons (cont.)

AUTHOR	DATE	THE CANTONS	BORDERS OF THE JEWISH CANTONS	COMMENTS
Douglas Duff	1936[k]	Two cantons in a federal state; members of the League of Nations	Coastal area plus the valleys, excluding a British colony in Atlit-Sidon and a "free" corridor from Jerusalem to Jaffa	Arab canton is part of Transjordan. The Peel report quoted his line; "Better half a loaf than none at all."

[a] A. Ruppin, "Jewish Autonomy in Eretz Israel—Thirty Years of Building in Eretz Israel" (memorandum to the Zionist General Council), Jerusalem, 1907, as quoted in Eliash, 1971, pp. 16–27. Ruppin repeated his proposition in a letter to Weizmann of May 1937. Ruppin, 1968, pp. 275–278.

[b] Itamar Ben Avi, "The Federated States of Palestine," New Palestine, 1920. This publication is mentioned in several sources (see Hattis, 1970, p. 116), but could not be found.

[c] Itamar Ben Avi, 1930.

[d] Hayom, March 13, 1932.

[e] P. Dickenstein, 1930, pp. 121–123.

[f] On the Jacobson plan, see Gabi Cohen, 1974, pp. 350–357; see also Eliash, 1971, pp. 24–25, as based on the Sharett and Arlozorov diaries; and Hattis, 1970, p. 120, as based on his letters to Weizmann.

[g] Anonymous, Filastine (December 27, 1937), as quoted in Hattis, 1970, pp. 123–125. See also note 37.

[h] Musa El-Alami presented a detailed memorandum on the cantonization program to the High Commissioner in September 1933. CO 722/257/37367 II, as quoted in G. Cohen, 1974, p. 307. He was also in touch with Ben-Gurion on the idea of federation (Porath, 1985, pp. 67–68). See also note 38.

[i] L. A. Cust, 1936.

[j] S. Kripps, Letter to the Manchester Guardian (September 8, 1936).

[k] D. Duff, 1936, pp. 266–269. See the map in Eliash, 1971, p. 184.

economic difficulties."[38] Cust wrote a summary of their meeting, according to which Weizmann maintained, in reaction to the canton plan, that separate land "reserves" needed to be created: for the Arabs on the hills and for the Jews in other areas. Cust later wrote that Weizmann agreed to discuss the proposal with his colleagues, and Cust would discuss it with the Arabs.[39]

By return correspondence, Weizmann asked Cust to correct the summary on a number of crucial points and then raise it in additional forums without obligating Weizmann.[40] In short, the exchange was tentative and rather informal. But clearly Cust's proposal was accepted as a basis for discussions, and Weizmann and Ben-Gurion knew that the contents of the discussion with Cust were transmitted to Ormsby-Gore.[41] The colonial secretary also mentioned the plan in a memorandum to the cabinet on July 4, 1936.[42] There is therefore a basis for the premise that "Weizmann did not reject outright the cantonization plan."[43] Nevertheless, one cannot conclude that "Weizmann had already weighed the other solution proposed by Ormsby-Gore—territorial partition between the two peoples" or that it had been agreed that the Jewish Agency and the mandatory government would prepare a joint plan along these lines.[44]

What is known is that Weizmann supported the idea of allocating "reserves" of land to the Arabs in the mountain region, where land purchase by Jews would be forbidden, in exchange for expanding Jewish settlement in the lowlands.[45] But there is no evidence that Weizmann proposed territorial and political partition of Eretz Israel at this stage. To be sure, there were attempts to advance geographical solutions, but there is no basis for assuming a grand conspiracy. It can be assumed, on the other hand, that Weizmann's agreement developed gradually: first, readiness to consider separate land reserves for Jews and Arabs; second, willingness to discuss concepts of cantonization; and third, in-principle agreement to the idea of territorial separation—partition in exchange for Jewish sovereignty. Indications of his thinking in terms of "land reserves" remain in Weizmann's statements as late as 1938, as well as in his testimony before the royal commission.

In Dothan's opinion, Lord Peel was chosen to head the royal commission because Colonial Secretary Ormsby-Gore supported Cust's ideas. Furthermore, behind-the-scenes discussions on the partition solution were taking place parallel to the process of establishing the royal commission, which began in Spring 1936, and Weizmann was a party to these discussions.[46] Again, there is no proof. Only ideas regarding a territorial solution had been exchanged before the British cabinet decided in May 1936 to establish the commission and before its official appointment in August 1936. As to previous contact with Coupland, we have only indirect proof: On July 31, 1936, Felix Frankfurter met with Coupland and reported to Ben-Gurion.[47] The contents of the discussion are unknown, but the context of Ben-Gurion's entry in his diaries is Jewish preparations for the royal commission. All of this strengthens the assumption that Weizmann was not being candid when he wrote that he first heard about partition during his testimony before the royal commission and subsequently in a secret meeting between himself and Coupland at Nahalal.[48] It does seem, however, that his commitment to the idea started at that time. There were prior feelers and exchange of ideas, particularly concerning the allotment of land, but partition was politically placed on the agenda only in early 1937. In any event, this debate about Weizmann's involvement does not detract from the crucial nature of the decision faced by the Zionist movement when partition was transformed from an idea to an official British proposal.

The idea of geographic separation between Jews and Arabs was bandied about in various forms, and we can summarize the process, until it became an official British proposal, as follows:

• It circulated rather early among British policy makers. For instance, the Colonial Office conducted a political evaluation in March 1934 and resolved to maintain the existing policy and reject other alternatives, one of which favored geographic separation of the Arab and Jewish communities in Palestine (E.I.). This option was again raised in 1936, when the riots began.

• As noted, Weizmann developed a gradual commitment, but he was previously aware of the idea and even discussed it in his meetings with Mussolini in 1933–1934.[49]

• A number of Palestinian Arab leaders, such as Mussa El-Alami, also considered territorial separation as a possible solution to the conflict (see Table 2.1). They proposed it to the British as a means of limiting Jewish expansion in Palestine.[50]

• Cust's efforts to raise support for the cantonization idea won approval as a possible solution to the land problem and became a subject of correspondence between Colonial Secretary Ormsby-Gore and High Commissioner Wauchope.[51] Wauchope stressed the subject of immigration and added that: "the solution to the problem of our dual obligations to the Arabs and Jews . . . can be found in partitioning Palestine into three categories, reservations for Arabs, for Jews and for mixed population."[52]

- Weizmann and Ben-Gurion met with the colonial secretary on June 30, 1936, after Weizmann's discussion with Cust. Ormsby-Gore raised the issue of cantonization, but Weizmann was opposed. Ben-Gurion wrote in his diary: "Weizmann replied that cantonization in this small land cannot be discussed from either an administrative or economic point of view."[53]

- After Ormsby-Gore's meeting with Weizmann, the secretary believed that the royal commission would also examine the cantonization proposal.[54] As noted, he brought Weizmann's comments on cantonization to the cabinet's attention on July 4, 1936.

- Wauchope asked Ben-Gurion and Shertok for their opinions on cantonization in a conversation in Jerusalem on July 9, 1936. Ben-Gurion replied negatively both to cantonization and the proposal to concentrate Jewish land purchases in the plains.[55] Ben-Gurion did not appreciate the canton proposal during this period, and vehemently opposed Cust's ideas.[56] He also expressed this position in conversations with George Antonius in April 1936.[57]

- It is not certain that all members of the royal commission were aware of the ideas of cantonization or partition. But some of them, notably Coupland, must have heard of it directly or indirectly. For instance, Lord Peel had begun to investigate the possibility of rescinding or changing the mandate while still in England.[58] In his letter to the colonial secretary of December 1936, immediately upon his arrival in Palestine (E.I.), Peel noted that the gap between the Arabs and the Jews apparently could not be bridged.[59]

In sum, various ideas raised in 1936 influenced British, Jewish, and Arab leaders to consider the possibility of utilizing geography to separate the two communities in Palestine (E.I.). The next phase in terms of the Jewish stance constituted an attempt to influence the royal commission's work. This began in August 1936 and continued until July 1937, when the report was published. Before discussing this in Chapter Three, we will present the chronological course of events until the idea of partition was formally dropped with the publication of the White Paper of 1939, on the eve of World War II, with emphasis on developments external to the Zionist movement.

Chronology of Main Events

The Predecision Stage

May 19, 1936 Colonial secretary's announcement in the House of Commons of the intention to establish a royal commission of enquiry to investigate the causes of the disturbances. The secretary announced that the commission's members would be appointed only upon the return of order to Palestine (E.I.)[60]

August 7, 1936 Announcement of the establishment of the royal commission, headed by Earl Peel. The other members were Sir Rumbold, Sir Hammond, Sir Carter, Sir Morris, and Professor Coupland. The Commission arrived in Palestine (E.I.) on November 11 and remained until the end of January 1937.

October 11, 1936 The Arab Higher Committee acceded to the request of the Arab kings and announced an end to the strikes.

January 6, 1937 The Arab Higher Committee acceded to the request of the kings of Iraq and Saudi Arabia and announced its willingness to testify before the royal commission.

The Decision Stage

July 7, 1937 The royal commission submitted its report and unanimous recommendations to His Majesty through the colonial secretary. The report was submitted to the House of Commons with a government "Statement of Policy," according to which the government was "in general agreement with the arguments and conclusions of the Commission."[61]

July 10–21, 1937 Debates in both the House of Commons and the House of Lords. Deliberations in the House of Commons ended not with a vote but rather with a majority decision authorizing the government to bring the matter to the League of Nations before preparing a final plan for parliamentary approval.[62]

July 30–August 20, 1937 Extensive discussions by the League of Nations' Mandates Commission raised many reservations to the proposal. The commission's preliminary recommendation to the league's council expressed willingness to continue to examine the advantages and disadvantages of "the new territorial solution." This recommendation to postpone the decision was authorized by the league's council on September 16, 1937.[63]

Postdecision stage

September–December 1937 Disagreement occurred within the British government: the Foreign Office opposed the partition proposal, whereas the Colonial Office continued to support it.[64] The cabinet held a secret discussion on December 8, 1937, and accepted Prime Minister Chamberlain's proposal to delay all immediate action for more than a year and meanwhile to appoint another commission to examine the plan and submit its opinion.[65] In retrospect, this cabinet resolution signified abandonment of the partition proposal, although this would be announced publicly only a year later.

January 4, 1938 A policy statement was made of the British government's intention to establish a "technical commission" to prepare detailed proposals for the partition scheme.[66]

March 1938 The Palestine Partition Commission, headed by Sir Woodhead, was established. The commission was secretly told that, in accordance with the cabinet's decision, it was within the commission's authority to recommend that "no workable scheme could be produced." That is to say, the government told the commission that it was prepared to accept a recommendation to retract the partition recommendations of the Peel commission.[67] The colonial secretary announced in the House of Commons that the government's policy had not changed since July 1937 and was still determined to see partition through. The foreign secretary reacted with a personal letter to the colonial secretary, dissociating himself from this announcement because the cabinet resolved to take a final decision on partition only if the Woodhead commission's investigation would prove that an equitable and workable scheme could be evolved.[68]

November 9, 1938   The Woodhead commission report was published. Its main point was that the partition proposal of the royal commission was not practicable for administrative and political reasons.[69] The report also contained majority and minority recommendations on other possibilities for partitioning Palestine, but these were immaterial. With the report's submission, the government published a policy statement that "partition is not a practical solution" and invited the Jews and Arabs to a conference in London.

February 7–March 17, 1939   The St. James "round table" ended in a deadlock. The final proposals submitted by the British government were rejected by both the Jews and the Arabs.

May 17, 1939   The 1939 White Paper was published stating that, instead of partition, the British government would implement a policy by which[70]

- An independent state would be established in Palestine within ten years. This would be conditioned upon Arab-Jewish cooperation and, meanwhile, the British Mandate would continue.

- Jewish immigration would be limited to 75,000 during the next five years. Further expansion of the Jewish national home by immigration would be subsequently conditioned on Arab acquiescence.

- Jewish purchase of land would be limited by "Land Transfer Regulations" to be published later.[71]

The publication of the White Paper was followed by a debate in the House of Commons (May 22–23, 1939); and the government policy was approved by a majority of 268 to 179, with 110 abstentions—including many Conservative members of the prime minister's party.

June 1939   Discussion of the British White Paper in the Mandates Commission of the League of Nations ended with a negative recommendation (four against, three in favor). The outbreak of World War II preempted discussion of this recommendation in the league council.

3 The Predecision Phase

Everybody seems to be quite irreconcilable. I have never been on any enquiry before where there was less suggestion of how to meet a difficulty. The thing we love so much in England, which is not liked here, is compromise, but we have had nothing of that sort put before us.

—Lord Peel, chairman of the royal commission,
during Weizmann's testimony

Jewish Testimony Before the Royal Commission

The announcement of the British colonial secretary on May 19, 1936, of the intention to establish a commission of enquiry generated intense trepidation in the Yishuv and the Zionist movement.[1] When its attempts to block the commission's establishment failed, the Jewish Agency tried to change the commission's terms of reference in order to link it to the original goals of the mandate.[2] At a meeting of the Mapai party Central Committee, fears were expressed that the commission's recommendations would result in a reduction of the area of the Jewish national home.[3]

A meeting of the enlarged Zionist General Council in Zurich on August 26, 1936, extensively debated the appropriate reaction. It was resolved to establish a special committee, headed by M. Ussishkin, to formulate the Zionist movement's position toward the royal commission.[4] An announcement by the general council included an appeal to the "civilized world" to support continuation of the mandate for Eretz Israel.[5]

The Jewish Agency began to formulate the positions and documents for presentation to the royal commission. However, serious quarrels—not entirely detached from the usual power struggle—broke out among members of the Zionist executive in London and Jerusalem concerning central policy issues. Finally, a memorandum prepared by L. Stein, the former political secretary of the London executive, was printed in London and served as the main document. A few days before the arrival of the royal commission, several pages from Stein's memorandum were removed and pages printed in Jerusalem were glued in their place. It was presented to the royal commission in this form. Neither cantonization nor the possibility of partition were raised in this internal dispute. It was agreed that the Zionist testimony would not relate to the possibility of terminating the mandate or drastically altering the political status of Eretz Israel.

We will first present the preliminary positions of Weizmann and Ben-Gurion, the two central leaders, whose unwritten 1937 accord on partition paved the way for the decision at the Twentieth Zionist Congress.[6]

Weizmann's Testimony

Weizmann was the main Jewish witness, towering above his colleagues in both stature and his prestige in the eyes of the commission. He testified five times, excluding informal meetings with commission members, between November 25, 1936, and January 8, 1937.[7]

Weizmann's initial open testimony was directed at public opinion and described the saga of Zionist revival. In the second, private testimony, he was more specific and mentioned Transjordan as a possible solution for settlement by Jews as well as by Palestinian Arabs who would move there in response to overcrowding in Eretz Israel. Weizmann noted two possible directions for British policy: to continue the original mandate, namely, to strengthen the Jewish national home; or to try to appease the Arabs by curtailing the Zionist endeavor. He rejected the second possibility and, instead, suggested placating the Arabs by promising them that the British would remain in the country always and would enforce a principle of nondomination of one people by the other, even if the Jews became a majority in Eretz Israel: "We do not want to reduce the Arabs to be bearers of wood and drawers of water," Weizmann told the Peel commission. They pressured him to state what he felt "constitutes completion of the development of a national home?" Weizmann evasively replied, "It is never completed."

In the third private testimony, Weizmann listed the reasons for the Arab revolt and their demand to halt Jewish immigration and land purchase and to establish a national Arab government in Palestine: The very existence of the Balfour Declaration; the granting of independence to neighboring Arab countries; the "inferiority complex on the part of the Arabs"; and their fears that the Jews would become a majority and force the Arabs out of Palestine. A hint of the need for separation between the two peoples can perhaps be found in Weizmann's comment that "the Arab is a totalitarian," to which commission member Coupland agreed, "He does not like minorities."

In his fourth private testimony, Weizmann was again asked: "What essentials are the establishment of the Jewish national home lacking at the present time?" Weizmann responded that the nucleus already existed, including national language and spiritual awareness, but that the national home had yet to solve the problem for a majority of the 16 million Jews throughout the world. Lord Peel asked to clarify the difference between a Jewish national home and Jewish national state. Weizmann answered that, even if the Jews became a majority, Palestine would not—and immediately corrected himself to say that is "should not"—become a Jewish national state. He admitted that it would automatically become a Jewish state if it contained no Arabs, but insisted that this was neither the overt nor covert intention of the current Zionist leadership.

In this testimony, Weizmann was for the first time asked directly by Sir Hammond: "Is cantonization in any form possible?" Hammond referred to a federated structure of Jewish and Arab regions under the aegis of the mandatory government. Weizmann had anticipated the question, knowing that the proposals of Cust and Kripps had been submitted to the commission.[8] He presented a long list of general and practical arguments against the whole idea, maintaining that cantons were an artificial solution. He reiterated the point that the Jewish people had lost Transjordan and would now lose the vast majority of Palestine, becoming a permanent minority in a small ghetto. Nevertheless, Weizmann promised the commission that the Jews would carefully examine any proposal even if it happened to run counter to the mandate. He immediately added two conditions: that the proposal allow immigration to continue and include Transjordan in some form.

Coupland asked if it was feasible to consider something more drastic than cantonization: division into two large areas of self-government. Weizmann responded that he could not answer right away and made a long speech explaining that there was no point in getting Jewish agreement as long as the Arabs were not a party to the process. In this situation, he hinted, any proposal would become only the starting point for Arab demands. Lord Peel requested clarification, and Weizmann replied that he was willing to examine Coupland's still unclear proposal.

Partition was discussed most directly in his fifth private testimony.[9] Coupland made his third and final progression—from cantonization to a regional federation and now to partition into two independent states. Weizmann mentioned his talks with Cust in London and emphasized that "this possible solution, perhaps in five or ten years time, would be an easier thing than the present situation." He then presented a series of counterarguments, some of them new, such as the lack of continuity between large blocs of Jewish-owned land, no Jewish land between Gaza and Jaffa, and financial and administrative problems. Weizmann closed his remarks by repeating his position that the proposal would mean the creation of "land reserves" for the Arabs in the hills, meaning: "You, the Jews, keep off the hills." He continued "If a tripartite agreement can be arrived at and this is the price which is demanded from us, I do not think that you would find us difficult. . . . I am saying this without any authority," he stressed, adding that it would not be easy to obtain Jewish support. The testimony at this point became a dialogue during which Weizmann hinted that he would personally assist a proposal based on the commission's full authority. Coupland saw this as an opportunity to clarify his proposal, stating that the intention is "to terminate the Mandate, split Palestine into two halves—the plain for an independent Jewish state, and the rest of Palestine plus Transjordania, an independent Arab state." "Permit me not to give a definite answer now," Weizmann replied. "Let me think of it."

The desire to buy time for the Zionist endeavor was central to Weizmann's lengthy testimony.[10] Weizmann would have preferred to continue the mandate (assuming it would suppress the riots) and postpone any decision for five years in the hope that the Jewish presence in Eretz Israel would meanwhile grow stronger.[11] Weizmann well understood, however, that the commission would seek a compromise, a tendency that he tried to go along with, while battling the danger that it would come at Jewish expense.[12] Accordingly, Weizmann did not reject the idea of partition. He argued against it (more aggressively against cantonization), but led the commission to understand that he personally believed partition could be discussed.[13] He thus paved the way for the prevailing opinion in the Colonial Office, and very possibly among the majority of commission members, that Weizmann—followed by the Jewish leadership—would ultimately agree to partition.

It should be noted that the Jewish leaders continued referring to cantonization even though they were familiar with the royal commission's partition proposal. Weizmann's official letter to the

THE PREDECISION PHASE 59

commission of January 19, 1937, whose purpose was to complete and correct his closed testimony, also related to "cantonization" without mentioning partition: "The Jewish people can only relate to the cantonization proposals as a plan for the gradual and on-going destruction of the Jewish national home."[14]

Weizmann was deliberately vague, but Shertok's record of a meeting of the Mapai Central Committee on February 5–6, 1937, proves that Weizmann clearly distinguished between cantonization and the proposal to establish two separate states.[15] According to Shertok, Weizmann attended the final hearing to oppose cantonization. When Coupland raised the two-state plan, Weizmann answered that he had to think about it. From the protocol of the testimony, it is clear that the two-state issue was raised earlier. Therefore, Weizmann and Coupland spoke about this matter for the third time during their secret discussion at Nahalal in January 1937.[16]

Therefore, Weizmann concealed from his associates and per-haps from Shertok that he did not reject the idea outright and even led the commission to understand that the matter was open for discussion. We know that in early 1937 Weizmann supported parti-tion. Shertok even said in the beginning of February: "I greatly feared Weizmann's excitement over this matter."[17] Weizmann cor-roborated this after his testimony to the commission: "The long toil of my life was at last crowned with success. The Jewish state was at hand."[18] He apparently spoke in a similar vein to settlers at Nahalal after his meeting with Coupland.[19]

The fact that Weizmann did not clarify the confusion over the distinction between cantonization and partition and his partial report about what happened during his testimony led to the formu-lation of a conspiracy theory regarding Weizmann's role. According to this theory, Weizmann began to consider the partition plan first in thought and then through feelers to British acquaintances, and also in his meetings with Mussolini in 1933–1934. Subsequently, the Arab riots caused Weizmann to solicit active support for parti-tion in meetings with Cust and the colonial secretary as early as June 1936. Weizmann's next campaign, according to this theory, was to "guide the Royal Commission toward the idea of partition,"[20] which he did in his closed testimony and in secret contacts with royal commission members. Thus Weizmann managed to convince the royal commission to recommend partition after the matter had been previously arranged with the colonial secretary and Lord Peel. This hypothesis even claims that Weizmann started the rumor that Coupland fathered the partition idea for two reasons: to leave himself room to maneuver, and especially to create the impression that partition was actually introduced by the honorable, independent royal commission—to increase its chances of acceptance by the involved parties.

The problem with this seemingly well-constructed theory is that there is no proof of it in the documents or testimonies. Moreover, this version credits Weizmann with virtually unlimited political maneuverability to enlist the colonial secretary and the high commissioner, to orchestrate the appointment of a prestigious royal commission that would act according to a predetermined plan, and to manipulate the commission to generate the partition proposal in a way that would increase its chances of acceptance.

In reality, however, political initiatives such as this are much more complicated and carried out slowly and circuitously. Furthermore, the existence of such a complex conspiracy between Weizmann and the colonial secretary should have been reflected in documents of the Foreign Office, which opposed partition from the start.

We therefore postulate that Weizmann had contemplated geographic separation as a possible solution before 1936. He was familiar with the subject before his testimony, but he began to consider the possibility seriously only when he realized that it had gained support among members of the commission as well as British policy makers, particularly the colonial secretary and the high commissioner.[21] Weizmann was above all a political pragmatist. He was familiar with British policy-making processes, and when he grew convinced that a new British policy was being formulated around partition as a compromise, he started to work for its advantageous realization. Accordingly, Weizmann acted from early 1937 on two levels: to do everything he could to ensure that the partition proposal would be the best possible for the Jews;[22] and to garner British and international support for the proposal.[23] This hypothesis is compatible with the analysis to be presented later, which shows that the Zionist movement's 1937 decision was not preordained. In this internal struggle, Weizmann found a determined and consistent ally in Ben-Gurion.

Ben-Gurion's Positions

The first time that Ben-Gurion expressed unequivocal support for the idea of partition was when he proposed the "two-state plan" in Mapai's Central Committee on February 5, 1937, after he was told that Weizmann and members of the Royal Commission had discussed the matter. Shabtai Teveth maintains that Ben-Gurion, and not Weizmann, was the first to view partition as a solution to political Zionism and a path to statehood: "The idea of partition fell within his conception of Zionism from the start and returned like a genetic code in each of its permutations."[24]

Teveth indicates that Ben-Gurion called for the establishment of a federated Eretz Israel based on national separation (i.e., partition), as early as 1929. Thus Ben-Gurion "unwittingly" prepared the ground for the partition plan. When, on January 8, 1937, Weizmann told him about the proposal being formulated in the royal commission, "nothing was needed, save a purely tactical adjustment from the complete Land of Israel to a part of it, in order to accept the concept of partition."[25]

Was this just a "tactical adjustment?" To answer this, we must examine Ben-Gurion's attitude toward the commission and his testimony before it. From his 1918 book with Ben-Zvi, where Ben-Gurion defined the boundaries of Eretz Israel, one can discern his initial territorial conception, as well as his willingness to adapt to changing circumstances: "there are significant differences of opinion on the question of the boundaries of Eretz Israel, and it is not easy to determine absolutely what is Eretz Israel and what is not."[26] He later notes that in the Bible there are different promised boundaries of Eretz Israel and that historically the actual lines changed in each era.

> Nevertheless, if we wish to determine the boundaries of Eretz Israel today, particularly if we see it not only in terms of the Jewish past, but as the future land of the Jews, of Jewish settlement and of the Jewish national home—we cannot consider only the *ideal* boundaries [emphasis in the original] promised to us by tradition. For they are too extensive in the present situation; and we cannot adhere only to the historic boundaries, which so often changed and were incidentally realized, because they are mostly too narrow and inconsistent with the natural features of the land.[27]

Ben-Gurion and Ben-Zvi accordingly outlined the boundaries (see Chapter Two), noting that "the breadth of the 'ideal' Land of Israel is almost twice that of the more narrow 'real' boundaries of the Land of Israel."[28] On boundaries, as on other issues, Ben-Gurion, very much like Weizmann, was a political pragmatist.[29] There is no evidence that Ben-Gurion thought in concrete terms of territorial partition in the years immediately before 1937, although he often dealt with questions of land and settlements.[30] Neither in his writings nor in his speeches of the same period did Ben-Gurion mention cantons, partition, or "land reserves" for the Arabs.

Ben-Gurion's initial attitude toward the royal commission ranged from negative to ambivalent suspicion. He later hesitated for personal reasons whether to appear before it, even though he believed the commission would have great influence.[31] Ben-Gurion's testimony before the commission on January 7, 1937, was brief and hardly impressive by comparison with Weizmann's.[32] There is also no indication that he impressed the commission, with the possible exception of his boldness in speaking about Palestine's capacity to sustain 6 million residents (with 4 million Jews). In his public testimony, Ben-Gurion vehemently espoused the need to continue the mandate and asserted that the Jewish goal was not "a state."[33] Behind closed doors, Ben-Gurion spoke mainly about relations with the Arabs and made no reference to territorial issues.[34] It would seem that Ben-Gurion's support for partition became concrete only after his testimony, when he realized the practical alternatives facing the Zionist movement. From this moment, in early 1937, to the end of his days, Ben-Gurion adamantly and consistently favored the principle of partition as the only viable political solution. He was also its architect in 1948–49.

This support was distinct from his public position, however. Ben-Gurion fought for continuation of the mandate and opposed any suggestion that partition would be presented as a Zionist proposal. At the Jewish Agency executive meeting of January 10, 1937, after—in Shertok's words—"getting excited" by Weizmann's account of the royal commission's discussion of partition, Ben-Gurion still believed that Weizmann's letter to the Commission had to include a negative response to cantonization.[35]

In February 1937, Ben-Gurion embraced partition and presented the "two-state plan" at a meeting of the Mapai Central Committee. This marked the beginning of the Zionist movement's internal process of decision making regarding partition.[36] Although twenty-three top party leaders were present at the meeting, the protocol shows that only five responded to Ben-Gurion's partition proposal.[37] Ben-Gurion began by listing various possible conclusions of the commission. First, ending or altering the mandate; second, cantonization; third, changes in immigration policy—total cessation, temporary stoppage, another way to perpetuate Jewish status as a permanent minority in Eretz Israel, or establishing immigration quotas in accordance with political absorption capacity; and fourth, reducing the authority of the Jewish Agency or creating an Arab Agency.

As to cantonization, Ben-Gurion sketched a general outline of Jewish, Arab, and mixed cantons plus areas of British control, a concept the commission had apparently already discarded. The commission's ambition was to find a radical solution to the issue of Palestine, Ben-Gurion said, causing him to fear a solution that would degenerate Zionism and the Yishuv. Still, as great as his fear was Ben-Gurion's willingness to voice the heresy that "there is nothing more dangerous to Zionism than a fatal belief in the 'Eternity of Israel.'" His conclusion:

In my opinion there is such a solution and it existed even before the Royal Commission and in my opinion this is the solution. The solution is the direction of the proposal of Sir Stafford Kripps—establishing two states in Eretz Israel, an Arab and a Jewish state. Partitioning Eretz Israel into two portions so that a Jewish state will be established in one part, and it will make a treaty with England following the Iraqi, Egyptian and Syrian examples. This is not a solution under all circumstances. But if the minimum land necessary for our growth in the near future will be set aside for the Jewish state, then this is the solution.[38]

Ben-Gurion then continued to present a plan whose details constituted a map of territorial partition. The Jewish state must include the entire coastal plain, the Jezreel Valley, the Galilee, the Jordan Valley to Beit Shean, and a portion of the Negev all the way to Aqaba. The Akko and Gaza districts, with practically no Jews, would be autonomous under British supervision for a transitional period, the same as Haifa and Jerusalem. The remaining territory would belong to an Arab state. This partition plan gave the Jewish state about 10,500 km^2, including 4,300 km^2 in the Negev. The Arab state would total 12,500 km^2, including 6,000 km^2 in the Negev as well as the corridor from Ramle/Lod to Jaffa. This was the first time a partition program was presented to an official body, not as a general idea, but as a proposed policy that, under certain conditions, would become operational. The plan was presented by none other than the head of the Jewish Agency executive. It should be noted that Ben-Gurion spoke of the minimal area needed for the near future, making a point that he would repeat again: "What will be after 3 million Jews enter this Jewish state we will see later. Future generations will take care of themselves. We must take care of the present generation."[39]

The protocol does not reveal whether Ben-Gurion surprised his colleagues or if they took him seriously,[40] but we do know that at this meeting he was outnumbered by those who expressed reservations or opposition. Moreover, the two other leading figures of Mapai at that time, Berl Katznelson and Yitzhak Tabenkin, were against it. Katznelson's reaction was important because he said that, had Ben-Gurion's proposal come from the royal commission, he would have thought it "very positive and important." He was against the plan because the British would propose a highly truncated area. Nevertheless, Katznelson concluded, "the principle in and of itself could under certain known conditions be desirable for us,"[41] indicating the eventual compromise that he would adopt at the Zionist Congress six months later. The resolutions of the Mapai Central Committee's February meeting made no mention of Ben-Gurion's "two-state plan." Ben-Gurion apparently did not press for a decision. To him, this was a trial balloon intended to measure his colleagues' reaction.

Ben-Gurion made his next attempt to gain internal support for his plan at the Mapai Central Committee meeting of April 1937.[42] The possibility that the commission would recommend partition had by then been made public in Palestine and abroad.[43] Of all the discussions leading to the Zionist Congress decision of August 1937, this April meeting was most significant. Partition was no longer only "Ben-Gurion's proposal, but rather a concrete possibility.[44] Ben-Gurion decided to address the issue as a series of questions: Is partition feasible? (Yes, he said.) Is partition desirable? (Again, yes.) By the time of this meeting the camps of the supporters and opponents were beginning to be clearly marked within Mapai. The debate among the central leaders of Mapai was very complex and highly sensitive. Those who took the floor were almost perfectly divided: thirteen for, eleven against. The Central Committee members were then asked to vote on two proposals: Bankover's, "Mapai will oppose all proposals for partition of the country in any form whatsoever", and Ben-Gurion's "To ratify the previous position [against cantonization], to demand intensified efforts [immigration, settlement, etc.] and to fight any attempt to limit the chances of the national home."

Bankover's proposal was defeated 9–3 and Ben-Gurion's was accepted by a clear majority of 11–2. This was the first formal rejection by an official body of total opposition to partition. And it was Ben-Gurion's first victory—characteristic in its ambiguity—on what would be a long obstacle course. Furthermore, in the discussion, almost all the arguments that would later be part of the great debate were raised. For example, the proponents of partition said that the territory would be a result of what we have done thus far.

We will not get all of it because we have not accomplished enough since the Balfour Declaration. The opponents agreed, adding that therefore, we should continue our efforts and will eventually acquire the entire territory.

The next decisive meeting took place on the eve of the Zionist Congress in August 1937, even though in the meantime the opponents were still trying to reverse the tentative approval of Ben-Gurion's tactical scheme for April. Ben-Gurion traveled to London in early May to try to influence the royal commission report. The opponents of partition intensified their demands to reconvene the Mapai General Council, and Tabenkin threatened to resign, accusing Weizmann of conducting disastrous negotiations with the British government without authorization of the movement.[45]

The Mapai Central Committee decided in June 1937 to request Ben-Gurion's presence at a council meeting on July 9.[46] After three days of discussion in Ben-Gurion's absence, the council resolved to reject the specific partition plan of the royal commission, but not to abandon attempts to improve it.[47] Again, a compromise resolution was reached. Meanwhile, Ben-Gurion and Katznelson held a "secret and exhaustive" conversation in London to overcome their differences. In his journal, Ben-Gurion concluded that Katznelson opposed only a "bad" partition plan and would consider any "good" plan recommended by the commission.[48] This conversation apparently paved the way for Katznelson's support of the compromise in the Mapai council as well as the compromise resolution at the Congress in Zurich.

Jabotinsky's Testimony

Disagreement as to the "correct" territory of the future Jewish state was only one of the reasons Jabotinsky opposed the leadership of the Zionist movement. He established the Revisionist party in 1925 to provide an alternative to the Zionist executive's stance on British policy toward the "national home," including its orientation in favor of the local Arab population. In 1926, Jabotinsky expressed the territorial component of this alternative as follows: "Zionism's first aim is the creation of a Hebrew majority in Eretz Israel on both sides of the Jordan River. This is not the final goal of the Zionist movement, which is committed to loftier ideals, such as the solution of Jewish distress around the world and creation of a new Hebrew culture. But a precondition for achieving these exalted final goals is a land in which the Jews will be a majority."[49]

Jabotinsky's proposal to declare Jewish statehood as the final goal of Zionism was rejected at the Zionist Congress of 1931. In 1935 the Revisionist party withdrew from the Zionist Organization to establish the New Zionist Organization (NZO). The NZO's purpose, as determined at its founding conference, was to strive for "the realization of *a state with a Jewish majority on both sides of the Jordan River*" [emphasis in the original].[50] By 1937, Jabotinsky was unaffiliated with the Zionist leadership and took no part in its decisions. Nevertheless, he was invited to testify before the royal commission in London (he was barred from Palestine) on February 11, 1937,[51] and we will discuss here only his role in the predecision process, as well as his special position. In his testimony, Jabotinsky referred only once to the possibility of partitioning western Eretz Israel:

> You have undoubtedly heard about the compromises and the proposed intermediate stages, among them the partition of the Land of Israel into cantons or the "parity plan" or cultural convergence or Jewish "concessions," etc. . . . We would want there to be the possibility of an intermediate stage, but this is certainly not possible. We cannot agree to partition of the country into cantons because many, and even you, would say that the greater Land of Israel might be too small for the human goal facing us. A corner of the Land of Israel, a "canton"—how can we promise that this would be enough for us? It would be a lie. And what other area would we forego?"[52]

Jabotinsky repeatedly emphasized that "Palestine" included the territory on both sides of the Jordan River, because of Jewish distress, the absorption capacity of the country, and Eretz Israel's geography. He also presented a number of legal references to prove that the national home cited in the Balfour Declaration, the mandatory charter, and declarations by British statesmen referred to both sides of the Jordan River. But the main thrust of his testimony was that an area large enough to "save millions, many millions" of Jews, was essential. He presented calculations and comparisons with other states supporting his premise that only the greater Land of Israel would be capable of absorbing the 3 to 4 million Jews crying out for permission to enter.[53] In this, Jabotinsky's argument was based on Jewish distress; however, when presenting Eretz Israel as a "geographical integrity," he came very close to the organic state concept prevalent in the literature of the time, as discussed in Chapter One.[54]

Jabotinsky used a mixture of arguments. But examination of his testimony and his political positions of the same period show that, despite his emphasis on the geographical integrity of the land on both sides of the Jordan River, he was ultimately an instrumentalist. The territorial framework was primarily intended to ensure absorption of the millions of Jews who might gradually reach the Jewish state. The only purely geopolitical argument in Jabotinsky's testimony was his mention of the importance of Eretz Israel as a land bridge between three continents. He intentionally avoided raising the argument about Jewish "historic rights" to the land and emphasized Jewish rights under international law, an issue that the commission members intensely questioned. First, Jabotinsky noted that the mandatory charter of the League of Nations did not prohibit Jewish settlement in the entire Land of Israel, including Transjordan. Second, the right to a Jewish state did not expire with British renunciation of the Balfour Declaration and the consequent policy reversal: "Not one sentence in the White Paper of 1922, not even one word, can be interpreted as preventing the Land of Israel from becoming a land with a Jewish majority, the 'Jewish state.' "[55]

Jabotinsky did not change his position toward Britain even after the outbreak of the Arab revolt of 1936. He still believed that the British government could be pressured to continue the mandate and fulfill its commitments to the Zionist movement.[56] His testimony before the royal commission and his subsequent opposition to the partition proposal should be seen in this light.

We do not know whether Jabotinsky influenced the commission's report. His testimony was apparently used largely to show that there were extremists on both sides and that the solution must therefore provide a compromise between polarized Jewish and Arab demands:

To the Jewish extremists the solution of the problem is as simple as that put forward by the Arab Higher Committee. Mr. Jabotinsky and the Revisionists demand that the expansion of the national home should continue at an accelerated pace. Trans-Jordan should be opened to Jewish immigrants and room quickly found in this larger Palestine for many millions of Jews. The whole country would thus become in fact Eretz Israel and in due course obtain its independence as a Jewish state. . . .

In present circumstances, the Revisionist programme is not merely at plain variance with our legal and moral obligations: its execution would convert the friendship of all the Arab peoples into implacable resentment and react beyond their borders throughout the Moslem world.[57]

The commission rejected Jabotinsky's (as well as Weizmann's) demands to allow Jewish settlement in Transjordan on the grounds that the legal commitment to the establishment of a Jewish national home did not apply to Transjordan and its independent government.[58]

Jabotinsky's testimony before the royal commission showed that his intense opposition to partition was a foregone conclusion. If he struggled against the separation of Transjordan, then how much more would he fight against any division of western Eretz Israel. Nevertheless, as we shall see in Chapter Five, the possibility of establishing a Jewish state immediately caused even Jabotinsky to hesitate before voicing a vehement "no" to the commission's proposals.

El-Husseini's Testimony Before the Royal Commission

This book deals with Jewish positions toward the partition proposal. Accordingly, the Arab positions require a separate discussion without ignoring the fact that the 1936 Palestinian uprising, caused by their opposition to Zionism, catalyzed the process that led to the commission's establishment and its conclusion of the need for territorial separation.[59] The internal Jewish debate, however, was much more concerned with British intentions and goals than with the Arabs. The paradox is that the partition debate took place among the Jews themselves, between the Jews and the British, and between the British and the Arabs, even though developments in the 1930s were rooted in what the Jews called the *Arab question* and some attempts were made to reach an Arab-Jewish understanding.

The Arab positions were considered only indirectly in the Jewish debate for two additional reasons. First, Britain was not about to abandon Palestine (E.I.) completely. The proposal to terminate the mandate did not imply discontinuing the British presence, in one form or another. British strategic interests, as seen from London, required this.[60] Second, although the Jews generally viewed the continuation of the British mandate positively, the Palestinian Arabs did not. When their political awakening intensified in the 1930s, they demanded not only termination of the mandate and its promise of a Jewish national home, but also the establishment of a Palestinian state alongside other independent Arab states.[61] This position effectively eliminated any possibility of discussing cantonization or partition and of finding common ground between the two sides.

The leaders of the Palestinian Arabs opposed the establishment of the royal commission from the outset, much as did the Jewish leadership initially. They later conditioned their cooperation on the cessation of Jewish immigration during the commission's investigation. When the British government refused to comply, the Arab Higher Committee resolved to boycott the commission and called on all Palestinian Arabs to do likewise.[62] The boycott was intended to stultify the work of the royal commission because the British government had conditioned its presence in Palestine upon an end to the riots. On October 11, 1936, the Arab Higher Committee complied with the request of the kings of Iraq and Saudi Arabia and announced an end to the strike. The kings' continued intervention eventually convinced the Palestinian leaders to appear before the commission.[63] The central witness was the mufti of Jerusalem, Amin El-Husseini. He testified before the commission on January 12, 1937, in his capacity as chairman of the Arab Higher Committee and not, as he emphasized, as president of the Supreme Moslem Council.[64]

El-Husseini opened by saying that the Arabs of Palestine desired national independence, according to President Wilson's principles of self-determination after World War I. These principles are incumbent on all Arab areas included in the former Ottoman Empire, he said, contradict the Balfour Declaration, and are inconsistent with Article 22 of the League of Nations Charter. Palestine is an Arab state because 93 percent of its inhabitants at the time of the British conquest were Arabs. The fact that this had decreased to 70 percent by 1937, with a larger drop in the percentage of Arab land ownership, emphasizes the problem with British policy, but does not alter the reality.[65] The two main causes of the 1936 revolt, in El-Husseini's view, were the negation of the natural and political rights of the Palestinian Arabs and the British policy directed at establishing a Jewish national home in Arab territory. He accordingly proposed the following steps:

- Abandonment of the "experiment" of the Jewish national home, which proved to be a failure;
- Immediate and complete stoppage of Jewish immigration;

- Immediate and complete prohibition of the sale of Arab land to the Jews;

- "Solution of the Palestine problem on the same basis as that of Iraq, Syria and Lebanon, namely by the termination of the Mandate and by the conclusion of a treaty between Great Britain and Palestine. A national independent and elected Palestinian government will be established, on which national elements will be represented, and which will guarantee justice, progress and prosperity to all."[66]

El-Husseini was repeatedly asked what would be the fate of the 400,000 Jews in an independent Palestinian state. He gave several different answers. He first said that Jews would have complete freedom as natives of the country, as they always had in Arab states. He then suggested that the matter be left to the discretion of the future government, on the considerations most equitable and beneficial to the country. In the end, when Sir Rumbold asked whether the Palestinian state "could assimilate and digest the Jews" or would "some of them have to be removed by a process kindly or painful as the case may be," he replied "no" to the first question and "we must leave all this to the future," to the second.[67] To the best of our knowledge, members of the royal commission did not raise the matter of territorial separation during the testimony of El-Husseini or any other Palestinian Arab. In Chapter Ten, we shall discuss the positions of the Arab leadership toward the commission report.

The commission report dealt extensively with the Arab opposition to a mandate that included recognition of the Jewish national home and rejected the legal bases of the Arab arguments.[68] It also rejected, however, the longstanding Jewish premise that economic well-being would gradually lead to moderation of Arab national demands.[69] The report notes "the sad fact" that British attempts to accommodate the Arabs not only failed to eliminate their opposition to Zionism, but that the Arabs were actually more hostile toward the Jews and the British after seventeen years of the mandate. The commission concluded that this was a political conflict between unreconcilable aspirations and that territorial surgery was the only solution.

Zionist Attempts to Influence the Commission's Report

The center of Zionist activity returned to London with the royal commission in January 1937 and for the next five months operated on several levels: first, attempts to influence the content of the report through members of the commission, the colonial secretary, the high commissioner, and senior officials in Whitehall; second, attempts to enlist support among British politicians and officials prior to their appearance before the commission;[70] third, mobilizing international support through friendly politicians, like Leon Blum, the French prime minister;[71] and, fourth, meetings with moderate Arabs.[72] We will focus mainly on the first and second aspects, which most affected the internal Zionist decision.

This period forged the unwritten alliance between the three Zionist leaders who favored partition—Weizmann, Ben-Gurion, and Shertok—and who worked to extract information on the recommendations being formulated by the royal commission to improve them insofar as possible.[73] Some delegates to the Zionist Congress would later charge that these contacts effectively obligated the Zionist movement to support partition. Weizmann was the dominant one, due to his status in London and his network of diplomatic connections. The Zionist movement was thus very involved in the final preparation of the commission's recommendations, including last minute changes in the proposed partition boundaries. Nevertheless, it is evident that details of the report remained unknown. Ben-Gurion described in his journal his tense anticipation and great excitement upon receipt of the report, as well as Weizmann's anger when the colonial secretary refused to provide him a prerelease copy for his perusal.[74]

Coupland was the only commission member with whom regular meetings were held. The others refused to meet or courteously rejected attempts to discuss the report. Weizmann's efforts to meet with Prime Minister Chamberlain and Foreign Minister Eden were also for nought. Weizmann knew that the commission was designing a partition plan in early March 1937. This was indirectly confirmed by the high commissioner in a meeting on March 14.[75] Weizmann wrote to Coupland on April 19 suggesting they meet to consider the "matters we discussed." Coupland provided Weizmann with details of the commission's deliberations on April 26.[76] Toward the end of May, Coupland wrote to Weizmann that last-minute changes had been made in the report. Other sources informed Shertok that the commission members disagreed on whether to include the Galilee in the Jewish state.[77]

Suddenly, a territorial decision was required: Would the Zionist movement prefer the Galilee or the Negev? At the executive's behest, Weizmann rushed to attain Leon Blum's support for a Jewish state that would include the Galilee and border the territory of the Maronites in Lebanon.[78] Thus, the troika in London—Weizmann, Ben-Gurion, and Shertok—made in fact a crucial decision: to give priority to the Galilee over the Negev in the Jewish state proposed by the royal commission.[79] The "north vs. south" question would again be raised by the Woodhead commission and a decade later in the 1947 partition proposal.

A number of parallel meetings were held with Colonial Secretary Ormsby-Gore. The possibility that the commission might recommend partition was mentioned in a meeting in early February, immediately upon Weizmann's return from Eretz Israel.[80] Weizmann and Shertok again met with the colonial secretary and two British senior civil servants on March 19. Weizmann raised the matter of the partition plan by saying that in his testimony before the royal commission they had discussed substantial territorial dimensions, an independent government, and a seat in the League of Nations, whereas the high commissioner was now talking about cantons. According to Shertok, the colonial secretary responded that he did not know what the commission would propose, "but he was clear that the Commissioner did not mean a limited plan mentioned by Weizmann."[81]

Attempting to enlist support for the Zionist position in the British House of Commons, Liberal party leader Sir Archibald Sinclair invited Weizmann, Conservative leaders Churchill, Cassalt, and Emery, Labour leader Clement Atlee, former minister Wedgewood, and Liberal MP Rothschild to a dinner at his home. Lloyd George, who was invited, sent his regrets and pledged to support any resulting decision. Two conclusions can be drawn from the fragmented testimonies of what took place at this famous dinner on June 8.[82] First, although everyone expressed readiness to support Weizmann, they did not clearly understand what they were being asked to do. Consequently, no decision for action was taken. Second, everyone except Emery opposed partition. They did not support the two-faced tactic that Weizmann proposed: to demand continuation of the mandate while simultaneously mounting a struggle for Jewish independence within realistic boundaries. There is no doubt that the strong reservations of most of this influential group, especially Churchill, greatly affected the parliamentary discussion of the commission's report.

At their next meeting, on June 13, the colonial secretary informed Weizmann that the Galilee would be included in the Jewish state, a fact he already knew from Coupland.[83] Weizmann told Ormsby-Gore that the Jews had not yet agreed to anything and that their position would be determined only after publication of the commission's report. The colonial secretary replied that Jewish rejection of the report would be a disaster. Weizmann stated a number of preconditions for acceptance, which Ormsby-Gore asked to receive in writing. Consequently, in his famous letter of June 15, 1937, Weizmann again emphasized that "I am not in any sense committed to any partition scheme," but raised a number of "minimum requirements" for his support. The Jewish state must include the whole of Galilee and the Jezreel Valley (including the Beit Shean area), and the coastal plain from Ras A-Nakura to northern Gaza. The eastern boundary must be strategically defensible and include the electric power station at Naharayim. Haifa would provide a British base within the Jewish state and Jerusalem would be British except for its Jewish quarters. If the Negev did not remain under British control, it would be demanded by the Jews. The Jews would be granted full sovereignty within their territory by treaty with Britain and, most important, full control of immigration. Weizmann concluded: "Unless the area and boundaries of the proposed Jewish state are such as to permit it to maintain itself, both economically and strategically, and to absorb a substantial Jewish immigration (with an adequate proportion settled on the land), it is, in my view, unlikely that the scheme would prove workable, and I doubt whether any responsible Jewish leader could ask his people to consider it."[84]

These were strong words, which nevertheless did not reject the partition. Moreover, British documents show that the colonial secretary said even earlier, at a closed meeting in his office on April 21, 1937, that there would naturally be a great outcry against the proposal of the royal commission by both Jews and Arabs, but "Dr. Weizmann and the official Zionist Organization would accept this solution without too much demur."[85]

Weizmann's letter of June 15 caused a stormy session of the Jewish Agency executive in Jerusalem on June 17.[86] Ussishkin charged that Weizmann and Ben-Gurion were already negotiating boundaries and threatened that all those who opposed partition would secede from the Zionist Organization. Shertok did his best to smooth things over by saying that Weizmann had made no commitment to partition and that, even if he did, the British government knew that his position was not binding on the Zionist Congress.

Weizmann took Ben-Gurion to his last meeting with Ormsby-Gore on June 28. Their purpose was to influence the governmental statement of policy that would be released with the commission's report. But the meeting came too late, as the colonial secretary had prepared his memorandum to the cabinet on June 25.[87] Still, the conversation was significant because the cabinet discussed the commission's report on June 30, and announced the government statement only on July 5, saying: "His Majesty's Government . . . find themselves in general agreement with the arguments and conclusions of the Commission . . . [and] the scheme of partition on the general lines recommended by the Commission represents the best and most hopeful solution of the deadlock."[88]

Later, after the British government changed its policy and dropped the partition proposal in 1938, the question was raised whether the Zionist movement had the ability to enhance the British commitment to the royal commission's report. Teveth claims that Ben-Gurion wanted to downplay Zionist readiness to accept the partition proposal, whereas Weizmann's public enthusiasm was too obvious.[89] Others blamed the "double message," which was understood only in the innermost circles, for preventing predisposed members of the House of Commons, like Churchill, from lending their support.[90] In either event, the closed contacts between the Zionist leadership and the British created the impression that the Zionist movement would not reject partition outright. However, Weizmann and Ben-Gurion had left themselves two routes of escape. First, they could refuse to support partition if the proposed territory was not "substantial." Second, they maintained that the final decision was the exclusive prerogative of the Zionist Congress and the enlarged Jewish Agency Council.

The Internal Debate Before Publication of the Report

The main internal debate began after publication of the report on July 7. During the royal commission hearings, the organized Jewish community presented a more or less unified front, and subjects like partition and the establishment of a Jewish state were not raised in public testimony. The notable deviant position presented by the Revisionist movement was generally insubstantial.[91]

As noted, Weizmann did not provide full details on his testimony before the royal commission to his colleagues. Ussishkin was already suspicious by the executive meeting of January 10, 1937, but he thought cantonization was still being discussed; and Shertok did not bother to apprise him of the difference between this and the partition plan. Therefore, at this stage partition was not on the agenda of the Zionist institutions. Leaders who did not belong to the inner circle were left groping in the dark despite Weizmann's review of his testimony in the Zionist General Council on January 13, Ben-Gurion's proposal of a "partition plan" at the closed meeting of the Mapai Central Committee in early February, and Shertok's February 7 report to the Zionist executive that the commission also discussed the possibility of "dividing Eretz Israel into two."[92] There was still no sign of alarm among executive members who would later oppose partition, perhaps because they were not privy to the ongoing contacts with the British. Ben-Gurion told the Jewish Agency executive on March 14, for example, that he believed the "Colonial Office in London is now preparing a cantonization plan. Not two states as was once proposed before the Royal Commission, but rather a Mandatory land containing two cantons, one Jewish and one Arab.[93]

The subject of partition was raised for real discussion only after this possibility was publicized in the press, first in England and then in Palestine in early April.[94] *Ha'aretz* also reported Shertok's official statement of the intention to launch a "diligent war on the partition of Eretz Israel."[95] Parties such as the General Zionists, the Mizrahi and the State party then announced their opposition to partition.[96] The first official discussion of partition by a Zionist institution was held only on April 20, at a closed Jerusalem gathering of the Zionist General Council. According to Shapira, this debate was rather authentic as it reflected first reactions, immediate and spontaneous.[97] Ussishkin and Ben-Gurion (Weizmann did not attend) clashed head on: the first against partition "in the name of the bones of our fathers in the grave" and the second in favor, in the name of responsibility for realizing Zionism and "concern for future generations."[98]

This debate also marked the division, which crossed most party lines, between the camps opposing and supporting partition. Because the debate returned during the Twentieth Zionist Congress, here we will present only the resolutions. The meeting ended with an agreement not to postpone the congress scheduled for Zurich in August, but elections to the congress were advanced to precede the anticipated publication date of the royal commission report. This would influence discussions in the congress, with the "opponents" charging that the congress was not authorized to make a decision because the delegates were not elected on the basis of their positions on partition.

The Zionist General Council made a unanimous decision on partition: "The Jewish people strongly opposes any attempt to limit the rights, options and territory of the national home." Furthermore, the Balfour Declaration's commitment should be fully realized and all obstacles to Jewish settlement in Transjordan should be rescinded.[99] To this was added an internal, secret decision authorizing the executive to use all necessary means to amend any partition proposal, if submitted, without making a commitment to accept it.[100] This formulation and the earlier (April 15) vote in the Mapai Central Committee that rejected total opposition to partition together illuminate the strategy of Ben-Gurion and Shertok: the coalition they had begun to form and the substantive position that would be taken in the Zionist Congress proposal.

Continued political activity in London intensified suspicion among the "opponents," led by Ussishkin. This struggle took place not within the Zionist institutions, but mainly in the press. Dothan sees this as evidence of Ussishkin's failure to coalesce the opposition within the Zionist leadership.[101] Ben-Gurion's trip to London transferred the burden to Shertok, who continued to update members of the executive and to withstand the growing opposition in both his and other parties.[102]

The next eruption within the Jewish Agency executive occurred on June 17, in the wake of Weizmann's letter to the colonial secretary. As noted, Ussishkin threatened to withdraw from the Zionist Organization; however, he later sought a compromise and agreed not to force a decision, but rather to forward the protocol of the discussion to London.[103] At the meeting of the restricted Zionist General Council four days later, it was rumored that the London executive had committed the "treason" of accepting the partition proposal.[104] Shertok again managed to forestall a decision and telegrammed London that the April position of the expanded General Council had in effect been accepted; namely, that any reduction in the territory of the national home would be opposed outwardly, and the executive would simultaneously work to limit the damage of any British government partition proposal. Ussishkin demanded to place partition at the crux of elections to the Congress, but even opponents like Tabenkin resisted this in the interests of preserving unity. Thus, the supporters averted the attempt to force a decision requiring the executive to declare that the Zionist movement is fighting against partition. It became clear that such a decision would indeed be made at the congress. Shertok remained loyal to the "double message" policy and, upon publication of the commission's report, asked Jewish newspaper editors to reject partition and support the mandate.[105] However, internally he and Ben-Gurion remained decisively enthusiastic: "I see in this plan *in its entirety* [emphasis in the original] not the lesser of two evils, but a political conquest and a historic chance which we have not had since the days our country was ravaged. I see in the realization of this plan an almost decisive phase in the beginning of complete redemption and an unsurpassed lever for the gradual conquest of the entire Land of Israel."[106]

The first round of debate within the Jewish institutions thus revealed a number of central points regarding partition:

- Weizmann, Ben-Gurion, and Shertok became personally committed to the proposals being formulated by the royal commission, principally because of their success in including the Galilee rather than the Negev in the proposed Jewish state. Their minimal commitment was not to reject outright the commission's recommendations on partition.

- The lines of fundamental disagreement among the Zionist leaders and parties were outlined even before publication of the report in July 1937.

- The ground was laid for framing both the coalition and the content of the compromise decision that would finally be accepted.

- The final decision itself was left open.

Recommendations of the Royal Commission

The commission was appointed to ascertain the "underlying causes" of the disturbances in Palestine (E.I.) and inquire into the manner in which the mandate was being implemented. This wording allowed the commission not to limit itself to findings and recommendations regarding the disturbances alone but to propose a new policy. A first hint of this is found in Lord Peel's opening statement that the commission would examine "wider issues."[107] The 404-page report was published on July 7, 1937. This document is unique in its authors' willingness to delve deeply into the fundamental issues of the Jewish national home, commitments to the Arabs, performance of the mandatory government, and causes of the Arab-Jewish conflict. And what of the British interests?

The commission was British and above all deeply concerned with the interests of the empire.[108] The strategic importance of Palestine grew in 1936–1937 due to the increasing strength of Germany in Europe and Italy in the Mediterranean and Red Seas (following its conquest of Abyssinia in 1935). At the same time, the insuperable "headache" of the Jews and Arabs in Palestine spurred a search for ways to reduce local British involvement in order to decrease the military and financial burden of the mandate. The royal commission's report is an attempt to bridge these two goals. British policy would later change principally in response to the increasing strategic importance of Palestine (E.I.) and the alliance with neighboring Arab rulers. The British indeed saw partition as a fair solution for both sides as long as it coincided with British interests and promised eventually to reduce the burden on the empire.

Revealing evidence of this approach is found in secret documentation of the "informal discussion" in early March 1937 between members of the commission and the British Chiefs of Staff.[109] Lord Peel opened the discussion by telling the military leaders that the commission was preparing to recommend the partition of Palestine. He showed them a proposed map of the territorial solution and stressed that the commission would not submit strategically impractical recommendations. The following is a summary of the reply of the Chiefs of Staff.

- *Naval Interests.* The importance of Palestine is rather small. The use of the port of Haifa and the protection of the outlet of the Iraqi oil pipeline must be assured.

- *Air Force Interests.* Palestine is important because it lies across the air communications to the East and for the Royal Air Force in Iraq. It also gives strategic depth to the defense of the Suez Canal.[110]

- *Military Interests.* Palestine is of great strategic importance. It provides a land footing in the eastern Mediterranean without which Cyprus is in danger. It is also a buffer between British vital interests on the Suez Canal and possible enemies to the north. Britain should not give up this dominating position as the importance of Palestine will increase, when in twenty years the Anglo-Egyptian Treaty would be due for revision.

Lord Peel made it clear that the British presence in Palestine would continue and that the Jews were aware they would have to trust Britain to protect them from the surrounding Arabs. The discussion concluded the following: The empire's strategic interests could be secured through bilateral treaties with the two nascent states; the Arab-Jewish conflict was already placing a heavy burden on the British forces, which would only be increased by endless

conflict between the two new states. By contrast, if an agreed partition would bring a stable peace, the British military obligation to
Palestine would be reduced. The Chiefs of Staff did not oppose the
proposed plan, and Lord Peel summarized by saying, "There are
many difficulties in any partition scheme," but he was much re-
lieved to find that if these difficulties could be overcome there were
no insuperable strategic difficulties in the way.[111]

The royal commission did not elaborate on the British interests in proposing partition, except by noting repeatedly that it was
intended to reduce the burden of military expenditure on the British Treasury.[112] Strategic interests are not mentioned explicitly and
were in fact reduced to a clause in the report according to which
military conventions (between Britain and the two new states) would
be attached to the treaties dealing with maintenance of naval, military, and air forces and "the upkeep and use of ports, roads and
railways, the security of the pipeline and so forth."[113]

The commission's report courageously and consistently noted
Britain's "double and contradictory obligations" toward the Jews
and the Arabs.[114] But the report's historic analysis, apart from its
practical recommendations, is closer to the Zionist positions. This
reading is based on the report's rejection of the position prevailing
among senior British officials, that Britain has no political obligation whatsoever to the Jews. In contrast, the report adopts the
equation that a national home means a Jewish state. For example,
"This definition of the national home [in the 1922 White Paper] has
sometimes been taken to preclude the establishment of a Jewish
state. But, though the phraseology was clearly intended to concili-
ate, as far as might be, Arab antagonism to the national home,
there is nothing in it to prohibit the ultimate establishment of a
Jewish state, and Mr. Churchill himself has told us in evidence
that no such prohibition was intended."[115]

This reading is reinforced by the reactions of senior Foreign
Office officials to the commission's recommendations, who felt the
report seriously damaged British interests in the Arab-dominated
Middle East.[116] Also, Ben-Gurion's reaction to the report, at first
apprehensive and fearful, gradually became most enthusiastic:
" . . . the book demands a second reading and deserves it. If its
central practical conclusion will not be proved false—this book will
serve as our proclamation of independence and will eclipse the
Balfour Declaration."[117]

We will now present the report's main points regarding territory, which served as the basis for the commission's partition
plan.[118]

Immigration   The commission presented alternate rates of Jewish immigration. For example, immigration of 30,000 Jews per year would create a Jewish majority in the country in the mid-1960s; 60,000 immigrants per year would achieve it in 1947. Accordingly, the report proposed replacing the previous principle of "economic absorptive capacity" with immigration quotas to be determined by a "political barometer." The commission nevertheless recognized that limiting Jewish immigration would not alleviate Arab opposition to the very existence of the national home, which blocks the establishment of a Palestinian Arab state.

Transjordan   The report reemphasized that the area east of the Jordan River was not included in the British commitment to a Jewish national home and that Arab opposition to Jewish settlement there would be as strong as in Palestine.

Self-Governing Institutions   The report concluded that there was no chance of establishing joint Jewish-Arab self-governing institutions, even though the population in Palestine deserved this no less than the neighboring countries that had won independence. Nevertheless, proposals for "political partition," based on joint representation in the government, were rejected, because the two communities were deemed incapable of cooperation.

Cantonization   The intermediate solution, division into autonomous regions under a central mandatory administration, was rejected because this could worsen rather than solve the internal security problems of the mandatory government. Moreover, the creation of separate cantons for Jews and Arabs was precluded by the geographical mix of the two communities, and a possible transfer of populations seemed more feasible within the framework of an actual partition. Finally, temporary arrangements would not eliminate the conflict between Arab and Jewish aspirations for independence. Thus, cantonization "presents most, if not all, of the difficulties presented by partition, without partition's one supreme advantage—the possibility it offers of eventual peace."[119]

The commission concluded that the Arab-Jewish deadlock was absolute and that the mandate itself could not bring about a satisfactory and stable solution. The conflicting aspirations of the two communities and the contradictory British commitments created a situation in which the 900,000 Arabs and 400,000 Jews of Palestine (E.I.) required a "clean-cut" solution with some chance of attaining peace. Therefore, the mandate should be terminated in its present form and the land divided into separate political entities.[120]

Following are the main recommendations concerning boundaries of the proposed Jewish state (see Map 2.1):[121]

1. Establishment of a Jewish state in Palestine (E.I.) along the coast, in the Jezreel Valley, the northern valleys, and the Galilee. Estimated area of the proposed state: 5,000 km²; that is, about 20 percent of western Eretz Israel.

2. The remaining area of Palestine (E.I.) would be annexed to Transjordan and form part of an independent Arab state.

3. The British mandate would be terminated and replaced with treaties between Britain and the two independent states, following the Iraqi and Syrian precedents. A new British mandate would be proclaimed over the holy sites; an enclave in the Jerusalem-Jaffa corridor; Nazareth and the Sea of Galilee. The mandate would meanwhile continue in the mixed cities of Tiberias, Safed, Haifa, and Akko.

4. Since 225,000 Arabs would remain in the proposed Jewish state, and 1,250 Jews in the Arab state (excluding the mixed cities and the other areas remaining under British control), the commission proposed that "sooner or later there should be a transfer of land and, as far as possible, an exchange of population."[122]

5. As the boundaries proposed in the report were not exact, the commission recommended the appointment of a "frontier commission" to determine the precise dividing lines between the states.

6. The report also included recommendations defined by the commission as "palliatives," in the event that the partition proposal was not accepted. These included serious limitations on immigration, settlement, and land purchase by the Jews.[123]

The riveting chapter of the Jewish response to the proposed solution began at the moment that the royal commission recommendations became British government policy on July 7, 1937. The partition proposal was explicitly presented as an "opening for the solution of the Palestine (E.I.) problem once and for all." That is, not a procedural arrangement of a joint legislative council or a temporary arrangement concerning cantonization, immigration ceilings, and land quotas, but a definite territorial solution of the Jewish-Arab conflict. The Jewish debate resulting from the report, primarily within the Zionist movement, can be considered a decision-making crossroad because most of the participants believed their decision would influence the final outcome. It is irrelevant that the British government soon began to rescind its plan, finally announcing a year and a half later that it would not adopt the partition plan because the "solution is not practical" (see Chapter Two). The Jewish leaders could not have predicted this outcome. When the Jewish Agency's representatives appeared before the Woodhead commission in March–August 1938, they still believed their testimony to be of utmost importance.[124] Moreover, the practicality of territorial partition was enhanced in the 1930s by two additional developments: First, the geographic profile of Jewish settlement became continuous and distinct.[125] Second, the Yishuv proved its self-governing ability during the disturbances, and this despite the near doubling of the number of Jews in the country between 1933 and 1936. Nevertheless, we can postulate that an independent Jewish decision, both within and outside the Zionist movement, would have preferred free immigration and unrestricted purchase of land, postponing the question of statehood and its boundaries to a more suitable date in the future.

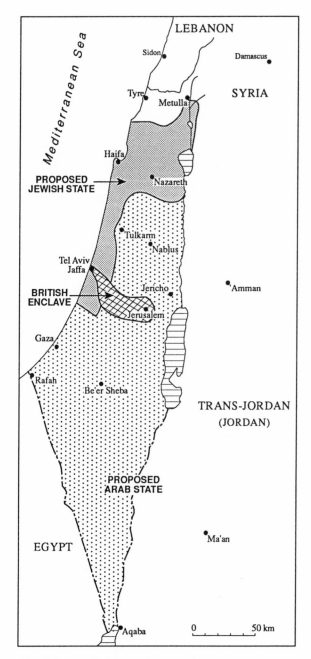

Map 2.1. Map Attached to the Report of the
Royal Commission, 1937.

4 Choice Analysis

In the preceding chapter, we outlined the efforts to influence the commission's report in the predicision phase, when options were still open. Yet, although the possibility of establishing a sovereign state through partition was still hypothetical, a very complex and fundamental dispute within the Zionist movement and among its constituents already began to surface in this phase. We have seen that the testimony before the royal commission raised basic issues: from the goals of Zionism (is the state a solution to the Jewish problem?) to political tactics (how to enlist the support of Zionist friends in Britain). The territorial question in the narrow sense—size and boundaries—was only one of the burning issues on the overburdened agenda of the Zionist movement. For example, some within the movement opposed the establishment of a Jewish state regardless of its proposed size. Others rejected the idea of formulating a purely "territorial" position and related it to their particular ideology or their assessment of the political situation. It is possible, therefore, to isolate the positions on territory and boundaries and submit them to a rather focused test of opposition to or support for the partition proposal.

The need to formulate a response to the royal commission proposal presented a moment of truth or, in our terminology, a "decision crossroad." The proposal did force an unprecedented, acute choice between a sovereign state and a truncated territory, and the reduction of the issue to this basic alternative is justifiable despite our awareness that the reality was, as usual, far more complex. This book, therefore, neither addresses all facets of the Arab-Jewish conflict nor purports to survey the state of the Zionist movement in that period. As we stressed in Chapter Two, the neglected aspects concern the international situation, the Arab positions, and the status of European Jewry on the eve of World War II. All these have been relegated to a category of "environmental constraints" and are discussed only in the context of their direct influence on the partition arguments, positions, and decision itself.

Obviously, those who participated in the polemos did not follow the structural-conceptual framework to be presented here. For example, most of them did not respond unequivocally to the question of whether they would support the territorial partition of Eretz Israel in exchange for the establishment of a sovereign Jewish state. They raised complex arguments, and some even maintained that the Zionist movement should avoid the trap of making a clear stand in a situation of such uncertainty. Moreover, when the "moment of truth" arrived, and the leaders were required to vote on the proposal at the Twentieth Zionist Congress, we do not know for sure whether they voted according to their convictions or out of party loyalty, fear of divisiveness, or other tactical reasons. Nevertheless, the decision was made; and the entire complex web of motivations, personal and movemental, was forcibly channeled into a vote that expressed a rather clear position on the territorial issue. It is therefore possible to focus on the decision itself, to compare it to the arguments raised during the debate, and to reach a number of conclusions concerning this choice in the first territorial crossroad of the Zionist movement.[1]

Limiting the discussion to the question of state and territory is legitimate not only from the vantage point of methodology, but also accurately reflects the political situation created by British policy in that period. In 1937, the Arab revolt and the royal commission created a situation that condensed all the complex issues, and not just for the Zionist movement, into the dilemma of the partition proposal. It was simply impossible to ignore, as those who suggested the creation of an "alternative agenda" to the commission's report soon discovered. For example,

• The Arab Higher Committee's complete rejection of the royal commission's recommendations was in fact a crucial decision, with vast implications for the territorial fate of Palestine.

• Some Jewish opponents of partition proposed to gain time by deciding not to decide. They soon realized that this too would be a decision, one that might bear the opposite result: the establishment of an Arab state in the entire area of the mandate.

• The Zionist movement's resolution included an alternative, tactical clause proposing continuation of the mandate. As noted, this double message influenced the movement's ability to garner support in Britain and the League of Nations on behalf of a Jewish state.

The choice was therefore very real, and even though the term *decision crossroad* does not appear in the wealth of documentation on the partition polemos, it is well-anchored in the subjective feelings of the participants. Many spoke with great emotion of the "impending historic decision" and were intensely conscious of the fateful responsibility on their shoulders.[2]

Main Choices

In the following analysis, the choices in the great polemos of 1937 are presented as "yes" or "no" theoretical answers to specific statements.[3] The advantage of this structured framework is that it demands identification of the hard core arguments and their presentation as a sequence of mutually exclusive answers. We will use a hypothetical "decision tree," which is retroactively applied to the various positions and in which a position-holder's "decision" (answer) on one question determines his or her decision (answer) for the next. The statements in Figure 4.1 are the main choices faced by the debaters and the decision makers at the decision crossroad forced upon them by the royal commission proposal.

Figure 4.2 presents the seven main choices in a framework of a decision tree. A negative answer to any of the first three statements removes the decision maker from the process and saves him or her the need to answer subsequent statements. With a positive answer to each of the first three statements, the decision maker moves to the next branch of decisive choice. The conditions and considerations attached to statement 4 and onward present more diverse options, and each answer, whether negative or positive, requires the decision maker to relate to an additional statement. From this point onward there are additional combinations that do not appear in the figure, including possible jumps between branches. For example, those whose conditions for agreement to partition are not fulfilled (in statement 4) would probably return to statement 3 and respond "no" to the principle of partition. They might even go back up to statement 2 and oppose the timing of a state now. As another example, tacticians whose agreement to the principle of partition was conditioned on the Zionist movement's outwardly negative response would probably change their minds if their actual support became public. Figure 4.2 is not intended to cover all possibilities, but rather to present the main choices and the implication of choosing a particular option.

---

1. Starting Point: A Jewish state should be established.

2. Timing: A sovereign Jewish state should be established *now,* insofar as is feasible and dependent on the Jews.

3. Partition Principle: Territorial partition of western Eretz Israel should be supported in exchange for a sovereign Jewish state.

4. Accompanying Conditions: *Territory*: Partition should be supported on condition that the size of the Jewish state will be "sufficient" for immigration, settlement and development.

Security: Territorial partition should be supported on condition of defensible borders.

Demography: Territorial partition should be supported on condition of a Jewish majority in the Jewish state, and as few Arabs "as possible."

Mutual Consent: Territorial partition should be supported on condition of Arab consent.

5. Tactics: In return for a Jewish state, agreement to territorial partition should be unconditional due to tactical considerations. But this should not be declared publicly.

6. Specific Proposal: The royal commission's territorial proposal for the establishment of a sovereign Jewish state in western Eretz Israel should be accepted.

7. Other Solutions: The creation of autonomous cantons; securing Jewish minority rights; establishing a Jewish spiritual center without territorial sovereignty—should be supported as intermediate or final solutions.

Figure 4.1 The Main Choices (in terms of "Yes" and "No" statements)

Figure 4.2 also shows the common denominator at the extreme two poles in their support of "other solutions," including a nonterritorial answer to the Jewish problem. Yet the positions at these two poles originate from totally different arguments and, as we will see later, are also contradictory. These poles will be used to designate the extreme positions in the continuum, but we will not discuss them in detail because they did not gain significant support among the Jews and because nonterritorial solutions are beyond the scope of this book.

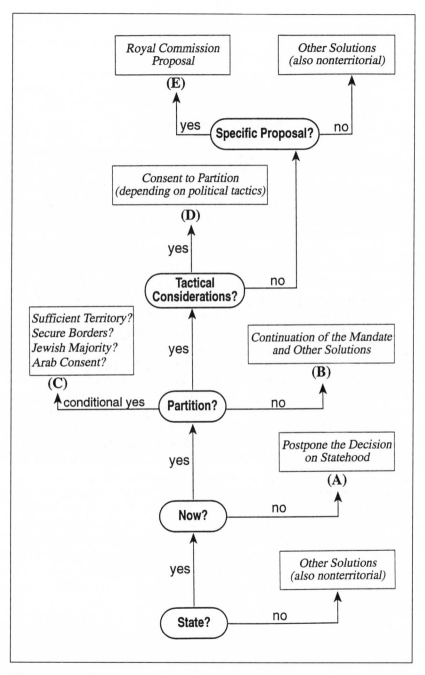

Figure 4.2 Possible Answers to Questions of State and Partition

Those who rejected territorial partition *outright*, because they opposed the establishment of a Jewish state at the proposed time, would be located at the position marked *A* in Figure 4.2. They in effect rejected the legitimacy of the equation—a state in exchange for territorial concessions—because they maintained, for different reasons, that the time for political independence had not arrived. Hypothetically, they would consider an immediate sovereign Jewish state, even within the boundaries of the greater mandate, including Transjordan, as premature.

Supporters of the "Greater Land of Israel" are found at position *B*. They opposed any partition of Eretz Israel, some referring only to the area west of the Jordan River, and others including Transjordan. In response to the dilemma presented by the royal commission recommendations, they demanded the continuation of the British mandate until complete fulfillment of the international commitments to the Jewish national home. Some also advocated a struggle with the British government and the local mandatory administration, even by force, to ensure free Jewish immigration, purchase of land and also self-government.

The conditional positions at *C* were, as we noted, more complex. If and when they were requested to give an unequivocal answer to the principle of partition, they usually vacillated. We listed the four main conditions that could set the final position of the undecided: territorial size, boundaries, the ratio between Jews and Arabs, and Arab consent to a Jewish state in exchange for partition. But not all the undecided presented all of these conditions. Moreover, as we will see later, subconditions can be added and tactical considerations can be integrated within the conditions.

The positions in category *D* are the clearest in their goal and the most obscure in their content. The holders of this position differ from the undecided primarily because they voiced an unconditional "yes" to the principle of partition of western Eretz Israel. Their only precondition was tactical, because they were great believers in the need to create political maneuvering room to allow the leadership freedom to negotiate the establishment of a state based on the best partition possible.

The few found in category *E* answered "yes" to the first three statements and "no" to the fourth, concerning the conditions, as well as the fifth statement, which grants absolute priority to the tactical consideration. They favored the immediate establishment of a Jewish state, even at the price of agreeing to a limited area of 5,000 km² in western Eretz Israel, as proposed by the royal commission. Here, too, there were various reasons: Zionist agreement would increase the chance that the British government would actually implement the commission's proposal; immediate sovereignty was critical to saving the Jews of Europe, making the question of territorial size essentially irrelevant.

When presented like this, the main answers to the statements in Figure 4.2 already indicate the heart of the problem faced by the decision makers, which is characteristic of political decision crossroads. The majority of the Zionist movement held strong ideological viewpoints, but were forced to choose between them and the readiness to compromise with political reality. The framework allows us to translate the "answers" to these difficult questions into less equivocal positions. Accordingly, Figure 4.3 places the main five answers in a bipolar schematic continuum that sorts the supportive and opposing positions in the partition polemos.

Positions at the Decision Crossroad, 1937

Figure 4.3 is a condensation of the choices (Figure 4.1) and the answers to the statements in Figure 4.2. Our discussion will concentrate on the positions marked A to E on the spectrum, which are based on the degree of readiness to support territorial partition of Eretz Israel in return for the establishment of a sovereign Jewish state. The main argument in each position, to be presented in detail in subsequent chapters, is summarized here:

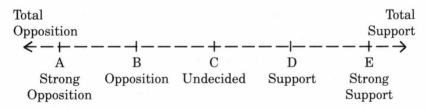

Figure 4.3 Distribution of Arguments and Positions on the Partition of Eretz Israel

Total Opposition. Fundamentally opposed to the establishment of a Jewish state in any place at any time.

A. *Strong Opposition.* Against the establishment of a sovereign Jewish state at the present time, even if they controlled the decision; consequently opposed any deliberation of territorial partition as premature.

B. *Opposition.* Against any territorial partition of western Eretz Israel,[4] even in return for the establishment of a sovereign Jewish state.

C. *Undecided.* Oppose or support partition depending on the practical answers to one or more of the following conditions— size of the proposed territory; security of the boundaries, existence of a Jewish majority or alternately, the proportion of Arabs to be included in the Jewish state; extent of Arab consent to the plan, both within and outside Eretz Israel.

D. *Support.* For the establishment of a sovereign Jewish state—even if the price is partition of western Eretz Israel— unconditionally, but subject to tactical considerations.[5]

E. *Strong Support.* For the immediate establishment of a sovereign Jewish state, even according to the royal commission's specific territorial proposal.[6]

Total Support. Support various forms of Jewish autonomy— self-governing cantons, a spiritual center, religious, cultural, and communal freedom of the Jewish minority—without sovereignty and regardless of the territorial aspects.

The Arguments

In Chapter One, we made a distinction between expressive and instrumental arguments for the need to possess a particular territory and linked it to literature on the nation-state, territory, and boundaries. We also stressed that political reasoning utilizes all types of arguments and that a particular position, therefore, usually combines expressive and instrumental—as well as tactical— arguments. Consequently, when we identify the argument most central to a political position, we must make do with the relative prominence of the type of argument presented and, most important, translate it into a position. In other words, we must put the arguments to a practical test of a political decision.

The participants in the polemos and the decision makers will therefore be positioned along the spectrum in Figure 4.3 according to their main arguments regarding the issue of 1937: partition of Eretz Israel in return for the establishment of a sovereign Jewish state. The positions of the policy makers in the decision itself will then be examined. We will also point out the degree of expressive-

Expressive Arguments

History. Historic rights to the land, collective consciousness, law of nature and historic mission related to territory.

Nation-People-Community. Land as a source of identity,[a]
ties of blood and land, common language, the nation-state as
a value, frontiers and living space for national development,
and territory as a shelter.[b]

Religion-Culture. Sacred land[c] promised boundaries, redemption of the land, religious commandments related to the
land, the religious "wholeness" of the land, cultural cradle.

Geography. Territorial laws, natural boundaries, "compact" states and geopolitical "wholeness" of the land.

Symbols.[d] Holy places, cemeteries, archaeological discov-
eries, landscape, and dates connected to historic places.

Instrumental Arguments

State. Territorial sovereignty as an expression of self-
determination and independence;[e] capacity to include the relevant population, national majority, legal rights.[f]

Defense and Security. Defensible boundaries, sea access,
strategic depth, security zones, effective control.

Societal. National, ethnic, religious and linguistic homogeneity; and a basis for social and cultural development.

Economic Viability. Settlement areas, water sources,
natural resources, markets, land and sea ports, economic self-
support (autarchy).

Transportation and Communication. Rivers, lakes, ports,
railways, and roads.

---

[a]Malmberg, 1980, p. 10.
[b]Gottmann, 1973, p. 1.
[c]On the connection between instinctive territorial behavior and religious
beliefs, see Maier, 1975, p. 18. When a community with a territorial culture
separates itself from its territory, it tends to develop an alternative nonterritorial
base of support. If it fails to do so, it loses its identity and assimilates. In
Maier's opinion, religion (the Torah) provides this support base for Diaspora
Jewry, a sort of portable territory replacing that which was lost. The Age of
Enlightenment loosened the religious bond. Consequently, he believes, the
need arose to return to the real territory of Eretz Israel.
[d]Gold, 1982, p. 48; Laponce, 1986; Gurevich and Aran, 1991.
[e]Sack, 1983, p. 55.
[f]See review of legal reasonings in Burghardt, 1973, p. 227.

Figure 4.4 Arguments for Territorial Attachment

ness or instrumentality in the arguments raised in the polemos; that is, was the attitude toward territory an axiomatic and independent value or could its benefits be weighed against other values? Figure 4.4 presents a general list of the main arguments divided into these categories.[7] Later chapters will present these arguments in detail and in the participants' own language.

The list of arguments in Figure 4.4 shows that it is not easy to separate expressive and instrumental arguments, and that they are usually used interchangably in territorial conflicts between states.[8] For example, is the argument for the need to possess a specific territory or for "compactness" to facilitate political or economic viability, an "expressive" one concerning the fate of the nation-state, or an "instrumental" argument designed to strengthen the state's ability to survive and compete?[9]

We can avoid most of these traps by putting these questions to the test of the choices faced by the decision makers and the specific decision adopted. Nevertheless, the decision makers' perception of reality may also determine their decision.[10] Take two examples. The tendency to employ expressive arguments increases if both parties claiming sovereignty over a particular territory believe that they are involved in a zero-sum game—what is given to one is necessarily taken from the other. This is indeed what happened in the struggle between the Jews and the Arabs in the Middle East. Conversely, the tendency to use instrumental arguments and to point out mutual benefit increases if the decision is aimed at an external factor that does not necessarily claim sovereignty over the territory, but has other defined interests. In 1919, the Zionist movement did not hesitate to use a mixture of arguments to persuade the British—the anticipated mandatory authority—to expand the boundaries of Palestine (E.I.). On the one hand, they talked of Jewish biblical rights "from Dan unto Beersheva," and on the other, raised colonial British interests.[11] By contrast, in 1937 the Zionist leadership generally emphasized concrete needs and avoided the historic arguments in the negotiations with the British government over the size of the proposed Jewish state.

This distinction between the instrumental-pragmatic as opposed to the expressive-ideological approach is relevant to the analysis of other international territorial conflicts.[12] This book will attempt to prove that this choice framework is applicable to the analysis of the 1937 territorial decision. But it can also be used to examine territorial decision crossroads that would later confront the Zionist movement and the state of Israel.

5 Predecision Positions

Excitement, excitement . . . flashes of speculations.
Rumors harvested like wild fields.
It is difficult to envision,
The determination of historic hours
As a concert program!

Natan Alterman, "Historic Hour," *Davar* (July 7, 1937)

The commission's report was published on July 7, 1937, and after one short month, the assorted arguments were translated into positions, votes, and decisions. In this chapter, the predecision positions of the parties and other organizations will be placed on the continuum presented in the previous chapter to enable later comparison between them and the actual positions and votes.

Initial Reactions to the Report

Prior to publication of the commission report, the tension in Palestine (E.I.) was palpable among both Jews and Arabs. Agreement of the Arab Higher Committee to testify before the royal commission had been accompanied by internal strife and rivalry, but that was held in abeyance in anticipation of the findings. The question now was whose needs and aspirations, if any, the recommendations would meet, and because they could not possibly suit both sides, whether they would touch off renewed "disturbances."[1]

The Jewish Response

Immediately upon publication of the report, the Zionist executive in London published a lengthy announcement presenting the official, public position of the movement, including

- A challenge of the report's basic premise, that the mandate could not be fulfilled, and a demand that its international obligations be pursued faithfully and resolutely.

- A pledge to examine the report in depth and to make a decision at the Zionist Congress and the Jewish Agency council meetings the following month.

- A call to the Jewish people "to remain calm and resolved in the justice of our cause . . . and to unite all of our powers to defend our right to our historic homeland and our national future in E.I., of which we cannot be deprived."[2]

On July 9, 1937, the Executive Board of the Va'ad Leummi resolved to send a telegram protesting the commission's decision to cut off Jewish Jerusalem. Shertok supported this announcement, after proposals for more extreme reactions were rejected.[3] Therefore the Jewish leadership preferred not to relate directly to the partition proposal other than the general mention of "our historic homeland," the customary term in Zionist documentation. But the public was much more agitated. At 9:00 P.M. on July 7, the mandatory radio broadcast an address by the high commissioner on the report, which would be published in London. By morning, Alterman's poem (quoted above) had already appeared in *Davar*.

Many declarations, articles, and commentaries by Zionists and non-Zionists alike appeared in the press in Eretz Israel and abroad, mainly against the partition proposal. One example was the proclamation of the Hebrew Writers Association:

[Our heart] . . . lies with the heart of the Jewish people in Eretz Israel and the Diaspora in fearing the royal commission's conclusion regarding partition of the Land of Israel, which amputates our land, cuts off entire limbs and robs us of Jerusalem, the cradle of our civilization in the past, our glory in the present, and our hope for the future. The Hebrew writers will fight together with the entire House of Israel for the reestablishment of Israel in its complete homeland. The association calls . . . on all ranks of the Yishuv to unite as one body with national discipline and a sense of responsibility and to avoid any action counter to our cultural position.[4]

Several characteristics of this response should be emphasized. First, fear of the uncertainty entailed in the impending change. Second, anxiety based on the past experience that British policy changes in the wake of governmental "reports" were never for the best. Third, the use of the analogy of Eretz Israel as a live body whose limbs would be torn from it. This image would be used repeatedly by opponents of partition.[5] Fourth, the call to behave responsibly and obey the national leaders, directed mainly against a Beitar leaflet calling upon the youth to demonstrate and embark on a "merciless war against the crushing of the body and soul of Zionism."[6]

Reaction to the publication of the report was a prelude to what would later be called *the partition polemos*. The explicitness of the report eliminated the previous confusion and contributed to the sharpness of the debate. It rejected the idea of gradual development of the Jewish national home and the concept of cantonization, thus focusing the debate on its proposal for a political-territorial partition, including boundaries and all, between Arabs and Jews in Palestine (E.I.).

The Arab Response

The commission's report recommended the establishment of two sovereign states, one Jewish and the other Arab, uniting Transjordan with part of Palestine. The commission proposed that Britain would negotiate treaties of alliance with the government of Transjordan and representatives of the Arabs in Palestine, but deliberately avoided mentioning who would govern the Arab state. This omission suggests either that the British did not regard Emir Abdullah as the suitable ruler of this state[7] or that they tried not to upset the kings of Saudi Arabia and Iraq by designating their rival to rule over Palestine.[8] On the other hand, it is inconceivable that the British thought Abdullah could be ignored completely. Although the British kept their options open, the Zionists clearly favored the "Hashemite option" both before and after the partition proposal (see Chapter Ten). There were constant contacts between the Zionist leaders and the ruler of Transjordan,[9] and it is important to note that some Jewish proponents of partition based their support on the assumption that Abdullah and moderate Palestinian leaders would agree to the proposal despite the expected opposition of the Mufti El-Husseini and his followers.

Abdullah indeed supported the partition plan, which recommended the annexation of 75 percent of Palestine to his kingdom, and made this explicit in a secret discussion with British High Commissioner Wauchope and representatives of the Jewish Agency,[10] but he was understandably wary of supporting it openly. Abdullah conducted talks with the mufti, Palestinian leaders, and leaders of Arab states, but primarily he waited to hear the reactions of the Jews, the British government, and the League of Nations. In contrast, the vehement opposition of the Arab states[11]—led by Iraq and, later, Saudi Arabia—increased opposition to the commission's proposal within the British Foreign Ministry as early as the summer of 1937 and fueled the quarrel between this ministry and the Colonial office.

The Arab Higher Committee, led by the mufti, rejected the Commission's recommendations and the British government declaration of policy accompanying the release of the report. The Committee's public statement published on July 8th 1937, listed the negative aspects of the report:[12] establishment of a Jewish state, and in the most fertile part of Palestine; partition of Palestine; leaving the holy places under permanent British mandate; and violation of Arab rights.

The statement also called upon the kings of Arab states to consult and support this stand, noting that Palestine belonged not only to Palestinian Arabs but to the entire Moslem and Arab world. If there was any implied opening for negotiations, it was quickly closed when the Arab committee said on July 23 that it saw no basis for discussion of the commission's recommendations and called for renewal of the revolt.

The Arab Higher Committee objected on principle to Jewish sovereignty of any sort in Palestine. The mufti's camp also intensely opposed Abdullah and the idea of incorporating any part of Palestine into Transjordan. Until then, there had been some internal debate among the Palestinian Arabs, but the general tone of the press was that "acceptance of the principle of partition is treason." A leaflet issued by the Supreme Muslim Council added the threat that supporters of partition are infidels and would be excommunicated.[13]

Opponents of the mufti, the Ma'arda party of the Nashashibi family, were more moderate in their approach to the British and the Jews in Palestine and closer to Abdullah. Their resignation from the Arab Higher Committee in early July 1937 was interpreted as an expression of support for the royal commission report. However, even the Ma'arda party rejected the partition proposal and indeed did so two days before the announcement of the Higher Arab Committee. In a July 21 memorandum to the British high commissioner, the Ma'arda party rejected a Jewish state outright, and demanded the establishment of an independent Arab Palestinian state. Porath raises another point: "Even if the Nashashibis had accepted the principle of partition, the proposed borders greatly disappointed them. Particularly disappointed were those who resided in areas to be incorporated into the Jewish state."[14]

Hence, even though the Nashashibi position resembled that of the moderate Jewish supporters, they were subject to pressure and death threats and preferred to condemn the partition unequivocally. The unified front against the commission's recommendations and the glossing over of differences eliminated an opportunity for a serious internal debate among the Palestinian Arabs about whether or not to make do with part of the land. Had such a debate taken place in 1937, it is possible that the Palestinians would have been more willing to come to grips with the partition proposal of the United Nations in 1947. In any event, the commission's recommendation to establish a Jewish state was regarded as a failure of the Arab revolt, particularly because renewal of the disturbances elicited a tough British response.[15] In October 1937, British authorities outlawed the Higher Arab Committee and the local national committees, causing their leaders, Amin el-Husseini and Jamal El-Husseini, to flee the country.

The initial Jewish and Arab responses to the report were decisively different. The moderate Palestinian Arabs eventually toed the line of unequivocal opposition, whereas among the Jews, the report shook some basic assumptions. Until 1937, most Jewish leaders, including Jabotinsky, assumed or hoped that the British would continue to oversee the realization of the national home despite their zigzagging policies and the inherent struggle.[16] For how long? Perhaps until the Jews would constitute a majority in the country or until most of the land would be Jewish controlled, or until the Arabs would agree to a Jewish presence in Palestine. The likelihood that the mandate was about to end fostered great uncertainty and especially fear that the British government was going to abandon the Zionist movement midway. Even advocates of active and open efforts to establish a Jewish state suddenly realized that their timetable might be greatly abbreviated and that this bore a painful price. No wonder the commission's recommendations fragmented the previous positions into new differences within the political parties, the Zionist movement, and the Jewish Agency.[17]

We will now present the initial positions of the Jewish parties and organizations, divided into four groups: the "Left," the "Center," and the "Right," the religious and the ultra-Orthodox, and the positions of some other groups.

Division Within the Labor Parties and the Left

Mapai's hegemony within the Zionist Organization began in the 1930s, with Hashomer Hatzair and Poalei Zion-Smol being on its Left and organizationally and ideologically independent.[18] There were also two Communist parties, the larger being the Palestine Communist party.

Mapai

The party's General Council convened from July 9–11, 1937, after those opposing partition stated insistently: "it cannot be that political action concerning 'partition' will be conducted without involving the movement in deliberating this question . . . [and without] an authoritative debate in the movement's institutions."[19] The council meeting lasted for more than two days, and a slight majority of the thirty-eight speakers supported the proposal.[20] But the "opponents" had prominent and outspoken representatives in B. Katznelson, Tabenkin, and others. At the end of the discussion, a ten-member committee (half proponents and half opponents) was appointed to formulate the resolution. Typically for Mapai, the 200 or so delegates unanimously accepted the committee's draft proposal at 4:00 A.M., and it was published the next day in *Davar* under a banner headline.[21] The heated debate within the committee centered on two main points, and resulted in the following unwieldy compromise:

> *Article 8.* Mapai sees no solution also in this plan, presented in the commission's proposals, even though the plan pretends to speak in the name of a Jewish state. Despite Mapai's great desire to lead the Hebrew nation to complete control of its fate—and to maximal independence in determining its own way of life in managing immigration, settlement and the development of Hebrew culture, and despite our deep commitment to the meaning of exile in the Herzlian term "state of the Jews"—which is not a state for purposes of national or class dominance, but rather for the purpose of economic, social and spiritual organized development—the party cannot consider this proposal of the commission anything but abuse of the idea of the Jewish state and its dilution.
> *Article 10.* Therefore, Mapai also does not see the possibility of accepting this royal commission proposal that refers

to the establishment of a Jewish state. It calls upon the leadership and the Zionist movement, with the assistance of its allies and those interested in the success of the Jewish endeavor in Eretz Israel, to do everything possible in order that the British government will faithfully fulfill its obligations to the Hebrew nation through sincere assistance in the establishment of the national home . . .

Thus, in July 1937, Mapai rejected the royal commission's conclusion that the mandate could not be fulfilled and declared that it was not the mandate that failed but rather the policies of the British administration. It denounced partition, but mainly because of the proposed size: The first truncation in 1922 reduced the mandatory boundaries to approximately 60 million dunam (15 million acres); the current proposal would leave the Jewish national home a fifth of the remaining area. Finally, there was an important statement concerning the purpose of establishing a Jewish state; it is not desired for imaginary prestige or honorific titles of government, but rather to solve the Jewish question.

Mapai council members so strongly felt the fatefulness of the hour that the compromise decision contributed to party unity despite the strong underlying differences. Mapai's pragmatism was illustrated in the decision's inclusion of most of the arguments of both camps, rejecting however only "this" royal commission proposal. The idea itself was not rejected, and the council was very careful not to mention the word *partition*. In terms of Figure 4.3, the council's decision avoided both clear-cut positions: opposition or support for partition depended on the practical answers to particular conditions.

Shertok thus managed to take another step in the direction that he and Ben-Gurion had charted: to oppose termination of the mandate, but not to reject the report outright as a basis for negotiations.[22] Ben-Gurion, who was in London, had no reason to oppose the Mapai council decision because it did not contradict his position, which he expressed in his diary as a detailed list of arguments—for and against the commission's proposal. He concluded that the positive aspects outweighed the negative "and therefore we should fight to fulfill the commission's proposals in general terms." He also compared the commission's proposal to his own partition recommendation, as presented to Mapai's secretariat in February and found the former generally superior.[23]

The ambiguous decision of the Mapai council marked a very important stage in the decision-making process, because the Labor movement's victory in the Zionist Congress elections (42 percent of the delegates) strengthened the party's and Ben-Gurion's personal influence. Ben-Gurion had a clear idea of what he expected from the Labor movement and the Zionist Congress, and he outlined a tactical plan for himself: to denounce Viscount Samuel's proposal to restrict the Jewish population in Palestine to a permanent minority; to reject the commission's proposals to restrict immigration and land purchasing; to refute the assumption that the mandate could not be fulfilled; and regarding partition: "the Congress need not yet say either 'no' or 'yes', rather it must empower the new Executive to discuss amendments to the commission's proposals with the government."[24]

Hakibbutz Hameuchad

Hakibbutz Hameuchad (KM) was affiliated with Mapai and part of the World Labor movement at the Congress. In 1944 they would split and establish the separate L'Ahdut Ha'Avoda party. In 1937, under Tabenkin's leadership, they were the most insistent opponents of partition within Mapai. Ever since their proposal to oppose partition was rejected by the Mapai Central Committee in April 1937, KM had demanded that the decision be transferred to a wider party forum. The Mapai council meeting in July was a result of this pressure, and all KM leaders spoke against partition.[25] Obviously, they were dissatisfied with the council's compromise decision and convened their secretariat on July 14, 1937, to express vehement opposition to the partition plan.[26] We will later examine the ideological reasoning of KM's opposition, mentioning here only that Tabenkin considered settlement the only way to establish the Jewish right to Eretz Israel. He therefore opposed any proposal to establish a truncated state on any other basis, political or opportunistic. His "maximalist Zionism" preferred a "bad mandate" to a "bad partition" and hence his readiness to forgo the premature establishment of a Jewish state.[27] The ambivalent attitude of Tabenkin and his colleagues toward the state also originated from a completely different source—the Marxist "theory of stages" and its conception of the role of the state in the socialist revolution: "The state is not an 'ideal of life' borrowed from German philosophy, because the state constitutes organized authority and repression. The Jewish state is a requirement until the day will come when Hebrew socialism will battle for its withering away."[28] Although this reasoning is antithetical to the German geopolitical theories, the arguments concerning the need for settlement space and expansive boundaries are quite similar. Therefore internal ideological tension already existed between those who completely opposed the state on purely Marxist grounds and those who, like Tabenkin, opposed a state "now" because of settlement ideology encompassing the "entire Land of Israel." Other practical arguments, such as a lack of confidence in the British or fears of a vassal state without actual sovereignty or independence, funneled into this debate of principles. However, Tabenkin outlined KM's ideological position on the eve of the report's publication.

The state is the outcome and the expression of real public forces in economic and social life and cannot be established before any other social organization.

This [partition] proposal does not stem from our way of life, it was never anticipated along the way and arose in contradiction to the movement's path. We did not yet demand the Land of Israel as a state. On the contrary, we proved that the Hebrew state is an illusion until actual strength will exist in Eretz Israel to make this possible.[29]

Beyond the ideological arguments lay a power struggle over the status of the kibbutz movement and its urban partners within Mapai. KM started to organize independent political action based on its opposition to partition, and it contributed to the formation of a faction and eventually to the split within Mapai in 1944.[30]

Upon publication of the report, KM opposed territorial partition, even in exchange for the immediate establishment of a sovereign Jewish state. Nevertheless, as we shall see, Tabenkin and his colleagues supported the compromise resolution of the Labor movement at the Congress in the name of unity and against the attempts to divide Zionism and split the Labor movement.[31]

Hashomer Hatzair[32]

The resolutions of the Kibbutz movement of Hashomer Hatzair (ST), which convened on July 9–10, 1937, expressed total opposition to the idea of partition.[33] They maintained that

- The partition plan and the proposal to terminate the mandate constitute an unprecedented assault on the foundations of the Zionist enterprise and a denial of the plans stemming from the Balfour Declaration and the mandate regarding immigration.

- The partition plan implies minimal Zionism, further concession of the possibility of opening Transjordan for Jewish settlement, and restriction of the territory of the Zionist enterprise—the subjugation of Zionism to foreign interests.

- It also implies the destruction of any chance for a Jewish-Arab peace and an additional sharpening of the confrontation in Eretz Israel.

- The Zionist movement vehemently rejects the royal commission's attempt to establish a divided, ephemeral "state" of pseudo-independence as the goal of Zionism. It should not be misled by the mirage of empty state-oriented solutions into surrendering the clear and only goal of the Zionist movement: the concentration of a majority of the Hebrew nation in the Land of Israel and its environs.

- The Zionist movement must reaffirm its commitment to the principle of equality between Jews and Arabs regardless of their present or future numerical ratio, as the basis for cooperation in an undivided Land of Israel.

ST called upon the Zionist executive to reject the commission's conclusions and warned it against replacing the war against the commission's plan with a war for an improved territorial partition; it also called on the labor movement to fight for uncompromised rejection of the partition at the Twentieth Zionist Congress. For them, the commission's plan was an imperialistic British plot intended to pursue a policy of *divide et impera* between Jews and Arabs. Instead, they urged continuation of the mandate to establish a socialist society in a binational state.[34] There was also, however, an additional element: "We cannot abandon one inch of the land of Eretz Israel. The needs of the tortured Jews in the Diaspora and, no less than that, the good of the Arabs in Eretz Israel, demand not a reduction of the territory of the Zionist enterprise but rather maximal development of the entire land.[35]

Ideologically, ST's opposition to territorial partition was more sweeping and absolute than that of the KM or the Revisionists because it also opposed the creation of an exclusive Jewish state within any boundaries. Such a state was seen as a dangerous deviation from Socialism, Zionism, and Judaism, even though its future establishment was not summarily ruled out. The following summary clarifies ST's position as it was published in English to the outside world, and also included nonideological arguments.

- From the very first moment, the Zionist executive adopted a positive attitude to the partition scheme or to the possibilities for a slightly improved one. But, as it is intended to safeguard only British interests in Palestine, there would be no major changes in the proposal.

- Maximal use should be made of the international obligations that compel Britain to abide by the terms of the mandate. Signing away any part of Eretz Israel may be for good.

- And finally, "the progressive character of Zionism is endangered! A sentiment of Messianism and 'hour of redemption' is sweeping Jewry." Consequently, the emphasis on pioneering is vanishing and instead dreams of a Jewish "empire," which would expand its borders through military might, are being born.[36]

ST leaders remained loyal to this position of absolute opposition to partition. They would join the opponents front, despite their chagrin at finding themselves together with the leaders from the Right.

Poalei Zion-Smol

This small movement was outside the Zionist Organization. In a statement following the publication of the commission's report, they completely rejected any partition scheme. For Poalei Zion, the "integrity of the land" implied a chance for the convergence of Jewish and Arab farmers and workers, "en route to a socialist Eretz Israel."[37] However, it was not far from ST in its opposition to the partition proposal: "The promise of a Jewish state is simply a ruse of British imperialism to conceal its real intention to end the ongoing, massive immigration of Jews and the realization of a Jewish territorial center in Eretz Israel."[38]

The negation of a Jewish state is absent both from the movement's general approach and from the preceding statement concerning the "territorial center." They emphasized the supranational identity of the proletarian society and the necessity to strive for complete Jewish-Arab agreement. This entailed significant differences between the small group of party members in Eretz Israel and the majority in Poland. The latter supported statehood and justified it in terms of a dialectic process. In its party council in Poland in November 1937, the following resolution was approved: "In protest of the plan to partition Eretz Israel and in battle against this plan, [we acknowledge] the enormous political importance of declaring a Jewish state, and not just in part of Eretz Israel."[39] In December 1937, Poalei Zion-Smol resolved to return to the Zionist Organization, and in 1946 it united with the Ahdut Ha'avoda movement.

The Palestine Communist Party

The Palestine Communist party (P.C.P.), anti-Zionist and mostly Jewish, was outlawed by the British government of Palestine. The Arab revolt plunged the P.C.P., and particularly its Jewish members, into a dilemma. They supported Arab nationalism and aspired to separate the Jews of Palestine (E.I.) from Zionism, but they were fearful of crossing the line between revolutionary ideology and Arab terrorism. In a manifesto they published in Arabic in May 1936, they declared that the P.C.P. would fight to attain Arab nationalist objectives: curtailment of Jewish immigration, self-government, prevention of the sale of Arab lands to foreigners, and the restoration of land sold to the Zionists.[40] The involvement of several P.C.P. members in terrorist activities at the end of 1936 brought mass arrests and the expulsion of many from Palestine (E.I.) by the British government. Fear of losing support among Jewish workers and the fact that the Arab leaders of the revolt were anti-Communist had a moderating effect on the views of the P.C.P. The party expressed criticism of personal terrorism waged by Arabs and emphasized the political character of the struggle of the Arab national liberation movement.[41]

In this context, it is clear why the P.C.P. supported a united Arab-Jewish boycott of the royal commission. With publication of the report, the P.C.P. aggressively opposed the idea of partition of the land as an imperialistic and Zionist conspiracy and demanded that the plan be repudiated, the mandate revoked, and an Arab state established in Palestine.[42] The P.C.P. favored maintaining the demographic status quo between the Arab and Jewish populations of Palestine (a 2:1 ratio) within a democratic representative framework.[43] This position was presented not just in the ideological terms customary in Communist propaganda (the Jews are not a people and do not deserve a state), but in the context of the wider struggle against Italian and Spanish Fascism and as an effort to prevent the destruction of the Jewish Yishuv. We will not present this party's positions in detail, as it had almost no influence on Zionist movement decisions, except to point out that this was the only party in Palestine (E.I.) to support the 1939 White Paper policy of Britain.[44]

Division Within the Center and the Right Parties

As opposed to the Left, dominated by Mapai, the Right and the Center were divided into many small bodies; and all attempts to create a permanent political organization among the Yishuv's so-called civic camp and the General Zionists within the Zionist movement failed.[45] We will present only the positions of the main parties.

The General Zionists

The General Zionists formed a party within the Zionist Organization in 1931.[46] In 1935, they split into the General Zionist Union (hereafter, Union), and the General Zionist Federation (hereafter, Federation). They reunited in 1946. The General Zionists' lines of division on the question of partition ran both between the two factions and within each of them. Menachem Ussishkin, the leader of the Union and chairman of the Zionist General Council, stood out among those who rejected the partition proposal outright. However, the political weight of this veteran Zionist leader had already diminished, but his personality and opinions came to symbolize the opponents camp. In a lengthy article in *Ha'aretz*, written before publication of the commission's report, Ussishkin presented his arguments against partition and raised a number of points touching on the decision-making process:

- Fear that leaders in Eretz Israel and London would present the Zionist movement with a fait accompli.

- The need for an immediate negative response to any partition proposal in order not to compromise the Jewish position. Silence would be interpreted as willingness to consider the proposal.

- Elections to the Zionist Congress should be on the basis of support for or opposition to the decreed partition.

- The dispute could destroy the Zionist Organization, which is the only asset unifying the Jews working for national revival.[47]

Many of the private farmers in Eretz Israel belonged to the more conservative Union, but the urban leaders such as Peretz Bernstein, editor of the *Haboker* newspaper, and educators such as Chaim Bograshov and Emil Shmurak expressed the most adamant opposition to partition. Union leaders were also prominent among the signatories to a declaration written by the "Rabbis, Party Heads and Heads of the Municipal Councils" against partition.[48] In contrast, Moshe Smilansky, a leader of the Farmers Union, was one of the few Union members who favored partition. He initially supported the concept of a binational state, but switched to support partition upon publication of the commission's report.[49]

The Federation was the larger party—moderate in its views, closer to the labor movement, and stronger among the overseas Zionists. Federation members generally espoused less ideological positions than their peers in the Union, on issues including the promotion of private enterprise or opposition to the Histadrut (General Federation of Labor). On the question of partition, the Federation's support was essentially pragmatic and identical to Weizmann's. Moshe Glickson, editor of the daily *Ha'aretz*, and leaders of American Jewry, Louis Brandeis, Stephen Wise, and Abba Hillel Silver, were prominent among the Federation opponents. By nearly unanimous decision, the Conference of American Zionists resolved in June 1937 to oppose the concept of partition.[50] We will detail the positions of the American leaders later, but it should be mentioned here that Weizmann directly influenced a number of them to change their positions just before the Congress opened.

Both factions of the General Zionists determined their positions only on the eve of the Zionist Congress. The majority at the Union convention firmly opposed the partition proposal, while at the Federation convention most demanded adoption of a positive position despite the opposing views of Silver and Glickson.[51]

The Revisionists

The Revisionist Zionist Union was founded in 1925, declaring that the goal of Zionism is to gradually establish Eretz Israel (including Transjordan) as a Jewish commonwealth. In 1935, they withdrew from the Zionist Organization to establish a separate

New Zionist Organization (NZO), and did not participate in the decisions of the Zionist Congress and the Jewish Agency council. Yet its positions did influence the Zionist and Jewish world due to its power overseas and Jabotinsky's leadership. For example, the Revisionists had the ability to organize demonstrations in Poland against the partition.[52] In May 1937, the NZO announced its opposition to the partition plan.[53] But when the commission's report was released, Jabotinsky composed a declaration that reflected his doubts about whether to reject a British proposal that, after all, espoused the establishment of a Jewish state:

> The document published tonight by the Mandatory government includes two basic and salient proposals: (A) the idea of the Jewish state, (B) the plan for partitioning Eretz Israel. The first constitutes an admission and a recognition that cannot be repudiated, that "a Jewish national home for the Jewish people" has only one particular and unique meaning, and that is a Jewish state. To be sure, this was the intention of the mandate, and this interpretation will come to life and persist. But the second matter is an attempt to reduce the size of the Jewish state intended by the mandate—from 100,000 km^2 to 3,000 km^2. Its implication is to kill the human essence of Zionism, which is—returning millions of homeless to their homeland.[54]

According to B. Akzin, then a leader of the NZO, publication of the report caused Jabotinsky "to hesitate for a day or two" because his longing for a Jewish state and the example of Italy's independence process led him to consider whether the small territory proposed would not serve as the nucleus for wider Jewish independence in the future.[55] Jabotinsky ultimately decided to oppose the plan out of his conviction that it was a British ruse that would never be realized. Some other Revisionists feared that Mapai's support for the partition proposal was totally based on its desire to assume governing power.[56] Beitar, the Revisionist youth movement, issued a harsh call addressed to the "national Hebrew youth":

> Our gift will be a pathetic strip of land wrapped in a fake royal Tallith [prayer shawl]. External assault is cruel, but worse is the shame of treason woven from within. Leaders are assisting the plot and preaching dissension.
>   Alert the masses of Hebrew youth united under the pure banner of Beitar's leader and national Zionism for a merciless war against dismemberment of the body and soul of Zionism.[57]

The Revisionists held massive rallies in Eretz Israel against the partition plan. At a meeting of the Jewish Agency executive in early July, Shertok expressed his fear that the demonstrations would become violent and that even Jabotinsky would not be able to control his followers.[58]

The Revisionist movement's final stance against the royal commission report was unequivocal. They continued to support the establishment of a sovereign Jewish state, in the present if possible, but without making any territorial concession on both sides of the Jordan River. If this could not be accomplished now, there would be a better opportunity in the future and meanwhile the Zionist movement should demand that the British government fulfill its obligations in accordance with the mandatory charter and international law.

With the hindsight of forty years, Akzin would later summarize his movement's opposition in four arguments. First, the Zionist movement could absolutely not surrender willingly any part of the land, in order not to compromise its right to the remainder of Eretz Israel under different circumstances in the future. Second, the state was not a goal unto itself, but rather a territorial shelter that should be big enough for a great number of immigrants, particularly after Hitler's rise in Germany. Third, it would be impossible to defend the state within the proposed boundaries. Fourth, the British government did not actually intend to implement the royal commission's proposal. Rather, it would use Jewish consent in order to establish an Arab state under British protection and leave the mandate in force on the microscopic area slated for the Jewish state.[59]

Jabotinsky failed to lead a united opposition to the partition proposal. Mapai members also prevented the Revisionists from participating in the "opposition front" to partition. This inability to influence the course of events led some Revisionist leaders to regret having left the Zionist Organization.[60]

The Hebrew State Party

This small party (nine delegates to the Twentieth Zionist Congress) was composed of those who did not leave the Zionist Organization with Jabotinsky. Despite its name, the party aggressively opposed the "state for partition" formula for reasons similar to those of the Revisionist movement. At the Zionist Congress, its head, Meir Grossman, virulently accused the Zionist executive and Weizmann of secretly negotiating Jewish acceptance of the partition proposal with the British government. His speech quoted the secret discussion between Weizmann and Ormsby-Gore of July 19, 1937, and accused Weizmann of conducting "two-faced" politics with or without the executive's agreement and certainly without authorization from the Zionist General Council or the Congress.[61] These revelations, spread by wide press coverage, strained relations between the Zionist leadership and the British government. Grossman was convicted in the Zionist Organization's court of honor and suspended from the Zionist General Council for two years.[62] But this did not prevent him from becoming one of the opposition's most extreme spokesmen against partition.

Division Within the Religious and Ultra-Orthodox Parties

The Mizrahi and Hapoel Hamizrahi were religious *Zionist* movements that participated in all the institutions of the Jewish community in Eretz Israel and the Zionist institutions abroad. Conversely, Agudat Israel and Poalei Agudat Israel were ultra-Orthodox *non-Zionist* movements that functioned outside these frameworks, socially and politically. However, the religious-ideological distinctions between these two camps are more complex, revolving around the internal bond and relative weight of the three components: the people of Israel, the Torah of Israel, and the Land of Israel.

Mizrahi and Hapoel Hamizrahi

Religious opposition to partition first appeared in *Netiva*, the official journal of Hapoel Hamizrahi, in April 1937.[63] In June, the declaration "against any partition proposal whatsoever" was signed by the two chief rabbis, the two chief rabbis of Tel Aviv-Jaffa, and representatives of the World Mizrahi Organization and World Hapoel Hamizrahi:

> The people of Israel did not surrender its right to the land of its fathers during thousands of years of exile, and will not now concede even one inch of the Land of Israel.
> We staunchly declare the external, complete and full right of the nation to its homeland within its historic boundaries, and absolutely reject any attempt to agree to the partition of Eretz Israel or to other proposals assaulting our rights.[64]

This declaration presented a religious and political position, but raised no definite ruling derived from religious law against partition. Nevertheless, rabbis associated with Mizrahi did not refrain from saying that the partition contradicted religious law, constituting "an intentional desecration of the holiness of the Land."[65] By contrast, the two chief rabbis of Eretz Israel refrained from issuing a religious directive against partition despite appeals to them to do so. Similarly, Mizrahi Leader Berlin was careful to present general reasoning based on his religious world view, rather than definite rulings.

The Fourteenth World Mizrahi Conference, which met from July 27–30, 1937, adopted an unequivocal stand against the partition.[66] Mizrahi and Hapoel Hamizrahi attended the Zionist Congress as a single faction (with seventy-one delegates), presenting a unified opposition to the idea of partition and voting accordingly. The few members who favored partition (several Mizrahi representatives from Germany and Hapoel Hamizrahi from Eretz Israel) agreed to leave the hall during the vote in order not to be counted among the abstentions. Moshe Shapira, who would later lead the National Religious Party in Israel, and Yehuda Fishman, a member of the Jewish Agency executive, were among their representatives who either supported partition or were undecided. However, the main leaders firmly opposed the plan and were active in the opposition both before and after the Congress.

Agudat Israel and Poalei Agudat Israel

Both the opponents and the proponents of partition attempted to sway these two ultra-Orthodox organizations, which were outside the Zionist movement, to their side. Yaacov Rosenheim, head of the World Union of Agudat Israel, met Jabotinsky in London and sent a joint letter to Weizmann requesting that the three organizations convene to discuss the partition proposal. The request was rejected, but members of the Zionist executive did meet Agudat Israel representatives to seek common ground concerning the partition. The religious Zionists also tried to form a united front against partition with the ultra-Orthodox, but without practical result.[67]

The official decisions of Agudat Israel were multifaceted and subject to various interpretations.[68] The Aguda's Council of Torah Sages adopted a clear position in favor of the integrity of Eretz Israel: "The boundaries of the Holy Land are drawn by He who bequeathed the countries in His holy Torah and are determined for generations eternal. It is therefore impossible for the Jewish people on its own to make concessions on these boundaries in any way whatsoever. Any such concession would be worthless."

However, the political decisions of the Third Great Assembly of Agudat Israel, which convened at the end of August 1937, were remarkably similar to the resolution adopted at the preceding Zionist Congress in their pragmatic adaptability. The Great Assembly

rejects the Jewish state proposed by the royal commission, with all due respect for the commission and its efforts to find an objective solution.

. . . believes that implementation of the mandate with a clear policy to attain peace between Jews and Arabs is feasible.

. . . empowers the Political Action Committee to negotiate with the British government and the League of Nations in order to find a solution fitting the spiritual and material needs of the Jewish people and their historic right to the Holy Land based on Torah principles.

The resemblance to the Congress resolutions stopped short, of course, at support for the Zionist aspiration to establish a state since the ultra-Orthodox could not consider a non-strictly religious state to be a Jewish state. But in Agudat Israel, opinions about partition were divided, as evidenced by Rabbi Dushinsky's testimony before the royal commission: "The holy Torah has promised the Holy Land to the people of Israel but it is by that very Torah that we are commanded not to inherit the country by force, and not to dominate others; but we are confident that when the returning exiles to Zion . . . will make the national home the abode of the Torah . . . the Almighty God will move the people of this country to greet us willingly . . . "[69]

Therefore, Agudat Israel's position does not fit onto the scale of opposition-support for territorial partition proposed in Chapter Four. Although it remained loyal to the promised boundaries and the religious commandment to settle the Land of Israel, Agudat Israel struggled with Zionism's premature schemes for political sovereignty, particularly for a secular state. It also acknowledged the bond between the local Arabs and the land. In contrast with Mizrahi, this "spiritual patriotism" attached more importance to the Torah of Israel and the people of Israel than to the worldly, territorial Land of Israel.

The other ultra-Orthodox party, Poalei Agudat Israel, was considered an ally of the Zionist leaders due to its association with the

Yishuv and its institutions. They rejected the Zionist idea of establishing a secular Jewish state, but their position on partition was less ambivalent and could be classified as moderate support. Like some Agudat leaders, their leader, B. Mintz, also claimed that it was possible to support the establishment of a Jewish state on condition that it would be a "Torah state": "Observance of the Torah in the Land of Israel is more important than the inclusion of one settlement or another."[70]

This variance of opinions makes it difficult to determine where exactly the ultra-Orthodox stood on the question of partition. Yet it should be noted that Agudat Israel also demanded to be included in any negotiations on the future fate of Eretz Israel, which indicates a certain willingness to be part of the political process.

Additional Positions

The Jewish debate lasted for one and a half years: from April 1937 until October 1938, with publication of the Woodhead commission report. Many more people and bodies participated in the polemos: writers, poets, journalists, rabbis, and intellectuals, as well as the major publications at that time.[71] The partition proposal aroused intense public opinion in Eretz Israel and around the Jewish world, as evidenced by the press of that period.

We will mention only another two groups whose positions influenced the polemos within and outside Eretz Israel: some former members of Brit Shalom (which stopped functioning in 1933)—now represented through Kedma Mizraha[72]—and the non-Zionists within the Jewish Agency.

Kedma Mizraha

The small intellectual movement of Brit Shalom (1925–1933) did not become a party, but its positions did have an important ideological influence throughout the Jewish world. It was influenced by the thought of Martin Buber concerning issues of nationalism, the role of the homeland in Zionism, and relations with the Arabs, but it also presented an alternative political program to that of the Zionist leadership.[73] Brit Shalom had sought a solution that would be national but not territorial, because it thought that Zionism would not be attainable without a political agreement with the local Arabs. Jews and Arabs should arrive at an agreement between them based on full equalization of political rights, and the state will be composed of two nations: "The Land of Israel does not have to be a Hebrew or an Arab state, but a binational state in which Hebrews and Arabs will live with equal civil, political, and national rights, without discrimination based on the majority or the minority nation."[74]

Kedma Mizraha (founded in 1936), added a regional orientation to Brit Shalom's ideas: cultural integration of Zionism in the Middle East (Mizrah) and political integration within the framework of an Arab federation. On May 18, 1937, Margalit Kalvarinsky explained at a meeting of Kedma Mizraha: "It is only necessary to find a way to reconcile the two national movements: the Zionist and the Arab. They seem to oppose and contradict each other, but in reality they complement one another and can dwell side by side in friendship and brotherhood."[75]

Kedma Mizraha had no clear position concerning the Peel commission proposal. It sought Jewish Agency approval to attempt to negotiate with the Arab states to formulate a compromise proposal. These efforts were rejected by Shertok, and Kalvarinsky continued in vain to seek Arab partners to the idea of a binational autonomous state in Palestine (E.I.), which would have institutions with parity, as transition to a federation of this state with Arab states.[76]

The role of Kedma Mizraha in the partition debate was rather marginal. Nevertheless, Yehuda Magnes continued to advocate these positions during this period, without officially belonging to any movement. In a widely quoted *New York Times* article published after release of the report, Magnes emphasized that the real test of any solution would be its ability to foster a Jewish-Arab agreement. The royal commission plan could not accomplish this, despite its many attractive features. He opposed on principle any attempt to erect artificial barriers between the two peoples and also feared that partition would create "terribly irredentist areas on both sides of the new border, the new Balkans."[77]

Magnes was not a socialist, but on this issue he was close to Hashomer Hatzair both in recognizing the political element in the Jewish-Arab conflict and in proposing a binational state as a solution. In his speech at the Jewish Agency assembly, Magnes most vehemently opposed the establishment of a Jewish state, partition, and population transfer.[78]

Non-Zionists

Ben-Gurion tried to adjust the line separating the proponents from the opponents to coincide with that separating the Zionists from the non-Zionists. He argued that the non-Zionists rejected the royal commission's proposal because they opposed any Jewish state, implying that such opposition is therefore assimilationist and "non-Zionist":

I am not completely ignoring the internal Zionist dispute: for or against the partition. It is serious and tragic enough even if somewhat overblown and artificial. This is not a dispute for and against a Jewish state, but on how to ensure the establishment of the Jewish state. Our dispute with Warburg (and his associates), although he too is phrasing the matter as if it is an argument for and against partition, is that it is basically and at its core an argument for and against a Jewish state . . .

The most serious danger comes from those Jews who see a Jewish state as dangerous to their property, status, rights and influence. This danger is even more acute when those subverting a Jewish state are led not by complete assimilationists and clear haters of Zion but rather half, third and quarter Lovers of Zion such as Samuel, Willy Cohen, Warburg and their faction.[79]

Reality was far more complex than Ben-Gurion's simplistic phrasing, especially since the Jews who called themselves *non-Zionists* were actually part of the institutions participating in the Zionist mission of "rebuilding the homeland."

The Zionist executive elected in 1935 at the Nineteenth Zionist Congress was a coalition of seven members: in addition to Weizmann as president, three from the Labor movement, three General Zionists, and one Mizrahi. Zionists and non-Zionists were represented equally in the enlarged Jewish Agency Council (224 representatives) and on its board of directors (40 members), and the Jewish Agency executive was composed of all members of the Zionist executive plus three non-Zionists. The representatives of Jewish organizations in the expanded Jewish Agency were entitled to present their positions on partition both because of their role in building Eretz Israel and because the agency was the official Jewish representative to the British government. Felix Warburg, a businessman, contributor, and leader of American Jewry, insisted that the agency council, and not the Zionist Congress, was the forum to discuss and decide about the royal commission's proposal. Ben-Gurion vehemently refused, claiming that political decisions on the fate of Eretz Israel could not be placed in non-Zionist hands.[80]

Although they supported the Zionist enterprise, the non-Zionists did not draw the conclusion that a state is absolutely necessary. Hence their fundamental opposition to the commission's proposal. Many of them denied the existence of a separate Jewish nationality and did not believe that the Jewish people, which is above all a religious community, embodied the characteristics that would allow it to demand territorial self-determination. Like Magnes and others, many non-Zionists therefore supported a nonsovereign arrangement between the Jewish and Arab peoples in Eretz Israel.

Many non-Zionist Jews in Britain also adopted a firm negative position, but from a different angle. Although they completely supported the mandate and the idea of a national home, they rejected the royal commission proposal as perilous to the interests of both the Jewish people and Great Britain. They maintained that Britain's colonial rule in Palestine was not over yet, and an independent state would isolate the Jews there from their European origin and swallow them in primitive Asia. Such attitudes were expressed in the London *Jewish Chronicle* before and after publication of the report.[81] It should be mentioned, however, that there were several non-Zionists attending the Jewish agency council who supported statehood.[82]

The non-Zionist stance against partition impaired the persuasiveness of those Zionist leaders from overseas who also opposed partition, but for different reasons. Stephen Wise, a leader of American Zionism and the General Zionist Federation, found himself attacked for a position that he did not support. Although he was accused of opposing the establishment of a Jewish state, like the non-Zionists, Wise actually opposed only a state based on territorial partition on the grounds that such a state would not be economically viable.[83] As we shall see in Chapter Nine, his proposal was rejected at the Zionist Congress, whereas the position of the non-Zionists did have a slight influence on the resolution adopted by the Jewish Agency council.

In sum, the opposition of former members of Brit Shalom as well as non-Zionists within the agency, like that of Jabotinsky and the ultra-Orthodox from outside the Zionist Organization, did not greatly influence the formation of the "rejectionist" camp. Despite Warburg's importance and Magnes's personal influence, they were not among the first line of leading opponents, which included insiders: Ussishkin, Berlin, Tabenkin, Ya'ari, Wise, and the ambivalent

Berl Katznelson. They were all members of the Zionist Organization, and they formulated the arguments against a partitioned state
that influenced the movement's final decision.

Positions on the Eve of the Decision

The initial negative reactions to the royal commission's report faithfully represented the instinctive fear of a possible plot being hatched
by the British government. Not one of the many parties that had
adopted positions and made public announcements at that time,
supported the commission's proposal or the principle of partition in
exchange for a sovereign state. Figure 5.1 presents the initial official positions of the parties and movements, as well as the main
divisions among their members, on the continuum of support vs.
opposition.

The Mapai Council's official decision of July 1937 was equivocal and is therefore placed in category C in Figure 5.1. By contrast,
the arguments raised by party members during the preceding five
months ranged across the entire spectrum: from strong opposition
to any proposal for the immediate establishment of a Jewish state,
unrelated to partition, to strong support for any type of sovereignty, even—if there is no choice—within the boundaries proposed
by the commission.

We separate Hakibbutz Hameuchad, even though it was then
affiliated with Mapai, because it had a different, uniform, and opposing position. The resolution it adopted upon publication of the
report places it in category A: rejection of the immediate establishment of the state, hence nonacceptance of the "sovereignty for partition" equation. There were, however, some moderate rejectionists
within KM who stressed only their opposition to partition.

It is more difficult to place Hashomer Hatzair because of its
support for a binational state in the entire mandate territory. Although this was a nonterritorial solution in terms of the "Jewish
problem," ST is in category A because ideologically it did not rule
out the possibility that, within the framework of a national revolution, a Jewish state could be established in the future. Its members
included "total opponents" whose position replicated that of Kedma
Mizraha and also moderate opponents who objected only to a partitioned state. This was also true of Poalei Zion-Smol, whose opposition to any territorial solution was more moderate than that of the
extreme left within ST. Thus, at the left-most extreme of the continuum we find only the P.C.C., whose opposition to Zionism and

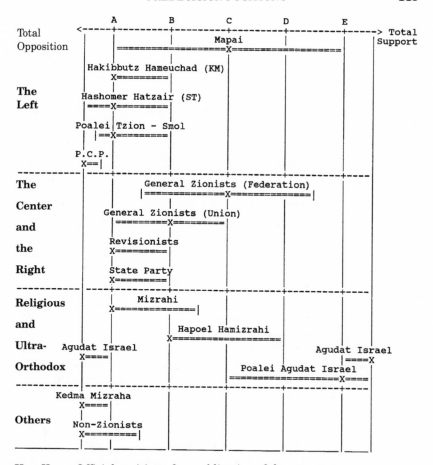

Key: X = Official position after publication of the report.
=== = Divergence of main positions within the party or movement.

Figure 5.1. Party and Movement Positions Toward Partition upon Publication of the Royal Commission Report

the identification of some members with the Arab revolt, as well as internal party discipline, did not permit a broad schism of positions. In sum, the official positions of the parties on the Left after publication of the report ranged between *C* and *A*. However, the positions of their members spread the length of the spectrum due to the differences within Mapai, the dominant party. Unlike Mapai, the positions and arguments were relatively uniform within the small parties.

This general picture is repeated among the parties of the Center and Right. The largest party, the General Zionist Federation, is in category C, midway between the position of Weizmann and his followers, who supported partition (D), and the contrary position of the American Zionists, who—except for several undecided and even fewer supporters—decided to oppose partition (B). The Union's official position was rather unequivocal and belongs to category B, but, again, there were decided members and a few supporters.

The Revisionists did not oppose the establishment of the Jewish state, but the movement's official position, as formulated by Jabotinsky after publication of the report, differed from the more instrumentalist approach he presented before the royal commission (see Chapter Three). It rejected outright the establishment of a small state even in all of western Eretz Israel and should therefore be placed in category A. There were also more moderate Revisionists who belonged to category B. On partition, the position of the State Party was identical to that of the Revisionists.

To summarize, like those on the Left, the positions of fringe groups on the Right were also more uniform and, as could be expected, more ideological in their opposition to partition by comparison with the Center. The unofficial positions within this grouping also stretched from A practically to E because the larger body, the Federation, was divided and included many supporters. The Revisionists' breakaway from the Zionist Organization weakened this camp considerably.

We have alluded to the great disparity between the religious Zionists and the ultra-Orthodox on the question of statehood and partition. Mizrahi officially rejected the proposal, despite a number of conditional supporters among its membership. Hapoel Hamizrahi did not adopt a separate decision, but retained the right to refrain from voting. It is therefore placed in category B of moderate opposition. Its members included not only undecided, but also moderate proponents of partition. Agudat Israel's exceptional position makes it very difficult to locate on the continuum. Although its stance against the deliberate establishment of a Jewish state would place Agudat Israel among the strongest rejectionists, these Orthodox Jews prayed for the kingdom of Israel, a fulfillment of God's promise to redeem his people. The Aguda also opposed the truncation of Eretz Israel for religious reasons. But it did not reject communal autonomy allowing Jews to live according to their religious precepts. Its position was essentially nonpolitical and, because it opposed (secular) Jewish sovereignty over any part of Eretz Israel, nonterritorial as well. Consequently, Agudat Israel is placed at both

Table 5.1. Official Party Positions upon Publication of the Royal Commission Report

	POSITIONS				
Party	Total opposition A	B	C	D	Total support E
Mapai			X		
Hakibbutz Hameuchad (KM)	X				
Hashomer Hatzair (ST)	X				
General Zionists, Federation			X		
General Zionists, Union		X			
State Party	X				
Mizrahi	X				
Hapoel Hamizrahi		X			

extremes of Figure 5.1. For our purpose, Poalei Agudat Israel's support for Jewish autonomy was relatively clear and places it in category *E*. Its members included proponents of the establishment of a religious state in exchange for partition, and others who wavered on the idea of partition itself.

Kedma Mizraha and the non-Zionists in the Jewish Agency held a more distinct nonterritorial position: unequivocal opposition to a separate sovereign-territorial solution to the Jewish problem.

The following chapters will analyze those groups whose positions placed them in categories A to E, principally those who belonged to the Zionist Organization and participated in the decision. Table 5.1 summarizes the official initial positions on the parties that participated in the Zionist Congress.

Had the vote at the Twentieth Zionist Congress been held according to the initial positions presented in Table 5.1, there is no doubt that it would have recorded clear opposition to the partition. This premise is strengthened by the fact that, upon publication of the report, all of the small factions at the congress shared a dual common denominator: they were not fragmented to the same extent as the two large parties and they opposed the partition, for differing reasons. Moreover, neither of the two major parties, Mapai and the General Zionist Federation, officially supported partition. However, they did not adopt binding, clear-cut decisions immediately following the report's publication, and the positional schism

among their membership was the widest. These two parties represented the ideological center of the political system within the
Yishuv's institutions, the Zionist Organization, and the Jewish
Agency. The equivocation of the center would directly influence the
character of the decision adopted at the congress a short time later.

6   The Opponents

> The partition plan . . . holds a shiny tin coin out to us—a 'state'. But its real meaning is: liquidation. It decisively separates Zionism from the question of exile.
> What will the partition of the Land therefore give us? A shaky state without land.
>
> Yehezkel Koifman[1]

The analytical framework presented in Chapter Four and the initial party positions in Chapter Five serve as the basis for Chapters Six, Seven, and Eight, which will detail the main arguments of the central organizations and leaders. We will use Figure 4.2 to classify the answers according to the following: opponents (categories *A* and *B*), undecided (category *C*) and proponents (categories D and E).

Those who answered "no" to the first question in Figure 4.2, on the actual need for a Jewish state, and favored alternate solutions are identified as the *total opposition*. Negative answers to one or both of the next two questions, concerning the appropriate timing for the state's establishment and the partition of Eretz Israel, identify the *opponents* camp. The third question defines the *undecided,* those who were prepared to examine the "pay-off" for territorial concessions. The fourth and fifth questions identify the *proponents* camp, those for whom tactical considerations took precedence, because they were in principle prepared for territorial compromise, and those who evidenced great willingness to make territorial concessions, including adoption of the royal commission's proposal as the basis for a sovereign Jewish state. The category of *total support* branches off from the fifth question because, similar to the "total opposition" at the other extreme, they supported alternate, albeit entirely different, solutions.

In presenting the arguments, we shall focus on what was said during the parties' debates over the royal commission's report and the deliberations of the Twentieth Zionist Congress and Fifth Jewish Agency Council.

Opposing the State

Nettl suggested that the term *state* be defined as a variable to facilitate comparative research and reveal the state's true functions and purposes.[2] This approach suits our needs, given the fact that some participants in the partition polemos rejected the basic premise that the state is a goal worth making concessions to achieve. We therefore open our examination with the "total opposition," those who on principle opposed the establishment of a Jewish state at any time for various, and sometimes contradictory, reasons. This definition seemingly excludes all "Zionists" because the Zionist movement, like other national movements, suggested an irrefutable bond between self-determination and a sovereign state.

The Zionist movement arose at the end of the nineteenth century, but from a political point of view relevant to the 1937 decision, it belongs to the category of nationalities that demanded self-determination following the post-World War I demise of the previous empires. Internally, the "Uganda Crisis" (1903–1905) eliminated other territorial solutions and focused the Zionist efforts on Eretz Israel.[3] Those who were called *territorialists* because they supported Jewish settlement (and autonomy) in Uganda or Argentina, as a solution to Jewish distress in Europe, remained by and large outside the Zionist movement. Externally, the 1917 Balfour Declaration and the 1922 League of Nations' British mandate on Palestine established the fact of international support for Jewish return to Zion. There were, to be sure, alternative avenues to Zionism and, practically speaking, the opponents camp includes diaspora Jews who chose other solutions: assimilation, emigration to America, universal ideologies, or Messianism.[4]

Yet caught between the anti-Zionist and Zionist camps were some exceptions mentioned in Chapter Five: the "non-Zionists," who were nevertheless connected philanthropically to the Zionist endeavor in Eretz Israel; as well as the Zionist and non-Zionist groups that favored a territorial solution, but not on a distinctly national basis. They were prepared to forgo one of the first two vertexes of the nation-state/sovereignty/territory triangle.

Without Political Sovereignty

The Zionist movement cooperated with non-Zionist Jews who wished to help build the land. The 1929 establishment of the expanded Jewish Agency, including non-Zionist Jews particularly from Britain and the United States, was the crowning achievement of these efforts. The non-Zionist presence in the Jewish Agency in 1937 allowed them to add their influence and votes to the opposition.[5]

Morris Karpf, a non-Zionist representative on the Jewish Agency executive, maintained that the proponents were "intoxicated by the idea of a Jewish State," whereas the non-Zionists opposed such a state on principle because it would endanger the Jewish people. For him, Palestine was a refuge and a cultural center for the Jewish people. He felt that the hypernationalism of both sides should be eradicated and the statement of the royal commission that Jews and Arabs cannot live together should be rejected.[6] Karpf explained that the non-Zionists feared the negative effect of a Jewish state on the status of world Jewry. For example, the Jewish state's representative in the League of Nations would supposedly speak in the name of all Jews, raising the problem of dual loyalty and antisemitism. Under such conditions, the non-Zionists, and perhaps most of the Jews in the world, would be forced to repudiate the Jewish state.[7]

This incisive position was expressed more ambivalently by Felix Warburg, a leading non-Zionist from the United States. He opened his address at the Jewish Agency council by declaring that he did not wish to argue the "philosophy of the Zionists or non-Zionists for or against statehood" and preferred to focus on the possible Jewish-Arab understanding in Eretz Israel.[8] He opposed the idea of Jewish sovereignty based on partition and warned against a situation in which "we will worry only about achieving a state, paying no attention to our obligations toward the neighbors." Warburg also threatened that the non-Zionists would leave the agency in such an event.[9]

We already mentioned the intricate position of the British non-Zionists. On the one hand, they feared Zionism would break away from the British mandate, which they saw as their historic achievement. On the other hand, the proposal to establish a Jewish state came from no less than a prestigious royal commission and, at least initially, had been approved by the British government. In the end, opposition prevailed. *The Jewish Chronicle* editorial against partition in April 1937 continued to set the tone for the main argument: the unsuitable timing rather than fundamental opposition to a Jewish state.[10]

The most outstanding Jewish opponent in Britain was Herbert Samuel, the first high commissioner for Palestine. Many conflicting opinions have been expressed about the degree of Samuel's Zionism.[11] Over time, Samuel's political views changed, from being one of the fathers of the Balfour Declaration and a partner to the efforts of the Zionist Organization in the 1919 Paris peace conference to his absolute opposition to the 1937 royal commission proposals. Nevertheless, Wasserstein emphasizes Samuel's consistent commitment to the Zionist idea and his desire to build for himself a home in Israel on Mount Carmel, a plan not realized due to the opposition of Lord Plumer, the high commissioner who succeeded him. Samuel's opposition to a Jewish state in 1937, explains Wasserstein, was not on principle, but stemmed from his perception that a state should be established gradually and not be forced upon the Arab majority.[12] Before publication of the commission report, Samuel tried to persuade Ormsby-Gore not to adopt the partition proposal. Although this was not successful, Samuel did have an influence on others through his famous speech in the House of Lords on July 20, 1937,[13] in which he vehemently attacked the royal commission proposals. Samuel listed almost all the opposition's arguments: lack of economic viability, untenability of transfer, and long, winding, and indefensible borders.[14] The following excerpt from his speech was quoted repeatedly: "It would seem that the Commission referred to the Versailles Treaty, excerpting all of the greatest difficulties and most senseless aspects. They took the Saar region, Polish corridor and half a dozen Danzigs and Memels and put them all into a land the size of Wales."[15]

Lord Samuel alternately proposed that the Jews agree to limit their immigration to a ceiling of a permanent minority of 40 percent in Palestine. As for the future, a "Greater Arab Federation" would be established to include Saudi Arabia, Iraq, Transjordan, Syria, Lebanon, and Palestine.[16]

There were, however, English Jews, especially those close to Weizmann, who supported partition and statehood. Simon Marks told the Jewish Agency council that rather than harm the interests of diaspora Jewry, a Jewish state would actually enhance their prestige.[17] Conversely, Neville Laski wanted Palestine to remain under an amended British mandate as a phase toward its inclusion as a member of the British Commonwealth.[18] Other prominent British Jews, Harold Laski and Norman Bentwitch, also opposed the idea of partition and favored a binational state.

Weizmann and Ben-Gurion mounted a personal attack against Samuel and accused him of betraying Zionism. They also opposed the non-Zionists' demand to refer the decision to the Jewish Agency council only. For them, the commission's proposal was first and foremost a Zionist matter. Still, under pressure from the non-Zionists, the Jewish Agency deliberated the proposal and its decision would differ slightly from that of the Zionist Congress and contain a call for Jewish-Arab understanding and dialogue. Warburg died shortly thereafter, but the "Warburg Group" in the United States carried on in the spirit of his positions.

Joint Sovereignty

Those who favored a binational state are included in the "total opposition" even though their arguments were quite different from those just presented. The binational state implied a recognition of both Arab and Jewish nationalism. They felt that both national movements must share the plot of land called Palestine—not along dividing territorial lines of partition, but rather in sovereignty and government. The binationalists were a very diverse group with many varied perspectives.[19] We will concentrate only on those who supported the establishment of a joint state in Palestine through Jewish-Arab agreement and cooperation and opposed the establishment of a partitioned Jewish state at any time. Among them, Kedma Mizraha was the most prominent group in 1937 and Yehuda Magnes, who was also a delegate to the enlarged agency council, the most prominent individual.[20]

A memorandum from Brit Shalom to the Jewish Agency in 1930 defined their goal: "the constitution of the Palestinian state in which should be formed a free Palestinian commonwealth composed of two peoples each free in the administration of their respective domestic affairs, but united in their common political interests."[21]

They advocated political unity and recognition of the cultural and national differences on the basis of complete equality of rights. Brit Shalom did not believe that separate territorial sovereignty would solve the Jewish problem and emphasized the spiritual role of the Jewish center in Palestine. Magnes's political importance, unlike that of his colleagues, stemmed from his attempt to translate his ideas into practical Zionist terminology. He presented his willingness to forgo a Jewish state (and a Jewish majority) as an alternative to the conventional formulation of choices confronting the Zionist movement, arguing that the Jewish people did not necessarily require a reclusive Jewish state to ensure its very existence. The Jewish goal in Eretz Israel is not to become "a nation like any other nation," but to develop its original character. A binational state ensuring autonomy to both peoples and part of an Arab federation or confederation in the Middle East would accomplish this.

In his address to the agency council, Magnes repeated the proposal to negotiate with all parties involved in Palestinian affairs, including the Arabs, "on the best way which will lead to the establishment of a binational, unpartitioned state in the Land of Israel."[22] His speech focused on the need to prevent war with the Arabs: "I do not want to see the birth of a Jewish state by war." These comments caused the council delegates to clamor:

Ben-Gurion: "Did you immigrate to Eretz Israel with Arab agreement?"

Berlin: "Did the Arabs agree to the opening of the Hebrew University?"

Magnes: "I did not come with their agreement but, first of all, then there was no Jewish state in the world, and secondly I did not even strive, as you know, for this state."[23]

Magnes's speech caused an outcry and calls for his condemnation.[24] Magnes would continue his unsuccessful attempts to bring about Jewish-Arab agreement. He even occasionally cooperated with the "opponents front" in hopes of defeating the partition plan. Magnes repeated his proposal to establish a binational state in a memorandum to the Woodhead commission on July 27, 1938.

Within the Zionist movement, Hashomer Hatzair also favored a binational state, but with important differences. Most members of Brit Shalom were committed to the idea of a Jewish spiritual center in Eretz Israel, to which a Jewish majority was meaningless. By contrast, ST regarded a Jewish majority in Eretz Israel as a precondition for the creation of a binational, socialist society. A majority was necessary both for the social revolution in Jewish life and for ensuring the socialist character of the binational state. Unlike Magnes, ST maintained that the Arab national movement was led by a handful of reactionaries who should not be the partners for an agreement. Its position was actually closer to that of the "strong opposition," which we will discuss in the following section.

The sources of binationalism ranged from liberalism and even pacifism to socialism and antiimperialism. Its advocates also included political pragmatists such as Arthur Ruppin[25] and Pinhas Rutenberg,[26] who maintained that Zionism has no choice but to accommodate itself to the reality dictated by geography and demography. One should bear in mind, however, that binationalism did not reach beyond a concept and, in any event, found few Jewish—and almost no Arab and British—supporters in the 1930s and 1940s. The kibbutz movement was largely united in its opposition to the partition plan whereas ST, like many socialist movements before and after World War I, was torn between the revolutionary vision and the practical needs of Jewish nationalism.[27]

Arab Sovereignty

Some Jews supported the creation of a separate sovereign state in Palestine, but not Jewish or binational—rather an Arab one. The Jewish members of the Palestine Communist party ideologically supported the Arab national movement and the legitimacy of its revolution against British imperialism. The party did not oppose limited Jewish settlement in Palestine, but did not recognize Zionism and its national demands until the establishment of the state of Israel in 1948. It represented the official position of Stalinist Communism, which at that time did not define the Jews as a nation with a right to self-determination, only to cultural autonomy.[28] The P.C.P. regarded the partition plan as a joint British-Zionist plot to create an artificial entity in the service of imperialism.

To summarize, the distinctive feature of the "total opponents," which set them apart from the positions to be presented, was their refusal to address the territorial question, because of their ideological rejection of the whole idea of Jewish statehood. Whether or not they recognized the Jews as a people, they denied their right to self-determination within a separate national territory. Based on ideology, cosmopolitanism, or cultural ethnocentrism, they defined the *Jewish problem* as different from that of other nations struggling for national statehood.

Statehood: The Question of Timing

There was a sharp distinction between those who rejected a sovereign Jewish state completely and those who rejected a state now. Although the latter identified with many arguments of the opponents of statehood, they did believe that the solution was a Jewish state. The formulae were different and contradictory, from divided sovereignty to a redemptive Israeli kingdom, but they all agreed that one day a sovereign territorial state would arise as the correct and perhaps exclusive answer to Jewish distress.

The vast majority of delegates to the Twentieth Zionist Congress stood on this side of the line in their support of a Jewish state, as did most members of the agency council, except for several non-Zionists. Accordingly, the congress resolutions contained a clause stating that "the possible development of the Land of Israel into a Jewish state was from the outset engraved in the purpose of the Balfour Declaration." By contrast, the defeated resolution proposed by the minority in the congress suggested an important change to this clause: "The idea of the development of the Land of Israel into a state *or a Jewish community* was from the outset included in the purpose of the Balfour Declaration and the Mandate" (my emphasis).[29] This resolution does not reject the idea of statehood, but it implies that the development of a Jewish community rather than a state was also a goal of Zionism. It reflected the presence of ST among the supporters of the minority resolution,[30] as well as other delegates who were ambivalent toward the idea of establishing a state, and particularly its timing.

The agency council voted on one resolution only. Magnes's proposal to strive for "the establishment of a binational, undivided state in the Land of Israel" was not brought to a vote. The agency resolution added a new phrase to the congress's resolution regarding a Jewish-Arab peace conference "for an undivided Land of Israel,"[31] but refrained from mentioning the Zionist goal to establish a Jewish state because of the non-Zionist opposition. Weizmann, however, expressed the position of a decisive majority of the Zionists in his speech to the agency council: "For us, the national home is The national home, with a capital *T*; for others, the national home is one of many immigration countries in the world: today Russia, Birobijan, tomorrow Argentina."[32] Directly addressing Warburg, the leader of the non-Zionists, Weizmann said: "What is the essential difference between a national home and a state? The state is only the legal form of the same thing that the English . . . did not want to define precisely. The national home was *from the begin-*

ning [emphasis in original] different from Birobijan. Of course we did not talk about a Jewish state. This state is not our suggestion; this suggestion is the fruit of the pressures of new conditions."[33] It should be emphasized that most of the opponents desperately wanted to establish a Jewish state, but were not willing to make any territorial concessions for it. Ussishkin put it this way: "Weizmann says we should in effect agree to the proposal for a Jewish state. Thus far I agree with him. . . . We did not want to use the explicit name *Jewish state* [emphasis in original]—so long as it is premature. Now that the English have expressed this term we are accepting it with both hands. But the question is: all or part. . . . I say in the name of many sitting here—no!"[34]

Even Jabotinsky, a sworn opponent, began his testimony before the royal commission by defining the term *Jewish state* as a state containing a Jewish majority on both sides of the Jordan River, within the original mandatory boundaries of Palestine.[35] Others, who also spoke against the establishment of a state at the congress, such as Tabenkin and Bernstein, did not reject statehood in principle. This was officially expressed in the resolution unanimously adopted (with two abstentions) by the Zionist General Council in 1938: "both supporters and opponents of the political decision of the Twentieth Congress reject outright any attempt to limit the Jews to a minority status in the Land of Israel as well as any activity of the opponents of Zionism aimed against the principle of a Jewish state in the Land of Israel."[36]

Despite the wide agreement on the need for a Jewish state, the question of timing was still before the Zionist movement:[37] time, in terms of the Zionist movement's internal perspective; time, also in the context of the fate of Eretz Israel and the Jewish community there, as opposed to the situation of world Jewry following the Nuremberg laws in Germany and the pogroms in Poland.

Revolution Precedes the State

As noted, ST's position on statehood was not confined to favoring a binational solution or to the Marxist dialectics about the tension between class revolution and the state. ST maintained that the establishment of a Jewish state would counter attempts to reach Jewish-Arab coexistence because, in due course, worker solidarity would overcome national alienation.[38] Its immediate negative reaction to the royal commission report was in time given a broad ideological base. However, in its opposition to the partition proposal, ST found itself in support of the continuation of the British "imperialist" mandate, a position that their adversaries, particularly Ben-Gurion, repeatedly derided. Members of ST replied that they were not sanctifying the partnership between the Zionists and the British, but that currently a "commonality of interests" exists due to the international obligations of the British through the League of Nations.[39] Conversely, they argued that the partition plan was intended to make the Land of Israel a permanent part of the British empire.[40]

ST's position toward the state was cut from a radical Zionist-socialist ideology, in that order.[41] The role of Zionism was not to attain separate political sovereignty but to settle the land through dedicated labor in cooperation with the progressive forces in the world and the Arab workers in the region "for the sake of the common battle for Socialism."[42] This means a confluence of goals: the Jewish revolution could carry the message of equality to the Arab peoples of the region; it means also a "theory of stages"—territorial concentration of the Jewish people in Eretz Israel, Jewish-Arab agreement, and realization of the revolution to establish a binational socialist society.[43] The socioeconomic revolution thus would precede the political one. Yet, because territory plays an important role in this revolution by stages, ST is included here in the category of the "opposition" rather than among the "total opposition," which rejected any territorial solution.

Indeed, the resolutions of the movement's council, a week after publication of the report, asserted that the sole purpose of the Zionist movement is the concentration of most of the Jewish people in the Land of Israel and its environs.[44] State and boundaries were not mentioned, but rather a creation of a territorial core through settlements as a means to building socialism. In Marxist terms, this implies recognition of the revolutionary potential of Jewish nationalism and its needs to acquire the necessary tools, among them territorial concentration. The local Arabs, on the other hand, were not seen as possessing a progressive national movement, but only institutions representing bourgeois interests. Alliances could therefore be formed only with the Arab working class and never with Arab feudal leaders: "We will not forget the future shore toward which we are rowing—an Arab-Jewish workers' alliance, a binational Socialist society."[45]

Accordingly, territory took priority over sovereignty in ST's ideology. Territory meant a Land of Israel large enough to absorb most of the Jews, yet the final purpose was the creation of a binational socialist society whose political framework would slowly wither away. En route, a binational socialist state, not the bourgeois Jewish state that some Zionists dreamed of, would emerge from an alliance of Arab and Jewish workers in Palestine, and eventually also in Transjordan and Syria.[46] Therefore, ST did not reject the establishment of a state with a Jewish majority. However, this binational state would be just a tool toward the revolution: spacious, based on a unified idea of Jewish-Arab cooperation, and independent of British imperialism. As to its immediate establishment, ST's opposition was intense and absolute.[47]

Three ST delegates participated in the partition debate at the Zionist Congress. Ya'akov Hazan, one of the movement's two leaders, emphasized the very limited area and security problems of the proposed boundaries, the dependence on Britain and, finally, the need for peace with the Arabs as a guarantee for Jewish existence in the Land of Israel. Concerning "political independence," he maintained that "it does not grow and cannot be created in this way." Hazan, always a pragmatist, did not reject the establishment of a Jewish state in principle, but added that "we have not yet reached this great day."[48] By contrast, Y. Riftin called the partition proposal a British maneuver intended to perpetuate their colonial rule by dividing the country into two dwarf states that would live in eternal conflict. His proposed solution left no room for political sovereignty: "We, the members of Hashomer Hatzair, still believe in the possibility of Jewish-Arab understanding within an undivided Land of Israel and are very sorry that many of the progressive Zionists, including Weizmann himself, who once had the courage to declare the Land of Israel a binational country, have weakened their belief in this understanding."[49] M. Ben-Tov expresses the strongest opposition to a Jewish state based on radical Socialism. For him, Zionism would not be realized in a small Jewish state "and not in any greater Jewish state."[50] After the congress vote, ST presented a seven-point declaration. The movement would continue to oppose any partition plan and any injury to the geographic and economic unity of the land or to the progressive character of the Zionist enterprise. The following points are the most significant for our discussion:

Considering the dangerous temptation and the illusion of false statehood and pseudo-independence in a partitioned state, isolated within a dangerous environment which cannot become anything but a toy ball in the hands of British colonial politics ... the path to Jewish-Arab peace is in the faithful recognition of the principle of political equality between Jews and Arabs in the Land of Israel, regardless of their numerical ratio today or in the future, as a basis for a binational regime in the undivided Land of Israel.[51]

ST adopted the concept of binationalism already in the early 1930s and continued to support it when the 1947 partition plan was debated. Its opposition to partition in 1937, and particularly to the immediate establishment of a Jewish state, catalyzed its ideological development in this direction. It also widened the gap within the kibbutz movement and with Hakibbutz Hameuchad, which was also among the opposition, but far from any idea of binationalism.

Statehood Follows

As we have seen, the question of timing encompassed a statement about the current phase of the Zionist revolution. This section will discuss those who, in terms of Figure 4.2, said "yes" in principle to the establishment of a sovereign state based on Jewish nationhood. The differentiating question is this: If the decision rests wholly in Jewish hands, should a sovereign Jewish state be established now? The vast majority of Zionists would have answered such a question positively, albeit with attached conditions, particularly concerning the size of the desired territory. Yet among the state proponents were those who opposed the timing not due to external constraints but based on an ideological position concerning the developmental phase of Jewish nationalism. They opposed the immediate creation of a Jewish state not only because of the miniscule number of Jews in Eretz Israel, but because for them it was premature Zionism.

Not all participants in the debate explicitly expressed their position on the question of timing. One way to extrapolate their position is to examine whether they supported the continuation of the mandate for a limited or longer period and on what grounds. In this group, once again, we will find combinations of movements and leaders who presented totally different reasons for postponing the establishment of a state. We already saw that some ST members based their opposition to statehood on unsuitable timing. Also, some Orthodox non-Zionists opposed the state with similar arguments. We will therefore discuss only the ideological positions toward the establishment of a Jewish state in 1937, detached from the specific "conditions" of territorial size, boundary lines, the extent of sovereignty, or the international situation. Only those who clearly answered "no" to the timing question presented in Figure 4.2 are included among the "opponents of a state now" or "advocates of a state later."

KM, whose initial positions and reactions we have already examined, was central to this category. Their main spokesman, Y. Tabenkin, said at the Mapai council in April 1937:

> The party council (and, in my opinion, also the congress) should make a decision demanding fulfillment of the mandate completely and faithfully ... but *not out of a negation of a Jewish state in the Land of Israel* [emphasis in the original]. I firmly oppose those positions that regard the very establishment of a Hebrew state—whatever its territory and extent—as a positive value unto itself, just because a Hebrew state of any sort grants the Jewish people an international status and official prestige. I see in this idea a distortion and castration of the Zionist idea. For me, the essence of Zionism is not the statehood attribute, but rather the concentration of the Hebrew nation and its settling in the homeland as a nation with equal rights in the family of free nations. ... I totally deny the value of a separate state and I believe that mankind's future is dependent on the establishment of one universal state, that is, the complete elimination of states.[52]

Did Tabenkin oppose the state on principle? His following comments clarified his intention: The state is just a tool, but a "supreme tool," for the realization of Zionism. The possibility of establishing a Jewish state therefore presents an unparalleled opportunity. Yet if its establishment did not require the cancellation of the mandate and partition, he would accept the smallest of states without hesitation. Thus, these were the two overriding arguments: the mandate safeguards Jewish rights to all of Eretz Israel; and gaining a state is not worth territorial sacrifices. Moreover, he would have preferred limited independence, with continuation of the mandate in the remainder of the country, to maintain the chance for Jewish independence in the entire land. The question of timing was central to KM's position because it considered the premature establishment of a state—almost like the Orthodox Jews—to be forcing the issue. It also precisely divided the roles of each generation: our generation, settlement; the next generation, Jewish majority and a state.[53] Statehood was seen as the end of a process, when "the vast majority of the Jewish people will be in the land of

Israel—most of them a working people in workers settlements."[54] Unlike ST's position, this was above all an exclusive Jewish national solution. Hence, KM's vehement opposition to any proposal legitimizing the establishment of an Arab state in Eretz Israel. Shertok attributed "doubts about the very idea of the Jewish state" to Tabenkin,[55] but KM's ideological position envisioned stages: from social development to an independent state. In retrospect (1956), Tabenkin maintained that this negation of the state as a precondition saved Zionism.[56]

The sequence of ideological arguments underlying KM's opposition to partition can be summarized as follow:

- Zionism is above all a social revolution.

- The revolution can be accomplished only through settlement and "redemption" of the land.

- Settlements will determine the scope of the required territory.

- The territory of Eretz Israel should be regarded as a geosocial entity.

- When this entity will be "ready," the state can and should be established.

Notwithstanding the ideological element and the socialist-revolutionary rhetoric, this position was crystallized as a direct reaction to the partition proposal, and its dominant component was national and territorial.[57] Thus KM should be positioned among the "strong opposition"—those who supported a state, but completely opposed partition because it imposes limitation of Zionist aspirations.[58]

This position was not very different from those of other opponents. No one suspected Ussishkin of rejecting a Jewish state, yet he too voiced pragmatic opposition to the timing because of his deep concern that the Zionist executive's policy would lead to the establishment of a truncated state. Similarly, P. Bernstein of the General Zionist Union spoke about the intense danger of premature statehood.[59] As a liberal Zionist, he was not concerned with the need to mold the society first. But, like the socialist opponents, he believed that the Jewish community was not yet ready for political independence. Brodetsky, a member of the Zionist executive who voted for the majority resolution at the congress, also warned, "There can also be false states."[60]

The arguments of these opponents of a "state now," however, rested on different world-views from those of KM because they usually contained an instrumental condition. The Revisionist movement and the State Party were also excluded from this category because they maintained that it was desirable to establish a Jewish state now. Had they believed it was possible to attain sovereignty on the entire Land of Israel, including Transjordan, they certainly would have joined the proponents' camp.[61]

KM was distinguished from other strong opponents by its ideological position regarding the proper timing for Jewish sovereignty. It did not share the belief that time was running out—for the Jews of Eretz Israel and the world—and suggested avoiding the decision being forced by the royal commission: "I therefore favor postponing the decision on the political fate of the land."[62] However, despite KM's secular socialism, it was an expressive position whose conclusion was not totally removed from that of religious Zionism.

Territorial Unity: The Religious and Historic Position

The opponents surveyed thus far were sincere in their desire for a Jewish state coupled with their belief that, even if the decision were left entirely in Jewish hands, this was not the proper time to establish a sovereign state. Their arguments were mainly ideological and social: an independent political framework is the apex of the Zionist enterprise and not the cornerstone for attaining other goals. The strong opponents among the religious Zionists, the Revisionists, and some General Zionists also belong to this category. Their arguments, although totally different, stemmed from religious, historical, or national world-views that attributed independent importance to territory (unity of the land) and transcended the immediate establishment of a state.

Territory and Redemption

Religious Jews share a belief in the unity of Eretz Israel as the Holy Land.[63] But there were important differences in the practical positions they adopted toward sovereignty and partition. We have pointed out that the ultra-Orthodox were divided in their position on partition. They regarded the Land of Israel as an indivisible holy unity, but because they were not particularly interested in the political framework, members of Agudat Israel were more open to political arrangements that were religiously immaterial to their attachment to Eretz Israel. Appearing before the royal commission, Agudat Israel's representative, Rabbi Dushinsky, emphasized the indissoluble covenant between the people of Israel and the Holy Land, explained that the fulfillment of more than half the Torah's commandments depend on being in Eretz Israel, and expounded upon God's promise of the land to the Jewish people. But then he added that "we are commanded not to occupy the country by force and not to strive to dominate others."[64] Thus, Agudat Israel believed in the unity of the land, but their patriotism was spiritual rather than territorial. Accordingly, its great assembly adopted a moderate resolution: not rejecting negotiations with the British government on condition that the Aguda would be included in determining the future of Eretz Israel.

As noted in Chapter Five, Poalei Agudat Israel was even more moderate on the question of a Jewish state. Their leaders did not regard territorial division as an unacceptable calamity because "it is more important to observe the Torah in the Land of Israel than to include this or that settlement."[65] Their only prerequisite was that the Jewish state be based on the Halacha, the Jewish religious law.

By contrast, Mizrahi and Hapoel Hamizrahi were Zionists, and their positions displayed a unique mixture of religious and political arguments. They opposed partition in principle, but not the Zionist goal of establishing a sovereign Jewish state. They too maintained that the timing was wrong, but for completely different reasons: The completion of the redemption process is in Divine hands. Meanwhile, one must exert every effort because the entire Land of Israel is a precondition for redemption. No leadership is authorized to forfeit the Promised Land. The religious and historic arguments of the religious Zionists were intertwined: Only the entire land of our fathers will bring the entire redemption. In the spirit of the slogan that today still serves them in the territorial debate: "the Land of Israel to the people of Israel in accordance with the Torah of Israel." The order of preference of these three components indicates very clearly the different positions within the religious camp. The ultra-orthodox do not hesitate to place the land last because, despite the essential centrality of Eretz Israel in religious observance, the Torah and the People of Israel come first. For them, the existence and continuity of these two elements outside Eretz Israel must be recognized. Religious Zionism, on the other hand, rejects the idea of ranking these three components, even though some of them attach supreme importance to the holy territory of the entire Land of Israel.

The religious Zionists' spokesman at the Congress, Rabbi Berlin, rejected Weizmann's request to examine partition in light of Jewish spiritual and physical distress. For him, the ultimate test was: "We have no right to surrender the Land of Israel, either a large or small part of it. And we must be ready to accept anguish, struggles and wars for a greater Land of Israel."[66]

Although Rabbi Berlin was employing religious arguments to underlie a pragmatic position, other rabbis submitted religious rulings against partition, some even ruling that surrender of any part of the Holy Land is heresy. By contrast, there were religious leaders who explicitly said that nothing in religious law or the *Code of Jewish Laws* (Shulchan Aruch) obligates opposition to the partition of Eretz Israel.[67] Religious Zionist opposition to partition often resembled that of the secular Zionists, and it was also of the strongest kind because it employed practically all of the opponents' arguments: the territorial unity of Eretz Israel as the religious, historical, and national basis for redemption.[68] It was very difficult for the religious Jews to reconcile the religious commandments concerning Eretz Israel with political pragmatism. Even the religious moderates felt obliged to say that "from a purely religious point of view there is no room for two opinions. Any willing concession constitutes a deliberate desecration of the sanctity of the Land and of the glorious Covenant of the Pieces which was sealed between the Master of the Universe and our forefather Abraham."[69]

In the end, the answer of most religious Zionists to the question of whether they supported the immediate establishment of a Jewish state entailing partition was a firm "no."

The significance of this reaches far beyond the religious camp's position toward the royal commission's proposal. Zionism was essentially a secular national movement. Yet the question of the link between Jewish nationalism and the Jewish religion, tortuous from the outset, remained largely unsolved. Zionism drew content and symbols from religious sources that served as a common denominator for Jews from different countries and with opposing worldviews.[70] Kimmerling adds two important points: The Jewish religion has a monopoly on the definition of the social boundaries of the Jewish collective, and as the struggle between Jews and Arabs increased, so did the importance of the exclusive Jewish religious identity.[71] Thus the absence of religious legitimization for partition influenced the secular positions as well, particularly through the fostering of a strong analogy between Jewish nationalism and the *entire* Land of Israel. It also created a natural alliance within the opponents camp based on a national-religious ideology.

The National Viewpoint

The Zionist-religious rejection stemmed from the insoluble link of religion, nationalism, and territory. Another important group of strong opponents totally rejected partition on secular grounds. Their credo was less organized and their arguments more intricate, but they responded with a resounding nationalistic "no" to the idea of partition and did not consider hinging their opposition on specific conditions. For this reason, some of the Revisionists and General Zionists, most of the opposition within Mapai as well as the moderate non-Zionists, whose arguments were essentially instrumental, are not included in this category of the strong opponents.

The General Zionist Union, headed by Ussishkin and joined by some overseas members of the General Zionist Federation, formed the central group within this category. The essence of Ussishkin's intense opposition was based neither on the practical arguments he expounded nor on a liberal-Zionist world-view. As a veteran Zionist leader, he was torn between his desire for a sovereign state and his loyalty to the greater Land of Israel. We have seen how Ussishkin confronted Weizmann after his testimony before the royal commission and how he consistently opposed the Zionist executive's support for negotiations with Britain. Ussishkin also headed the coalition of opponents to partition, but refused to fight the issue to the end, because he feared dividing the movement. At the congress, Ussishkin pitted himself against Weizmann and presented a historical deterministic view regarding the bond between territory and the national state. For Ussishkin, already in 1929, Eretz Israel was above all a locus of self-identity intertwined with a romantic motif:

> The first period [was] that of the poetic love of nature, but this was insufficient. The second period arrived, the period in which the new Jew stood up and said: Yes, land is important, but the land must be that of the homeland, and the homeland is not the rich and fertile expanse of Russia or the Ukraine, but indeed a small, poor and meager land, the Land of Israel. Here came the second moment, the movement to redeem the homeland, the movement to commune with the nature of the homeland.[72]

At the congress, Ussishkin refused to put the issue to a fundamental test: a yes or no answer on whether he supported a Jewish state in a limited territory. Instead, his appeal to the congress delegates was emotional:[73] "Two proposals were placed before us:

One would strangle us, the other cut our country into pieces. And we must discuss which is easier." His answer: "The Jewish people strives to return to its land, to *all* [emphasis in original] of its land, in all of its parts. It will not surrender even the smallest part of the land that belongs to it, both historically and in accordance with the mandate. Our mission is to say this openly and honestly for both moral as well as tactical reasons."

Ussishkin did not hesitate to raise religious arguments, including the "Messianic promise." He even argued with Mizrahi, which thirty years earlier had supported the Uganda Plan for pragmatic reasons. He rejected the realistic approach, interested only in the "needs of the hour," because there is a limit to realism and calculations—a living people may not openly and happily forego its inheritance in front of the entire world. Ussishkin's position rested mainly on his belief that the land is the foundation for building Jewish nationalism in Eretz Israel. In this he resembled KM, not for socialist reasons of settlement and labor, but rather because he viewed himself as the redeemer of the land of Eretz Israel. The word *land* was repeated many times in his speech, as in the dramatic appeal to the president of the Zionist Organization: "My friend Weizmann, this is not the way! Leave the prophecy of the 'End of Days' to Isaiah. The 'End of Days' is in the world of the prophets, and we want the land."

In his closing address before the decisive vote at the congress, Ussishkin sharpened his position to weigh the establishment of a Jewish state against partition: "They give us a Jewish state, but I don't think we are capable of accepting it. . . . I don't think we can build a state without land under our feet."

The concepts of Ussishkin and others closely resembled the religious position, even though they preferred to discuss the "promised land" in historical terms. Their determinist, as well as romantic, view of the role of land in the process of nation-building was very reminiscent of the approach relating "the spirit of the nation" to the homeland: "with logic alone, without mystical emotions, no national movement can be built."

To summarize the position of the strong opponents, we shall now briefly present the counterarguments of those who favored a "state now." For the strong opponents, these arguments inverted the natural order of events by regarding the political framework as a primary means to attain other Zionist goals. First and foremost among them was Ben-Gurion. His anxiety in February 1937 of a change in British policy and the possibility of a world war had grown even stronger by April 1937.[74] Ben-Gurion was bold enough to state that, under certain conditions, the Zionist movement would deteriorate and shrivel into a small, insignificant group of admirers. This fear spurred him already to propose a partition plan in early 1937 in the belief that a sovereign Jewish territorial entity, in even a part of Eretz Israel, would prevent a dangerous halt in immigration. At the congress, Ben-Gurion presented himself as "an absolute proponent of statehood, not at some future point or in all of the Land, but a state now. Even in a single part of the land."[75] He repeatedly claimed—with a consistency that would last a decade—that practical action was needed now because there is no such thing as deterministic organic development, only political opportunity.

Weizmann also felt the pressure of the decisive hour. More than Ben-Gurion, he emphasized the need to save millions of Jews threatened in Europe, which could be accomplished only through the framework of a sovereign Jewish State.[76] All of his activities since testifying before the Peel commision had been directed at strengthening British government and international support for the idea of a state under the best partition plan possible. His sense of urgency increased even further after the congress in Zurich, and all of his communications in 1938 evidence his desperate commitment to the need to achieve any form of Jewish sovereignty from the British before everything collapsed.[77]

The debate also stemmed from different time perceptions: the proponents' emphasis on future developments vs. the opponents' preoccupation with the lessons of the past.[78] Remez, a proponent, said at the Congress: "The Land of Israel cannot wait."[79]

The strong opponents maintained that the Land of Israel must wait, because religious, historical, and national reasons compelled them to tie the unity of the territory to the attainment of sovereignty. Sovereignty on only a part of Eretz Israel would not even be thinkable, because a state on a truncated Land of Israel is not really a state. There was a certain ambivalence in this position because, unlike that of KM and ST, it was concerned not with the creation of practical conditions for the establishment of a political framework, but rather presented a religious and historic determinism almost independent of Jewish action. This was their reasoning: If a Jewish state could be established immediately in all of Eretz Israel, it should be supported because this would indicate that the "conditions" (the redemption or historic development) did in fact exist. Because this is not the case, the opportunistic position of a "state now" should be firmly opposed.

Sovereignty, Yes; Partition, No

The strong opponents presented in the previous section display one main difference from the more moderate opponents to be discussed here. The former would not have supported the immediate establishment of a Jewish state, even if they completely controlled the decision. They opposed the idea of a premature state because they wanted it to be preceded by a social revolution, by the possession of more land through settlement, or by territorial unity from a religious, historical, and national point of view. The moderate opponents also rejected partition, but not on the basis of an overall belief system and without the same determinist, historic, and geographic premises. They were prepared to establish a Jewish state immediately, but on the uncompromising condition that it would include the entire Land of Israel. In their opinion, there could be no substitute for the complete territory, which is a prerequisite for providing a refuge, economic viability, and security. The state, they claimed, is not just a spiritual, national, or religious center, but a territory that should allow a majority of the Jews to immigrate to it, live and protect themselves within it, and sustain themselves from it. The 5,000 km^2 proposed by the royal commission (perhaps even the 28,000 km^2 of western Eretz Israel) would in no way meet these goals.

A Refuge for the Jews

As noted, the Revisionist movement linked its support for territorial unity in the entire Land of Israel to historic and religious arguments. It firmly and consistently opposed those leaders of the Zionist movement who supported partition in exchange for sovereignty, and from this point of view, the Revisionists were among the strong opposition. Nevertheless, because our discussion is limited to the positions presented during the 1937 partition polemos, and particularly those of its leader, Zeev Jabotinsky, we will show that it entailed a more moderate negation based primarily on instrumental arguments.

In his royal Commission testimony, Jabotinsky defined *Palestina* as the area on both sides of the Jordan River, as implied by the Balfour Declaration and as determined in the original mandatory charter.[80] His main argument, as explained in Chapter Three, was that a large enough area was needed to absorb many millions of Jews. He limited himself to technical calculations of absorption capacity and avoided mentioning Jewish "historic rights" to the land. Jabotinsky himself outlined the difference between his approach and that of other Zionists on the importance of territory: "The New Zionist Organization is distinguished from the other Zionist viewpoints in its integrality: Its purpose is—to eradicate *all* Jewish distress. The basis for this is the *entire* Land of Israel" [emphasis in the original].[81]

Jabotinsky's premise was his aim to achieve a Jewish majority in the Land of Israel. A land in which the Jews would be a minority, even with sovereignty, "would be nothing but a new version of the exile."[82] The "Ten-Year Plan" he presented at the founding conference of the New Zionist Organization in 1935 called for the immigration of 1.5 million Jews within a decade to establish a Jewish majority in the entire Land of Israel.[83] This was the first and most decisive phase of Zionist realization, after which 9 to 10 million Jews would concentrate in Eretz Israel. When the commission's report was published, Jabotinsky called it "an amazing example of a document which goes on for 400 pages and is nothing more than a feuilleton."[84]

He proposed his Ten-Year Plan in its stead, adding many details on the country's absorption capacity and population density.[85] According to Jabotinsky's calculations, the population density in the noncrowded European countries—France, Poland, Switzerland, Czechoslovakia, Italy, and Germany—ranged between 76 and 140 people per km^2. In Holland, England, and Belgium, the density was 240 to 270 people per km^2. Already in 1937, there would be 140 people per km^2 in the area of the Jewish state proposed by the commission. Because the Land of Israel is less developed than the European countries, little space would be left in this area for the new population. Therefore, only the territory on both sides of the Jordan River, encompassing an area of approximately 100,000 km^2, could sustain a population density similar to that of a medium-sized European country (Poland or Czechoslovakia): approximately 90–100 people per km^2.[86] The total population in this area could reach up to 10 million—out of them 6 to 8 million Jews—"without driving out any Arab or his descendant."[87]

Jabotinsky reserved very harsh words for the commission's proposal of population transfer: The idea is "irresponsible" and also "criminal" from a Jewish point of view.[88] His virulent opposition stemmed from the fear that this "precedent" would lead to Jewish expulsion from Europe. Moreover, he saw no practical or moral benefit in the commission's proposal to move Arabs from one part of Eretz Israel to another.[89] Jabotinsky was also very apprehensive about the establishment of an Arab state in Transjordan and Eretz

Israel, whose basic purpose would be to swallow the "Jewish cor-
ner" of the partitioned state. Heller believes that Jabotinsky later
took back his absolute opposition and in 1939–1940 even expressed
"surprising support" for "voluntary transfer."[90] We will return to
this in the next chapter.

These pragmatic arguments, which Jabotinsky emphasized in
the 1937 polemos, show him to be a relatively moderate opponent
of partition. Theoretically, Jabotinsky might even have conceded
Transjordan had he been convinced that 10 million Jews could be
fully absorbed in western Eretz Israel alone. The same logic could
be applied to the partition of western Eretz Israel: if the main
purpose were purely instrumental, namely absorption, even part of
this area could be compromised on the condition that it be Eretz
Israel and not some territory in Uganda or Birobijan.

It is left for us to clarify the function of territory generally and
the Land of Israel particularly in Jabotinsky's definition of Jewish
nationalism. The answer regarding Eretz Israel is forthright:

"To the Jews, the idea of settlement for the purpose of creating a state is related to the Land of Israel. For the Land of
Israel they find people, huge sums of money, tremendous energy and unprecedented insistence which is not intimidated
by any blow. There were no takers, even for completing the
negotiations, on Uganda or Angola, which were much more
attractive than Birobijan."[91]

But on the question of the link between territory and nationalism, Jabotinsky emphasized two different points. First, nationalism is above all national consciousness. "Nation is will" the young
Jabotinsky wrote under Mazzini's influence, and he dismissed the
value of objective factors such as territory, language, religion, common origin, and historic tradition.[92] Second, much later Jabotinsky
maintained that territory plays a decisive role in molding the character of a people. The land, climate, and landscape create basic
traits and shape the nation's personality.[93] Thus Eretz Israel molded
the character of the Jewish "race," and Zionism is an expression of
the continuing national singularity of the Jews—"a pure fruit of
the Land of Israel."[94] A trace of Jabotinsky's romantic core is also
found in his writings about "the ideal Jewish race" or when he later
added religious and historic arguments to his position against
partition.[95]

Everything considered, Jabotinsky's stance toward sovereignty
and territory was pragmatic: He attempted to prove "scientifically"

that only an expansive land would solve the Jewish problem. He raised almost no symbolic or religious arguments in the 1937 partition debate and even wrote about himself: "I did not have a romantic love for the Land of Israel. I am not sure that I do even now."[96] How did his concept of territory differ from the other opponents reviewed previously? Jabotinsky's preoccupation with the absorption capacity of Eretz Israel and the desired ratio of population to area recalls the writings of the German geopoliticists in the 1930s who pointed to the overcrowding of the German population as the justification for expanding its living space. But Jabotinsky did not think in terms of settlement frontiers. He required the entire Land of Israel as a secure shelter for the majority of diaspora Jews. To him, partition meant dividing the people between those few who would find a place in Eretz Israel and the majority who would be condemned to remain in exile. In presenting the Land of Israel as a "geographic whole," however, Jabotinsky came very close to Tabenkin's concept of "unity of the land." But Jabotinsky maintained that the "complete" territory would ensure Zionist fulfillment, whereas KM saw settlements as the workbench for achieving the "complete" geographic and social entity.

In sum, Jabotinsky's Revisionist movement opposed partition, regardless of the proposed territorial size, boundaries, control of immigration, or Arab consent. They considered territorial "wholeness" a condition for protecting the "wholeness of the people." Nevertheless, it can be posited that their opposition was not total: They did not negate the idea of a state, and they used the pragmatic argument that Britain had no intention of implementing the partition proposal. We already noted that Jabotinsky initially hesitated over how to react. Hence the assumption of his "weakness" toward the royal commission's proposal.[97] Ben-Gurion wrote in his diary: "If I am not mistaken, Jabotinsky avoided clearly stating that he was against. He just declares again and again that the partition plan would not be implemented. . . . But it seems to me that if the plan would be realistic, the Revisionists would turn to support it."[98] A sovereign state enchanted Jabotinsky and his associates, but not to the point of agreeing to partition Eretz Israel.

Economic Viability

There was a direct connection between opposition to partition based on the need to prepare a refuge for all of the Jews and its rejection on economic grounds. The difference is that the "economic opponents" held largely liberal capitalist views and presented them without the strong national overtones of Ussishkin and Jabotinsky. We have already discussed the non-Zionist opposition to the very idea of a Jewish state. But there were also many overseas Zionists whose opposition to partition and to the timing of the state's establishment were intertwined. The most outstanding among them were the American Zionist leaders Brandeis, Silver, and Wise. In June 1937, the conference of American Zionist leaders voted against partition, mainly on the grounds that current conditions would allow the establishment of only a tiny, economically dependent state. Silver's speech at the congress concentrated on his demand to fulfill the mandate: "If we once forfeit four-fifths of the Land of Israel, it will be impossible to get it back."[99] Wise was more decisive and resolute in his opposition to the partition and responded emotionally to Ben-Gurion's accusation that whoever opposed a state now is a non-Zionist: "A man can oppose the report of the royal commission, reject the partition proposal stemming from it and not be accused of opposing the foundation of a Jewish state. It is possible to oppose now a Jewish state also as a Zionist without being influenced ... by assimilationist and anti-Zionist arguments."[100]

Wise rejected the claim that the Zionist movement had reached its moment of truth and must immediately decide only on the conditions accompanying the establishment of a state now. In his opinion, the benefit from establishing a truncated state would prove only temporary. It was therefore preferable to continue to strive for a future state in the entire Land of Israel. A member of the Jewish Agency executive said directly that he opposed partition "not out of fear of the Jewish state, but rather on purely economic grounds."[101] Many proponents suspected that the diaspora Zionists' rejection of partition was only a camouflage for their fundamental opposition to a Jewish state. Only a few were willing to admit that the disagreement revolved on opposing evaluations of the historic opportunity in the royal commission's partition proposal.[102] Opponents of partition within Mapai happened to share Brandeis's hope that a change in the world situation would improve the prospects of establishing a larger Jewish state and therefore "the essence of our political contribution today is to forestall a radical solution."[103]

The General Zionist Union opponents broadly expounded on the economic nonviability of a small country. Whereas Ussishkin presented his opposition with thunderbolts and lightning, his colleagues quietly explained the importance of territory in more detail. Some emphasized the need for an area large enough for development, but did not contend that only the *entire* Land of Israel could meet this requirement.[104] Bernstein, who would come to lead the General Zionists in the state of Israel, presented it this way: "Any fulfillment before its time, and certainly the realization of the Jewish state in limited areas, presents a great danger."[105]

For him, this danger was primarily economic. A partitioned state could not solve the Jewish problem in the diaspora, because Jews would not want to come to a land devoid of an economic basis. As a result, the Yishuv would be sentenced to remain a permanent minority in Eretz Israel. Other opponents added detailed calculations of agriculture, water resources, industry, minerals, and transportation to this general argument of the country's economic capacity. For example, Bart of Mizrahi, who would eventually be one of Israel's top bankers, believed that an agricultural infrastructure capable of supporting a people living on its land could not be created in the proposed territory. He also refuted Ben-Gurion's vision that the Jews would make their living from the sea, because fishing and shipping could support only a few.[106]

The common denominator of this position, shared by some undecided and even supporters of partition, was that a sizable territory was prerequisite for ensuring the economic (as well as social, military, and political) strength of the state. The difference between them and the undecided, who will be discussed in Chapter Seven, was that this group largely believed that the entire Land of Israel (west of the Jordan River) was the required minimum for such economic viability. The undecided were satisfied with the demand for "a large enough area" and therefore did not reject the possibility of partition.

Security

Almost all participants in the 1937 polemos shared the fear that the proposed boundaries would be highly dangerous to the Yishuv's security. They believed that citizens of every state need to feel instinctively that it has "natural boundaries," that its boundaries are as short as possible, and that it is "compact" as to shape and area; hence, the demand that the Jordan River constitute the eastern border and that the Negev be included in the Jewish state.

Nevertheless, it is surprising how little attention was paid in 1937 to the question of the proposed state's security, a subject that would become so central to the future Arab-Israeli conflict. The "disturbances" in 1929 and in 1936 raised the security issue to the top of the agenda, but efforts were directed toward securing the settlements and transport lines. As we shall see, the commission's proposal to establish a state created a territorial reality with potential borders, and this fact had a great impact on the settlement policies and the perception of security from late 1937. It was also assumed that security affairs would remain in the hands of the British Army, which would stay in the area to supervise implementation of the partition and to ensure the defense of the fledgling states. Shertok, for example, included neither security arguments nor the need to shorten borderlines on his detailed list of areas not included in the royal commission's proposal, which he felt the Jews should fight to hold onto.[107]

We will return to the security issue in the next chapter, focusing here only on the position that held that partition should be completely opposed on security grounds. The differences between Eliahu Golomb, who was a moderate proponent, and Shaul Meirov, a security-oriented opponent, cover the matter. Both of them were Mapai leaders who, as the heads of the Haganah,[108] were highly involved in the Yishuv's security problems.

Golomb's approach was political, not military. Already in April 1937, he asserted that the mere establishment of a Jewish state would be such an important contribution to creating a "strong and significant security power" that the disadvantages should be overlooked.[109] At the stormy July meeting of the Mapai council, Golomb said even more decisively that independence is "the most tangible weapon that we can have in our hands in the coming period."[110] He did not support acceptance of the royal commission's specific proposal because he felt the partition boundaries would not allow the state to stand and survive on its own. He maintained, however, that territorial partition in itself would not determine the fate of the state's security, but rather the political circumstances and the plan's chance of acceptance by the Arab states.

By contrast, Meirov placed his belief in the security value of territory and the creation of facts in the field. He felt that "small facts determined the map of the Land of Israel," and the northern settlements determined the northern border.[111] In this approach he was closer to the leaders of KM who maintained that "winding and long boundaries cannot be defended."[112] When Meirov added his anxiety that Britain would prevent the Jewish state from defending itself, the following dialogue ensued:

Meirov: "Where will we obtain weapons?"

Ben-Gurion: "The War Office will give us weapons."

Meirov: "Why would England give us weapons? . . . I don't believe they will arm us in a serious manner."[113]

Meirov supported natural boundaries as the best defense of the Jewish state, because Eretz Israel is one geopolitical unit and any harm of its unity entails a security risk. As for partition, any radical solution should be rejected, waiting instead for political conditions favoring the establishment of the state without cutting the land into pieces.

Summary of the Opponents' Positions

This chapter detailed the distinction between the three types of opponents categorized in Chapter Four. The first, the total opposition, rejected the establishment of a separate, sovereign Jewish state—in the land of Israel or anywhere else and at any time. This group included those who favored Arab sovereignty with an enfranchised Jewish minority in Palestine, as well as those who supported joint Jewish-Arab sovereignty. The second, the strong opposition, opposed the state's establishment not only because of the partition proposal, but due mainly to its premature timing. And the third, the relatively moderate opposition, focused on the territorial issues: "It is forbidden to divide the Land of Israel" because of security, economic, and refugee reasons. Table 6.1 summarizes the arguments of the latter two groups.

The strong opposition shared an expressive loyalty to the unity of Eretz Israel (with different definitions) stemming from their belief system, ideology or religious faith. By contrast, the other opponents based their instrumental positions on practical arguments: why the territory was necessary.

Zionism, as we have said, was a pragmatic movement. In retrospect, it is clear that the process of building a state was carried out brick by brick, practical decisions taken in the wake of external events. Written texts from this period do not fully reveal the internal codes because they were self-evident. For example, for both proponents and opponents, the ideal was a large Jewish state with a large Jewish majority. But political decisions are often based on compromises with reality and the hope of fully realizing this

Table 6.1   Main Arguments of the Opponents (who did not oppose establishment of the Jewish state)

	ARGUMENT	MAIN MOVEMENTS
Strong Opposition	Social	Hashomer Hatzair, Hakibbutz Hameuchad
	Religious	Mizrahi (Agudat Israel)
	Historic and national	General Zionist Union, Revisionist movement, (Hakibbutz Hameuchad)
Opposition	Refuge	Revisionist movement
	Economic	American Zionists, part of the General Zionist Federation
	Security	Part of Mapai, Hakibbutz Hameuchad

ideal was minuscule. The 1937 debate brings these layers to light, as well as contradictions in the internal codes of the Zionist movement. These feelings are dramatically reflected in the positions of the undecided.

7   The Undecided

The tragedy is rooted in the inverse relationship between the enormity of the Jewish problem and the size of the Land of Israel. The greater the problem, the more the territory shrinks.[1]

Hesitation concerning the advantages and disadvantages of the royal commission's proposal was also expressed by those who did not reject the concept of partition. Ben-Gurion defined this dilemma as early as April 1937: "There is partition and there is partition. And there is only a hair's breath between partition that constitutes rescue and partition that constitutes destruction.[2] Nor did Weizmann conceal his doubts from the congress delegates. He rejected the commission's specific recommendation, but still advised acceptance of the proposal to establish a Jewish state in a limited territory of Eretz Israel because it contains a new idea and a bright perspective.[3] This premise was not shared by the extremists, and indeed, the intense debate over the pay-offs of "territory vs. sovereignty" took place mainly between the moderate opponents and moderate proponents and between these two groups and the undecided. Those who did not oppose partition in principle, but were very apprehensive of the specific proposal of the royal commission, presented four main conditions that would determine their support or opposition (see Chapter Four): the size of the territory of the Jewish state, the boundary lines and their security ramifications, the existence of a Jewish majority or the number of Arabs to be included in the Jewish state, and the extent of consent to the plan by the Arabs within and outside Palestine.

A fifth condition can be added: the extent of independence or sovereignty to be granted to the new Jewish state by the British. As already noted, many Zionists deeply suspected that the British had no intention of actually awarding sovereignty to the Jews, but wished only to attain Jewish consent to truncate the territory of the national home. The more moderate skeptics expressed their fear that sovereignty would be severely limited by the continued British presence in Eretz Israel and their global interests in the Middle East. There would be almost no advantage in forgoing territory to attain sovereignty, they maintained, if, for example, the Jewish state would not be given full control of immigration. Weizmann himself voiced this suspicion in an internal discussion: "Concerning the entire matter of the partition, we can commit ourselves to nothing without knowing what we are receiving. The questions are twofold: the boundaries and the essence of Zionism. . . . Of course, we will agree only to independence and not to a farce."[4]

However, this issue is not included in the preceding list of conditions simply because it is integral to the definition of a "sovereign state." The mere semblance of sovereignty, particularly on subjects critical to Zionism, would immediately have turned all the undecided and the proponents into absolute opponents.

The four conditions were not outlined so sharply in the debate. They were interwoven with various arguments of values, history, and religion and with tactical considerations. The question of how far the British government could be trusted and how changes in the international situation would affect the realization of its policy continuously floated in the background. It is also impossible to assess the relative intensity of each of the conditions or to grade the undecided according to the number of conditions they presented and with what salience. What distinguished this group from the opponents in the previous chapter was that their position could well be altered by the practical answers to one or more of these conditions. The undecided were a varied group that crossed party lines more than in the other groupings. We will present only a few central spokespersons on each of the four conditions.

Extent of Territory

What territorial size would be "enough" to ensure the viability of a sovereign state? Even if we assume that this refers only to economic viability, we must examine a long list of indicators, such as the structure of the economy, availability of raw materials and water sources, the extent of industrialization, transportation, and shipping lines, trade with neighboring countries, and the desired standard of living. However, for the Zionist movement, the most important factor at that time was population size and the predictions (and hopes) for its future growth through immigration, settlement, and development.

In the map it submitted to the Versailles Peace Conference of 1919, the Zionist movement claimed a total area of 45,000 km^2, an area similar in size to Northern Ireland or Latvia before World War II. This included approximately 20,000 km^2 in Transjordan and in southern Lebanon to be later placed under French mandate. The total territory awarded to the British mandate by the League of Nations on both sides of the Jordan River encompassed approximately 120,000 km^2. In European terms, this was slightly larger than Czechoslovakia or Greece. The separate status of Transjordan was determined in 1922, after which the main territorial conflict focused on western Eretz Israel. The Zionist movement continued to demand that the British allow Jewish settlement in Transjordan, but did not define explicit boundaries or territorial demands. The Revisionist movement, dissatisfied with the limited Zionist demands for Transjordan in 1919, requested that the entire mandate area east of the Jordan River be included within the Jewish national home. According to Jabotinsky's calculations, "the Land of Israel on both sides of the river" covers over 116,000 km^2.[5]

Those who were satisfied with western Eretz Israel, but opposed its partition, often compared it to Belgium, both in its size of 30,000 km^2 and its high population density. They maintained that there is an essential territorial minimum without which a state cannot survive. In Eretz Israel this minimum had to include the entire area west of the Jordan River because the arable land within this area, in effect, amounts to a very limited 7,000–8,500 km^2.[6]

The question of the territory necessary for a Jewish state related to the continuous argument between the Zionist movement and the mandatory authorities concerning the economic "absorptive capacity" of Palestine. Because estimates of the absorption capacity determined immigration quotas (the "schedule"), the Jewish Agency almost always used higher estimates than the British. The royal commission's report mentioned no less than a dozen investigations of the land issue since 1920 and doubted whether anyone could prescribe a "minimum subsistence area" for a farming family.[7] As to the controversial question of how much of Palestine was suited to agricultural cultivation, the commission submitted an estimate 20 percent lower than that of the Jewish Agency—and argued that there was no economic justification in upgrading additional land for agricultural cultivation. However, the commission recommended that a "political ceiling" of a Jewish immigration of 12,000 per annum for the next five years be used as a criterion, instead of economic absorption capacity, if the partition proposal was rejected.[8]

In any event, the commission recommended an area of about 5,000 km^2 for the Jewish state.[9] Would this be "enough" for the state to stand on its own and to absorb millions of Jews?

The Zionist movement struggled with this issue from the outset, and its patterns of purchasing land for settlement indicate two approaches. First, assuming that the entire mandate area was intended for the establishment of a national home, settlement should be spread throughout the country, with particular emphasis on the frontier and areas with sparse Jewish presence. This approach was favored by leaders in charge of settlement, such as Ussishkin and Weitz, who would subsequently oppose the partition plan. The second approach aimed at establishing nuclei of Jewish majority in order to create a solid territorial base for future dispersion and expansion. Other leaders in charge of settlement, such as Ruppin and Wilkansky, favored this approach and became supporters of partition. Obviously, Jewish policy of land purchase during the mandate years (1921–1936) created a settlement map that influenced the commission's partition proposal. The proposal was based on the principle of territorial separation between Jews and Arabs and therefore delineated boundaries that generally matched the land and settlement concentrations in 1937. Yet, the match was only partial. The commission proposed that the Arab-populated Galilee be included in the Jewish state (for future Jewish settlement and for forging territorial continuity with Christian Lebanon); and that the very sparsely populated Negev be included in the Arab state, despite the Zionist movement's demands to leave it as the land reserve for future Jewish immigration.

The considerations that guided Jewish land and settlement policy until 1936 were primarily economic, social, and inward oriented.[10] The goal, in the terminology of the time, was "redeeming the territory, conquering the soil and settling it," by purchasing as much land as possible, subject to availability and financial constraints.[11] The Arab revolt, the royal commission proposal, and the opportunity to establish a Jewish state caused a reversal—political and strategic considerations began to play a primary role in the acquisition of land.[12] The new goal was to expand the land holdings especially along the proposed boundaries and in the areas that the Zionist movement hoped would be added to the Jewish state, even though they were excluded by the commission. These efforts defined a certain map that, as we will see later, would be presented in the Zionist testimony before the Woodhead commission. However, these concrete efforts, carried out in response to external pressures, did not answer the general question of what is "enough" territory for the future state.

The Twentieth Zionist Congress rejected the commission's specific proposal to narrow the territory of the Jewish state to 5,000 km². The commission's alternate proposals were also rejected: to determine a "political ceiling" for Jewish immigration, to close parts of Palestine to Jewish settlement, and to tighten land acquisition policy.[13] We will now consider the positions of those who demanded "enough" territory, excluding those who opposed partition because they wanted all of western Eretz Israel or the entire mandatory Palestine. We will only note that many opponents were equally concerned with the future state's viability.[14]

Those favoring partition were generally hesitant to state explicitly what is "enough" territory, stressing instead what was lacking in the commission's proposal. Ben-Gurion was an exception. As early as February 1937, he told his Mapai colleagues that he would be satisfied if the Jewish state would be provided with the minimal area needed for short-term expansion. Under his proposal, the Jews would be given approximately 4,300 km² of territory and the Arabs some 6,500 km² in the first phase. In the future, the territory of the Jewish state would cover 10,000 km² (with another 2,000 in "reserve"), and that of the Arab state 12,500 km².[15] After first reading the commissions report, Ben-Gurion wrote to his son that two aspects of their plan were better than his: the entire Galilee was given to the Jews; and it proposed to "transfer" the Arabs out of the valleys intended for the Jewish state.[16] Ben-Gurion's willingness to accept only a small portion of Eretz Israel was a temporary provision. What would come next? When "the small proposed state will reach the saturation point of its population, what will be the response that we will give then to the masses of the Jews crying out to immigrate and for whom there will be no room in the Jewish state?"[17] Ben-Gurion's response sidestepped the question of territorial expansion: if, he said, in another fifteen years there would be a Jewish state containing 2 million Jews, this would be preferable to continuing the mandate.

Shertok's approach to the "survivability" of the Jewish state was also practical. He did not hesitate to say that if he must choose between the British regime as it is and the partition plan of the Peel commission, he would choose the latter.[18] The advantage of the commission's report is that the Jewish state would receive the best parts of the land, most of the coast and the future possibility of annexing the Negev. He then enumerated the changes that should be requested in the partition proposal: inclusion of new Jerusalem in the Jewish territory; continued British control of the Negev, so that it would remain open to future Jewish settlement; expansion of the Jewish area in the south toward the Gaza Strip; cancellation or reduction of the interim period that the "mandate cities" (Haifa, Akko, Safed, and Tiberias) were to remain in British hands; and inclusion of the area south of the Sea of Galilee, to the Yarmuk River, ensuring Jewish rights on the Jordan River and the Dead Sea enterprises.[19] This list makes it difficult to estimate the precise size of the territory that Shertok considered the essential minimum. However, despite his struggle to obtain an improved partition plan, Shertok was prepared to negotiate with the British government on the basis of the royal commission's proposal, with the addition of the Negev.[20]

And what did the experts on land, immigration, settlement, and development say? Kaplansky, an engineer and leader of Mapai, posed the question: What is the economic value of a state of 5,000 km^2? He maintained that 70 percent of this area is arable, and assuming that 20–25 percent of the total population would be employed in agriculture, it could sustain a total Jewish population of about 1.5 million. Therefore, the proposed state would allow the absorption of up to 1 million additional Jews over fifteen to twenty years.[21] This implied a population density of 300–350 people per km^2, more than in England or Belgium. Accordingly, his calculations did not provide an answer to those who hoped that the state would be a refuge for more than 2 million Jews, as many had hoped.[22] Kaplansky himself greatly feared what would happen in twenty years and therefore supported a federated political structure affording self-determination to both Arabs and Jews. Vilkansky (Volcani), a member of Mapai and an agricultural economist, was the most adamant in his defense of the economic absorption capacity of the proposed tiny state: "If you could settle 3 million in the [entire] country over the next twenty years, you can settle 3 million in the tiny state."[23]

Vilkansky's position is a good example of the pragmatism among the undecided. His comment would place him among the supporters of partition, but Vilkansky also demanded that the proposed boundaries be adjusted to add specific areas to the territory of the Jewish state. On the one hand, he presented these demands as a sine qua non for acceptance of the partition principle. On the other, he was furious with those trying to prove that the partitioned state would not solve the Jewish problem, and he thought that they were weakening the Zionist case concerning the objective absorption capacity of the country.

Despite his moderate opposition, Weitz of Mapai and the Jewish National Fund can also be included among the undecided. He strongly emphasized the economic importance of insisting on the inclusion of the mountain ridge in the Jewish state, however, inclusion of the Galilee in the commission's proposal captured his heart, splintering his position toward partition.[24]

But the man who more than any other symbolized the undecided in the partition debate of 1937—those whose consent to partition was almost ultimatively conditioned on the size of the territory, in addition to other considerations—was Berl Katznelson. He was torn between his fears that any Jewish consent to partition would become a basis for additional concessions and his political realism, which led him to believe that the proposal might present a singular opportunity.[25] Katznelson repeatedly emphasized his adherence to "the ideal and the content of the Jewish state," but concluded that what was being proposed was a "state without land." The Balfour Declaration promised 66,000 km² to the Jewish people, and they were now being offered 5,000, which, in effect, amounted to 2,000 only because the rest would be in the hands of the Arabs remaining in the Jewish state.[26] Katznelson equated the lack of land with the lack of a chance for economic independence. There would be no adequate basis for agriculture, industry would be devoid of markets, and the result would be a dearth of immigration. His list of reservations also included separation from the water sources of the Jordan River and the Yarmuk, turning Jerusalem and the corridor into a British enclave, and the tearing off of the Negev from the territory of the Jewish state, causing its segregation from Sinai and Egypt.[27] Nevertheless, Katznelson did not oppose partition in principle: "I am not one of those who declare that they are against the idea of partition under any circumstances, in any form or at any price. No, I do not say this." On the question of absorption capacity, he added: "The contraction of the territory dilutes the economic resources of the state, reduces its ability to absorb immigration, severs its agricultural character and weakens its defensive power. And we should not delude ourselves that the borders determined today will change tomorrow."[28]

From his speech at the Twentieth Congress, one cannot determine precisely where to position Katznelson between the supporting and opposing camps. He demanded that his colleagues suffer the pain of partition, stressing the value of one's love of the homeland, and reminded them of being cut off from the mountains and the settlements that would be robbed from the Jewish state. He echoed Ussishkin when he said: "Let us not forgo the mysticism of the historic land of Israel in favor of the mysticism of the Jewish state."[29] At the same time, Katznelson sought a compromise. He formulated the ambiguous resolution that was adopted by the Labor movement, and largely due to him, all the opponents in Mapai consequently voted for the majority proposal at the congress.[30] Shertok hurried to include Katznelson among the moderate supporters, but in fact he remained ambivalent. He did not reject partition in principle, but greatly feared the British intentions. He therefore had many conditions and restrictions. Katznelson was willing to authorize the executive to conduct negotiations, but mainly to test the British government's intention to implement the proposal; to determine whether the proposal could be improved territorially, and whether real independence could be attained, particularly regarding Jewish control of immigration policy.

To conclude this section, we will mention those who were more explicit on the necessary size of the territory required for the Jewish state. Writer Moshe Smilansky, a member of the Farmer's Union, supported partition and believed the proposed state could support 3 million Jews. Still, he demanded that the commission proposal be altered to include the Negev in the Jewish state.[31] Another representative of the General Zionist Federation said explicitly that it was not the principle of partition that troubled him, but rather the "extent of the partition." Surely, he argued, all of the opponents, too, would be satisfied with a Jewish state that covered five-sixths of the country.[32] Professor Brodetsky, a member of the Zionist executive, did not believe that many Jews could be absorbed in the small territory proposed. But in contrast to other British Zionists, he did not oppose the Jewish state and did not reject the principle of partition: "The first condition is territory—not because the Arabs have more, but because a state cannot survive in the territory proposed to us: neither economically nor from a security point of view." Brodetsky supported the proposal to authorize the Zionist executive to conduct negotiations with the British. But he was also prepared to define the extent of territory that should be demanded: at least half of all the Land of Israel and no less.[33]

Brodetsky demanded a state of approximately 14,000 km², including the Negev, and his position resembled Ben-Gurion's first proposal, which included some 12,000 km². It can therefore be assumed that those who demanded "enough" territory for immigration, settlement and development as a condition for accepting the partition principle thought in terms of at least half of western Eretz Israel.

But the debate concerned more than quantitative measurement of the land and touched on the question of the importance of territory to Zionism. Note the following exchange between Mapai leaders:[34]

A. Katznelson: "Without Jerusalem and without Haifa this is no Zionism but rather territorialism."

Remez: "Territorialism is the foundation of Zionism."

P. Lubyanker (Lavon): "The realization of the vision means outlining boundaries limiting it in area and time, and—in short—making it territorial."

As already noted, Ben-Gurion and Shertok were the only central leaders who stated how much territory was "enough," in the meantime, for a Jewish state. Other proponents stopped at generalizations: the proposed territory is too small or they hoped future developments would expand it.

Boundaries and Security

The stipulation on this issue is more ambiguous than that relating to the size of the territory. None of the undecided maintained support for or opposition to partition solely according to the defensibility of the borders. Nevertheless, the physical features of the borders and the ability to defend them concerned many, in addition to the Haganah members mentioned in the preceding chapter. Some pointed out strategic considerations, such as the importance of territorial adjacency to one Arab country or another. However, security concerns at that time were influenced mainly by the "disturbances" that began in 1936 and the need to defend Jewish settlements and transportation. The issue of boundaries and security, to become of primary importance in future territorial decisions of the Zionist movement, still played a secondary role in the 1937 debate. They argued passionately about statehood, independence, and the need for a Jewish army, but most of the leaders still believed in the continued protection of the empire and the extended presence of the British Army in the country (at least in the corridor, the mandate cities, and Transjordan).

We know now that this position was not off the mark. The royal commission attached great importance to Britain's strategic considerations in the region. This concern was expressed in secret contacts with the British military command. We mentioned the royal commission's secret meeting with the British general staff on March 1, 1937, to receive informal advice: "because the Commission does not want to put forth any proposals that will be impractical from a strategic point of view." And indeed most of the military experts favored continued British presence in Palestine because of its strategic importance.[35]

In their testimony before the royal commission, the Jews emphasized that the fundamental causes of the "disturbances" were political. This was not a problem of individual safety, but rather of Arab opposition in principle to the Jewish national home. The commission quoted a Jewish witness as saying "The underlying cause is that we exist" and adopted this explanation in its report: "These riots, troubles, disturbances, or as in 1936, rebellions, are symptoms of the disease. They are not the disease itself, the cause of which goes much deeper."[36]

This premise led the commission to conclude that there was no long-term military solution for the lack of security in Palestine. Hence their recommendation that "partition seems to offer at least a chance of ultimate peace. We can see none in any other plan."[37] The commission believed that the establishment of two states in the territory of the mandate, the continued British presence in certain areas, and the signing of military conventions (regarding the maintenance of the British forces, transportation, the oil pipeline, and so forth) between the two states and the British government would also solve the security problem. British support for the two states' membership in the League of Nations was intended, among other things, to make them parties to the world organization's defensive agreements and international security guarantees. The partition boundaries were intended to separate the quarrelsome adversaries and not to protect them from each other. In time, separation would engender acceptance and acceptance would eventually lead to reconciliation. The British army would meanwhile be charged with keeping the peace, after which the Jews and Arabs would have to manage on their own. This solution was characteristic of the separation policy later adopted by the British in different parts of the empire: India-Pakistan, Egypt-Sudan.

How did the Jews react to this approach? Opponents of partition emphasized the security problems to be caused by the proposed boundaries. Most of them rejected any boundary that was not "natural" enough (the Jordan River) or distant enough (the desert) as a satisfactory guarantee of Jewish security. Nevertheless, most of the opponents did not present defensive grounds as the main cause of their opposition to partition. In his testimony before the royal commission, Jabotinsky raised the issue of internal security and maintained that Jews should be allowed to create a defensive force in the Land of Israel. He repeatedly demanded that the Jews be allowed "self-defense" and said that "if you had enlisted 5,000 young Jews in April–May [1936], you would have put an end to the riots."[38] After publication of the report, Jabotinsky related directly to the question of security within the proposed boundaries of the state: "From a strategic point of view, how is it possible to defend this 'enclave' from serious attack? It is mostly lowlands, while the territory preserved for the Arabs is mountainous. It will be possible to place artillery on the Arab mountains a distance of 15 miles from Tel Aviv and 20 miles from Haifa. Within a few hours, it will be possible to destroy these cities, to paralyze the ports and to invade the valleys."[39]

Jabotinsky would later raise another interesting point. He estimated that most of the bombs thrown in Eretz Israel after publication of the partition plan were in the area apportioned to the Jewish state or the British corridor. He concluded that partition, proposed as a solution to the problem of security, would actually require the Jews "to drown an Arab population of 300,000 in blood," referring to those who were to remain within the Jewish state.[40] Similarly, Zeev von Weisel, a founder of the Revisionist movement, already in April 1937 raised a number of security arguments against partition. He argued that a state with a width of 12 km. is an invitation to external attack, with the result that the Jews would abandon their scattered settlements to live in cities protected by the British military.[41]

Members of KM were prominent among those who opposed the partition on security grounds. Tabenkin predicted that the boundaries of the partitioned state would have far-reaching national and social consequences. The Jewish state could not be defended well within the proposed boundaries; therefore relations with the Arab state would become solely military. Tens of thousands of Jewish soldiers would be needed to defend the artificial boundaries, draining personnel from the settlement enterprise. The result would be national totalism, chauvinism, and endless cultivation of militarism.[42] For him, Eretz Israel including Transjordan was one geographic unit, because the Jordan River binds together rather than separates the two parts of the country. Hence, for security reasons, the water sources must be controlled and the desert must be the security boundary of Eretz Israel.[43]

These arguments are original in two regards. First, the senior leader of KM was anxious about a situation in which the Jewish state's total energy would be directed into its army and security. This seems to be a position against Jewish militarism; eventually, however, Tabenkin and his followers would be known for their security orientation, which took precedence over any other consideration. Second, Tabenkin emphasized natural borders as a basis for the integrity of the land, a sort of addendum of geographic determinism in the terminology of the geopolitical school in Europe, to his ideological belief that settlement would determine the boundaries of the Jewish state.

Idelson (Bar Yehuda), another leader of KM, similarly raised the fear that we are "setting ourselves up to become a second Ireland" because of the internal war anticipated between Jews and Arabs in the Jewish state.[44] He also maintained that the "length of the border is astronomical . . . there is absolutely no chance of defending such a border."[45] Bart, a leader of Mizrahi, raised security-oriented geopolitical arguments based on the unnatural ratio between the exaggerated length of the borders and the smallness of the territory of the proposed state.[46] Similarly, the American Zionist Stephen Wise said of the proposed Jewish state: "A truncated, torn apart and dismembered state, with borders that create in advance a situation of insecurity."[47]

Berl Katznelson, presented previously as undecided on the question of the territory's size, also placed more emphasis than others on the security stipulation. He was ready to support partition, on condition that the adjusted borders be defendable: "The strategic situation of the proposed Jewish state is very serious and its defensive capability is very limited. The people around us are not pacifists like we are. The Executive must have the strength to declare that the question of the borders is primarily a question of security and defense, and we cannot agree to boundaries that we will not be able to defend."[48]

In his letter to Weizmann, Katznelson gave priority to the strategic issues: Land contiguity should be established with Lebanon and Egypt to prevent the Palestinian Arab state from coming between the Jewish state and these two countries, thus surrounding it on three sides.[49] He considered the concession of the Negev not only a territorial loss, but also a renunciation of a joint border with Egypt and a distancing from Sinai, which he considered to be of economic and security importance. Katznelson also raised doubts about the importance for security of the proposed sea boundary, which he said would not constitute a defense against the Arab state or against Italy: "I do not see our fortresses on the sea happening so quickly."[50]

The starting point of the proponents, on the other hand, was completely different. Although they did not disregard the security concerns of the opponents and the undecided, they maintained that political power is also the means of building military strength. Golomb, a moderate supporter of partition, believed that political independence is above all an opportunity to build Jewish military power, hence its advantage over the security liabilities of partition, including the "shape of the proposed state."[51] Nemirovsky (Namir) directly answered Meirov's arguments of security by saying that if the existence of the Jewish state depends only on artillery not being fired at it from the mountains, then Switzerland has no right to exist. In his opinion, having a state is the most solid security guarantee.[52] A. Katznelson similarly maintained that statehood could only improve the present security situation, in which Jewish life depended on the British army.[53]

Ben-Gurion first tried to shatter Tabenkin's thesis of "territorial unity" of Eretz Israel, the concept of "natural boundaries," and his laws of "correct" defensive lines: "Where is it said that there cannot be two states in Eretz Israel? There is no such law."[54] Nevertheless, Ben-Gurion repeatedly charged that the commission's proposal should be corrected to create "defensible" boundaries and particularly to provide the Jewish state with a defensive foothold in the hills.[55]

As to the regional strategic situation, the proponents raised the question of what is preferable: continuation of the British mandate and its international obligations or a sovereign Jewish state. They too feared the fate of a miniature Jewish state without British protection in a deteriorating international situation. They shared the anxiety of the threat of Italy, Germany, and the newly independent Arab states. And, as accused by the opponents, they had no clear answer to the long-term strategic problems of a Jewish state under extremely uncertain international conditions. Yet the proponents believed that the option of maintaining the status quo under British protection, thus avoiding the gamble on self-defense, was disappearing and perhaps no longer existed at all. Further, there was a more frightening and very real possibility: the establishment of an Arab state in the entire Land of Israel. The supporters of partition hoped that Britain would continue to need the world Zionist movement as an ally. However, in case of a drastic change in this commitment, the Jews should be prepared by immediately increasing their political strength and their ability to defend themselves.

Considerations of strategy became increasingly central to British policy making in the region and played a critical role in their retraction from the partition plan on the eve of World War II. As the value of the Arabs as regional allies increased, British policy placed little importance on the strategic value of the Jewish state within these or any other boundaries.[56]

As for the Jews, it is difficult to assess the size of the territory demanded in the interest of secure boundaries, because some extended it eastward to the desert. If we ignore the security arguments of the opponents and focus only on those who hesitated, conditioning their acceptance of partition on more secure boundaries, the map submitted to the Woodhead commission (see map 9.1) can be seen as a true reflection of these demands.[57] It presented three main conditions: an addition of 500–2,000 km^2 to the royal commission's proposal, mainly to include in the Jewish state hilly areas overlooking the valleys and the coastal plain; control of railways and main roads; and adjoining the future boundaries with Egypt by leaving most of the Negev under British mandate.

Demography and the Question of "Transfer"

In 1937, approximately 900,000 Arabs and 400,000 Jews lived in Palestine (E.I.). Some 320,000 Arab residents were estimated in Transjordan.[58] In this entire area, Jews totaled approximately 23 percent of the population. The natural birthrate among the Arabs was 24 per 1,000, and among the Jews 21 per 1,000.[59] The commission thus calculated that the percentage of Jews in the population of Palestine (E.I.), assuming only natural increase without immigration, would be 30 percent in 1970. That is, they would number 750,000 out of a population of 2.5 million.[60]

The idea that the Jews would remain a minority in their national home contradicted the goals of Zionism. Therefore many of the undecided conditioned their support of partition on the existence of a Jewish majority in the sovereign Jewish territory. This could be achieved in two ways: increased Jewish immigration or transfer of the Arabs to outside the Jewish state. Before considering these two subjects, we will briefly mention another question: the addition in Arab population as a result of "illegal" immigration through the land border of Palestine.

Arab Immigration to Palestine (E.I.)

The Zionist movement maintained that Jewish settlement caused the immigration of many Arabs to Palestine. Shertok and Epstein testified before the royal commission that approximately 20,000–25,000 people had moved from the Horan region in southern Syria to Eretz Israel in the 1934–1935 agricultural year and that most of them had remained in the country.[61] The Zionist position toward immigration from Transjordan was more ambivalent because, if they demanded to stop the passage of Arabs from east of the Jordan, this could imply that the river constituted an international border and that the Jews forgo their right to settle in Transjordan. In any event, Jewish Agency representatives argued that the British government should prevent such illegal immigration "in order to preserve the absorption potential which we are creating for the absorption of Jews."[62]

The Arab representatives conversely maintained that Arab immigration in general, and specifically from the Horan region, was nonexistent, with the exception of seasonal migration of workers who subsequently returned to their homes.[63] This was largely confirmed by the director of the Immigration Department of the mandatory government, who stated that the number of Arabs remaining in the country did not significantly supplement the population.[64]

The Jewish estimates of total Arab immigration to Palestine (E.I.) were much higher than those of the Arabs or the British. The first official British census in 1922 counted approximately 670,000 Arabs in Eretz Israel. This population had doubled toward the end of the mandate in 1948, and most researchers agree that the growth stemmed mostly, but not entirely, from natural increase, a drastic reduction in the infant mortality rate, and an increase in life expectancy. This conclusion counters the high estimates that 300,000 Arabs entered Palestine from neighboring lands during the mandate, as well as the low estimates referring to an insignificant addition. It can be conjectured, but not proven, that approximately 100,000 Arab immigrants entered Palestine during the mandate period. This estimate is based on the fact that the number of Arabs in the country in the mid-1940s had already reached the level that the commission predicted for 1950 based solely on natural increase.

In any event, the Zionist movement demanded from the British government not only the prevention of Arab immigration to Eretz Israel, but also to take past Arab immigration into account and increase Jewish immigration quotas accordingly. Furthermore, this issue became entangled in the discussion of the exchange of land and population known as *the transfer proposal:* Is it just to return the new Arab immigrants to where they came from? And, if so, why to other parts of Eretz Israel (or Tansjordan) rather than to Iraq or Syria?

Jewish Immigration and the "Transfer" Proposal

Table 7.1 presents the Royal Commission's assessment of the effect of changes in Jewish immigration rates on the demography of Palestine (E.I.) for a thirty-year period.

Table 7.1   The Royal Commission's Forecast of the Ratio between Jews and Arabs in Palestine (E.I.)

	RATE OF JEWISH IMMIGRATION PER ANNUM	NUMBER OF JEWS[a]	NUMBER OF ARABS[b]	PERCENTAGE OF JEWS IN POPULATION	MAJORITY
1940	10,000	445,000		30	Arab
	30,000	528,000	1,038,000	34	Arab
	60,000	653,000		39	Arab
1950	10,000	660,000		34	Arab
	30,000	986,000	1,290,000	43	Arab
	60,000	1,479,000		53	Jewish
1960	10,000	926,000		37	Arab
	30,000	1,550,000	1,558,000	49	Arab
	60,000	2,486,000		61	Jewish
1970	10,000	1,253,000		41	Arab
	30,000	2,246,000	1,821,000	55	Jewish
	60,000	3,735,000		67	Jewish

Source: Royal Commission Report, pp. 201–203
[a]Immigration plus natural increase
[b]Natural increase only

The estimates in Table 7.1 indicate that, at an immigration rate of 10,000–20,000 Jews per year, Arabs would remain the majority also in 1970; 30,000 immigrants per year would create Jewish majority in the mid-1960s; and the immigration of 50,000–60,000 Jews annually would already make them a small majority in the

1950s. The commission concluded from this data that, if economic absorption capacity would continue to be the sole determinant of Jewish immigration, the struggle begun by the Arabs in 1936 would only worsen. Hence the recommendation to determine a "political ceiling" for immigration not to exceed 20,000 Jews per year, a level that would only offset the natural increase of the Arabs and leave the percentage of Jews in the population at around 30 percent. The commission added that this measure was only a "palliative," because the Arabs in Palestine already considered the Jewish national home too large and a barrier to their achievement of independence.

Within the boundaries outlined by the commission, 225,000 Arabs would remain in the area of the Jewish state and 1,250 Jews in the Arab state, not including the residents remaining under British protection. Thus, the Jewish majority in the planned Jewish state would be slightly over 60 percent. To address this problem, the commission raised the possibility of land and population exchanges, a proposal known ever since as "transfer": "If partition is to be effective in promoting a final settlement, it must mean more than drawing a frontier and establishing two states. Sooner or later there should be a transfer of land and, insofar as possible, an exchange of population."[65]

It is important to emphasize several points in this proposal:

- The commission cited the enforced population exchange between Greece and Turkey in 1923 as a precedent, noting the main difference between the two cases: Palestine contained insufficient arable land on which to settle the Arabs who would move.

- The commission was careful not to establish that transfer of all concerned Arabs would have to be carried out forcibly. It specified that voluntary transfer in the Galilee based on the free will of the population would be sufficient. However, in the plains, where Jewish and Arab population is mixed, "it should be part of the agreement that in the last resort the exchange would be compulsory."[66]

- It called for an intermediate survey to determine the possibility of settling the Arabs transferred out of the Jewish state in areas of the Arab state, including Transjordan.

- The commission emphasized a point that was overlooked by the proponents of transfer: If the Arab and Jewish leaders could achieve a bold agreement on transfer, this would be implemented under the supervision and control of the mandatory government. The report contains no recommendation whatsoever that Britain would implement a forced transfer.

A secret memorandum prepared by commission members Coupland and Hammond outlined the considerations behind the transfer proposal: If the commission would not propose exchanges of land and population, even the moderate Jews would reject the proposal. Therefore, "the ideal would be the evacuation of all Arabs and Jews from the Jewish and Arab states respectively."[67] The exchanges of land and people would at first be voluntary, but would then become enforced, based on agreement between Arab and Jewish leaders.

In the internal Jewish debate, the attitudes toward transfer generally coincided with the position on partition. Almost all the opponents and the majority of the proponents opposed transfer, but a great number of the undecided and the proponents were in favor.[68] The opponents used the transfer issue to prove that it was impossible to establish a state that would be truly Jewish. The proponents pointed out the internal consistency of the commission in recommending both territorial partition as well as territorial concentration. Some of the undecided saw the question of transfer as determinant of their position on partition. These positions also cut across camps and parties, and we will classify them according to the main points raised in this specific debate.

First, should transfer be supported from the ethical and ideological perspective? These arguments were generally raised by the opponents of partition, particularly from the Left, but including Tabenkin and Jabotinsky. Second, is it feasible to implement the transfer of Arab residents from the territory of the proposed Jewish state? This question was raised primarily by the pragmatic opponents of partition, who argued that the Arabs would not willingly leave their land and that the British government would be incapable of implementing the transfer by force. Third, the undecided questioned whether they should support the establishment of a Jewish state with an Arab minority of 300,000 or about 40 percent of the total population.[69] This included those who tended to condition their support for partition on precisely this point: that there be as small a number of Arabs "as possible" in a Jewish state.

"Transfer" as an Issue of Principle

The ethical and ideological arguments of those who rejected the transfer proposal were espoused by people of entirely different world-views. Magnes, who favored a binational state and opposed separation of the Jews and Arabs in the country, rejected the proposal as unethical.[70] Similarly, Buber remained steadfast in his belief that relations between the two peoples must not become a political problem of majority and minority.[71] By contrast, Ruppin, who in 1937 favored partition and separation of the peoples, was willing for ethical reasons to reduce the territory of the Jewish state to limit the number of Arabs within it and eliminate the need to consider transfer.[72] Members of ST emphasized the antisocialist element of the plan:

Peace with the Arabs is the guarantee of our existence in the Land of Israel. This is a socialist role for us and a Zionist necessity.[73]

Expulsion of Arabs from the Land of Israel—is not only an assault on the Zionism of today: it will raise a wall to 'the end of days' between Zionism and Socialist justice and liberty.[74]

Tabenkin too noted the contradiction between transfer and the international socialist ideals that make it impossible to suppress and exploit other peoples.[75] This position saw no contradiction between Jewish national liberation and Arabs remaining in the Land of Israel. Jewish settlement does not require the evacuation of Arabs, and therefore Tabenkin rejected the comparison with Greece and Turkey principally because the Turks in effect carried out a massive and cruel expulsion of the Greeks. Nevertheless, in the same sentence in which he opposed the transfer of Arabs, Tabenkin also said: "not that I will oppose it if the Arabs agree and if we are able to transfer them. But if this does not occur, it would create an eternal abyss. A nation which can only establish a state based on the necessary transfer of a people from its place is not a nation which can create a state."[76]

The end of this sentence implies that Tabenkin opposed transfer categorically on ethical and ideological grounds. But the beginning makes clear that he opposed *forced* transfer only. He did not oppose transfer accomplished voluntarily or by agreement: it is a "wild and immoral idea if it is to be carried out through the use of violent force."[77] Other members of KM did not oppose forced transfer in principle, but maintained that it was unfeasible.[78]

Rabbi Berlin, the Mizrahi representative and a sworn opponent of partition, refrained from any explicit statement on the transfer proposal. He compared the rights of Jews and Arabs in Eretz Israel and maintained that only Arabs living there have certain resident rights. "For us, the Land of Israel is the land of our forefathers, while for the Arabs it is only a place of residence. . . . We must be given the right to be a majority in the Land of Israel [and] the Arabs will then be a minority."[79]

This implies support of the Arabs' right to remain in the country, while leaving open the possibility that the way to create a Jewish majority was by moving the Arabs' place of residence outside the Land of Israel. Ussishkin expressed a similar position against transfer, but also with an ambiguity stemming from his desire for a Jewish state without Arabs: "We do not want to expel even one Arab from Eretz Israel; we would not want this even if we had the power to do it. We have the right to this land as a nation; as the Arabs, who have been living in it for hundreds of years, also have the right to remain here."[80]

But Ussishkin prefaced this explicit statement with the comment that the concepts of ethic and law in the life of nations change and pass with time. He termed it immoral for one people (the Arabs) to have much land and another (the Jews) to have nothing. He opposed forced transfer as unfeasible, particularly because it served as an argument in favor of partition. He explicitly raised the question of the internal demography in the proposed Jewish state: " We will have 300,000 Arabs whose high standard of living will improve from year to year. They will multiply by 'internal immigration' and polygamy and their numbers will grow very quickly in the coastal Jewish state. And how will we treat them? Will we really believe in an illusory dream and think that they will leave the land, this state, when they have equal rights?"[81]

Among the opponents of partition, Jabotinsky was the most consistent and outspoken in his opposition to transfer. As early as 1932, he wrote that he would consider expulsion of the Arabs unacceptable: "I am willing to swear in our name and the name of our descendants that we will never violate this equality of rights and will never attempt to force anyone out."[82]

In his testimony before the royal commission, Jabotinsky declared that the Arab would have equal civil rights and cultural autonomy in the Jewish state. Upon publication of the report, he attacked the commission's transfer proposal and the comparison with the forced population exchange between Turkey and Greece.[83] Unlike most opponents of partition, Jabotinsky opposed the transfer of Arabs "voluntarily or by force, whether on a large or small scale."[84] His public statements leave little room for interpretation: "This babble about 'transfer' of the Arabs is even more irresponsible. From a Jewish point of view this is criminal.... We must ensure that the Jews reject this ugly and abhorrent thought as soon as possible. We want to be a majority, but not to show the minority the way out."[85]

There is, however, disagreement about Jabotinsky's real position on transfer. Teveth presents a number of examples before and after 1937 in which Jabotinsky did not reject the concept of transfer raised by others.[86] Heller suggests a distinction between Jabotinsky's public opposition and his private support for voluntary transfer, even in 1937.[87] Moreover, he maintains that Jabotinsky also changed his public position when he wrote just before his death in 1940: "We shouldn't be alarmed by the possibility that 900,000 [Arabs] would leave the country. This writer has already said that there is no need for this exodus; in fact, it would be highly undesirable from many points of view; but if it becomes clear that the Arabs prefer to emigrate, this possibility can be deliberated without any trace of sorrow in our hearts."[88]

These words indicate that Jabotinsky, like most Zionist leaders, aspired to a state of many Jews and few Arabs, to the extent possible. The tone of his words clearly change: if the Arabs prefer to emigrate, they should not be prevented from doing so, although it would be undesirable from many points of view. However, his attitude carries no recommendation whatsoever of a *policy* of transfer, or even support for the idea that leaders of both sides could come to an agreement about this matter. In terms of practical positions, the change in tone carried no weight, particularly when we compare them to his clear written and oral statements condemning transfer. Moreover, in the same 1940 essay, Jabotinsky repeated that "turning Eretz Israel into a Jewish state can be fully realized without uprooting the Palestinian Arabs."[89]

In 1937 Jabotinsky presented a sharp public stand against the transfer proposal of the royal commission based both on his world view and his opposition to partition of the country. First, he anticipated 8 to 10 million Jews, and a minority of 2 million Arabs, on both banks of the Jordan River within a few generations. Any partition of this territory, any attempt to separate the peoples artificially would mean sabotaging the central Zionist vision. He believed that, within the broad solution of the Jewish problem, which required an expansive territory for settlement, there is sufficient space for 20–25 percent Arab residents with full equal rights. Jabotinsky did not say what would happen if millions of Jews did not settle in Eretz Israel: Would less territory then be necessary? And what if the Jews did not become a majority in greater Eretz Israel? Would the Arabs be granted full equal rights in this case also, including the possibility of establishing a non-Jewish state? This omission apparently led to the interpretation that Jabotinsky opposed transfer only on condition that millions of Jews would settle on both banks of the Jordan and to an acrobatic leap to the conclusion that he would have favored transfer "if he would have lived and experienced the Holocaust, which laid to rest the hope of 8 million Jews in the Land, and if he had foreseen the Arab demographic explosion in the Land of Israel which threatened the existence of the Jewish state."[90]

But Jabotinsky did not think in these terms. We therefore must remain within the framework of what he said and wrote, in which his opposition to transfer was a logical and consistent conclusion stemming from his particular Zionist program.

Second, Jabotinsky greatly feared that the Zionist agreement to transfer would be used by antisemites as an excuse to expel Jews from their own countries. He supported and organized "evacuation" of millions of Jews to the Land of Israel, but not at the price of their expulsion from their homes and the confiscation of their property. He explicitly wrote that his opposition to the transfer proposal also stemmed from the danger that it would become an "instructive precedent" for all enemies of Israel in the world.[91]

In general, the opponents of partition who also opposed transfer on ethical and ideological grounds regarded a joint territory for the two peoples as a basis for solving the conflict. From this point, the positions diverge into opposing extremes: On the one side were those who believed in Arab-Jewish coexistence with almost no connection to their numerical ratio: and on the other were those for whom a broader territory was a precondition for the formation of a Jewish majority. They opposed separation of the two peoples because it would limit the area intended for the Jews. The second group also include those who did not reject the possibility of decreasing the number of Arabs in the Jewish state on the condition that this would not be linked to territorial concessions. Some of them maintained that transfer should not be opposed in principle, but that it was impractical.

"Transfer" Is Unfeasible

Those who maintained that transfer was desirable and even ethical, but unfeasible, are not divided according to world-view. This position was based on the premise that there was no prospect for voluntary transfer by agreement with the Arab leaders or through economic incentive to families and individuals. The Arabs would oppose it vigorously and the British government would not implement it through armed force. Golda Meyerson (Meir), among the opponents of partition, said of forced transfer: "Can we think for even a moment that, without Arab consent, England will suddenly come, after our bitter experience with her, and do something out of concern for us which could well provoke the entire Moslem world? I would agree for the Arabs to leave the country and my conscience would be utterly clear, but is there any chance of this?"[92]

A similar evaluation reverberated in the speeches of other Mapai members: The suggestion that an agreement on transfer with the Arab state could be achieved was a basic fallacy.[93]

The other argument for agreement to transfer was the desire to achieve Arab legitimacy, or at least acceptance, to the Zionist enterprise. Whoever raised this argument believed that physical separation through mutual agreement and without force would ultimately engender peaceful relations between the two peoples. Indeed this was the argument of the royal commission—that the proposal is ethical because it is intended to avoid Jewish and Arab bloodshed by eliminating the direct points of friction between them. Accordingly, they conditioned their agreement to transfer on it being negotiated, conducted in an organized manner, and in exchange for full compensation to everyone involved. But the result of these conditions was that it increased the number of skeptics who asked whether the matter was at all feasible: "My belief in transfer, in population removal, is small even though this solution is certainly ethical and fair. It will be good for the Arabs in the Jewish state, much better than in the Arab state, and no one moves freely from good to bad. And what of force? I don't see the power that can accomplish this."[94]

Remez's preceding comments are typically ambiguous and even self-contradictory. On the one hand, he supported territorial reduction and political separation of Arabs from Jews as a possible solution to the conflict. On the other, he harbored great doubts as to whether the other side would agree to it. Hence the importance for him and others of a Jewish-Arab agreement settling their differences, including the question of transfer, something that would have implied Arab consent to a Jewish state.

The royal commission noted the *possibility* of transfer as part of the solution to the problem between Arabs and Jews, and this posed a difficult moral and political dilemma to the Zionist movement. To the credit of many participants in the debate, they did not shy away from exposing their struggles with this issue. There were precedents for such solutions in those years, when the fate of nations and communities was determined by colonial interests or the arbitrariness of totalitarian rulers. At any rate, in the decisions of the Zionist Congress and the Jewish Agency council, transfer was not mentioned at all.

The Demographic Issue

According to the royal commission's recommendation, a ratio of three Arabs to four Jews would be created in the Jewish state, based on the population numbers as of 1937. The debate among the undecided revolved around this: Should agreement to partition be conditioned on the prospects of a Jewish majority in the Jewish state? And, if so, what is an essential minimum Jewish majority? The answer to this question related to other complex issues: rates of immigration, land ownership, and where to transfer the Arabs, if they were to be transferred.

The clearest expression of the dilemma in demographic terms was presented by A. Katznelson, who saw no chance that the Jews would become a majority in the entire Land of Israel. The natural Arab birthrate would double their numbers within twenty-two years, and only an immigration rate of 70,000 per year would enable the Jews to reach equality with the Arabs, still without becoming a significant majority.[95] Katznelson rejected the possibility of a binational regime because he believed that the wall between the two peoples had already become more tangible than political boundaries, and he supported separation, even seclusion, as the only way to realize Zionism. Time was working against the Jews because the international situation would lead England to a policy of reconciliation with the Arabs. Therefore the partition proposal should be accepted in order to increase the Jewish community to 800,000 within five years and create a clear Jewish majority of 70 percent in the Jewish state. This would eliminate the need for transfer.

Berl Katznelson and Ben-Gurion both favored transfer and regarded it as an appropriate and fair solution to the conflict. But

Katznelson did not believe it was feasible and was unwilling to condition his agreement to partition on transfer, whereas Ben-Gurion believed it to be possible under specific circumstances and was therefore willing—for tactical reasons—to condition Jewish agreement to partition on the implementation of transfer. Katznelson saw the transfer of Arabs from the Land of Israel as a long-term solution that would have to occur someday.[96] Still, he opposed the royal commission's proposal because, for him, transfer out of Eretz Israel referred to Syria and Iraq, rather than to other areas in the mountains of Eretz Israel or Transjordan.[97] Moreover, he did not state that he supported only voluntary or agreed transfer, hence the conclusion that he supported forced transfer. However, Katznelson's practical side led him to emphasize that he considered the transfer proposal to be no more than empty chatter: "The historic solution will be an exchange of population," but because the commission's report contained no plan for accomplishing this, it is hard to believe that the matter is at all feasible.[98] In his speech to the twentieth congress, Katznelson mentioned transfer only in a fleeting comment that one of the achievements of holding out for the international guarantee in the mandate charter is that "today, the transfer of thousand of Arabs from one place to another is being discussed."[99] For him, it was enough that the British royal commission had exposed the idea to the world. He did not consider its realization a condition for his agreement to partition.

In contrast, when Ben-Gurion finished reading the commission's report, he wrote in his diary that there was a tremendous advantage in the transfer proposal. But he questioned whether transfer by force was at all conceivable and whether the British government would carry it out even with Emir Abdullah's agreement.[100] In his usual fashion, he immediately began to make calculations: What is preferable, evacuation of Arabs or inclusion of the Negev in the Jewish state? Or perhaps the transfer proposal should be seen as a bargaining chip to be used in return for a larger Jewish state? The next day he wrote in his diary with great excitement about *forced transfer* (emphasis in the original) of the Arabs from the valleys proposed for the Jewish state. He felt this proposal was more important than any of the other positive points and cancels out all the negative points in the commission's report. It would seem that all of Ben-Gurion's prior doubts had vanished and he praised the real Jewish state that would emerge following the evacuation of the Arabs: creation of an agricultural continuum for settlement, a solution to the question of external labor, increased security, a better planned economy, and so on.[101] One gets the impression from Ben-Gurion's private journal that all his arguments in favor of a sovereign Jewish state in return for partition rested on the issue of the transfer proposal:

> We should first extricate ourselves from the feebleness of willpower and thought and from preconceived notions that this transfer is not possible.
> We should grasp this conclusion like we hold onto the Balfour Declaration. More so, like we held onto Zionism itself. We should insist on this conclusion with all of our force, will and belief because, of all the commission's conclusions, this is the one which contains some compensation for tearing off the rest of the land.
> In my eyes, the transfer clause is more important than all of our demands for additional territory. This is the largest, most important and most essential addition of land.[102]

These were Ben-Gurion's private thoughts, but he was a politician and did not state them in public. During the month before the congress's resolution, he did not change this position, but the centrality of the transfer issue, even its tactical leverage, would eventually dissipate.[103] Ben-Gurion listed the positive and negative points of the commission's proposal to crystallize the demands for adjustments. Based on the assumption that the Zionist movement would not be able to expand the territory significantly, he formulated two ultimatums: real sovereignty for the Jewish state, particularly concerning immigration and settlement, and evacuation of Arab residents from the coastal and valley areas.[104]

In his speech to the Labor party council, Ben-Gurion stated that the commission's plan could be better than the continuation of the mandate, if the British would only fulfill these two conditions. However, he tried to distinguish between "eviction" and "transfer," arguing that he supports only transfer that involves no damage to the economic existence of those being transferred and no deterioration in their standard of living.[105] In his congress speech, Ben-Gurion strongly emphasized demography as the reason for his opposition to the status quo and for his support of a partitioned sovereign state. By his calculation, even if the Jewish immigration rate of recent years would continue, it would cause only a small improvement in the Jewish percentage of the population, from 30 percent in 1937 to 33 percent in the early 1950s. Nevertheless, he refrained from drawing the conclusion that transfer should be a condition, despite the fact that he repeated his support for a forced solution.[106] At the end of his address, Ben-Gurion listed the subjects according to which the Zionist movement should examine the amended partition proposal in the future: extent of territory, boundaries, and authority. He thus returned to the three conditions he presented in the first internal discussions in Mapai and did not add the demand to implement the commission's transfer proposal, neither as a condition nor as a tactical ploy. And while the criticality of the matter passed, Ben-Gurion continued to support transfer throughout the debate, if it would be implemented by the British and authorized by the League of Nations.

We will briefly mention several other ramifications of the transfer proposal to complete the picture. In late 1937, a Population Transfer Committee was established in the Jewish Agency to prepare material for the hearings of the Woodhead commission. The main document suggested two goals: reducing the Arab population in the territory intended for the Jewish state, and freeing agricultural land for Jewish settlement.[107] It also contained a detailed plan for the voluntary transfer of about 100,000 Arab farmers to the Gaza district, Transjordan, and Syria. The committee found it very difficult to reach clear recommendations and made do with the general declaration that "the transfer of Arab population on a large scale is a precondition for establishing the state." However, "if the Arabs vehemently oppose transfer and it is not implemented by England with or without the cooperation of the international agencies, the transfer is not attainable."[108] Eventually, it became clear that there was no possibility of enforcing transfer, and among the thirty memoranda submitted by the Jewish Agency to the Woodhead commission, there was nothing on transfer.

At the end of 1937, the Colonial Office rejected the royal commission proposal for forced transfer, even in essential cases of Arab populations.[109] Consequently, the Woodhead commission set out from the premise that as few Arabs and Arab enterprises as possible should be included in the Jewish area, and vice versa, without, however, forced transfer.[110] The commission investigated the possibility of voluntary populations and land exchanges and the prospects of finding solutions for those who would be moved and reached the conclusion that it is "impossible to assume that the minority problem will be solved by a voluntary transfer of population."[111] Incidentally, the commission also concluded that the Jews opposed forced transfer.[112]

Transfer as a concrete politcal possibility never exceeded the bounds of the 1937 royal commission report—it was born and buried there. It was not even mentioned in the United Nations partition plan of 1947. Had transfer not been included in the Peel commission report, it would not have been placed on the political agenda of the Zionist movement, even though the idea itself had been mentioned occasionally in the past.[113] When the commission proposed the possibility of transfer, the matter became a mini-debate within the larger debate on partition. It divided the central Zionist leaders into those who completely rejected the idea on prin-ciple and those who were willing to adopt it, those who talked about voluntary transfer and others about forced transfer. On the level of practical politics, however, transfer did not become a condi-tion for accepting or rejecting the idea of partition.

Territories for Peace

Among the undecided there were those whose main concern was whether territorial separation would indeed lead to peace with the Arabs. A few even conditioned their consent to partition on its implementation with Arab agreement. Using current terminology, we may say that they supported the "territories for peace" formula, adjusted to the different circumstances of 1937. Obviously, the Royal Commission did not view the matter from the Jewish perspective, and it sought a solution that would distance neither of the two peoples from Britain. The commission's central reasoning in favor of the partition proposal: "There is little moral value in maintain-ing the political unity of Palestine at the cost of perpetual hatred, strife and bloodshed, and there is little moral injury in drawing a political line through Palestine if peace and goodwill between the peoples of either side of it can thereby in the long run be attained."[114]

In his opening address at the congress, Weizmann stressed this point from a different angle: "Greater opportunities are open-ing before us for peaceful relations with the Arabs. Until now we had nothing to offer them: for the first time we will be a certain power and will be able to offer them something in return."[115]

Jewish opinion was divided on the prospect for peace. One group maintained that agreement to the commission's proposal would leave the Jewish state without territory and without peace. The other agreed with Weizmann, but demanded "proof"—in the form of Arab consent—that territorial separation would open an opportunity for peace between the two peoples. The first group included many who feared the security and demographic ramifica-tions of partition: the existence of a large Arab minority within the proposed Jewish state. They argued that the proposed boundaries would only invite continued Arab attacks. Moreover, because the transfer proposal was not feasible, the 300,000 Arabs remaining in the Jewish state would become a fifth column, ultimately raising irredentist demands for their annexation to the Arab state.[116]

The opposing poles of the Zionist political spectrum shared this position, for completely different reasons, that partition would not bring peace. Jabotinsky believed peace in the greater Land of Israel would prevail only when a state with a Jewish majority would be established and the Arabs would become convinced that they could not defeat the Zionist enterprise.[117] At the other extreme, ST believed that peace would be attained only in an undivided, binational state expressing the needs of the two peoples. In between were many members of Mapai who spoke of separation as a means of reducing the friction between the two peoples and of seeking solutions acceptable to both sides, such as a federated structure.[118]

There was distinct difference between those who saw separation as an opportunity to protect the Jews from Arab hostility and those who strove to base separation on Arab consent. Golomb said that the Arabs of Palestine would oppose the plan, but that there nevertheless was a chance that it would be accepted by the Arab states.[119] Ben-Gurion also believed that the Jewish-Arab conflict over the right to the land would not quickly fade, however, the Arabs would ultimately come to terms with the power of the Jewish state, and this would enhance the possibility to reach an agreement with them.[120] As for 1937, he did not believe that the Arabs would agree to any Jewish sovereignty whatsoever, unless forced to by the British.[121]

Rubashov (Shazar), a Mapai leader and later the president of Israel, should be mentioned among the more optimistic. Already in February 1937, he told his party of his hope that, at the price of territorial compromise, accommodation with the Arabs could be achieved immediately or subsequently.[122] Yitzhak Greenbaum, of the General Zionist Federation, echoed this in his speech at the congress: "In the Jewish state and only in the Jewish state can we prove to the Arabs that we are not building our lives on the rubble of their lives."[123]

But it was Berl Katznelson who, more than any other, conditioned his agreement to partition on Arab consent. And because he was convinced that the Arabs would not respond, he was highly doubtful about the advantages of Jewish willingness to support it: "Partition does not absolve us of the Arab question." He then said at the congress, "If a Jewish state would arise as part of a comprehensive and agreed arrangement in the Middle East, this would create a hope for lasting peace. But the present partition is not a result of Jewish-Arab agreement, but rather an English invention,"[124]

The congress resolution reflected the positions of those who were ready to support the principle of partition, either out of necessity or hope that the establishment of the state would increase future prospects for peace with the Arabs. This position signified a major change in the attitude of the central stream of the Labor movement, which had previously maintained that Arab agreement should precede Jewish sovereignty.[125]

To summarize the positions of the undecided, those who were concerned principally with territorial reduction and the security problems were closer to the moderate opponents; whereas the issues of a Jewish majority and Arab consent were of more concern to the proponents of partition.

8 The Proponents

The Zionist movement was nursed by irrational sources, by a great vision. However, the realization of the vision means drawing boundaries, limiting it in space and time, in short, making it territorial.[1]

Unlike the conditions put forth by the undecided, the proponents answered the question concerning the "partition principle" (see Figure 4.2) unequivocally. They said a sovereign Jewish state should be established even in return for territorial partition of western Eretz Israel. They shared the grave concerns of the undecided but, after weighing the pros and cons, disassociated themselves from the restrictive conditions and answered "yes"—with a particular urgency.

The line distinguishing between the moderate and the strong supporters is a fine one, dividing them by their type of reasoning: the moderate supporters, including the leaders of the Zionist movement, were great pragmatists; whereas the strong supporters held more ideological views. The arguments of the proponents were antithetical to those of the opponents, with one essential addition: they maintained that Jewish sovereignty presented not only a singular opportunity, but also a starting point for the realization of Zionism's other goals. They believed that sovereignty would rally the entire Jewish people to immigrate and provide resources, thus creating the desired conditions for settlement, economic development, security—perhaps even for peace with the Arabs.

Some of the proponents' arguments have been presented in previous chapters. This chapter will therefore focus on the political tactics of the moderate supporters and the readiness of the strong supporters to adopt even the royal commission's partition proposal.

183

Partition Without Preconditions

These proponents gave the following positive answers to the questions raised thus far:
A sovereign Jewish state must be established, and now.
Territorial partition is imperative.
Is the territory large enough? Are the boundaries defensible? Is it possible to attain a Jewish majority? Arab consent? All of these questions would have to wait. They would all become clear in the course of negotiations with the British, which would aim to improve the royal commission's partition proposal and ensure full Jewish sovereignty.

The proponents first responded positively to the principle of "sovereignty in return for partition" and then turned their sights to promoting and improving the specific proposal. Their considerations were largely tactical: the partition proposal could not come from the Jews, continuation of the mandate and improvement of the partition proposal should simultaneously be demanded of the British, the agreement to partition should be in the present, and no commitment should be made as to future boundaries.

Tactical Pragmatism

Ben-Gurion and Shertok were the architects of what was called in Hebrew *HaTachsis*, from a Greek word for "tactics." Weizmann was full partner but, to their great regret, occasionally deviated from the common line. Berl Katznelson was a confidant too, and despite his disagreement with Ben-Gurion, the two managed to reach an overall understanding of the policy required for the Zionist executive.[2] However, Katznelson was a reluctant partner because he believed it would be impossible to improve the partition proposal and particularly feared that the establishment of an Arab state in part of Eretz Israel would create immutable facts; that is, permanent boundaries.

Weizmann's public declarations and official position reflected the tactical line. We mentioned already his letter to Ormsby-Gore of June 15, 1937, in which he wrote: "I am not in any sense committed to any partition scheme."[3] In a letter to Stephen Wise on June 29, he wrote: "Partition was never, is not now and will never be my scheme."[4] But, in reality, it was known that Weizmann supported partition. In his letter to the colonial secretary of July 20, 1937, he detailed the changes in the royal commission proposal that he had requested in their meeting the day before and concluded: "If the points which I had raised in the interview were settled to our satisfaction, I personally would look with favour on the scheme."[5] The secret protocol of this meeting was leaked to the twentieth congress and caused a general uproar.[6]

In their testimony before the royal commission, as noted in Chapter Three, Weizmann and Ben-Gurion asserted that the mandate must be fulfilled. But Weizmann maintained parallel contacts with commission member Coupland and Colonial Secretary Ormsby-Gore regarding the partition proposal. As the commission report was being prepared, representatives of the Zionist executive held ongoing contacts with the British in an attempt to improve the pending partition proposal. These contacts led the British to understand correctly that the Jewish leaders did not rule out the idea of partition; hence the opponents' accusation that Weizmann, Ben-Gurion, Shertok, and Goldman had actually agreed to partition before the matter was resolved in the official Zionist bodies.

Publication of the commission's report magnified this controversy: What should the official response of the Zionist Organization be? For what purpose could the friends of Zionism in England be activated? What is the desirable decision by the Mandate Committee of the League of Nations? We saw that this tightrope walk of contradictory demands—that the British fulfill the mandate while simultaneously negotiating with them for an improved partition proposal—confused the friends of Zionism within the British House of Commons. Moreover, the house decision not to adopt the commission proposal, but to empower the government to submit it to the League of Nations caused a further dispute: Is it good or bad for the Jews?[7]

The underlying reasoning for tactical pragmatism was expressed thus: "The basis of Zionism is in making use of every opportunity to act. Its basis is in making use of every possibility to gain more power."[8] Ben-Gurion began building a coalition to support the tactics in April 1937 by asking two questions: What is the plan? And, more important, what are the tactics?[9] Many, however, were unhappy with this approach. If the plan seemed inappropriate, they said, one should answer with an absolute "no" and bring all force to bear against it: "We should reject in our movement, and regarding Jewish public opinion, any hidden tactic of 'yes' in the heart and a fictitious 'no' toward the outside world."[10]

Others argued that the movement's position toward the plan should be presented truthfully, that there is no real opportunity to be seized, that the decision should be delayed for as long as possible, and that Mapai should not even hint at agreeing to partition too hastily.[11] As we noted, this opposition was considerably weakened after publication of the commission's report, when the vast majority of Mapai members adopted the tactical line formulated by Shertok and Ben-Gurion.

And what were the arguments of the opponents and the undecided who opposed this tactic? They argued that only an immediate and explicit Jewish rejection of partition would prevent its implementation at some future time. They opposed, as we stressed earlier, the presentation of the dilemma in terms of "sovereignty in return for partition" and had strong reservations on the issue of timing. The opponents who were members of the Zionist institutions witnessed the formulation of the tactical approach and tried to nip it in the bud. They consistently opposed any tactic that implied agreement to partition, as Ussishkin explicitly stated at a Zionist executive meeting: "If the executive proposes that the congress not decide for or against, but rather that it authorize the executive to continue the political negotiations, then the whole world will understand that this decision means agreement to partition and that we are just struggling to expand the boundaries. It is also impossible to notify the Mandate Committee [of the League of Nations] that the congress decided—not to decide."[12]

Ussishkin also did not hide this opinion at the twentieth congress. In opposing the majority proposal, he said: "No realistic approach to the needs of the hour, no convenience for the day."[13] Conversely, Tabenkin voted in favor of the majority proposal, maintaining that the resolution did not imply a position for or against partition, only a postponement of the decision until the next congress.[14] Eventually, the essence of the tactic was adopted and it was embodied in various clauses of the Zionist congress and Jewish Agency resolutions. The moderate proponents won the debate. They overcame the opponents and swayed most of the undecided to forgo their preconditions and vote for the resolution.

Partition Cannot Be Proposed by the Jews

This first component of the "tactics" was also the most difficult to implement. Ben-Gurion noted this in February 1937, when he first presented his own partition proposal to Mapai: "If this plan will appear to be a Jewish proposal—it is lost. It must be made an *English* plan [emphasis in the original]."[15]

Berl Katznelson agreed, "This plan first of all cannot be our plan,"[16] and thus laid the foundation for his compromise with Ben-Gurion on the congress resolution six months later. On the eve of publication of the commission's report, Shertok formulated the tactic of public repudiation of the partition proposal in a more picturesque way: "We must be in a situation to deny paternity of the child."[17] Accordingly, the Zionist movement would state that it prefers the British government to keep its prior obligation under the mandate charter and the international guarantees contained therein. If it wishes to propose an alternate route, this can be discussed. Practically, this created a difficult problem of how to convince the Jewish public that its leaders were willing to discuss an unacceptable proposal. How to influence international public opinion that continuation of the mandate is preferable, but not push it too much, in order to gain support for amendment of the partition proposal. Shertok recognized the contradiction inherent in these tactics. If the partition plan is British, he reasoned, the Jewish public might well see it as a "monster of incomparible danger," which would make it almost impossible for the leadership to work toward an amended plan.[18]

This complex move brought mixes results. The partition proposal was published by a prestigious royal commission, and the involved parties were asked to respond. So far so good. The plan was British and was initially adopted by the British government, although not by the British Parliament or, ultimately, by the League of Nations. Nevertheless, it was already clear to the British government, to the governments represented on the Mandate Committee of the League of Nations, and most probably also to the Arabs of Palestine as well as to other Arab states that most of the central Jewish leaders supported the idea. When the Zionist movement did not reject the idea of partition outright, and even passed a resolution to this effect at the Zionist congress, it was exceedingly difficult to continue to say that the plan was and remained solely British.

Thus charged the extreme opponents, who rejected the "tactics" outright. They accused Weizmann of transforming the commission's proposal into the *maximum* attainable and not the minimum, as the proponents maintained. Moreover, they said, the Arab leaders within and outside Eretz Israel who rejected the partition proposal would not form a united front against the "British plan" that was hatched, the Arabs would charge, in conspiracy with the Zionist movement.[19]

The congress resolution strove to make a sharp distinction between the two parts of the equation: partition, on the one hand, and statehood, on the other. It first declared that the partition scheme proposed by the royal commission was unacceptable; and then went on to empower the Zionist executive to conduct negotiations on the proposal to establish a Hebrew state in Eretz Israel. Hence, the commission's specific proposal was never formally adopted by any official Jewish body. But the distinction was artificial. Did anyone really believe then that a Jewish state could be established without partition? Also, to pick a fine legal point, the congress resolution said a "state *in* Eretz Israel" and not in the entire Land of Israel.[20] In any event, even though the 1937 partition proposal was British, the Zionist movement did not reject the idea outright, as the opponents demanded in the minority resolution they proposed to the congress. Thus, the possibility of partitioning western Eretz Israel was placed as a precedent on the agenda of the Zionist movement. Within a decade, this possibility would become explicit agreement.

Fulfillment of the Mandate and an Improved Partition Proposal

The "double formula" just explained was inspired by Ben-Gurion; and he would use it again on many future occasions. Teveth believes Ben-Gurion invented this verbal tool as a reaction to intractable situations, a sort of poor man's wisdom and weak man's ingenuity.[21] It was intended to help him think in antithetical situations, to say and even do one thing and its opposite at the same time. This is how Teveth reconstructs Ben-Gurion's double formula in 1937: "We will fight for the continuation of the Mandate as if we do not agree to a state in part of Eretz Israel; thus leading the British to force a state upon us—and we will take advantage of this for expanding the boundaries proposed by the Peel Commission— as if we forgo the Mandate."[22]

As early as February 1937, Ben-Gurion was already convinced that the mandate in its original form was coming to an end. Katznelson's fierce reaction and his call "to plan with all our might for a war on behalf of the status quo"[23] apparently persuaded Ben-Gurion that the mandate and its international guarantees should not be forfeited easily. The formulation of the two conflicting demands went through many changes, but its content remained similar: we do not forgo the mandate as long as a more acceptable plan is not proposed to us.[24] The opponents willingly agreed to the first part of the formula, as leaders of vastly different positions— Ussishkin, Tabenkin, and Hazan—all stressed the importance of the mandate's continuation. The proponents seized on this, ridiculing the sudden "loyalty" particularly of the anticolonists, to the British empire.

However, the opponents' arguments were rather consistent in this regard: The mandate represented international guarantees that were attained with great effort by the Zionist movement. Perhaps it could be exchanged for another mandate, but the component of international recognition must not be conceded: "We did not see the mandate as a Garden of Eden. But for out sorrowful people, the mandate is still the best practical framework in the international arena."[25]

The proponents, by contrast, regarded the demand to continue the mandate as just a logical extension of the tactical position that the partition proposal could not originate with the Jews. Some of them did recognize the stumbling block inherent in such a position: "When they say *status quo* concerning the continuation of the mandate, surely they are defending a lost position from a historical point of view."[26]

Nevertheless, they also recognized that Zionist willingness to abandon the mandate would make it easier for the British government to ignore its obligations and also to worsen the partition proposal of the royal commission. Accordingly, they said, we should not, for the time being, "minimize the importance of the mandate by even one iota."[27]

It is important to note that adherence to the mandate exceeded tactical considerations. In retrospect, the greatest achievement of the Zionist movement was not the Balfour Declaration, but its incorporation in the mandatory charter that the international organization bestowed on Britain: "The Mandatory [government] should be responsible for putting into effect the declaration originally made on November 2, 1917 by the Government of His Britannic Majesty, and adopted by the Powers, in favour of the establishment in Palestine of a national home for the Jewish people."[28] The League of Nations recognized the historic bond between the Jewish people and the Land of Israel and its right to reestablish the national home. No Zionist was willing to surrender this recognition, particularly in light of the storm gathering in Europe before World War II. It was this approach which triumphed in the congress resolution: "The congress rejects the assertion of the Palestine royal commission that the mandate has proved unworkable, and demands its fulfillment. The congress directs the executive to resist any infringement of the rights of the Jewish people internationally guaranteed by the Balfour Declaration and the mandate."[29]

The minority resolution proposed to "force the mandatory government" to fulfill the mandate and say no more.[30] In the end, the "double formula" was adopted, and it contained a certain concession by Ben-Gurion to Katznelson, who demanded not to tear up the mandatory IOU but rather to cash it. Conversely, Katznelson's concession to Ben-Gurion was the clause in the resolution concerning negotiations with the British government, which included the possibility of agreeing to exchange the mandate for a partitioned Jewish state.

Did the double formula achieve its tactical purpose? The real position of the Zionist leadership in 1937 was that the establishment of a sovereign state based on a corrected partition plan was preferable to continuation of the mandate. Hiding this position in contradictory language paved the way to an important compromise on the elite level. The value of this compromise should not be underestimated, because there had been real concern that the issue would split the Labor movement, the Zionist movement, and the Jewish Agency. Indeed opponents and proponents all expressed the need to close ranks in the face of the Arab revolt domestically and the situation of European Jewry abroad.

But the double formula confused the Zionist public and its international supporters and was not taken seriously by the British government. As noted earlier, Churchill, who was then a warm friend of the Zionist movement, was not persuaded by Weizmann to support an improved partition plan if the British mandate would not continue. Lord Samuel's firm opposition to the royal commission's report made sense to him. In a letter to Samuel on October 6, 1937, Churchill noted, "The more I think of this Partition Scheme, the more sure I am it is folly."[31] If there was a chance of dislodging Churchill from his position that a British presence was important for both Britain and the Zionists, it would take more than the double formula that Weizmann offered.

It is difficult to gauge the damage of Ben-Gurion's double formula to the Zionist leadership's efforts to win support for its position, and it is impossible to blame it for the failure of the partition proposal in 1937. The British government know the true position of the Zionist movement, and it still retreated, for its own reasons, from the commission proposals. The British mandate continued another ten years, to be replaced, when it ended, with a Jewish state in a partitioned Palestine.

Unspecified Future Boundaries
of the Jewish State

The two tactical components presented thus far were aimed outward. By contrast, this component—concerning the desired territorial boundaries of the Zionist enterprise—was intended to allay the fears of the domestic opposition. Perhaps this was not a tactical move at all, because most Zionists emotionally aspired to a large Jewish state. They formulated it ideologically in stages: what could be achieved now and what should be left for future generations. This debate focused on the historical interpretation of the fate of the Zionist movement and on lessons of its own past and that of other peoples in similar situations. The conclusions therefore were split between two distant poles. The opponents regarded the boundaries of a Jewish state covering some 5,000 km^2 as final and the end of the Zionist revolution as a solution of the Jewish problem. The proponents, by contrast, spoke of the opportunity to create a sovereign Jewish entity as a lever for the gradual realization of greater Zionism.

The cleavage within the Labor movement had an additional dimension. The opposition of leaders such as Ya'ari and, to a certain extent, Katznelson and Tabenkin, was not tactical. They wished to delay the decision on the political framework out of ideological conviction.[32] But most of the other Labor movement's leaders, those in charge of policy making, concluded that the time had come to choose the best from among bad alternatives.

Jabotinsky can be included among the ideological opponents on this issue because he claimed that partition would be the death knoll of Zionism. This is no "Jewish Piedmont," he warned, which would be followed by the liberation of the rest of Eretz Israel. Once there is consent to partition, "military expansion is not at all possible . . . and there is no serious chance of expansion by peaceful means."[33]

There was also a tactical element in the Revisionist opposition to partition, as Akzin suggested years later. They did not believe that the British government really intended to establish a Jewish state and feared that Jewish agreement to and Arab rejection of the plan would lead to the removal of the "Arab part" from the mandate area, as was done earlier with Transjordan.[34]

The religious opponents also pointed to the danger of Jewish willingness to forgo part of Eretz Israel. We have noted that, as far as religious law was concerned, opinions were divided. Some of the Mizrahi rabbis quoted the interpretation of "thou shalt not show mercy unto them" (Deuteronomy 7:2)—and ruled that non-Jews should not be allowed to possess any land in Eretz Israel. Many Othodox rabbis, on the other hand, distinguished between the Jewish people's attachment to the Land of Israel and ephemeral political sovereignty. As for the latter, neither religious prohibition nor commandment is involved. Accordingly, religious opinion was divided: The opponents maintained that it was forbidden to establish a Jewish state prematurely and the religious proponents, like their secular peers, believed that a political solution was provisionally appropriate, particularly when the commandment of "Saving a life" (of endangered European Jews) applies.

The opponents of partition argued that agreement to a reduced territory would determine final boundaries. In response to Ben-Gurion, who said that partition is a solution only for this generation, they said: "Setting boundaries—this is a tragedy for generations to come. Boundaries cannot easily be changed. Certainly a world war can change many things. But who knows if our changes will be better in this war . . . and if borders are established they will remain for many years and perhaps forever."[35]

Another argument raised was that the proposed partition was between three states based on three religions: A Jewish state, a Moslem state, and a Christian state (the Jaffa-Jerusalem corridor, which was to remain under British control). Such a division, founded on religious separation and especially on the Christian interest in Jerusalem, would be eternal.[36] Members of KM angrily confronted Ben-Gurion when he said that agreement to partition now does not surrender the larger Zionist vision. They presented their own perception of the generational division of responsibility: "Our generation will first carry out the settlement enterprise on the distant lands of Eretz Israel, and the state will be left to future generations."[37]

Berl Katznelson, who was party to the other parts of the tactical scheme, did not believe, however, that the system of gradual settlement ("another acre, another goat") could also be applied to territorial sovereignty. "We should not delude ourselves that borders set today will be changed tomorrow," he emphasized.[38] He opposed the desire to seize the opportunity and establish a fait accompli of sovereignty, even on a limited territory, because he both was suspicious of Britain and believed that "it is an elementary matter in international relations that you should not want to take the territory of your neighbor."[39] The opponents were deeply convinced that Zionism had to concern itself with all Jews in both this and future generations and that it should not rely on the unlikely chance for territorial expansion.

The proponents did not regard their agreement to partition to be a purely tactical position. They were aware of the possibility that the territorial reduction would not prove temporary and with some of them it is difficult to distinguish between wishful thinking and political assessment. The exception was Ben-Gurion, whose tactical aims remained consistent throughout the debate, and included all of the components, both external and internal—Jewish agreement to the partition principle, leaving the issue of future boundaries open:

There is nothing permanent in boundaries. I doubt whether [you] can show one border on the earth which never changed. By the time we complete the settlement of our state to its full density, many things will happen which I cannot predict in advance.[40]

And what will happen in fifteen years (or some other number of years) when the proposed state, with its small area, will reach the "saturation point" of its population? What answer will we give then to the masses of Jews desperate to immigrate—when there is no room for them in the Jewish state?

For now, only one answer can be given: In another fifteen years our situation will be better—if a Jewish state is meanwhile established and 2 million Jews meanwhile are concentrated in that state—than if the British mandate will continue for the next fifteen years.

What will be in this land after fifteen years depends on what will happen in this land during those fifteen years. Just as I do not regard the proposed Jewish state as the ultimate solution to the problems of the Jewish people, I do not regard partition as the ultimate solution to the problem of the Land of Israel. Those opponents of partition who argue that this land cannot be divided because it is one unit not only historically, but also naturally and economically, are correct.[41]

These comments brought Ben-Gurion much closer to the opponents, especially Berl Katznelson and Tabenkin, whose support he desperately required to win the crucial vote at the congress. Never again throughout the debate did he speak about the Land of Israel as an indivisible historical unit. He would later explain that this does not mean it cannot be divided politically. The distinction

Ben-Gurion set forth in his book of 1917 shows that the statement about the land as "one unity" amounted only to a tactical exception. In the book, Ben-Gurion distinguished between geographical and political "wholeness" and emphasized that in most historical periods the Land of Israel was not one political unit.[42] Although he spoke of a small Jewish state now as a decisive phase toward the realization of greater Zionism, Ben-Gurion quickly pointed his audience northward and not eastward: The first possibility for expansion based on the complete agreement and goodwill of our neighbors may well be in southern Lebanon, which borders the Jewish state.[43] Ben-Gurion's position that "we can merely decide the fate of the next stop" secured the support of the opponents and the undecided within his party and thus led to the in-principle decision at the twentieth congress in favor of partition.

Others added their own personal touch to this tactical line. Luffbahn supported partition because he believed it was essential to Jewish historical development. After all, he reminded his Mapai colleagues, Joshua's "flow of conquest" also stopped after a series of victories; and he bequeathed an area no greater than that intended for the Jewish state in the partition plan. He explained that initially an independent political force should be created on the conquered territory "so that it could subsequently inherit the remaining parts of the land." He concluded that settlement of people is always gradual: "A people has never conquered a homeland in one fell swoop in one or two generations. It always was and will be that a first conquering thrust held onto the edge of a particular land, and this formed the core of the expansionist force of this people."[44]

Thus, Ben-Gurion's political maneuvering was turned into the hidden hand of the master of history. Therefore partition should be accepted willingly and not only out of necessity. In addition to Tabenkin, he was one of the few Mapai members who used the terminology of the romantic geopolitical school that developed in late nineteenth century Europe. As we have seen, these arguments were more prevalent among the opponents, particularly the religious Zionists and the Revisionists, who maintained that political intervention in the natural process of expansion and conquest prematurely determines constraining boundaries.

However, the tactic of the leadership was essentially political, and directed inward, and also nourished by underlayers of hidden aspirations, which were not tactical at all. For Weizmann and Ben-Gurion, the establishment of a state essentially entailed seizing a political opportunity. Their arguments contained no trace of conceptualizing the state as a living body that grows organically.[45] On the contrary, just as the boundaries are determined by present circumstances, unpredictable historic opportunities for change may also arise.[46] As Shertok said at the Mapai central committee meeting after the congress, regarding the anticipated political activity in London and Geneva: "We do not now have a more effective strategic position than the demand for a Jewish state. Whether or not they want it to be established, tactically we have no more powerful tool than this."[47]

Territorial Demands

Although the moderate proponents refused to state whether the proposed territory was "enough" and held that everything would be determined by negotiation with the British, their position regarding the desired territory can be deduced from the changes they demanded in the royal commission's partition proposal.

When the commission was preparing its report, an argument broke out among its member regarding the land reserves to be given to the Jewish state: the unpopulated but arid Negev or the fertile Galilee populated by Arabs. We may assume that the royal commission recommended inclusion of the Negev in the Arab state because of British interests in Sinai and Transjordan, rather than in consideration of Zionist preferences. But either way, the Zionist leaders preferred the fertile and populated Galilee to the Negev (see Chapter Three), perhaps assuming that it might be easier to acquire the empty Negev desert later. The insistence on the Galilee was unequivocal, whereas Weizmann demanded only that the Negev not be included in the Arab state and that it remain under British control and open to Jewish settlement.[48]

In early June 1937, before the publication of the commission's report, Rutenberg formulated the main condition he believed essential to Jewish support of the partition plan: that the territory of the Jewish state enable it to sustain itself economically.[49] It therefore must include extensive arable land and hence the need to transfer Arabs voluntarily to the territory of the Arab state. In addition, he suggested including the Galilee to create a common border with Christian Lebanon; the elevated territory east of the coastal plain, for security reasons; and the area north of the Sea of Galilee, including his power station at Naharayim. The Negev, including the Dead Sea Works, could meanwhile remain under British protectorate. These demand were formulated with Ben-Gurion's full agreement and were sent to the director-general of the Colonial office, in the hope that they would reach the royal commission.[50]

Shertok more fully detailed the "essential corrections" demanded after publication of the report: leaving the Negev under British control and open to Jewish settlement, inclusion of the proposed four mandate cities in the north of the Jewish state, inclusion of the southern tip of the Sea of Galilee and the power station at Naharayim as well as the Dead Sea Works, expansion of the southern border, and inclusion of new Jerusalem in the Jewish state.[51] Subsequently, the Jewish Agency presented the expanded "map" to the Woodhead commission. Except for the demand that the Negev remain British, these Zionist claims involved relatively marginal territorial changes—an addition of some 10 percent to the Jewish area proposed by the royal commission. Thus it can be concluded that moderate support for partition did not revolve intrinsically around the size of the territory intended for the Jewish state. Shertok made this explicit:

> There is also a danger in abstract mysticism, as it may raise a devil in the path to Zionist realization. A clear example of this: if we ignore the realistic Land of Israel and are influenced only by the "mystical" meaning of Eretz Israel—from the sea unto the desert.
>
> I cannot accept opposition to the partition plan on "mystical" grounds . . . just to prevent us from surrendering the wide and abstract boundaries of Eretz Israel, or to avoid reconciling ourselves with the excision of Jerusalem. The Jewish test for me is: What framework and what political regime will facilitate our rapid growth and real consolidation, and allow us the maximum power.[52]

To summarize the positions of the moderate proponents, we will quote two leaders who did not belong to the Labor camp: Greenbaum, a member of the Zionist executive and General Zionist Federation, and Rutenberg, who was an unaffiliated industrialist. Greenbaum, a central leader of the Polish Zionists, felt that the hour of decision had arrived. In response to the opponents and the undecided, who argued for continuation of the status quo, he said that it was impossible to force Britain to fulfill the mandate. For him, the options were these: "a Jewish state in part of Eretz Israel" vs. "a Jewish minority in Arab state on the entire Land of Israel." His choice was sharp: "We require the power of a state, of a government! A state means not only a piece of land but also power, government, the possibility to arrange life according to our own needs and ways. . . . We have now reached this stage of our development, when we already require governmental power. And this only a Jewish state could give us."[53] Greenbaum was the most outspoken in his opposition to what he termed "the insufferable religious and mystical" arguments of the opponents. The following is Ussishkin's account of an exchange comparing partition with the proposal to settle Jews in Uganda: "Greenbaum told me at a Zionist executive meeting: Don't make a tragedy of this question. This is not Uganda. I answered him: I know that the Sharon (region) is not Uganda. I know geography as well as you. But I also know that it is much more difficult to distinguish between holy and holy than between holy and profane . . "[54]

Rutenberg's position was characteristic of the moderate proponents who supported partition almost against their own will. In May 1936, immediately after the first Arab riots, he was one of the "Five" who tried to reach a Jewish-Arab agreement even at the price of restricted Jewish immigration for a limited period. He also believed that "the Jewish community in Eretz Israel is not ripe for the institution and operation of an independent state" and favored continuation of the British empire's patronage.[55] However, from the moment the commission's report became a fact, Rutenberg devoted himself to improving the boundaries and conditions proposed for the Jewish state. Moreover, although he held a lifelong disdain for "politics" that force people to say "yes" and "no" in the same breath, he supported the ambiguous resolution of the congress. He welcomed the majority's readiness to say a conditional "yes" to the principle of partition and was sharply critical of Katznelson and others who vacillated until the last moment.[56]

To summarize, even the unconditional proponents of partition had their doubts but, unlike the undecided, they were willing to take a risky step that could create the fulcrum for Jewish independence now. Their demanded changes in the commission's proposal and their suggestions of how to present Jewish consent to partition stemmed from a tactical definition of the problem. They felt that the door to the fulfillment of Zionism had opened slightly and that they should act very quickly so that it would not close again. Accordingly, the appropriate political tactics must be found, but under no circumstances should fundamental conditions be raised that might subvert the entire scheme. This was not a cohesive group, but the pragmatic arguments that they raised and the personal weight of Weizmann, Ben-Gurion, and Shertok gave them considerable influence among the undecided. They ultimately managed to convince the majority to vote for the tactical resolution proposed at the Zionist Congress.

Partition as the "Right" Solution

By comparison with the moderate proponents, the strong proponents constituted a tiny minority that generally did not dare voice its opinion aloud. They were not influential in the Zionist movement or the Yishuv, principally because the commission's proposal was territorially minimalistic and because of its other components, which were hard to swallow. The majority saw no reason to support a proposal about which the British Parliament had its reservations, that the League of Nations had not yet discussed, and that most Arabs rejected as unacceptable. Therefore, few prominent Jewish leaders publicly adopted the commission's proposal without reservations. Some implied this possibility indirectly or hypothetically. Others expressed a positive inclination as an extension of the "tactics" presented in the previous section. But against the thunder and lightning of the tactical proponents, it was difficult to expect strong support for the immediate establishment of a tiny sovereign Jewish state, as proposed by the royal commission. Hence this position could be presented as a hypothetical question: Would you support the royal commission's proposal without amendments if it would become clear, beyond a shadow of a doubt, that this was the only way to achieve Jewish independence?

The opponents were against the *principle* of partition and are thus exempt from answering this hypothetical question. They rather preferred continuation of the mandate to partition. The undecided set forth specific conditions and therefore would not accept the commission's partition proposal. This question is therefore relevant only to the proponents, whose tactical goal was to alter the commission's proposal. Ben-Aharon, of KM, pointedly presented this very question to his Mapai colleagues to pressure the proponents and the undecided to address the commission's proposal directly:

We have a specific proposal before us, a proposal with alternatives and to which we must answer yes or no. And this "yes" or "no" must be accompanied by a simple pronouncement: yes or no under any circumstances? With all of the corollary expressions that have been accompanying every speech, it is impossible to know if they are just for the sake of eloquence, if they serve to reduce or soften the blow, or if they are said for the purpose of an iron-clad, ultimate position. . . . But since this is not stated clearly, I can draw one conclusion: from everything I have heard from the supporters, it seems to me that—after they have added the changes they desire, they are prepared to support this partition plan as it was proposed in the conclusion of the royal commission.[57]

Nemirovsky agreed that the demand for a clear response was justified. He stated that he favored territorial separation of Jews and Arabs and the establishment of a Jewish state based on partition and did not agree to the partition proposal in its present form, which must be corrected. He then added that Ben-Aharon and the other opponents must likewise answer the parallel question: Would they accept an amended partition plan?[58] Shertok, too, was one of the few leaders who was willing to examine the ramifications of this hypothetical possibility: "If I have to choose between the mandatory government as it is or the partition plan as it is in this book [the commission report], I choose the latter."[59]

There are also indications that, under certain conditions, Ben-Gurion was willing to make do with the commission's plan: "I see this plan in its *entirety* not as the lesser evil, but rather as a political triumph and historic chance that we have not had since the day our land was destroyed. . . . I prefer this plan in its *entirety* over the existing regime" (emphasis in the original).[60]

Ben-Gurion also said that the commission's proposal was generally superior to his February 1937 proposal, due to its inclusion of the Galilee and most of the coast in the Jewish state as well as its proposal of transfer.[61] And although he emphasized the importance of struggling to correct the commission's proposal, he also saw fit to write: "We should decisively clarify the position of the movement and where it is headed. I see only one desirable path: partition and establishment of a state along the general lines of the commission."[62] At the congress, by contrast, Ben-Gurion spoke in the spirit of the compromise formulated with the opponents' camp and stressed that the commission's proposal was unacceptable.[63] He also reiterated Weizmann's preceding comment that the proposal could serve as a basis for negotiations with the British government only after the essential changes were made.[64]

But Weizmann, too, expressed totally different tones in his private letters. For example, when, toward the end of 1937, he became anxious that the British government was about to retract the whole partition idea, he wrote to Colonial Secretary Ormsby-Gore: "I am very well acquainted with the Jewish people, and I am certain that 95 percent of the Jews would agree to partition on the basis of an improved Royal Commission proposal. But they will not accept a distorted plan, a concoction of the Palestinian governmental offices."[65]

In this letter Weizmann was still fighting for "improvements" in the commission's proposal, but already feared that a further reduction would be proposed by the new partition commission (Woodhead) with the concurrence of the high commissioner. In a March 1938 letter to the new colonial secretary, Halifax, Weizmann explicitly warned against reducing the Peel commission proposal and particularly the excision of the Galilee.[66] It can be posited that Weizmann and Ben-Gurion would have been willing to accept the original royal commission's proposal during this period of British government retreat from the partition plan.

N. Goldmann was the only senior member of the Zionist organization to state in his speech at the congress that it was forbidden to reject the Peel commission's plan. He believed that "we cannot wait" and that "every partition plan has its negative aspects." He understood those for whom "the present plan is a leap into darkness," but maintained that they must take the risk.[67] When Goldman wrote his memoirs many years later, he bitterly attacked the fanaticism of the opponents who in 1937 did not understand that reality demanded "to sacrifice some precious historical ideas as a means to independent designing of the future." Moreover, in his opinion, had the Zionist movement accepted partition without delay in 1937, it might have been implemented and possibly millions of European Jews might have escaped.[68]

For the strong proponents, partition was a "right" solution because the Jews, being a people without a recognized territory, must adopt an approach unlike that of other peoples fighting for independence. As long as there is not patch of sovereign Jewish land, there is grave doubt as to the sheer prospect that the Jews can achieve their self-determination. Therefore, self-government and perhaps even autonomy under British patronage should supersede other considerations. The extent of the territory was almost irrelevant, because even a small island of Jewish independence would create the conditions for social, economic, and cultural development. Lavie, alone among the members of KM who openly supported the partition proposal, spoke in this vein: "I wanted to prove that even this partition, which all of us are still fighting in its present form, is better for us than any other alternative, even the best. . . . Indeed, any partition is better than the present status, which it is hopeless to change decidedly in the coming years to our benefit."[69]

Lubyanker foresaw quite accurately the alternatives that would unfold: "A truncated state or an anti-Zionist Mandate."[70] He chose the first; and even though the sovereignty granted to the Jewish state would be largely fictitious, the most important goal was self-government in the internal matters that would determine the country's development: immigration, land, taxes, and security.

The arguments of the strong proponents presented thus far emphasized Jewish self-interest in adopting the partition plan. But another argument deserves mention, even though it was not held by many: the contribution of separation to Jewish-Arab coexistence. Those who stressed this point were, in effect, adopting the logic of the royal commission that "good fences make good neighbors," hence the need for painful territorial surgery. Among the Jewish leaders, Ruppin came closest to adopting this position, which the commission proudly called "one of the finest" British features—resolving competing national claims through compromise and partition.[71] He said in his speech at the congress: "If you ask me what I think would be best, what I think in general about partition and isolating these two people, I would say: this idea of partition is good in and of itself. If the two peoples reside in different parts of the land, the chances for friction between them will be lessened."[72]

Ruppin, who belonged to Brit Shalom in the 1920's, changed his position regarding a binational solution, but continued to favor a restrained Zionism that would convince the Arabs that the Jews were not expansionists. He therefore supported complete separation even at the expense of territorial reduction, both to establish a homogeneous Jewish state and to build Arab confidence in the possibility of coexistence with the Jews.[73]

We have seen that some proponents conditioned their readiness to support the partition on Arab consent. There were also a few, like Ruppin, who reversed the order of the argument, saying that Jewish willingness to reduce their territorial aspirations would convince the Arabs that Zionism stood for peace. Weizmann himself spoke similarly at the end of his speech at the congress: "We now face greater new possibilities also for peaceful relations with the Arabs. Until now we did not have much to offer them; for the first time we will be a certain power and will be able to propose something in exchange to them. This is the first basis for friendly negotiations between peoples and one of the main advantages of the plan."[74]

Total Support

Completing the continuum of the positions, we will mention that there also were nonterritorial solutions on the supporting side: various forms of Jewish autonomy, self-ruling cantons, the establishment of a spiritual center in Eretz Israel—all these without demanding sovereignty over the territory. The premise was that the British mandate would continue and the goal should be autonomy as a means of communal development with different emphases: social, cultural, and religious. The ultra-Orthodox groups who were mentioned among the "total opposition" appear at this pole, too. Their lack of interest in the present political status of Eretz Israel and their adherence to their local religious autonomy can be interpreted as willingness to allow autonomy for every group in its own area, until messianic redemption would rebuild the kingdom of Israel.

Among the proponents of partition who agreed to any solution that would grant autonomy to the Jewish community in Eretz Israel was Itamar Ben-Avi. As noted in Chapter Two, he was one of the first to raise the cantonization possibility and became one of the strongest supporters of the royal commission's proposal.[75] He envisioned a Jewish state as an "eastern Switzerland" in which Jews and Arabs would live in peace. So the circle was complete: the "total proponents" backed any expression of Jewish self-rule almost regardless of territorial size; whereas the "total opposition" was in principle against the establishment of a Jewish state anywhere, also regardless of the territorial question.

Summary of the Proponents' Positions

The debater's presentation of the arguments listed in Table 8.1 was jumbled and inconsistent. Nevertheless, the moderate proponents, whose position completely rested on political pragmatism, can be distinguished from the strong proponents, who believed in the principle of separation as the basis for the solution. From this perspective, there is a similarity between the more pragmatic moderates on both sides of the continuum. There is also a similarity between the strong opponents and the strong proponents, whose positions were more ideological and consequently uncompromising.

Table 8.1 Main Arguments of the Proponents

Proponents: Support partition without preconditions	Political sovereignty as a means for achieving Zionist goals
	Preeminence of tactical considerations
	Final borders to be determined in the future
	Royal commission's proposal could be improved
Strong proponents: Support the principle of territorial separation	Partition would serve Jewish self-interest
	Partition would increase the prospects for Jewish-Arab coexistence
	Self-rule is more important than the size of the territory

A comparison of the positions of the proponents (Table 8.1) with the opponents (Table 6.1) indicates an important difference. Among the opponents there were political movements that rejected partition almost in their entirety. In the proponents' camp, on the other hand, we find divided parties and movements, especially Mapai and the General Zionist Federation. They were the two largest parties in the Zionist movement at that time and the political basis of most of the predominant leaders. This is why the proponents bore greater political weight and ultimately succeeded in forming a majority for their position. Another factor was the division of labor between Ben-Gurion and Weizmann: the former emphasized the importance of sovereignty for creating a place to absorb Jews, and the latter, the situation of the Jews who needed refuge. Both sensed the urgency, that some opportunities in political life do not recur and must be seized. There was no guarantee that the Zionist movement would again face the option of a Jewish state.

The partition debate formed a deep cleavage within the Zionist movement, between the "neinsager" (no sayers) and the "jasager" (yes sayers), despite which a decision was reached in 1937.

9   The Decision

Unanimity is not a precondition for action, action is taken in accordance with the majority resolution. There is a large majority resolution at the Congress—and the Executive acts in accordance with this resolution.[1]

The atmosphere at the opening of the Zionist congress in the Tonhalle in Zurich was festive and tense. The delegates were celebrating the fortieth anniversary of the First Zionist Congress in Basel, and for the first time in Zionist history, on the agenda was an official British proposal to establish a Jewish state. In his opening speech, Weizmann knew how to link the festive occasion and the proposed resolution: "Today we conclude forty years of wandering in the desert. Now we ask—is its end in sight? . . . I think I would hardly be exaggerating if I said that we are today facing a decisive turning point."[2]

The congress protocol, within the constraints of an official document, attempted to describe the tension and excitement of the delegates. This is evident even in the congratulatory telegrams read at the opening, which hinted at the difficult debate to come:

> . . . We will not budge from here. We will expand our boundaries. We will move eastward and southward. (telegram from Kibbutz Tirat Zvi)

> Accept our congratulations. We will concede no portion of the land in which years of work were invested to conquer it for the Hebrew people. (telegram from Yishuv Darom, Dead Sea)[3]

The polarized positions made the debate drawn out and painful, but the congress ultimately recorded a significant achievement by reaching a decision. This achievement was exceptional for several reasons. First, the debate did not proceed, of course, according to the systematic structure set out in the preceding chapters, although there was clearly a common denominator. Party lines were crossed, an attempt was made to respond to each other's arguments and convince one another. Some delegates even changed their positions as a result of the debate. In a political struggle of this kind, there is a tendency to ignore rival positions, but at the congress it seemed as if the delegates were laying out their arguments before the tribunal of history, in hopes of attaining a worthy decision. Second, the decision-making process in the Zionist movement was always very complex, reflecting the complicated organizational structure and a political culture that favored "understandings" and informal agreements over unequivocal decisions, which could be divisive. Third, the decision was made in a relatively short period of time, less than eight months after Weizmann's testimony before the royal commission in December 1936.

This chapter will discuss the decision itself and how the various arguments surveyed in the previous chapters were cast into a concrete resolution. The discussion will continue to focus on events internal to the Zionist movement, rather than its interaction with the other participants in the process: the British, the Arabs, the League of Nations, and other involved countries. The main questions are how the alternatives presented in Chapter Four became a resolution and how the participants overcame the deep internal schism on partition (see Figure 5.1) that surfaced upon publication of the commission report. To this end, we must first detail the texts of the decisions themselves, as well as the secondary decisions that preceded them.

The Main Resolutions

The most significant resolution, and in this case also the official one, was adopted at the "parliament" of the Zionist movement that convened in Zurich in August 1937. It was critically preceded by a resolution at the world council of the Labor movement (Union of Poalei Zion), which convened in Zurich just before the congress, even overlapping its deliberations. After the congress, the Jewish Agency council, the official body recognized in the mandatory charter, passed a resolution that was forwarded to the British government. We shall present the main passages from these resolutions concerning the royal commission's recommendations.

I. Resolution of the World Council of the Union of Poalei Zion—August 5, 1937[a]

(1) The Congress instructs the Executive to insist on the international recognition of the historic bonds between the people of Israel and the Land of Israel and on the full rights of the Hebrew people incorporated in the Mandate.

(2) The Congress empowers the Executive to conduct negotiations for the purpose of clarifying the specific content of the government's proposals concerning the establishment of a Jewish state in the Land of Israel.

(3) The Executive will present the results of the clarification to a newly elected Zionist Congress.

(4) Prior to this decision, the Executive is not authorized to commit or link the Zionist Organization to any plan or proposal that contradicts or impairs the Mandate.

II. Resolutions of the Twentieth Zionist Congress— August 11, 1937[b]

(1) The Twentieth Zionist Congress solemnly reaffirms the historic connection of the Jewish people with Palestine and its inalienable right to its homeland.

(2) The Congress takes note of the findings of the Palestine Royal Commission with regard to the following fundamental matters: first, that the primary purpose of the Mandate, as expressed in its preamble and in its articles, is to promote the establishment of the Jewish National Home; second, that the area in which the Jewish National Home is to be established was understood, at the time of the Balfour Declaration, to be the whole of historic Palestine, including Transjordan; third, that inherent in the Balfour Declaration was the possibility of the evolution of Palestine into a Jewish State; fourth, that Jewish settlement in Palestine has conferred substantial benefits on the Arab population and has been to the economic advantage of the Arabs as a whole.

(3) The Congress rejects the assertion of the Palestine Royal Commission that the Mandate has proved unworkable, and demands its fulfillment. The Congress directs the Executive to resist any infringement of the rights of the Jewish people internationally guaranteed by the Balfour Declaration and the Mandate.

(4) The Congress rejects the conclusion of the Royal Commission that the national aspirations of the Jewish people and

of the Arabs of Palestine are irreconcilable. The main obstacle to cooperation and mutual understanding between the two peoples has been the general uncertainty that, as stated in the Report of the Royal Commission, has prevailed in regard to the ultimate intentions of the Mandatory Government, and the vacillating attitude of the Palestine Administration; these have engendered a lack of confidence in the determination and the ability of the Government to implement the Mandate. The Congress reaffirms on this occasion the declarations of previous Congresses expressing the readiness of the Jewish people to reach a peaceful settlement with the Arabs of Palestine, based on the free development of both peoples and the mutual recognition of their respective rights.

(5) The Congress condemns the "palliative proposals" put forward by the Royal Commission as a policy for implementing the Mandate, such as curtailment of immigration, fixing of a political high-level in substitution for the principle of economic absorptive capacity, closing of certain parts of the country to Jewish settlement, limitations on the acquisition of land, etc. Those proposals are a travesty of the Mandate and a violation of international pledges, and would prove destructive of the future of the National Home.

(6) The Congress enters its strongest protest against the decision of His Majesty's Government to fix a political maximum for Jewish immigration of all categories for the next eight months, thus sweeping away the principle of economic absorptive capacity, in violation of Jewish rights and of the undertakings repeatedly given in this regard by His Majesty's Government and confirmed by the League of Nations.

(7) The Congress declares that the scheme put forward by the Royal Commission is unacceptable.

(8) The Congress empowers the Executive to enter into negotiations with a view to ascertaining the precise terms of His Majesty's Government for the proposed establishment of a Jewish State.

(9) In such negotiations the Executive shall not commit either itself or the Zionist Organisation, but in the event of the emergence of a definite scheme for the establishment of a Jewish State, such scheme shall be brought before a newly elected Congress for decision.

III. From the Resolution of the Fifth Jewish Agency Council—August 21, 1937[c]

(1) The Fifth Jewish Agency Council session accepts for consideration the policy resolution that was passed by the Twentieth Zionist Congress and expresses its agreement with its main conclusions.

(2) The Council rejects the Royal Commission's conclusion that the Mandate for Eretz Israel cannot be implemented. The Council instructs the Executive to oppose any infringement on the rights of the Jewish people as they were pledged and internationally guaranteed by the Balfour Declaration and the Mandate . . .

(3) The Council reaffirms the declarations that were accepted at its previous meetings and that expressed readiness to reach a peace agreement with the Arabs of Eretz Israel on the basis of assured freedom of development to the two peoples, Jewish and Arab, and of mutual recognition of their rights. The Council instructs the Executive to continue its efforts in this direction and for this purpose to request that His Royal Majesty's government convene a joint conference of Jews and Arabs of Eretz Israel in order to examine the possibilities of attaining a peace agreement between the Jews and Arabs within and for an unpartitioned Land of Israel on the basis of the Balfour Declaration and the Mandate.

(4) The Council sees no possibility of accepting partition as proposed by the Royal Commission, and empowers the Executive to enter into negotiations in order to determine the precise conditions of His Royal Majesty's government for establishing the proposed Jewish state. In these negotiations, the Executive is not authorized to obligate itself or the Jewish Agency. If a specific plan for the establishment of a Jewish state can be concluded as a result of these negotiations, the Executive must bring this plan before a special session of the Council for examination and decision.

[a]*Paths of Our Policy*, 1938, p. 219.
[b]Protocol of the Twentieth Zionist Congress, pp. 201–202. The text is an official translation of the resolution to English and is slightly different from the Hebrew text.
[c]Protocol of the Fifth Council of the Jewish Agency, 1937, p. 79.

Within two weeks, the majority coalition of the Labor movement, the largest and dominant faction in the Zionist Organization and expanded Jewish Agency, passed a resolution that enabled consideration of the partition of western Eretz Israel, or at least forestalled its outright rejection. The resolution of the Labor movement was accepted unanimously, except for paragraph 3 (postponing the final decision to a newly elected Zionist Congress), which was accepted by a majority of ninety-seven to sixty-three. This paved the way for similar resolutions at the congress and Jewish Agency council. The editor of the protocol summarized the Labor movement resolutions in the following introduction:

> And thus, once again, our movement's character asserted itself: its great moral force, the deep rootedness of the feeling of unity impressed within it, and the awareness of its great responsibility to the fate of the entire liberation movement. After eight days of strenuous ideological struggle in our council, its political resolutions were adopted almost unanimously and served as a guiding path to the Zionist congress and a basis for its resolutions.[4]

The "double formula" is repeated in different combinations in all three resolutions: insistence on continuation of the mandate and the rights contained therein, and a parallel expression of willingness to negotiate with the British government on the basis of the royal commission's proposals. This is the most important point, but there were a number of differences between the resolutions. First, the Labor movement's resolution includes no declaration rejecting the royal commission's specific proposal. Characteristically, "partition" is not mentioned at all, and the emphasis is on the decision-making procedure. Second, the congress resolution attempts to accommodate the "opponents" on the declarative level. Indeed, the opponents could easily accept all the clauses in this resolution, other than paragraph 8, which grants authority to the executive to discuss partition. Kaplansky, who presented the majority proposal to the congress, tried to placate the opponents by saying that the difference between the majority and the minority "is not the difference between the proponents and opponents of partition."[5]

Third, the Jewish Agency's resolution adopted the congress resolution, but inserted an additional paragraph, at the behest of the non-Zionists, concerning the need to reach a peace agreement with the Arabs of Eretz Israel.[6] This is the only clause in the resolutions that does not address solely the British government, but also implies recognition of the Arabs as a party to the matter. The mention of the Arab community of Eretz Israel in paragraph 4 of the congress resolution is utterly different because it does not instruct the executive to act to reach an agreement with the Arabs. The Jewish Agency's resolution does contain explicit recognition of the freedom of development of the Arabs of Eretz Israel and their rights, but not their political rights. This resolution also added a request to convene a joint conference of Jews and Arabs "to examine the possibilities of attaining a peace agreement" between them, a meeting that did take place in 1939, but by then not in connection with the partition plan.

Although the non-Zionists in the Jewish Agency hoped to prevent a pro-partition resolution, they left feeling that they had achieved a declaration concerning the need to reach an agreement between the Jews and Arabs, and that they had "stopped the rush toward partition, at least temporarily."[7] On the other subjects, the Jewish Agency resolutions echo those of the congress, including the restrictions on the executive's negotiations with the British. This closed the circle that began with the unwritten alliance between Weizmann and Ben-Gurion to advance the possibility of establishing a sovereign Jewish state, even at the cost of accepting the idea of partition. Both decisions, however, amount to an official authorization of the executive to conduct negotiations with the British government. To evaluate the significance of this authorization, it should be contrasted with the following minority resolution that was rejected by the Congress:

---

1. The Twentieth Zionist Congress notes the conclusions of the Royal Commission for Eretz Israel in the following basic matters:

(a) That the principal goal of the Mandate, as it was defined in its preamble and clauses, is to facilitate the establishment of the Jewish national home;

(b) That in the Balfour Declaration, all of the territory of the historic Eretz Israel was intended for the establishment of the Jewish national home;

(c) That the idea of the development of Eretz Israel into a state or Jewish commonwealth was included a priori within the purpose of the Balfour Declaration and the Mandate;

(d) That the return of the widest Jewish masses to their homelands was effected while bringing important beliefs to the Arabs of Eretz Israel and while strictly protecting their civil and religious rights.

2. The Congress rejects as baseless the Royal Commission's claims that the Mandate cannot be realized and that cooperation between Jews and Arabs to the benefit of the entire land cannot be realized, and expresses its deep conviction that it is not the Mandate that failed, but rather the Palestine Administration, a view also expressed in the Royal Commission report.

3. The Congress rejects just as decidedly the two political alternatives proposed by the Royal Commission: The partition of Eretz Israel, on the one hand, and on the other, the "palliatives" that are intended to prevent economic advancement and delay the development of the national home.

4. The declaration of the new policy of His Majesty's government is intended to fulfill the Royal Commission's proposals concerning the partition plan as follows:

(a) Cancellation of the Mandate for Eretz Israel and disavowal of the Balfour Declaration;

(b) Dissecting Eretz Israel into pieces;

(c) Allocating the lion's share of Eretz Israel to a new Arab state;

(d) Transferring several parts of it to permanent British administration;

(e) Establishing a Jewish state in the western part of Eretz Israel under conditions that do not ensure the satisfaction of vital political, economic and strategic requirements, and that do not take into account the essential needs for the immigration of the widest masses of the Jewish people.

The Twentieth Zionist Congress regards these proposals as a breach of the commitments that were given to the Jewish people before the entire world. The Congress solemnly declares that it unequivocally opposes partition of the land and that it is prepared to oppose it vigorously and with all the means at its disposal, because the inalienable rights of the Jewish people to its historic homeland cannot be abrogated by any signature; and because any plan for partition of Eretz Israel cannot serve as a basis for negotiations on the new policy in Eretz Israel.

5. The Congress instructs the Executive to stand firm on the solid ground of the rights and achievements of the Jewish

people in Eretz Israel, which once again were awarded recognition and full legitimacy in the Royal Commission report. In addition, the Congress calls on the Executive to redouble its efforts to force the Mandatory government into a constructive policy for the realization of the Mandate by the Mandatory government and for the revival of the Jewish people in their historic homeland.

Source: Protocol of the Twentieth Zionist Congress, pp. 205–206.

The fundamental difference was that the minority proposal, unlike the majority resolution, unequivocally opposed any partition. It even contained a veiled threat: that the right to Eretz Israel cannot be voided by any signature whatsoever, even, it hints, if this signature is that of the authorized Jewish leadership. The second difference is that the congress resolution empowers the executive to conduct negotiations with the British to clarify the royal commission's proposal. This compromise formula allowed the two sides at the congress not to make too sharp a decision, under the assumption that the final resolution was delayed. The adopted resolution, which instructed the executive not to make any final commitment during the negotiations, was the main concession of the proponents, which allowed the undecided and some of the opponents to concur. It allowed Berl Katznelson and others to vote for the majority proposal, while continuing to maintain that they did not accept the idea of partition because

- The Executive was authorized only to *clarify*;
- The clarification pertains only to the specific content of the British government proposal to establish a Jewish state. That is, not to the partition proposal but rather to the sovereignty proposal;
- The final decision would be made at the next congress.

Conversely, the minority proposal makes no attempt at compromise. It decisively rejects both partition of Eretz Israel, even detailing the reasons for this (paragraph 4), and the premise that the British proposals provide some basis for negotiations on a new policy for Palestine. The alternative proposed by the minority was that the Zionist executive act "to force the Mandatory government

Table 9.1   Faction Votes at the Twentieth Zionist Congress
Regarding the Royal Commission's Recommendations

	MAJORITY PROPOSAL	MINORITY PROPOSAL	ABSTENTIONS	TOTAL
Mapai (including KM)	181	—	1	182
Hashomer Hatzair	—	23	—	23
General Zionist Federation	79	20	4	103
General Zionist Union	10	28	1	39
Mizrahi and Hapoel Hamizrahi	—	66	—	66
State Party	—	9	—	9
Others	18	6	—	24
Subtotal	288	152	6	446
Unclear	11	8	—	19
Total Votes	299	160	6	465

Note: According to the protocol of the twentieth congress, there were 484
delegates. According to the official calling of the vote, 465 delegates voted,
of whom only 446 delegates were identified by their vote and faction
membership. Ben-Gurion quotes slightly different numbers regarding the
majority proposal: 300 in favor, 158 against and 30 abstentions or
absences. Ben-Gurion, 1971–1982, vol. 4, p. 420.

into a constructive policy for the realization of the Mandate" (paragraph 5). It should be pointed out, however, that for the opponents,
such as the New Zionist Organization, the Congress resolution was
perceived as an in-principle Jewish agreement to the "amputation
of their land," because the resolution did not reject any discussion
of partition outright.[8] Similarly, opponents in Hashomer Hatzair
also interpreted the congress resolution as an endorsement of the
idea of partition.[9]

    We will now focus on the congress resolution, and compare it
to the initial division of the positions upon publication of the royal
commission's report and before the decision. Table 9.1 summarizes
the parties' votes at the Congress as recorded in the protocol.

    The decisive majority assembled by Ben-Gurion and the other
proponents in the Labor movement, together with Weizmann's support in the Zionist Organization, resulted in acceptance of the congress resolution by a 64 percent majority, nearly two-thirds of the

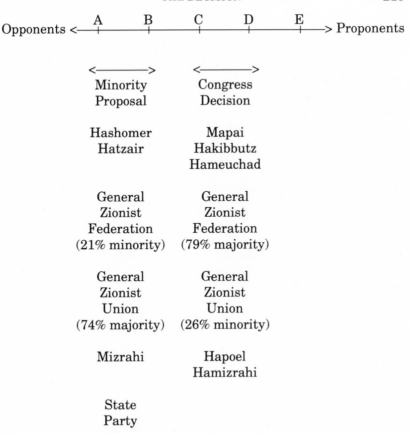

Figure 9.1 The Votes at the Twentieth Zionist Congress

voters. However, had the opponents within Mapai (approximately sixty delegates) and a few more General Zionists voted in favor of the minority proposal at the congress, the proponents would not have had a clear majority. Moreover, acceptance of the majority proposal by a small margin would have been a defeat for Weizmann and Ben-Gurion's leadership and for the policy that the executive had followed since the beginning of 1937. If the congress delegates had been asked to adopt or reject the partition proposal as it was, the forces would have been evenly divided or tended toward opposition. It should nevertheless be emphasized that the minority resolution was explicitly rejected by the Congress because it was too extreme for the undecided, and even for some of the moderate opponents.

Figure 9.1 presents the breakdown of voting at the Congress according to factions. Comparison with Figure 5.1 indicates how the positions of the various factions changed after publication of the commission report in July 1937. Even considering that an open and noncommittal public debate differs from a vote, namely, that the need to vote at the congress forced delegates to adopt much clearer stands, the fact remains that the positions changed significantly.

First, the Mapai representatives, whose initial positions at the time of the report's publication covered the entire range of the continuum, converged at the time of the vote around the compromise formula. Of course, the Mapai members' vote was also influenced by party considerations. They feared that a victory by the opponents would damage Ben-Gurion and Shertok's leadership as well as the party's dominant standing in the Zionist Organization.

Second, all members of Hakibbutz Hameuchad voted for the resolution, with the exception of one. Of all the factions at the Congress, they made the longest journey from a position of fundamental and ideological opposition (A) to a vote that amounted to qualified support (D), even though they themselves did not interpret their vote in this way.

Third, ST, which was part of the World Labor Movement, did not support the compromise. Its ideological opposition to partition and the establishment of an exclusive Jewish state remained steadfast. There was no difference between its preliminary position and its vote at the Congress.

Fourth, most of the delegates in the two General Zionist streams remained firm in their positions. A large majority of the Federation supported Weizmann and voted in favor of the resolution at the Congress, but approximately 20 percent voted for the minority proposal. The Union was also divided. Despite Ussishkin's attempt to enforce a uniform vote, 26 percent voted in favor of the majority proposal.

Fifth, neither Mizrahi nor the State Party changed its fundamental opposition; both voted unanimously against. But the representatives of Hapoel Hamizrahi, who were part of the World Mizrahi movement, were absent from the vote, thereby expressing their opposition to the minority proposal.

The Congress resolution is therefore located between (C) and (D), between the undecided and the moderate proponents. Although the resolution's wording included a declaration of "the historic connection of the Jewish people with Eretz Israel," the political message of the resolution was entirely pragmatic. The minority proposal is located between (A) and (B), and it is a fundamentally expressive position even though it also includes many instrumental arguments. Ben-Gurion summarized the congress resolution in his diary: "Today the internal battle ended. 300 versus 158 voted in favor of empowering the Executive to conduct negotiations for the establishment of a state . . . all of our 'opponents' were among the 'proponents' except for Idelson, who abstained. Therefore we should not interpret the entire support of the proponents of negotiations as a vote in favor of the state."[10]

How should the vote be interpreted? On exactly what was the executive empowered to conduct negotiations with the British government? According to the strict wording of the resolution, the negotiations would concern the establishment of a Jewish state and not partition. However, because the only relevant proposal then on the agenda linked the establishment of a Jewish state to partition, it was obvious that the mere readiness to negotiate implied acceptance of the partition *principle*. This is the political significance of the congress resolution, even though some of the opponents disagreed, as we will see later. The other interpretation, that the congress resolution rejected the concept of partition, is grounded neither in the political reality in 1937 nor in the text.[11] Had this been the intention, then the minority resolution would have been adopted stating that the congress "unequivocally opposes partition of the land."

In contrast, the adopted resolution rejects the specific territorial proposal of the royal commission, but it does not rule out partition. It demands only that the executive not make any commitments and that it bring the final decision to the next congress. Therefore, in August 1937, a majority of the Zionist movement was prepared to accept responsibility for the establishment of a sovereign Jewish state even in return for territorial concessions. The full importance of this decision can be measured only in consideration of the significant weight of the opposition.

The Opposition

Each of the parties that participated in the congress included representatives who opposed the idea of partition, including leaders at the highest echelon. Leaders from outside the World Zionist Organization—the Revisionists, the non-Zionists in the Jewish Agency, Poalei Zion-Smol, the Communists, Kedma Mizraha, and some of Agudat Israel—were also among the opponents. All of Mapai's delegates voted for the majority proposal at the congress, but the opponents among them did so because they interpreted it as a postponement of the decision and because they rejected the extreme minority resolution. The strength of the opposition indeed derived from the moderate opponents to partition.

At the Zionist general council meeting of April 1937, Ussishkin referred to the Uganda debate at the beginning of the century, thus hinting at the possibility of a serious schism within the Zionist movement. The public campaign of the opponents and the silence of the proponents, but mainly the leadership's official rejection of the report, prepared Jewish public opinion before the congress to oppose the royal commission's plan. We have also seen that the declarations of many parties and other bodies strongly expressed opposition to partition.

The opponents began to organize upon publication of the commission's report in July 1937. Ussishkin played a central role, due both to his vehement opposition and his personal reputation. He tried to convene a conference of the opponents in Eretz Israel even before the delegates left for the congress, but Berl Katznelson opposed the idea and was only prepared to establish a "Liaison Committee."[12] Cooperation with the Revisionist party was also proposed, but this was strongly opposed by the Mapai members. The founding meeting of the "Opposition Front" took place only on August 10 in Zurich, on the eve of the congress resolution. According to reports, 150 representatives from all the parties participated in the meeting. They included practically all those who subsequently voted for the minority proposal. To make their presence felt, they decided to continue their activities after the Congress and elected a presidium of distinguished representatives from all the parties, a political and geographic expansion (from Eretz Israel and the diaspora) of the Opposition Front.[13] Concurrently, the Revisionist movement initiated an organization of the opponents in cooperation with the State Party to strengthen the position of the nay sayers outside the Zionist Organization.[14]

Despite its organization and public support, the Opposition Front failed at the congress, even though it enlisted one-third of the delegates in favor of the minority proposal. As noted earlier, the main reason for this was that the moderate opponents and the undecided within Mapai and the General Zionists voted for the majority compromise proposal. This was more of a victory for the leadership than a failure of the opposition.

But efforts by the opponents did not end there. A short time after the vote, sixty of them submitted a protest memorandum to the congress administration after the official newspaper of the congress printed a statement that the adopted resolution implied agreement to partition.[15] The opponents published a counterdeclaration in the congress newspaper, pointing out that the essence of the resolution lay in delaying the decision until the next elected congress. Thus began a new debate over interpretation of the congress resolution, which continued for one year, until partition was buried by the Woodhead report in October 1938. Two of the main questions in this new debate were inextricably linked: Had the idea of partition been accepted? And exactly what was the executive authorized to conduct negotiations about? Ben-Gurion expressed his position in this regard:

> There were two things at the Congress: (A) The decision that was rejected. (B) The decision that was accepted. That which was rejected . . . said that the Zionist movement would not discuss anything connected with partition of the land; and that the Zionist movement would only support a policy of maintaining the Mandate. This is a very clear position; it defines what it rejects and what it desires. . . . But the fact is that this proposal was rejected. The second fact—that a resolution was adopted at the Congress and that resolution does not mean agreement in principle to establishing a Hebrew state on the basis of partition of the land . . . [meaning] that the Executive must do everything it can so that the next Congress will be able to choose one of these two: either the Mandate or a state based on partition.[16]

Weizmann had a similar explanation: The Congress instructed them "to do everything so that the proposal for a state would be the best. The question itself would be decided at the next Congress."[17] But there were other interpretations of the resolution. The strong proponents emphasized that the idea of partition was not rejected outright. Although the Executive was authorized to negotiate only a "specific proposal" for establishing a Jewish state, practically the only matter being considered was the possibility of a state based on partition. This meant that partition was a fact and that the negotiations were intended to extricate a better territorial proposal than that proposed by the royal commission.[18] This was in fact the position presented by the Zionist executive in its discussions with the British government.[19]

The strong opponents—those outside the Zionist Organization and those who voted for the minority resolution at the congress— offered a similar interpretation. They maintained that the executive had effectively agreed to the royal commission's proposal and that it might agree to something even worse. Therefore, when the congress empowered the executive to enter into negotiations, it had in fact authorized agreement to partition and the forgoing of the mandate.

Some opponents maintained that the executive was not authorized to conduct negotiations on partition, only on independence,[20] or only to conduct "passive" negotiations—to hear the British government's proposal and relay it to the Zionist bodies,[21] or not make any commitments that would "tie the hands" of the Zionist movement.[22] For still others, the significance of the congress resolution lay in opposition to the specific partition proposal of the royal commission, leaving all other options open, including the executive's ability to oppose the proposal to establish a Jewish state.[23] The range of opinion concerning interpretation of the congress resolution is more indicative than a fine analysis of the resolution text itself. Obviously, each faction tried to interpret the resolution according to its own position, but one fact strengthens our conclusion that the congress did indeed make a decision. The strong proponents and the strong opponents maintained that the resolution adopted the partition principle; the moderates on both sides and the undecided maintained that the matter remained open. No one claimed, however, that the resolution *rejected* the idea of partition outright.

The Decision-Making Process

In terms of the choices that confronted the decision makers (Figure 4.2), the significance of the congress resolution was that a majority in the Zionist movement answered positively the series of questions placed on the agenda by the royal commission's report. They expressed willingness to establish a Jewish state immediately, even at the cost of partition, without rigid preconditions. They also showed a clear preference for a pragmatic policy based on tactical considerations. Did this willingness also pertain to the specific proposal of the royal commission? On the one hand, the congress resolution clearly rejected the proposal. The issue was never raised even as a decision of last resort. On the other hand, the official Jewish Agency delegation to the Woodhead commission was willing to accept a relatively small territorial addition (less than 1000 km^2) to the original partition proposal.

Lack of Consensus

The decision-making process was influenced by the brevity of the period in which the positions about the partition principle were formulated. The Arab revolt in Palestine that began in 1936 created a sense of crisis and the need to reevaluate previous positions. The readiness of the royal commission to propose the establishment of a Jewish state nevertheless came as a surprise. When it became clear that the trade-off would be partition, the Jews initially reacted with shock, strong abhorrence, and rejection. At this point, even before publication of the report, serious discussion began among the leadership, the parties, and the attentive public, revealing deep differences between the opponents and proponents. At the time of publication of the report, the main bodies were divided internally, with a certain advantage to the opponents (see Figure 5.1).

On the eve of the congress, it was still unclear what the decision would be. Ben-Gurion, the main architect of the internal coalition supporting the partition principle, was very anxious about the pending outcome. In his diary, he wrote that Weizmann's position at the congress would be most difficult. He also sent an uncompromising letter to Shertok demanding that every member of their own party must adopt a *clear* position on the question of partition, hinting that otherwise he might resign:

> I do not know what will take place at the Congress. But I consider myself absolutely obligated, at our movement's first gathering at Zurich, to present a sharp and clear choice: yes or no!
>
> If Yitzhak [Tabenkin's] position is accepted—I will submit to it. And the members who believe in this will be our representatives. . . . I am willing to take upon myself our movement's political mission—but on the condition of clear and decisive support.[24]

When they arrived in Zurich, Mapai's central leaders were not certain of the decision, mainly because it was difficult to foresee the mood of the congress. Fifty-six delegates participated in the debate on partition at the congress: twenty-nine spoke against and twenty-seven in favor. It was evident that the major parties were themselves divided: Among the opposing speakers were six from the General Zionist Federation, five from the General Zionist Union, and five from Mapai. Therefore, when the congress convened, the initial conditions were lack of consensus and division within all the relevant circles: the diaspora concerned with the Zionist enterprise, the Zionist movement, the leadership, the main parties, and public opinion. Accordingly, the resolution itself, particularly one based on a slim majority, threatened the unity of the movement. Some of the opponents explicitly raised the threat of a split, recalling painful precedents, such as the secession of the Revisionists from the Zionist Organization.

Compromise

Five days after he wrote to Shertok in such a forceful manner, a complete turn occurred in Ben-Gurion's position. He abandoned his confrontational tone and the demand that each member of the movement make an unequivocal choice and began to outline the compromise formula: "Regarding partition—the Congress need not yet say either 'no' or 'yes,' but it must authorize the new Executive to discuss with the government revisions in the Commission's proposal."[25]

When the Labor movement convened, Ben-Gurion was still uncertain whether Katznelson and Tabenkin would support the compromise. The former remained "doubtful" and, as to the latter, fear of a split increased when Ben-Gurion was told that "the opponents to partition will not accept the majority decision—if the majority will favor partition."[26] Eventually, the compromise both in the Labor movement and at the congress was, above all, a masterpiece of delicate and carefully conceived draftsmanship. It included, as noted, the "double formula" (continuation of the mandate and improvement of the partition proposal) plus a concession by the majority: to bring the final decision before the next congress. Also a significant compromise was made regarding substance: First, the position expressed in the congress resolution situates it not far from the center of the continuum, between (C) and (D) in Figure 9.1. This formula facilitated support by the undecided and a large portion of the moderate opponents. Second, the resolution refrained from any determination concerning the final territorial and boundary requirements of the Jewish state. Ben-Gurion promised, and many understood, that this matter remained open for decision by future generations. The significance of the compromise was later summed up by Berl Katznelson: "The dual decision in Zurich—that many do not agree with and many did not understand—was the only possible Zionist decision."[27]

The Coalition

Two overlapping coalitions ensured the majority decision at the congress. The first was within the Labor movement and its

Figure 9.2. Schematic Structure of the Leadership's Process of Coalition Building in 1937.

main architects were Ben-Gurion and Shertok. The second was within the Zionist movement and the Jewish Agency, at whose center stood Weizmann (see Figure 9.2).

The Labor movement coalition was built slowly and in a pattern of widening, concentric circles. As we showed in Chapter Three, Ben-Gurion first floated the idea of partition within his party at a meeting of the Mapai central committee in February 1937. In the second important round, held at the central committee meeting in April, he failed to pass a clear decision in favor of partition, but the resolution that "Mapai would oppose all proposals for partition of the land" was rejected by a majority. Out of this general "no" grew the seeds of the eventual "yes." The third round took place in a wider public forum, the Mapai council convention in early July 1937, and the resolution adopted there (see Chapter Five) is of great significance for what it contains, what it omits, and its ambiguity:[28]

- The resolution did recognize the "allure" of the royal commission's proposal "which purports to speak in the name of the Jewish state." But the party rejected it because the proposal itself was none other than "abuse of the idea of the Jewish state and its depletion."

- It contained the rudiments of the double formula, even though Ben-Gurion was not one of its formulators, calling on the British government to fulfill its obligations to the Jewish people by establishing the national home.

• It responded to the opponents of a "state now" by emphasizing that the aspiration to establish a Jewish state is not based only on the desire for artificial prestige, trappings of statehood, and honorary titles, but rather for resolving the Jewish problem.

• It recoiled from the "territorial stress," recalling that the first surgery took place already in 1922, when the removal of Transjordan reduced the territory of the original mandate from its original 60,000 km². Now, only one-fifth of the remaining territory was under consideration.

The Mapai council resolution rejected the specific partition plan of the royal commission, but did not close the door on attempts to improve it. It made no mention of rejecting the partition principle. This obfuscation in the party's broadest forum created the basis for the compromise formula in the Labor movement, in accordance with which all of its members (excluding ST) subsequently voted at the congress. In 1937, the representatives of the Labor movement constituted 45 percent of the total delegates at the Twentieth Zionist Congress, and their vote was decisive.

Although Mapai never had an absolute majority, its clear hegemony in the coalition and leadership positions, which would continue for more than forty years, was determined by two additional facts. First, the second largest party was very far from threatening Mapai's position. Second, Mapai controlled the pivotal coalition position and, practically, the parties to its left and right could not form a coalition without it. This created the pattern that was to rule Zionist and Israeli politics for many years: no resolution could be passed without Mapai, but Mapai had neither the majority nor the inclination to decide alone. The Zionist and Jewish Agency executives always relied on a coalition of several parties. Accordingly, the greatest achievement represented by the 1937 resolution was that Ben-Gurion and Shertok managed to consolidate the full support of their movement. This endorsement, supplemented by Weizmann's support in the General Zionist factions, created the two-thirds majority in favor of the congress resolution.

The coalition-building process outside the Labor movement was segmented and less critical to the final resolution. Weizmann was not very active in the party arena and did not have the full support of his own party—the General Zionist Federation, of whom

20 percent voted for the minority proposal. Nevertheless, Weizmann's leadership of the overall Zionist movement was then uncontested, and a large majority of the delegates supported him regardless of their party affiliation. Weizmann's speeches at the congress had a direct impact on the votes of many delegates, particularly the undecided.

The absolute support for the resolution in the Jewish Agency council must also be credited mainly to Weizmann.[29] The council was composed of half Zionist delegates (representatives of the Zionist Organization) and about half non-Zionists (who were chosen by their communal institutions). Ninety-four Zionists and eighty-nine non-Zionists participated in the Fifth Jewish Agency Council Meeting in Zurich in 1937. In effect, there could have been a majority against the resolution had the non-Zionists, most of whom opposed partition, combined with the Zionist opponents of partition. As noted, Philip Warburg led the non-Zionist opponents of partition and came to Zurich with an ultimatum against empowering the executive to negotiate with the British government for the establishment of a Jewish state, or else they would resign.[30] Weizmann's conciliatory stance toward Warburg on the matters of representation in the Jewish Agency executive paved the way for a political compromise. Consequently, the proposed resolution was unanimously adopted at the Jewish Agency Council Meeting, except for paragraph 4, which was passed with thirteen delegates abstaining.[31]

Just as it is important to identify those who were included in the widening circles of the resolution coalition, it is important to recall those who remained outside. On the Right, all the religious delegates of the Mizrahi party opposed the resolution, whereas the Socialist delegates of ST were their equivalent on the Left. The opposition of these parties to the 1937 resolution was politically very significant because they were part of the coalition that led the Yishuv and the Zionist movement. Other important opponents represented various parties, including leaders who were members of the Zionist general council. They also had allies outside the Zionist Organization, such as the Revisionists and some of the non-Zionists in the Jewish Agency. Accordingly, although the coalition assembled around the decision was strong numerically and in terms of the support of the major parties, the opponents included not only the "defectors" of the New Zionist Organization or small groups like Kedma Mizraha, but also bodies wielding significant weight within the Zionist movement.

This fact further emphasizes the criticality of the congress decision in terms of patterns of political action. It was, as we have said, a majority resolution adopted without initial consensus and facing the threat that it would split the leading parties of the Zionist movement and the Jewish Agency. The political achievement of the leaders who supported the partition principle was that they did not hesitate to present the matter for decision despite the danger of division. An additional achievement was in finding a compromise formula acceptable to a sizeable majority and in the ability to reach a decision that did not cause the minority to withdraw. Nevertheless, Ben-Gurion was firm in his willingness to be satisfied with merely a majority resolution: "I would under no condition be ready to sacrifice the state on the altar of peace [within the Zionist movement]."[32]

In retrospect, the unofficial alliance between Weizmann and Ben-Gurion granted the coalition its essential leadership. The argument among researchers as to which of the two was the "father of the partition plan" misses the point: There was an effective division of labor between them despite the personal rivalry that, rather than dissipating, would actually grow stronger in the future. Moreover, the adoption of such a critical decision via a majority resolution in the largest representative bodies, the congress and the Jewish Agency council, contributed to the democratic character of the Zionist movement.

The Option of Nondecision

"This state of yours is a mirage," Winston Churchill told Weizmann at that famous meal in June 1937 at which they discussed the royal commission's proposal. Likewise, many opponents demanded that the decision be delayed as long as possible—some because they were undecided and some because they believed that time, if not improving the situation, would at least help improve the decision. Meanwhile, they argued, certain important points would be clarified: Are the British serious in their intentions? Would the Arab opposition undermine the proposal? Could the proposal be significantly improved from a territorial point of view? What would be the extent of the sovereignty to be granted to the Jewish state and, in particular, would it control immigration?

There were additional arguments in favor of the understandable tendency to stall for time: the fear of internal division in the Zionist movement; and the desire to force the "other side" (mainly the British, but also the Arabs) to show their cards first, because implementation of the plan was not in Jewish hands. This was the implicit tendency of the Zionist general council's conclusions in June 1937, as Shertok wrote in his diary:

Outward resolutions: Opposition to a reduction in the territorial size of the Jewish national home, whether by partition, cantonization or any other way.

Internal resolutions: Authorization of the Executive to do everything in its power to ensure that any resolution proposed by the [Royal] Commission and adopted by the government would be as little damaging as possible and—under prevailing conditions—be the most advantageous to Jewish concerns.[33]

The opposition of Weizmann, Ben-Gurion, and Shertok to any postponement of the decision was consistent with their approach to the dynamic nature of political processes. On the one hand, they believed that unequivocal endorsement of the partition proposal would harm its chances of realization and turn the "Peel map" into the minimum demands of the Arabs. On the other hand, they regarded the idea of trying to gain time as equivalent to saying "no." Postponing the decision would not defeat the partition proposal, but a delay, they feared, might pave the way for the worst possibility of all, an end to the mandate and establishment of an Arab state in the entire territory of Eretz Israel. Politics allows one to stall for time when there is a reasonable chance of improved results. But, as these leaders read the reality, the probability of worse alternatives was actually greater, such as deterioration of the mandate provisions, which would suffocate the Zionist enterprise and prevent a solution to Jewish distress in Europe. They therefore proposed a third alternative—neither opposing partition nor delaying the decision, but instead negotiating on the basis of a qualified "yes." Their main goal was to tie the British to the commitment, uttered publicly for the first time, to establish a Jewish state. Obviously, they wanted the British to offer a more generous territorial proposal and preferred secret negotiations with the government over unilateral publication of the plan by the prestigious royal commission. However, once the British step had been taken, the leaders struggled against the great temptation to build a wide consensus around a decision "not to decide," and thus avoid the great internal difficulties. Characteristically, they preferred involvement with an opportunity to affect events to passivity with no chance of having an influence. For Shertok, saying "no" or delaying the decision meant "that we would condemn ourselves to impotence and lack of any influence."[34] And for Weizmann, "Sometimes you have to want what is possible when it is impossible to attain what you want."[35]

Secrecy

The 1937 partition debate was public and encompassed all of the parties and other bodies. Nevertheless, the formula that evolved as a solution to the painful dilemma enlisted two proven political techniques in decision-making processes. The first was what Shertok labeled as *outward as opposed to internal resolutions.* In the conclusions of the Zionist general council presented earlier, for example, the "internal" portion was adopted by the political committee and was not mentioned in the plenum. This technique was also used in the private testimonies before the royal commission, the discreet connection with commission member Coupland and the secret contacts between Weizmann and Colonial Secretary Ormsby-Gore. To this end, the plenum at the Zionist congress was declared a closed "Political Committee" meeting during the debate on partition, allowing participation by all the delegates but without a public audience or the press. The contents of these deliberations were leaked, but an effort was made to conceal the internal disagreements without limiting the number of participants in the discussion itself.

The second technique was that decisions were made at the very last minute, both to enhance secrecy and to create the appropriate psychological pressure. The outstanding example of this is the decision adopted by the Labor movement after the congress deliberations had already started.

The Decision: Instrumental Pragmatism

The process that led to a decision at the congress was so tortuous, and the formulation of the resolution so irresolute, that Colonial Secretary Ormsby-Gore, who had been kept informed, expressed disdain when he heard the resolution. As expected, he was annoyed by that part of the resolution calling for continuation of the mandate.[36] Nevertheless, he had no doubt that Weizmann had delivered on his word and that the congress resolution would enable progress toward realization of partition. How can it be explained that a movement as ideological as Zionism took such a pragmatic decision?[37]

This can be attributed to both the weak position of Zionism at that time, which dictated absolute dependence on Britain; and to its strength, which drove the movement to stick to its main goal—the establishment of a state—even at the expense of other goals. Thus the decision was a mixture of dependence and firmness and of revolutionary fervor and political soberness. This fusion was also, as noted, the political hallmark of Weizmann, Ben-Gurion, and Shertok. Weizmann's realism stemmed from being essentially "nonideological," in the European terminology of the day, and from representing the "general Zionists," as he and his associates called themselves before circumstances forced them to form a party. Striving to establish a Jewish state stood at the center of his spiritual and practical world.

By contrast, Ben-Gurion defined himself as a socialist—even a radical one, initially, before the establishment of Mapai. But Ben-Gurion was above all a national Zionist, and a Zionist-socialist in that order. When the two conflicted, such as over the question of partition, which meant separating Jewish and Arab "workers," he rejected the "socialist solutions" of the Left-wing parties, adhering to Weizmann's brand of political Zionism.

It is important to stress again Berl Katznelson's contribution in this context. As Shertok pointed out, Katznelson won the opponents' support for the joint resolution by cooling the excitement of the proponents. As a result, the decision bears the opponents' imprint, what we defined as qualified support, located between positions (C) and (D) on the continuum. Katznelson was more ideological and more socialist then either Weizmann or Ben-Gurion. But Katznelson was also an intellectual involved in practical politics, and as such he was highly pragmatic. We will recall that in his opposition to partition, which was not a matter of principle, Katznelson usually avoided using the purely ideological reasoning of the socialist Left or the religious fundamental arguments of the Right. Because Katznelson's hesitation stemmed from political considerations, he was able to share the responsibility for formulating a politically oriented compromise resolution encompassing a qualified support of partition.

Indeed, many congress delegates were unsure about how to vote. The general atmosphere in the conference hall wavered back and forth until the institutional resolution of the Labor movement (excluding ST), in favor of qualified support, turned the tide. Beyond the personal contributions of the leaders, this was also the first time that Mapai stood at the center of such a critical decision in the Zionist movement, and the decision bears the pragmatic imprint that would further develop in Mapai throughout the years. The Arab revolt of 1936–1939 and the shift of the Zionist political activity from London to Eretz Israel strengthened this orientation in Mapai, as it began to bear responsibility for the leadership of the national institutions. One of its central patterns, of which Ben-Gurion was a principal designer, was avoiding the pursuit of declarative policies, particularly policies based on a passive or self-righteous stand. Of course, extreme declarations were made for external bargaining and mobilizing internal support, but they did not crystallize into maximal positions in the actual policy-making process. It is not by chance that the central motif of Ben-Gurion's speech in the Labor movement council was "We are not helpless."[38] The instrumental pragmatism reflected in the 1937 decision would also characterize critical decisions of Mapai under Ben-Gurion's leadership in the future: the impulse to take advantage of every political opportunity. The political significance of this urge in 1937 was to prevent the door to Jewish statehood, which had opened a crack, from closing again.

The pragmatists' main argument in favor of qualified support was that the agreement in principle to partition would pave the way for political sovereignty or at least lead to recognition of the legitimacy of this Zionist goal. It was also aimed at preventing the establishment of an Arab state in all of Palestine, and perhaps, many hoped, it would also help moderate the Arab-Jewish conflict.

This position, and its accompanying political tactics, managed to convince most of the undecided and even some of the moderate opponents. These were instrumental opponents who did not believe that the British actually intended to establish a Jewish state or to grant such a state real sovereignty. They preferred continuation of the mandate because partition would not solve the Jewish problem in the diaspora and might even reduce the chances for peace with the Arabs. The pragmatic proponents directed their main argument toward these opponents because the two groups had a common ground: the willingness to examine the advantages and disadvantages of territory as well as the trade-off: territory in return for sovereignty. By contrast, the strong opponents adopted an ideological, national, or religious position, and the argument with them was not conducted on common ground, as reflected in two articles published in 1938. Moshe Kleinman, the editor of *Ha'olam*, the newspaper of the World Zionist Organization, defined the dilemma in the following language:

Should we accept "partition" because of its reward, establish-ment of a Jewish state; or should we reject the "state" because of the entailed loss, cutting off a great part of the land from the area of our national aspirations? And the "reward"—is it worth such a big sacrifice? And even the "loss"—is it a real and absolute loss for eternity, which forces us to forgo the great historic perspective of establishing a Jewish state?[39]

Kleinman was a moderate proponent, and he responded to his own queries clearly and unequivocally: "If the land will initially be small, but sovereign, that is better than a large land without sover-eignty."[40] By contrast, biblical scholar Yehezkel Koifman was among the strong opponents for whom partition was a tautology for the destruction of Zionism. He did not believe in the proposed sovereign state and, for him, reducing the territory meant sacrificing the only chance that Eretz Israel would solve the problem of Jewish exile.[41] These two views reflect the gap between the instrumental and ex-pressive positions and the difficulty in bridging between them, even for the sake of a common ground for debate. Be-Gurion sarcastically described the proximity between the extreme opponents in the Jew-ish and Arab camps: "Ussishkin and the Mufti—no comparison be-tween the two—have a common platform—the unity of the land."[42]

We should add that the pragmatists, too, generally ignored the Palestinian Arabs as relevant partners with whom a compro-mise should be negotiated directly. We discussed this in Chapter Seven, when we presented the various positions on the "transfer" proposal. Qualified support of the partition principle was directed essentially at the British, under the assumption that they alone would determine whether or not the proposed solution would be implemented.

Table 9.2 indicates the complexity of the positions. The main arguments are presented here, but reality, as usual, is richer than any analytical framework. Moreover, surprising paradoxes were revealed in the debate itself.[43] The opponents who were generally anti-British favored continuation of the mandate. The expressive opponents, whose arguments were based on values, were willing to form political alliances with ideological rivals; whereas the instru-mental proponents displayed stronger organizational loyalty to their parties. The debate revolved mainly around the future develop-ments in Eretz Israel, and the argument focused on whether time was working in favor of the Zionist endeavor. A. Shapira points out that "it is surprising how little the debaters of partition dealt with the

Table 9.2 "Partition in Return for Sovereignty": Main Positions and Arguments

POSITION	MAIN ARGUMENT	MAIN OPPOSING ARGUMENT
(A) Strong opposition	Prevent a precedent for partition of the land	Rejection of partition would result in an Arab state in the entire Land of Israel
(B) Moderate opposition	Chance to continue the mandate and international sponsorship of the national home	The mandate would continue under worsened conditions
(C) Delay the decision	Prevent an internal rift and clarify the conditions for implementing the commission proposal	Lack of influence on events increases the chance of worse options
(D) Moderate support	Create a commitment for establishment of a state and improve the territorial proposal	Agreement to territorial concessions will become the minimum demand of the other side
(E) Strong support	Create a sovereign territorial hold, especially to rescue European Jews	A state of 5,000 km^2 has no right to exist; boundaries cannot be changed in the future

situation of the Jewish people in Europe."[44] An analysis of the speeches at the congress in 1937 confirms this general conclusion, despite the fact that Weizmann and many other delegates did not ignore the events in Europe. However, the decision to support the principle of partition in return for a sovereign state could not be understood without the strong belief that the state would enhance immigration, both for rescuing European Jews and as a realization of Zionist goals.

In the Wake of the 1937 Decision

To complete the picture, we shall review the developments until the beginning of World War II to examine the postdecision internal dynamics and the practical implications of the decision after 1937.

The Internal Front

The differences exposed in the Zionist movement's great debate of 1937 could not disappear after the majority resolution. In the previous chapter, we noted the opponents' different interpretation of the congress resolution. They continued their struggle and even presented a sort of double formula of their own in an attempt to derail the congress decision. Internally, they mounted a consistent opposition within the Zionist executive and the Jewish Agency to prevent any commitment to the British government on partition. Externally, they continued to organize public actions aimed at presenting an alternative plan. The first goal had to be attained through the "Political Committee," which was appointed at the Congress to supervise the negotiations in London between the Zionist executive and the British government. However, the committee was never convened, and Berl Katznelson demanded that Ben-Gurion disband it officially to avoid "an insult to its members and an insult to the movement."[45] Within the institutions of the Zionist movement, Ussishkin demanded that the congress resolution be implemented verbatim and that the partition proposal of the royal commission not be supported. He also began to organize the opponents for the technical "Partition Commission" recommended by the royal commission.

The first post-Congress meeting of the opposition took place in Jerusalem on November 22, 1937, and was attended by twenty-seven representatives of various parties. They decided to embark on a worldwide public campaign to explain the opponents' position. Assemblies were subsequently held with wide-ranging participation, but without the central opponents from Mapai, who had been advised by Berl Katznelson to wait and see if partition became a concrete issue.[46] Nevertheless, speakers from Mapai, Mizrahi, the General Zionist Federation, and ST participated in mass rallies in Tel Aviv on December 8, 1937, and in Haifa on January 6, 1938.[47] These activities intensely annoyed Mapai leaders, who were concerned that the opponents might take over the party's central committee as a result.[48] The campaign also worried members of the executive. Weizmann told a meeting of the Jewish Agency executive on December 12, 1937, that the status of the Zionist movement in England had been strengthened by international events and reported optimistically about the possibility that the Negev would not be included in an Arab state. He regretted, however, that the opponents—and particularly Ussishkin—were doing everything in their power to defeat the plan for establishing a state.[49]

There were also many Zionist and non-Zionist opponents in the diaspora, and they took a strong stand against partition, as Ben-Gurion and Berl Katznelson discovered during their autumn 1937 visits to the United States and Britain.[50] Attempts were also made to organize opponents in Europe, such as the "World Convention of All Opponents of Partition," which was to convene in Amsterdam in September 1938, but it was cancelled upon publication of the Woodhead commission report.[51] Nevertheless, the opposition from within the Zionist movement, and especially among the members of Mapai, bore much greater influence than the external opposition and increased when the time came to consider what position to adopt in testimony before the Woodhead commission.

The opponents in Mapai, led by Berl Katznelson, then began to indicate their strong dissatisfaction with the executive's contacts with the British government in London. Twenty-one opponents gathered in Tel Aviv on February 23, 1938, and unlike previous occasions, this meeting was attended by the central leaders of the opponents from all of the parties, including Berl Katznelson. The prevailing opinion was that the opponents should appear separately before the Woodhead commission.[52] Consequently, the controversy again broke out within the Zionist movement and particularly between Ben-Gurion and Berl Katznelson. The Mapai opponents decided not to participate in the Zionist general council meeting in London on March 9, 1938 as a means of expressing their dissatisfaction with the proponents' interpretation of the congress resolution. The exchange of correspondence on this matter between Berl Katznelson and Ben-Gurion, as well as the Mapai "Opponents' Letter," were circulated among the party's local branches and testify to the atmosphere as well as the nature of the controversy following the congress's decision.[53]

The "Opponents' Letter" was signed by eleven Mapai members, delegates and alternates to the enlarged Zionist general council, and expressed their fury at the disbandment of the "Political Committee," the incorrect interpretation of the congress resolution, and the lack of joint responsibility: "Since the Congress, no political events have taken place which would require us to change our position. Our nonattendance does not indicate our abandonment of our opposition to the partition plan and our struggle against it within the movement. But it does contain a demand for more involvement by the movement in all phases of the discussion and decision.[54]

Prior to this, Berl Katznelson wrote to Ben-Gurion that he feared the discussion would include demands to change the "status quo established in Zurich," and he did not wish to be part of it. Ben-Gurion was personally and politically insulted by the "strike" declared by his colleagues. He maintained that he remained loyal to the line agreed in Zurich and that he had even been accused by the proponents of sacrificing the state on the altar of peace and unity within the movement. He was infuriated by the accusation that he had breached joint responsibility and concluded with a threat to resign because he could not function without the support of his colleagues. Katznelson tried to placate Ben-Gurion, but repeated his personal position toward "the dual decision of Zurich," which, he said, must be fully implemented.

Meanwhile the debate concerning the testimony before the Woodhead commission continued. In the Mapai central committee meeting on May 17, 1938, and the Zionist general council session the following day, the proponents (and some of the opponents, including Berl Katznelson) managed to pass a resolution that allowed exclusive testimony before the Woodhead commission to the official Zionist delegation.[55] Still, Ussishkin submitted a memorandum to the commission expressing his opposition to partition, as did opponents from outside the Zionist movement.[56]

What was the influence of the opponents' efforts? Clearly, they could not be ignored—the formula of the congress resolution could not be explained otherwise. They also had a deterrent effect after the congress, causing Ben-Gurion's reaction and the proponents' struggle for a unified appearance before the Woodhead commission. In the end, the confrontation did not come to a head. Instead of the "amended proposal" for a Jewish state, which had to be voted on by a newly elected Zionist congress, the Woodhead commission and the British government rejected the ideas both of a state and of partition. In January 1938, Ben-Gurion warned that circumstances had already changed since the adoption of the congress resolution.[57] He himself did not then know how right he was, because the British government had already begun to retreat from the royal commission's recommendations. In his letter to Berl Katznelson of March 1938, Ben-Gurion wrote, "The possibility of establishing or not establishing a Jewish state depends not only on subjective intentions, but on objective forces and factors. In fact, Arab, English and international forces, which are many times stronger than our proponents, fought the Jewish state for whose establishment a great portion of our movement and people prayed."[58]

With regard to the decision-making process, the priority given to maintaining the unity of the movement must again be emphasized. The issue was a critical one; the positions were polarized;

and each side tried to veer the political moves in its own direction. And still, the majority did not use its power to oust opponents from the leadership of the movement; the minority, although continuing to fight for its position, did not cross the line into external opposition. A confrontation was avoided because of external events, but in the history of the movement it was recorded that, even after the decision, channels remained open for dialogue, bargaining, and a willingness to compromise.

Both the proponents and the opponents later claimed that their positions in 1937 had proven themselves, with each side emphasizing a different aspect of the events. The former stuck to their position that the congress resolution paved the way for the establishment of a Jewish state; the latter believed that they defeated a British plot and paved the way for a larger Jewish state in the future.

Other Decisions Following the Congress

After the congress, the executive began negotiations in London with the British government, with the goal of improving the royal commission's proposal. Weizmann met with Malcolm MacDonald, the new colonial secretary, on September 15, 1937, to ensure that "they would not try to touch the northern border" and then with Coupland concerning the status of Jerusalem.[59] A concurrent flurry of activity surrounded the mandate commission and the session of the League of Nations council in Geneva.[60] Attempts were also made to contact moderate Arabs.[61] Weizmann had received information concerning the disagreement within the British government and the possibility of a retreat from the idea of partition, but he had no details on the impending change and did not know of the British cabinet meeting on December 8, 1937, in which the Foreign Office succeeded, with Prime Minister Chamberlain's support, in beginning the process of revising the royal commission's recommendations.[62]

The preparations of the Zionist movement for testifying before the Woodhead commission should be viewed therefore within the proper context of that time—an attempt to improve the royal commission's proposals or at least to forestall any erosion in them. The internal discussions and the activities of the opponents clearly show that no new options were on the agenda. Rather, the Zionist movement was preparing itself to present its case once again before the new commission. The following resolution was passed at the enlarged Zionist general council meeting in March 1938, in which the Mapai opponents did not participate: "Both the proponents and the opponents of the political resolution of the Twentieth Congress resolutely reject any attempt to limit the Jews to a minority status in the Land of Israel, and they reject any activity of the opponents of Zionism directed against the principle of a Jewish state in the Land of Israel."[63]

At that time, Weizmann still believed that "the [British] government does not intend to withdraw from partition but rather to base itself on the Peel plan." Ben-Gurion, speaking at the same meeting, emphasized his willingness to accept even the Peel plan, with a number of changes, in place of continuation of the mandate.[64] As we will see in the next chapter, a concentrated effort was also made at that time to purchase land and "not just regular lands for settlement, but rather land that has political value";[65] that is, to improve the partition map.

In the first round of testimony before the Woodhead commission, the Jewish Agency representatives emphasized the negative aspect of the royal commission's proposal and managed to avoid submitting maps.[66] In due course, they were asked to specify where they wanted the boundary lines to be drawn in the improved partition plan. As a result, the Jewish Agency saw no alternative to submitting a list of specific territorial demands to the Woodhead commission. These were based on the recommendations of the boundaries committee established in the Jewish Agency in early 1938 to prepare materials for the Woodhead commission.[67] To avoid internal criticism, a map was not submitted, and qualifications were attached to the list of territorial demands, noting that these were temporary, minimal demands; that the Zionist movement had not changed its position concerning the Jewish right to settle in the entire Land of Israel; and that any decision would require ratification by the Zionist congress. Nevertheless, these territorial demands did constitute a "map"—the first submitted by an authorized Zionist body since 1919 (see Map 9.1).[68] The main changes in this map, by comparison with the map of the Jewish state proposed by the royal commission's report, were a several-kilometer expansion of the territory of the Jewish state in the north, east, and south; inclusion of western Jerusalem within the territory of the Jewish state; and a demand that the entire Negev remain under British control rather than being included within the Arab state.

The royal commission proposed about 5,000 km² for the Jewish state, and the Jewish Agency's additions demanded from the Woodhead commission totaled less than another 1,000 km².[69] The main changes match the preliminary demands listed by Shertok upon receipt of the Royal Commission's report (see Chapter Seven), including the tendency to limit the territory intended for the Arab state by leaving it under mandatory control. A special chapter in the Woodhead commission report explained that the Jewish Agency's expansion proposal was rejected because it was unreasonable to include Arab areas of residence or land ownership within the territory of the proposed Jewish state.[70] All of this proved irrelevant, however, because the Woodhead commission rejected the idea of partition, concluding its report by saying: "We are unable to recommend boundaries for the proposed areas which will give a reasonable prospect of the eventual establishment of self-supporting Arab and Jewish states."[71]

How did the Jews react to the Woodhead report? In August 1938, information began reaching the Jewish Agency executive that the Woodhead commission was preparing a proposal for a Jewish state that would be even more truncated than that of the royal commission.[72] Ben-Gurion still believed, or hoped, that in the immediate future "we have one central task: a struggle for a Jewish state now"; whereas Berl Katznelson maintained that partition is no longer on the political agenda.[73] Meanwhile, the international crisis in Czechoslovakia began, bringing with it changes in global British policy. After Weizmann and Ben-Gurion's meeting with Colonial Secretary MacDonald in September 1938, Ben-Gurion wrote in his diary that the British government had decided "to hand us over to the Arabs: no state and no immigration." He raised for the first time in writing the question of whether "the entire purpose of sending the Partition Commission was not indeed a delusion."[74] In mid-November, the possibility of an Arab-Jewish conference in London, with the participation of representatives of the Arab countries, was already being discussed.[75] Ben-Gurion bitterly pointed out in his diary: "It is difficult to understand the opponents' joy. More than once did I warn: your war against the Jewish state may well succeed, because you have very powerful helpers; the Arabs and the British."[76]

Days of total gloom for Weizmann and Ben-Gurion followed the publication of the Woodhead commission report. Their dream of establishing a Jewish state evaporated as if it had never existed.[77] The statement published by the Jewish Agency executive said: "There can be no doubt that this report cannot serve as the basis for any negotiations, either between the Jews and the Arabs or between the Jewish Agency and the [British] government."[78]

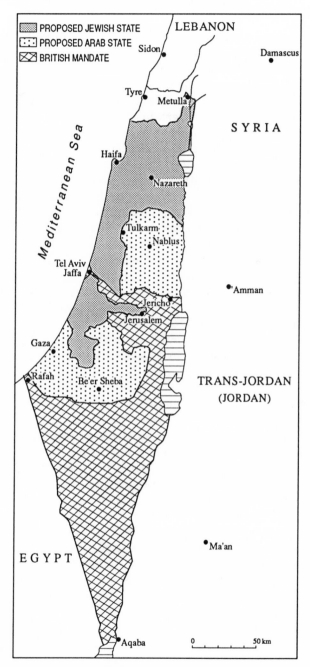

Map 9.1 The Territorial Demands of the
Jewish Agency According to the
Woodhead Commission, 1938

And so the chapter ended. Even the ardent supporters of partition no longer saw any possibility that a Jewish state would indeed be established. The Zionist executive agreed to participate in the "round table" discussions (St. James Conference) that took place in London February 7–March 17, 1939, only after great hesitation and out of intense fear. At a certain stage during the discussions, the Jewish Agency raised alternative plans: a Jewish state in part of Palestine in a territory that would be sufficient for large-scale immigration and settlement or a federal arrangement that would afford continued growth of the national home.[79] The Arab delegation demanded the establishment of an independent Arab state in Palestine and also discussed the possibility of a federal solution, with or without the neighboring Arab states. But all this was of fleeting importance, because the talks failed, and the White Paper of May 17, 1939, contained a vague declaration about the intention to establish an independent Palestinian state within ten years.[80] The thrust of the new British policy was to limit Jewish immigration and land acquisition. This represented a withdrawal not only from the partition plan, but also from the perception that the Jewish national home serves the interests of the empire. Britain's desire to continue its presence in Palestine was unchanged; but in 1939 its strategy was based on the hope of an alliance with the Arabs.[81]

Kimmerling and Migdal note the irony in the fact that the Palestinian leadership, led by the exiled mufti, also rejected the White Paper. The heavy toll taken by the Arab revolt on their own ranks (5,000 dead) may have made it impossible for them to agree to any proposal initiated by the British. The revolt helped build up Palestinian nationalism, but its fading and the rejection of the White Paper left the Palestinian national movement at a dead end.[82]

The partition plan was taken off the agenda until after World War II. Nor was it raised in deliberations of the twenty-first Zionist congress, which convened in Geneva in August 1939. Nevertheless, Weizmann and Ben-Gurion, the patrons of the partition idea within the Zionist movement, refused to regard this as the end.

10 1937 and Its Aftermath

Weizmann believes, as do I, that even if the partition plan would be revoked now, it would inevitably return sooner or later.

Ben-Gurion, 1938[1]

In this chapter, we will complete our discussion of two key issues previously mentioned only incidentally: the Zionist policy "on the ground," as manifested in land acquisition and settlement in 1937 and thereafter; and the significance of "the Arab question" in the territorial decision of 1937 from the perspective of the Zionist movement. At the end of this chapter, we shall return to the general issues raised in Chapter One: What can be learned from the 1937 decision about the attitude of the Zionist movement toward state, territory, and boundaries, and what general comparative hypotheses can be drawn about each of these, on the basis of the case study presented?

Land and Settlement Policy: 1936–1939

The decision at the Zionist congress in 1937 and the political activities surrounding it do not reflect all of the decisions and "territorial activity" in the period under discussion. Purchase of land and settlement paralleled the political actions, because the Zionist movement always believed that "activities on the ground" were more important than anything else.

In Chapter Seven, we pointed out how the partition proposal of the royal commission took into account the settlement map and the concentrations of land held by the Jews at that time.[2] The proposed Jewish state included the Jewish concentrations on the

241

coast, in the valleys, and in the Kinneret region.[3] But this proposed state deviated from the settlement map in two very significant areas: the "empty" Negev was not included, whereas the Galilee, which had an Arab majority, was. Indeed, the United Nations partition plan of 1947 reversed the situation by excluding the Galilee and including the Negev.

Until 1936, there were conflicting policies within the Zionist movement regarding "concentration" versus "dispersion" in the settlement program. The policy was not uniform, and there was also a tacit division between private capital, invested mainly in urban construction and citrus orchards on the coastal plain, and public capital, which was invested in other economic branches and in settlements in other parts of the country. The constraints of British policy and the availability of land for purchase together determined more than anything else the map of land acquisition and Jewish settlement.

This situation changed after 1936. The "disturbances" increased the weight of security considerations in settlement policy, shifting attention to problems of how to defend the Jewish settlements and the transportation routes. Concurrently, the partition proposal that began to engage attention increased the importance of political goals in settlement considerations. As a result of the security situation and the chance of political change, the Jewish National Fund became the main tool for purchasing land after 1936. With the increased uncertainty, holders of private capital were less eager to make investments.[4] In 1936, four settlements were founded, and in 1937, by the publication of the commission report, another thirteen went up, five of which were rudimentary settlements established in early July.[5]

Upon publication of the royal commission report, the Jewish Agency and the Jewish National Fund began a policy of land purchase and settlement based on two central considerations. First, accelerated purchase of Arab-owned lands in areas intended for inclusion in the Jewish state and, alternately, attempts to induce government expropriation of these lands. Second, an effort was made to "*establish facts*, such as in the frontier areas, in order *to strengthen* our position for the time when the territory and the extent of the Hebrew state will be determined" [emphasis in the original].[6] Accordingly, the accent in Jewish land policy shifted from settlement to political considerations. The amount of land openly purchased between April 1936 and publication of the 1939 White Paper was as follows:[7]

April 1936–September 1936		5,400
October 1936–September 1937		13,500
October 1937–September 1938		35,000
October 1938–April 1939		33,000
	Total	86,900 dunams*
*(1 km² = 1,000 dunams)		

An additional 60,000 dunams or so purchased by the Jewish National Fund were not recorded in the Land Registry to maintain secrecy.[8] These were very large acquisitions, in comparison with previous years, though in absolute terms, the total was only about 2 percent of the arable land in western Eretz Israel (excluding the Negev), or about 3 percent of the 5 million dunams earmarked for the Jewish state in the royal commission proposal.

The intention of Yishuv policy was to consolidate territorial continuity in areas already in Jewish hands, especially on the coast and in the valleys, for purposes of settlement and transport; to "establish facts" in other areas designated for the Jewish state, but defined as problematic (e.g., in the western Galilee, the Beit Shean Valley, and southern Judea); and to give lower priority to the Negev both because of the sparse population and in the hope that it would not become part of the Arab state, but remain under the mandatory government. It should be noted that the purchase of land was not limited to the territory designated for the Jewish state by the commission's report. The Jewish Agency also targeted territories it intended to claim in negotiations with the British government to improve the commission's proposal, such as the Jordan Valley and around the Tel-Aviv-Jerusalem corridor. Ultimately, most of these acquisitions were in the north, mainly above the Haifa–Beit Shean axis.

The goal was political: improving and populating the partition area. Economic and settlement considerations were secondary. And land *purchase* was only part of the effort: "Uncultivated and unsettled land does not yet 'establish facts' that are relevant for political decisions. Land on which there are settled Jewish villages is politically worth a great deal more."[9] Accordingly, fifty new Jewish settlements were established between April 1936 and May 1939.[10] Nevertheless, in these three years, the settlement map did not reach much beyond the commission's partition boundaries. The purpose of the settlement policy was to consolidate that which existed and to push out at the margins, in hopes of modifying the partition plan in accordance with settlement, transportation, and defense considerations. No attempt was made to break through to areas previously unsettled by Jews (on the mountain ridge, for example) or to locations far from the territory designated for the Jews in the partition plan.

Did the "settlement strategy" really set the future boundaries of the Jewish state, as is commonly believed?[11] There was, in theory, a policy of spreading out: The position of Ruppin and others—that it is preferable to create a Jewish majority in specific areas rather than to spread out to new areas—was rejected.[12] But in fact the land acquisition plan of the Zionist movement, which grew increasingly political from 1936, did not drastically change the map of Jewish presence in Palestine. Compared to the past, the amount of land acquired and the number of settlements established were impressive achievements—the Jewish National Fund more than doubled its land holdings between 1936 and 1948[13]—the result, however, was insignificant. It constituted a tiny percentage not only of the entire area of western Palestine, but also of the area designated to be the Jewish state. When the royal commission allocated to the Jewish state some 20 percent of the area of Palestine in 1937, the Jews held some 5 percent of it. When the United Nations allocated some 55 percent of the area to a Jewish state in 1947, the Jews held some 7 percent. Acquisition of land was therefore not a significant factor in shaping the boundaries of partition.

Oren believes that what affected the partition proposals in 1937 and 1947 was not only the amount of territory and Jewish settlements, but their *location*. This claim is based on Zionist premises and ignores the fact that Arab settlements were spread throughout the country. Had the criteria for the proposed partitions been the location of the settlements (both Jewish and Arab), the proposed Jewish state would have been much smaller. Hence, the starting point of both partition proposals was political. The British proposal of 1937 ignored the fact that the Arabs were a majority in Palestine (E.I.) and ignored the map of Arab settlements. Because Britain supported a Jewish state, the only way out of this dilemma was to create a Jewish majority by the prudent allocation of territory. Hence the lines were drawn to include the majority of Jewish settlements and additional areas in the Galilee where the Arab population was relatively sparse. On the other hand, where British interests so dictated, the royal commission completely ignored Jewish population concentrations, such as

Jerusalem and Haifa. The United Nations plan in the main followed this precedent: creation of two states, each with a territorial majority population. It took into consideration more population concentrations, which is why the Galilee was excised from the Jewish state; and the lion's share of the 9,000 km^2 added to the Royal Commission proposal were in the sparsely populated Negev. The settlement geography of the Jews and Arabs was, therefore, just one component in shaping partition boundaries. And, in the final analysis, the partition lines of 1948–1949 were set by military power and cease fire agreements . . . which were again redrawn in 1967.

The "Arab Question" in the Zionist Decision

The Jewish debate on partition focused on British intentions, whereas the Arabs within and outside Eretz Israel were generally regarded as secondary partners. Although the Arab revolt was recognized as the reason for the turnaround in British policy, Jewish leadership maintained that British interests would ultimately determine the fate of Eretz Israel. Most Arab leaders could not agree more. As we saw in Chapter Three, the testimony of el-Husseini and others before the royal commission left no doubt that they did not recognize the Jews as potential partners to a political solution. Using the analytical framework presented earlier, Arab positions ranged from A to C: from total opposition (the majority) to indecision (the minority). The Arab Higher Committee adopted a position of extreme opposition to the royal commission's partition proposal. In the end, the proposal was also rejected by the moderate Palestinians (see Chapter Five).

In retrospect, it can be said that throughout this period, there was no serious Jewish-Arab negotiation toward a solution that would be acceptable to both sides. The implications of this were far-reaching for the decision on the eve of World War II as well as the subsequent events that led to the establishment of the state of Israel and the de facto partition of 1948–1949. An asymmetry was created between both sides: the Palestinian national movement adopted a position of absolute opposition, whereas the Zionist movement chose to give moderate support that partially coincided with the British position. This created a total confrontation that undermined the chance for cooperative territorial partition, as the royal commission had hoped. From the British point of view, and eventually also from the perspective of the Arabs and Jews in Palestine, the struggle became a zero-sum game: whatever is gained by one side would be lost by the other. This conceptualization of the conflict applies not only to territorial partition, but primarily to the issue of political sovereignty: either a Jewish state or an Arab state. Arab positions did more to foster this situation than did Jewish positions. For the Arabs in Palestine, the reason for this was evident: They regarded themselves as the victims, to whom everything should be restored that had been taken from them. In any event, the absolute opposition to the partition principle by the Arab Higher Committee, under el-Husseini's control, eliminated any discussion within the Palestinian movement of whether the Arabs should be satisfied with sovereignty over just a portion of Palestine.[14] The result of this was of signal importance: The Palestinian Arab public and its leadership were "unprepared" for a substantive consideration of the advantages and disadvantages of the partition plan proposed to them in 1947.

Other factors also influenced the definition of who the partners to the political process should be. First, the two communities in Palestine (E.I.) were segregated culturally, religiously, linguistically, and socially. In the 1930s, the cleavage became an impenetrable national and political barrier, despite the small-scale economic relations between Jews and Arabs and the ad hoc interactions between intellectuals and politicians.[15] If not for the fact that two separate communities existed in Palestine, it is doubtful that the royal commission would have suggested that their separation be legitimized territorially and politically. In fact, such a separation presented the greatest difficulty of all, because "no line can be drawn which would separate all the Arabs from all the Jews."[16]

Second, the commission had actually recommended partition into three, not two, entities: Jewish, Arab, and British. According to the proposal, Britain would be given a new mandate on the Jerusalem-Jaffa corridor (nicknamed the *Promenade des Anglais*) and, for an unspecified period, on five northern cities. The Jews assumed that this presence would affect the sovereignty of the two states as well as the future territorial map. Hence their pressure to include the Negev in the area of the mandate rather than in the Arab state.

Third, the proposal was not to establish a separate Palestinian state, but rather an "Arab state" combined with Transjordan. As the emirate in Transjordan was under British control, the Jews preferred Abdullah and his British patrons as partners to the political process over the local Palestinian leadership, which was more extreme and had more insistent claims on all of western Eretz Israel. In contrast, opposition to allowing Abdullah control over

Palestine was one of the key factors in the Arab Higher Committee's decision to reject the proposal. Porath notes that the pan-Arab viewpoint also played a role in this context.[17]

Jewish Positions Toward the Palestinian National Movement

Our analysis of the partition debate indicated the two extreme approaches to "the Arab question" as defined by the Jews. The strong opponents, who claimed the entire Land of Israel (with or without Transjordan), did not recognize Palestinian Arab nationalism as a legitimate partner to any political solution. They also opposed the idea of transfer, as proposed by the commission, arguing that it meant transferring Arabs from one part of Eretz Israel to another. At the other extreme were Jews who supported the demand for full Arab sovereignty over Palestine (see the discussion of the Palestine Communist party in Chapter Six), granting the Jews a minority status with specified rights. Next to them were those who favored a binational state, opposing the premise that territorial partition would lead to a resolution of the conflict. Those who held this position were careful, for ideological reasons, not to plunge into the issue of a separate national Palestinian identity.

The position that triumphed at the Zionist congress essentially argued that a piece of sovereignty could be obtained from the British in return for conceding a piece of territory to the Arabs; that is, in return for Jewish agreement to partition. In other words, the policy of the majority in the Zionist movement was directed toward Britain, and the Palestinian Arabs played a secondary role. The predominant perception maintained that Zionism had benefited the Arabs in Eretz Israel, who would ultimately recognize this and even be grateful for it. A characteristic example was the chapter "The Situation of the Arabs" in the memorandum of the Va'ad Le'ummi presented to the League of Nations in 1930, in which the Zionist enterprise is described as having "improved in a significant way also the standard of living of the other population in the country."[18] Mentioned in the memo were improved agricultural methods, improved economic tools, expanded markets for Arab agricultural produce, increased wages, increased purchasing power, and an improved standard of living of Arabs in Palestine, compared with Syria and Egypt. In this memorandum, the Palestinian Arabs are regarded as a collection of private individuals or, at most, an economic community without national aspirations.

Gradually and increasingly after the Arab revolt and the royal commission recommendation, the Palestinian Arabs began to be regarded as a political enemy and even, for a few Jews, as a potential partner. Chapter Seven noted that some of the undecided conditioned their consent to partition on the Jewish state having a solid Jewish majority, and others considered Arab consent (local and regional) to coexistence with the Jews as a precondition for partition, a kind of deal that would today be called "territories for peace." Still others believed that the establishment of a Jewish state would ultimately engender Arab recognition and de facto acceptance of a Jewish presence in Palestine. But for Jews, the big question aroused by the Arab "disturbances" was this: Is there a national Arab movement? The term *disturbances*, as noted by A. Shapira, was an attempt to strike a neutral position between *revolt* (meaning national uprising) and *pogrom* (of individuals and gangs).[19]

The opponents refused to acknowledge the existence of local Arab nationalism and claimed that this was a British-Arab conspiracy or alternatively incitement of the Arab public by the landlords (effendis) and religious leaders. By contrast, the proponents did recognize the nationalist elements in the uprising and were aware of the fact that the Arabs were gathering collective political strength that could transform them into masters of the land. Golomb suggested that "we are in a country with a war between two peoples. . . . There is talk of gangs as if they are only murders, but among them are people who are giving their lives for their nationalism."[20] Whether the Arab revolt marks the beginning of the transition in the Zionist movement from an ethos of defense and self-restraint to an ethos of offense, reprisal, and belligerence is outside the scope of this discussion.[21] Clearly, however, the revolt marks a turning point in the Jewish perception of "the Arab question" and in the definition of the nature of the rivalry between Jews and Arabs in Eretz Israel.

The royal commission recognized explicitly that what was taking place in Palestine (E.I.) was a conflict between two contradictory national aspirations, and it noted that the roots of the Arab demands were political. It also noted that the Jewish national home brought substantial material gain to the Palestinian Arabs, but that this would not end their opposition to Zionism. The report quotes the figurative language of one Arab witness: "You say my house has been enriched by the strangers who have entered it. But it is *my* house, and I did not invite the strangers in, or ask them to enrich it, and I do not care how poor or bare it is if only I am master in it."[22]

The royal commission remained committed to the British promises to the Jews and did not propose the establishment of a Palestinian state in the entire area of the mandate. It went some distance in its willingness to recognize the aspirations of the Arabs in Palestine, but refrained from recommending a separate state, and instead suggested attachment to Transjordan. The change in attitude of the Zionist movement was also in that direction, but for different reasons. In the first half of the 1930s, Mapai and Ben-Gurion still strove to attain any sort of Arab agreement to the establishment of a Jewish state. The "disturbances" led them to abandon their belief in a Jewish-Arab agreement and to intensify their efforts toward the British in the hope that they would enforce a desirable solution (establishment of a Jewish state) on both sides. Nevertheless, despite the willingness to recognize the principle of partition and thus to respond to a British solution, the Zionist movement was very careful not to say explicitly that it recognized the political claims of the Arabs on Eretz Israel or even on part of it. The royal commission's proposal to establish an Arab state, which significantly was not mentioned in the congress resolution, was also one of the deepest points of contention among the proponents of partition. Was there a willingness to recognize the fact that not only were territories in the Land of Israel "taken" from the Jews, but that they would be "given" to Arab sovereignty? This is why so many strongly favored continuation of the British mandate as the best of all the bad alternatives, particularly the possibility of Arab sovereignty in Eretz Israel. In the congress resolution, the Palestinian Arabs and the Arab question were mentioned in the following way:

* Jewish settlement significantly benefited the local Arab community and brought economic advantages to all of the Arabs;

* Rejection of the royal commission's conclusion that it is impossible to reconcile the *national aspirations* (my emphasis) of the Jewish people and of the Arabs in Eretz Israel;

* The Jewish people are willing to reach a peace agreement with the Arab community in Eretz Israel on the basis of mutual recognition of rights and freedom of development of the two peoples.

Thus, although the resolution was aimed principally at the British government, it deviated from the prior attitude toward the local Arabs merely as individuals with economic interests and noted their national aspirations, rights, and freedom of development. This formulation did not, however, acknowledge symmetry in the national aspirations of the two sides. it mentioned the Jewish *people*, on the one hand, and the "Arabs" and "Arab community," on the other. In this respect, the Jewish Agency's resolution went a step further. It called on the British government to convene a joint conference of Jews and Arabs of Eretz Israel to reach a peace agreement (based on the Balfour Declaration and the mandate) and to forestall the need to partition the land. This was the closest that a Jewish formulation at that time came to defining the problem in terms other than a "zero-sum game" between Jews and Arabs, which inferred territorial separation and division of political sovereignty.

In sum, the majority in the Zionist movement, including the Revisionists, focused their attention on the colonial power in the hope that Britain could be convinced to resume its support of the Zionist goals. Over the course of time, important factions within the Revisionist camp would abandon this British orientation and call for unilateral steps to achieve Jewish independence, with the assistance of other powers, such as Italy and Germany.[23] As for "the Arab question," Zionist policy changed in practice and began to view Palestinian Arabs as an adversary whose bargaining power with the British required territorial concessions, but not necessarily a recognition of their separate national identity. The royal commission report did recognize Palestinian national aspirations, but sought to resolve the problem by looking east, toward Transjordan.

The Hashemite Option

Within and outside the Zionist movement, a number of prominent individuals continued their efforts to reach an understanding with moderate Palestinian leaders. We have already mentioned the separate efforts of Magnes, Rutenberg, and Hyamson.[24] The executive tacitly agreed to their actions, but the senior leaders, including Weizmann, remained highly suspicious.[25] From the beginning of the mandate, the British presence on both sides of the Jordan River invited, and perhaps even dictated, an arrangement that would exceed the borders of western Eretz Israel. From the point of view of British colonial interests, the administrative division between the two mandate regions was not very significant. Among the Palestinian leaders were those who supported Abdullah's plans for the establishment of a large Arab state that exceeds the boundaries of Palestine. Also in the Zionist movement were many who looked east in hopes of a solution. It is not surprising, then, that when the royal commission proposed that the Arab state be composed of parts of Palestine and Transjordan, the "Hashemite Option" became even more attractive.

Close contacts had been maintained with Emir Abdullah over a long period before 1937, but the commission report strengthened the tendency to regard him as a central partner to a Jewish-Hashemite-British solution, that would bypass the local Palesinian leadership.[26] Therefore, the Zionist leaders did not follow the lead of the royal commission, which was very careful not to mention Abdullah as the ruler of the future Arab state to avoid arousing the opposition in the mufti's camp or in Arab states such as Iraq.[27] Shertok, who was a fervent believer in the Hashemite orientation, recognized this problem and wrote to Weizmann:

> Another factor which can be important in the new situation is, of course, our friend the Emir. It seems that he is not without courage. According to the messages that I receive from him, he is full of energy and waiting impatiently to take advantage of the great opportunity if only we can fulfill our commitments. And this point I am very doubtful since, in the final analysis, we are not certain if the British committed themselves to a policy of supporting the Emir against all his enemies from without and within, and especially those from without.[28]

As noted in Chapter Five, additional contacts with Abdullah came to nought. He could not enforce his will on the leaders of the Palestinian national movement or, alternately, convince Britain to establish a greater Arab state headed by him in the whole mandate territory. The rejection of the royal commission's proposals by the Palestinian leadership and the Arab states led Abdullah to take a cautious and evasive approach to conceal his support for partition. In a memorandum to the Woodhead Commission, he proposed the establishment of a unified Arab state in Palestine and Transjordan under an Arab ruler and autonomy to the Jews in their regions. This plan stood in absolute contradiction to the agreements of his emissaries in their secret contacts with the Jewish Agency. In additional meetings, Abdullah tried to clarify that he actually had not retreated from his support of the partition plan, but it was too late. The change of British policy in 1938 reshuffled the deck of both the Zionist leadership and Abdullah, including their secret understanding on partition.[29] Abdullah was no longer of primary concern when Great Britain revised its policy. Moreover, they tried to accommodate Palestinian demands in the 1939 White Paper only because they believed that curtailing Zionism would aid Britain in the entire Arab and Moslem world. The mandatory territory on both banks of the Jordan River was of limited importance in this broader context.

Abdullah had some achievements in the years 1936–1939: His involvement in Palestinian affairs was established; opposition was created to the mufti's control of the Palestinian national movement; and a framewok for political cooperation with the Jews was put in place. It is also possible that a base was thus created for Abdullah's taking control over the West Bank in 1949.[30] But this is not how matters stood in 1939, not in the perception of Abdullah nor of the Jewish Agency leaders who were in regular contact with him. The Zionist movement gained nothing from the Hashemite option in 1937–1938, but cooperation with Abdullah would surface once again after the war.

In sum, the 1937 Zionist agreement to partition in exchange for sovereignty was aimed primarily at Britain. The Hashemite option and the willingness to negotiate the plan with the rulers of the Arab states was part of this orientation, whereas the Palestinian Arabs played a secondary role in the process.

Positions of the Palestinian Leadership

The Arab Higher Committee, headed by the Husseinis, was not the only body to reject the commission's recommendations. The more moderate Nashashibis, who were close to Abdullah, despite their hesitations and the "secret political preferences" of the recommendations, published a resolute declaration against them on July 21, 1937.[31] Whether we attribute this position to Palestinian public opinion and press, which condemned the commission, or to the evaluation that the British had made no concessions to Arab demands, two important facts are evident. First, all factions of the Palestinian national movement officially rejected the partition principle outright. Second, from their point of view, the Arab revolt that had led to the establishment of the commission failed to achieve its goals and ultimately turned into a bloody internal struggle within the Palestinian camp.[32]

The Arab Higher Committee viewed agreement to the royal commission's proposal as untenable surrender to both the Jews and

Abdullah. Despite differences of opinion on other subjects, the Palestinian leadership clung to the demand to establish an Arab state in all of Palestine and opposed partition for reasons similar to those of the extreme opponents among the Jews.[33] As far as they were concerned, the Jews had no legitimate claims to their territory, and the sheer idea that a Jewish state would be established on any part of Palestine was unjust and unacceptable. In retrospect, this Palestinian expressive position of absolute opposition was one of the consistent causes of missed opportunities.

The main goal of the Jewish leadership's position was to attain legitimization for a Jewish state, even at a heavy territorial cost— regarded by the opponents as a betrayal of Eretz Israel. Choosing between subjugation in the entire Land of Israel or sovereignty over a portion of it, the Zionist movement chose sovereignty. Moreover, it rejected the choice as framed by the opposition; namely, that between the chance of future sovereignty over the entire Land of Israel or temporary subjugation in part of it, the latter is preferable.

In reverse, the choices could equally apply to the dilemmas faced by the Palestinian leadership. Agreement to any Jewish territorial control would have implied recognition of their rights in Palestine and would have constituted a dramatic turning point in the consistent Palestinian position. Indeed, such a development, caused by Jewish immigration, was precisely what the Arab revolt was intended to prevent. In retrospect, however, it can be seen that the tenacious adherence of the Palestinians to their traditional position ignored the emerging political reality. In 1937, there were 400,000 Jews in Palestine—too many to ignore, but still too few to threaten the hegemony of about 900,000 Palestinian Arabs. The Palestinian leadership resolved to choose between all or nothing: rule over *all* of Palestine or continued subjugation to the British. As a result of this reduction of the choices, the first option was selected, leading to the adamant but impractical demand to replace the mandate with an Arab-Palestinian state in the entire territory. The prospect for realizing this was extremently poor, despite the veiled promise contained in the White Paper of 1939.

In the short term, the second option materialized—continuation of the mandate. But in the long term, all of Palestine was lost. The choice could have been formulated differently; for example, Arab rule in most of the land versus subjugation to the British (or even to the Jews in the future) in all of Palestine. Such a formulation would have forced the Palestinians, like most of the Jews, to wrestle with more practical alternatives, for example, "territory in exchange for sovereignty." It can even be postulated that the Palestinians would have advanced their own interests further if they had then agreed not to partition, but to a certain extent of Jewish autonomy (or cantonization) in return for an independent Palestinian state in the remainder of the land. These theories do not ignore the Palestinians' feeling that they must not recognize the rights of the usurper nor their deep anxiety that Zionism would flood the land with Jews. British power in the region had already begun to wane and the Palestinians were hoping that Britain would accommodate them as a way to strengthen its strategic position.[34] They observed the precedents of the nearby Arab states—Iraq, Egypt, Saudi Arabia, and Yemen—which had already achieved independence, and Syria and Lebanon, which were soon to follow. The 1936 uprising strengthened their hopes that Arab independence could also be attained in Palestine.

Yet in retrospect, it is clear that the Palestinian leadership did not read the political map correctly. As George Antonius said in his testimony before the royal commission, the Palestinian position was determined more by moral and psychological than by practical considerations.[35] This expressive position won nothing in the end and certainly not legitimacy for the establishment of an independent Palestinian state in the future. In contrast, the central achievement of the Zionist position was just that: legitimacy for the concept of a Jewish state and placement of the issue on the international agenda. The year 1937 shapes up as a critical year in this respect. Had there been Palestinian concessions toward the British and the Zionists, they might have been able to close the door then against the Hashemite dynasty's aspirations in Palestine.[36] The Arab Higher Committee's initial lack of cooperation with the royal commission made it easier for Abdullah to present himself as the patron of the Palestinians. The commission's recommendations to attach Arab Palestine to Transjordan can be interpreted as a concession to Abdullah. Yet, we noted that the omission of Abdullah as the ruler of the future Arab state was not accidental, and it left some maneuvering space for the Palestinian leadership. But they ignored it, and we know now that the Palestinians' failure to take advantage of the slight opportunity to advance their chance for independence contributed to the elimination of this option for more than fifty years. The next partition proposal, in 1947, would be much worse for them from a territorial point of view. They would reject that one, too, and then most would find themselves under Hashemite and Egyptian rule until 1967, and Israeli rule following that.

The Palestinian position in 1937 also legitimized the direct and dominant involvement of the Arab states in their affairs. It is debatable whether turning the local confrontation into a regional conflict served an interest of the Jewish or the Palestinian side, or perhaps of neither. In any case, it was mainly the neighboring Arab rulers who turned the "Palestinian problem" into an Arab problem, and their involvement was intended primarily to serve their own interests. The British partially pulled and were partially pushed into supporting the intervention of the Arab rulers.[37] It began with the call by the three kings for the Palestinian Arabs to end their strike of October 1936 and to cooperate with the royal commission and continued until representatives of the Palestinians and neighboring Arab states were invited to the round table conference in London in February 1939.[38] British hopes that the Arab states would moderate the uncompromising Palestinian position were unfounded, as was the Palestinian's hope that the Arab leaders could attain from the British government what they themselves had no power to achieve from the royal commission.

The White Paper of 1939 was seemingly a victory of the Palestinian Arabs in its severe restriction of the Zionist endeavor. But as this document was mainly intended to placate the Arab states in the interest of broader British goals in the region, it also deepened the Arab states' involvement in Palestine, which ultimately thwarted Palestinian interests. Furthermore, the Arab Higher Committee also rejected the 1939 White Paper because it did not determine a practical timetable for awarding full and immediate independence to Palestine as an Arab state.[39] All in all, the involvement of the Arab states in the Palestinian conflict contributed to the Arab rejection of partition in 1937 and 1947. Moreover, the history of the conflict records that the Arab states replaced the Palestinians from then on as the address for both international and Zionist politics.[40]

One of the British arguments on behalf of the Arab states' involvement was that world Jewry's support of Zionism should be balanced by the Arab world's support of the Palestinians. But world Jewry did not place insurmountable obstacles before the pragmatism of the Zionist leaders and often gave enthusiastic support. By contrast, the Arab states complicated the conflict by imposing additional interests, some of them very extreme, and did not contribute to its moderation. The decisive Jewish-Zionist coalition in 1937 succeeded in mobilizing some of their opponents by integrating national interests with pragmatic political maneuvering. By contrast, the Arab-Palestinian coalition adopted the most extreme position toward the royal commission's recommendations and even toward the White Paper of 1939. As a result, partition would be implemented ten years later by force and would receive international legitimacy and regional acquiescence without the consent of the Palestinian Arabs.

State, Territory, and Boundaries: The Meaning of the 1937 Decision

A number of general questions were raised in Chapter One about state, territory, and boundaries. We will examine here what can be learned from the 1937 decision of the Zionist movement regarding these issues. Several comparative hypotheses will be drawn based on an analysis of the case study presented. In the chapter that follows, we shall place the 1937 decision on the continuum of other territorial decisions taken by the Zionist movement up to the founding of the state of Israel.

Territorial Behavior

The territorial decision in the Zionist movement has a general significance, because the dispersed Jewish people is often presented as a case of "nonterritorial nationalism."[41] We noted the positions of Magnes and Buber who opposed the territorial solution in the partition debate of 1937. Hannah Arendt maintained, after the state of Israel was established, that the Jews are a nation even in the absence of territory.[42] On the other hand, the Zionist ethos was entirely one of territory. At the end of the nineteenth century, the Zionist movement adopted the western nationalist orientation, including the centrality of territory and even the concept of the formative role of the homeland.

The homeland for Ussishkin and Jabotinsky was intended to reshape the Jewish nation, whereas a different kind of geographic determinism was offered by Yonatan Ratosh and the "New Hebrews" (later called the *Canaanites*). In this movement, territory and language are the sole basis for national identity, and the rest is peripheral.[43] Although the nationalism of Ratosh appeared to be neither Jewish nor Zionist, it sought to impose the (nationalist?) vision of one people (the Hebrews?) on the other peoples of the region. It was, in the final analysis, territorial (and linguistic) etatism, of a rather primitive variety, which was intended to underscore the claim that "a land belongs to its conqueror."[44]

Elements of territorial nativism were interwoven in the 1937 debate, as the arguments raised were a rich amalgam of emotions and needs, values and interests. However, the approach that regarded parts of the territory as a trade-off—a means to attain political sovereignty—captured the majority vote. From 1937 to 1947, the Zionist movement was embroiled in an ongoing debate of these issues, to the extent that the political department of the Jewish Agency formulated a "doctrine" of how to present the Jewish arguments in three points: the *right* of Jews to immigrate to the Land of Israel; the *need* for a state of their own; and the *actual achievements* of Zionism.[45] This combination of arguments integrates the instrumental need with the expressive right. It also points out the actual achievements to validate both the right and the need.

The 1937 debate and the resulting decision reflect the duality presented in Chapter One: territorial attitudes as both emotional, inseparable from a sense of collective identity, and as a means for satisfying specific needs. On the one hand, territory is fatherland, motherland, and homeland. On the other, it is a source of livelihood, a natural treasure, and a resource like any other. We have seen how even the most practical instrumentalists recognized the symbolic significance of the Land of Israel and hoped that, despite the necessary concessions, it would be possible to expand the state's territory in the future; and how the most emotional expressivists wove into their presentations practical arguments about economic viability and secure boundaries. We have also seen that the struggle was mostly over winning the hearts of the undecided, who were torn between their emotional link to the entire Land of Israel and their political realism that called for seizing the opportunity to attain a bit of Jewish sovereignty. The 1937 choice of the Zionist movement was a painful majority decision in favor of instrumental pragmatism. By contrast, we have noted that the expressive component won the upper hand in the decision of the Palesinian national movement. This strengthens the assumption that territorial decisions can be compared according to the emphasis placed on these two components.

The general hypotheses derived from an analysis of the Zionist decision in 1937 is as follows: the territorial behavior of a human collective reflects the existence of the two components, and perhaps the struggle between them: territory as an emotional component, inseparable from the sense of common identity, and territory as a means to attain other human objectives.

Political Sovereignty and Territory

It is surprising how little of the vast quantity of written material relates to the essence of the "Jewish state" around which the
argument revolved in 1937. Perhaps this was unnecessary because
the longing for a Jewish state "after 2,000 years," as was often
said, was so self-evident that it required no explanation. Indeed,
the state was regarded as a powerful tool that would enable the
Jews, at last, to determine their own destiny, particularly through
control of immigration, land purchase, and settlement.

Which of the four definitions of state (see Table 1.1) including
their perceptions of territory was espoused by the leaders who made
the 1937 decisions? From the little they said on the issue, we can
deduct that two of the possibilities were not on their minds. They
did not think in terms of MacIver's "civic state" as a sort of "association" with limited functions, whose territory delineates no more
than the boundaries of legal sovereignty. The Zionist leaders were
too involved in the struggle with the British and the Arabs to adopt
such a purely instrumental view of both state and territory. Further, most of them did not regard the state as an organic unity,
whose natural boundaries and territory are determined by geographical or historical imperatives. Some important groups within
the Zionist movement did proffer these arguments, and we have
surveyed them extensively. But the leadership behind the 1937
decision belittled and degraded the mystical ideologies of their
opponents, even though they themselves utilized this reasoning
both internally and outwardly. Ben-Gurion, for instance, who told
the royal commission that "the Bible is our mandate," would not
think of presenting such arguments at internal Mapai meetings.
Another interesting question in this context is the degree of willingness of the leadership to hold to a pragmatic position and to
justify it to the general public, which by nature tends toward more
expressive arguments.

In the eyes of the pragmatic trio—Weizmann, Ben-Gurion,
and Shertok—state formation was seen as a process of power
struggles. And, by inference, the extent of the territory and its
precise boundaries were also the result of power contests. However,
for them *power* meant actual force, as well as political, organizational, and spiritual strength. When they repeatedly asked "what
is our strength?" they referred to the number of Jews in the land
and the economic power of Zionism, as well as to the movement's
political skill and determination.

The state that they conceptualized was that which they knew from the formation of European nation-states in the nineteenth century and from European imperialism in Asia and Africa. From this perspective, they, and Zionism as a whole, presented an un-equivocal solution to the Jewish people: sovereignty in a territorial state. Hence there was clear overlap in the dominant Zionist perception between political sovereignty and territorial control—similar to the European views during this period. We will also note the strong etatistic element in this approach, the state as an end in itself. That eventually evolved into Ben-Gurion's well-known "statism" policies after the establishment of Israel in 1948.[46]

The general hypothesis drawn from an analysis of this case concerning the connection between territory and political sovereignty is well known: At the revolutionary stage, national movements view the state as the revelation of everything and strive for sovereignty over as much territory as possible. Because this stage usually entails a power struggle, expressive arguments are used to mobilize public support, though at the end of the process, political sovereignty is what defines the territory and not vice versa.

The Nation-State

Zionism achieved its goals in the first half of the twentieth century. It missed the "spring of nationalism" in Europe and appeared a bit too early to be part of the liberation movements in Asia and Africa. This is not the only oddity. One of Zionism's riddles was the difficulty in conceptualizing and defining the *Jewish nation,* particularly because of the initial lack of that essential component of nationhood: common territory.[47] For Zionism, unlike other national movements, the problem was not merely how to define the geographic legitimacy of the nation-state or where to run the "line" separating itself from others. It also could not rely on the present territorial situation, but only on the past and the future. A people with too much history was looking for a little geography, it could be said. Hence the attempt to combine arguments of historical rights with the need to solve the current Jewish problem in the Land of Israel. Zionism's claim to a nation-state was therefore based on a future situation in which the Jews would become a majority in the land.

Why, of all places, Eretz Israel? The Zionist movement had previously struggled against the "territorialists" who favored a Jewish-national solution, not necessarily in Eretz Israel. Although this debate never completely disappeared, it was not on the agenda of the Zionist movement after the sixth congress in 1903 had rejected Uganda as a shelter for the Jews. It was practically resolved by the Balfour Declaration and the mandate, which established that the Jewish national home would be located geographically in Palestine. In this respect, 1937 was a turning point because, for the first time, the debate was not over the location but rather the extent of Jewish sovereignty in Palestine, even though the Jews had just begun the process of demographic concentration. Almost all the participants in the 1937 debate saw the Land of Israel as the sole solution, even if there remained some "territorialists" among the opponents of partition.[48] However, some opponents accused the proponents of espousing "territorialism" *within* the Land of Israel: If a state is so important, why not establish it somewhere else?

The answer of the proponents indicates the mixture of arguments and that an instrumental territorial claim can be derived from expressive attachment. They said that Jewish nationalism, like any nationalism, requires a common locus of identification: in this case, Eretz Israel. Moreover, Eretz Israel is this emotional and intangible component without which there is no Zionism and no Zionist practical politics.[49] The most ardent pragmatists agreed with Ussishkin's emphasis on the symbolic significance of "our meager and poor homeland," by contrast with other rich places. But they opposed the political conclusions that he derived from this emotional identification. In short, the Zionists no longer disagreed about the Land of Israel being the only proper site for realizing the goals of the Jewish national movement. The argument was and remains whether this requires *all* of the Land of Israel. As noted, the proponents of partition made a distinction between the emotional identification with the Land of Israel and the practical issue of the sovereign boundaries of the Jewish state.

The proponents were prepared to make territorial concessions, provisional or permanent, to expedite and found the Jewish nation-state. Facing them, however, was the opposing claim of the Palestinian Arabs based both on the past (historical rights of about 1,000 years) and on the present (a majority presence) as the basis for establishing their own nation-state. Those among the Palestinians who held out for separate independence (from Transjordan, Syria, or a Pan-Arab framework), pointed out that the borders of the neighboring Arab states had also been set in an arbitrary manner by the colonial powers. The Palestinian Arabs were not willing to define the problem in terms of boundaries between two (Arab and Jewish) nations. They rejected the concept of partiton because they did not recognize that the Jews have legitimate rights like their own to Palestine. Both movements were in an embryonic stage of realizing their right to self-determination, which explains the importance they attributed to terrritory as a focus of identity and the exclusivity of their claims. Most of the national Jewish movement, which was then fewer in number than the Palestinian Arabs, were willing to compromise and share. The majority of the Palestinian national movement preferred to cling to the concept of "all mine."

The general hypothesis drawn from analysis of the case concerning the territorial nation-state derived to a great extent from the centrality of Eretz Israel to Jewish self-determination. First, we said that nationalism is a very powerful collective impulse that found an ally in the state. Now we can add that the Jewish case, despite all of its nongeographic aspects, also testifies to the importance of the territorial basis in the nation-state-territory triangle.

Second, the new explanations for the growth of nationalism as a social and economic process (see Chapter One) also apply to the accelerated wave of Jewish immigration to Eretz Israel in the 1930s. Yet emotional identification with the people and its designated territory was the most important element in this developmental stage of the Jewish national movement.

Third, it is evident in hindsight that the binational solutions proposed by small Jewish groups with no Arab support didn't stand a chance or came long before their time. The nationalist impulse among Jews and Arabs was too strong and demanded expression in separate territorial-political frameworks. It seems that voluntary concessions of separate national self-determination within distinct sovereign frameworks could be considered only later, it at all, when the self-confidence of the national movement would grow with respect to its identity and ability to survive. The protracted Arab-Israeli conflict indicates that this is still not the case for either side.

Fourth, Zionism rejected the thesis that the Jewish nation could survive without a state. It strove for the fullest possible correspondence between the territorial state and the Jewish nation and rejected binational or multinational solutions. This is also true of the aspirations of the national Palestinian movement, even though it did not realize its goal. In other words, the European model of the territorial nation-state served as the basis for imitation (and clashes) for both these movements, though they were so different from each other.

Fifth, the 1937 decision verified our initial hypothesis that there are contradictory collective loyalties that compete among themselves. But national loyalty is clearly paramount as long as a particular nationalism struggles to achieve and maintain territorial sovereignty in the international arena.[50]

Geopolitics

Did the geopolitical thought of that period influence the positions of the leaders who participated in the 1937 debate? We have no evidence, for example, that Tabenkin read the writings of Ratzel and Kjellén, or that Jabotinsky was familiar with the theories of MacKinder and Spykman. We should also point out that only states and leaders powerful enough to move pieces on the international chessboard were able to translate theoretical geopolitics into practical politics. Zionism at that time was a small, embattled movement, totally dependent on the colonial power, and could conduct only defensive geopolitics. The central leaders were aware of the fact that the geopolitical assets of 400,000 Jews in Eretz Israel are rather limited, and the Jewish Agency made an effort to increase the leverage of the Zionist enterprise by representing world Jewry. The physical presence in Eretz Israel, despite its centrality to the Zionist ideology, was only one element in the international politics of the Zionist movement. In contrast with other national movements (including the Palestinian) whose territorial presence was the basis of their claim to self-determination, Zionism emphasized the anomaly of "the Jewish problem" in the world, and thus sought to make up for the inferiority of its geographic claim.

Because of these realities, and possibly under the influence of the liberal and socialist ideologies, determinism in general and the geographic variety in particular were alien to leaders such as Weizmann and Ben-Gurion. They harbored no images of an organic state or society that behaves according to immutable laws of evolution, including territorial expansionism. They did not regard human history, or at least political history, as an amalgamation of geographic facts. We did, however, note several threads of geopolitical determinsim within the Zionist movement:

- Hakibbutz Hameuchad wavered between the Marxist approach that attributed a limited (and temporary) role to the state and the geopolitical approach of the Kjellén school, which held that states strive to reach natural boundaries externally and harmonious unity internally. On the one hand, the social revolution was for them the essential goal and the state was not the ideal; on the other hand, Eretz Israel was considered one geographic unit, with the desert forming the security boundary of the Jewish state that would arise in the future.

• The religious camp was divided. The "patriotism" of the ultra-Orthodox toward the Land of Israel was spiritual, as opposed to that of the religious Zionists, which was also national and territorial. Mizrahi's combination of land and redemption was political, religious, and suffused with romantic symbols of the ancient connection to Eretz Israel, integrating holiness with national revival and statehood. This combination of uniqueness (of people and the land) and divine promise can also be found in other religious movements. We have also seen how the Nazi ideologues turned this into a slogan of "religious unity" between race and God.

• The most deterministic, however, were those secular Zionists who presented the grand vision of the bond between nation and history. For them, the homeland was the beginning and the end—the essence of national identity and even a substitute for the vision of the "end of days." Their romantic worship of the land was semireligious and called to mind German geopolitical writings that emphasize the mystical bond between the "nation's spirit" and the tangible territorial homeland. To this group can be added the "Hebrew movement" of Ratosh, who dreamed of founding a state in the geopolitical borders of the "fertile crescent," called by him the *Land of the Euphrates*.[51]

• In the 1937 debate on partition, Jabotinsky was defined as an instrumental opponent because his central argument concerned the need for a large territory as a refuge for millions of Jews. We noted that this position also reflected geopolitical attitudes concerning the unity of the land, and historical and religious arguments assigning to the Land of Israel a vital role in shaping the character of the Jewish nation.[52] Population density as a motive for territorial expansion was a central theme in German geopolitics. Jabotinsky thus laid the foundations for the perception among his followers that the greater Land of Israel, on both banks of the Jordan River, is a necessary "living space," thereby combining needs of nationalism (the wholeness of the people), economics (natural resources), and strategy (secure boundaries). The obfuscation of the distinction between "German land" and the "German state" would also turn up in the form of desired unity between geography and sovereignty, between the "Land of Israel" and the "state of Israel."

Geopolitical reasonings have played a role in the Zionist debate regarding state, territory, and boundaries ever since 1937. However, no Zionist stream or leader adopted the theories concerning the natural "unity" of the organic state constructed upon the links of blood and land, land and nation, nation and race, race and God. Demographic-political determinism and mythology of blood and land (*blut and boden*) appeared in many national movements that arose under the influence of the western model of the national-territorial state.

The general hypotheses drawn from the analysis of the "geopolitical currents" in Zionism is that geopolitics as a scientific attempt to explain the behavior of states is but a reflection of the deterministic elements of territorial ideologies. National territorial ideologies are therefore multipurpose for varied forms of political behavior.[53] To this should be added a corollary concerning the use of maps in the service of territorial ideologies. In Nazi Germany, maps were constantly used as propaganda by the pseudo-geographers. One such map distributed on the eve of World War II showing the giant British empire beside the puny German territory, was captioned, "Who is the aggressor nation?" The phenomenon of putting cartography in the service of territorial ideology exists in various forms in other places as well.[54]

Strategy and International Relations

Did Zionism have strategic "assets" that it could trade with the great powers? After the Balfour Declaration, Zionism saw itself as an ally of British interests in the Middle East. And, while the shifts in British policy during 1922–1937 expressed a search for allies among the Arabs, these were not necessarily at the expense of the Jewish national home. Unsuccessful attempts were also made to separate the contradictory British obligations in Palestine from those toward the neighboring Arab states established after World War I. Similarly, the royal commission's 1937 proposals evidence a British experiment to satisfy the conflicting Jewish and Arab claims to Palestine while safeguarding central British interests. On the eve of World War II, when Britain decided to change its allies in the region, it presented the Zionist movement with a fait accompli. The other European powers—Italy, not to mention Germany—did not strike the Zionist leadership as potential allies for advancing the Zionist cause. Contacts between Weizmann and Mussolini in the early 1930s came to naught, and Italy was never regarded as an alternative to Great Britain.[55] From 1939, however, the Zionist movement began to look around for support from other quarters, principally in the United States.

The lessons from these events, as regards our subject, are far from unequivocal. On the one hand, the British government, particularly the Foreign Office, considered the Jewish community in Palestine to be a very limited strategic asset and did not hesitate to trade it away. The same holds true for the Palestinian Arabs, also regarded by the British as of minor importance or totally insignificant if not for their connection to the interests of neighboring Arab rulers. On the other hand, the British found themselves in a deadlock between the Jews and Arabs in Palestine and, in a wider sense, between Zionism and the Arab and Moslem world. The British mandate for Palestine (E.I.) was, first and foremost, a realization of essential strategic and international interests that the British had the required strength and geographic presence to preserve. Yet, the non-geopolitical factors—the intercommunal local conflict and the external Jewish and Arab interests—ultimately led to British abandonment of Palestine. This took place after 1945 and is usually attributed to the general demise of the British empire, but these "other" factors were active and influential even before the war.

From this point of view, the 1937 royal commission proposal is an instructive lesson in international relations. Britain strove to reduce its global military and financial obligations and, to this end, was willing to risk a certain reduction of its direct control in Palestine (E.I.). This was the main reason for the 1937 policy, which was briefly adopted by the British government. But this was not the only reason. As opposed to the strategic considerations, less concrete factors such as nationalist feelings of the local communities also played an important role.[56] A quick examination of the partition map of 1937 demonstrates that the royal commission violated almost all the "rules" of geopolitical theories: three types of sovereignty in one tiny territory; long and circuitous artificial boundaries;

indefensible borders; and the establishment of two states lacking even minimal compactness. Accordingly, this case requires an analysis of the impact of the independent political variables upon the dependent spatial variables, and not vice versa, as suggested by the geopolitical model.[57] More broadly speaking, the political processes are much more important for understanding the Israeli-Arab conflict than the geopolitical or the geostrategic component.

Hence, the general hypothesis from this case concerning the international partition of the geographic space was formulated by Gottmann as early as 1952: "It is people and not state territory that determine the web of foreign relations. . . . The uniqueness of [a state's] 'geographical status' is principally a political outcome."[58]

Boundaries

The preceeding conclusion is even more applicable to the question of boundaries. We said in Chapter One that the search for a natural, sharp, and "correct" delineation of boundaries will never be successful. This was well-evidenced by the practical alternatives facing the Zionist movement in 1937 and by the decision that it adopted.

First, in contrast with the map submitted by the Zionist movement in 1919 (see Map 1.1), the map of 1938 (submitted to the Woodhead commission) lacked any geographic logic whatsoever (see Map 9.1). This was primarily a result of the willingness to compromise with political reality. It could be argued that the debate itself proved how geographically unreasonable the 1937 partition proposal was, and of course, it was never realized. But Zionist agreement to the 1947 partition boundaries (see Map 11.1) and particularly to the armistice lines of 1949 (see Map 11.2) reinforces the conclusion about the uniqueness of each boundary and that generalizations in this regard are highly dubious. The counterargument that political machinations always ruin strict geographic logic is insufficient to refute this conclusion.

Second, the royal commission's delineation of the boundaries and the debate itself placed little emphasis on the security aspect. What does this mean for the prevailing assumption that security and defensive needs are the most important motivators of territorial behavior? Some of the opponents of partition raised security arguments and demanded that the Jordan River be the eastern boundary, with borders as short and natural as possible. They also believed that the proposed state would be strategically untenable. In contrast, the proponents of partition, among them some security-minded members of the Haganah, played down the overriding importance of this argument and claimed that it was not the boundaries that would determine security, but rather the political circumstances and the prospects for peace with the Arabs. Some even said that if the existence of the Jewish state depended only on cannon fire not coming from the hills, then it had no right to exist. This position triumphed within the Zionist movement in 1937, 1947, and 1949. It represents an attempt to combine tangible physical security (military control positions, fortification lines, natural barriers, and defensible borders) within the wider context of political, economic, and military power.

Third, the shape of the state proposed in 1937 contradicted the accepted norms regarding the relation between territory and boundary length (see Table 1.2). Had the partition accepted by the Zionist movement in 1947 been implemented, it would have resulted in the most uncompact state in the world, even compared with Chile and Thailand. This is equally true of the boundaries of the State of Israel formed on the basis of the 1949 armistice lines, which resulted from a military campaign and diplomatic negotiations. These boundaries were long and winding, and Jerusalem—the capital city— was not in the center of a territorial circle, but at its most exposed edge.

In the first phase of Jewish nationalism in the nineteenth century, the still-unsettled argument began about the most complex question: the actual *need* for a separate territory for the Jews. There were advocates of other nonnational and nonterritorial solutions to the Jewish question: assimilation, emigration, universal, and antinationalistic ideologies. In the second phase, among the supporters of Jewish territorial concentration, the question of the *place* was raised: Where would the collective solution be located, in the Land of Israel or elsewhere?[59] This question was answered when the great majority in the Zionist movement rejected Herzl's Uganda proposal and declared itself "Zionists for Zion." In the third phase, the central question was *international recognition* of the Jewish right to a "national home" of their own, namely, territorial concentration in Palestine. The mandatory charter of the League of Nations, which included the Balfour Declaration, constituted the first international legitimization of the bond between the Jewish people and the Land of Israel. In the fourth phase, which we examined in this book, the practical possibility that the process would result in the establishment of a *sovereign territorial state* in the Land of Israel was placed on the agenda. The fifth phase continued from then on, and has not yet ended, despite the establishment of the state of Israel and its wide international recognition. It touches on the question of *delimiting* exactly how far the territory of the Jewish-Israeli state extends in the eyes of its residents as well as its neighbors.

The questions relating to the role of territory in the realization of Zionist goals were raised from the beginning of this long process. The arguments raised in the 1937 debate demonstrate the combination of expressive and instrumental components in collective territorial behavior. This strengthens the proposition that territorial behavior is built layer upon layer, at the base of which lie the most sensitive matters of self and collective identity. This rudimentary layer feeds the feelings of there being some sort of geographic determinism, national or cultural, that dictates territorial behavior. The assumption that this layer of primordial feelings is also a code that explains political behavior requires substantiation. It is very doubtful that these feelings are monolithic, particularly in the heterogeneous Jewish collective, which included not just religious and secular people but also some who denied the very existence of Jewish nationalism. What is more, the transition from "the holiness of the land" to determinism that dictates political decisions requires mental acrobatics and contradicts the facts of Zionist history. The decision presented in this book testifies that the attempt to create a necessary link between self-identity and the entire land of Israel was rejected. As a result, instrumental pragmatism prevailed in the Zionist movement in the decade following 1937. The divergence of arguments and positions (Figure 5.1) reflects the complex attitudes toward the state, territory, and boundaries. By contrast, the distribution of the votes (Figure 9.1) proves an ability of the majority to cluster around a compromise resolution that favored the partition principle. This approach of giving in on a longed-for aspiration in exchange for political sovereignty in a portion of Eretz Israel dominated in the Zionist movement and the State of Israel until 1967.

The general hypothesis drawn from this case has already been noted and is evident to anyone who looks at a map of the world with its mosaic of political sovereignties, still changing in the twentieth century. Boundaries between states are the result of political decisions. Even when lines that distort the topographic or demographic reality are imposed, the separation itself gradually assumes its own reality. After all, linguistic, religious, cultural, and national barriers between human beings are also artificial boundaries created over the years in response to specific circumstances. The sudden concreteness of imposed political boundaries, in contrast with the gradual evolution of other human barriers, is that which bestows a seemingly greater importance to territorial boundaries. Hence the central role of nationalism in determining human lines of separation in the modern era. The modern nation-state was intended to create a visible correspondence between territorial control and the identity locus. Yet, as we have emphasized in this book, the nation-state-territory triangle is a relatively new (200 year-old) combination, and there is no guarantee of immutability.

Territorial Decisions

The decision in the Zionist movement required a choice between incommensurable values. Territory is tangible and measureable, its possession and control either exist or do not. Forgoing territory is viewed as irreversible and contradictory to the prevalent image of human territorial instincts. Sovereignty, by contrast, is intangible and conditioned on many external factors that determine whether or not it exists and to what extent. Hence, the difficulty in forgoing territory in return for promises of sovereignty or other values.

The interesting comparative point stemming from the analysis of the 1937 decision is the choice formulation. When the proposal to postpone the decision was rejected, two possibilities were left. One was to continue to claim the entire Land of Israel, all or nothing. The other was to seize the opportunity to legitimize sovereignty through a willingness to accept an "appropriate" part of the land. The second approach prevailed in 1937 and also determined Zionist policy toward the United Nations' partition resolution of 1947 and, to a large degree, the armistice agreements of 1949, when international recognition of the state of Israel was the central goal. By contrast, in the Palestinian national movement the first approach prevailed.

The answer to the central question presented in this book is the following: In 1937 the Zionist movement was willing to consider a trade-off—territory for other values.[60] The primary "other" value for which willingness was expressed to limit (or delay) the territorial aspirations of Zionism was political sovereignty. From the point of view of the Zionist movement, the long-term achievement of the decision in 1937 was the beginning of external legitimacy to a status change: from a national home to a Jewish state. To the Palestinian movement, the Zionist achievement marked a defeat, especially because they could not record any progress in attaining international legitimacy for Palestinian sovereignty.

This conclusion rests on the fact that we know in retrospect, of course, that a Jewish state was founded ten years later, whereas the national Palestinian movement did not achieve its aim. But even if we posit for the sake of argument a different hypothetical situation, the conclusion still stands. Let us assume that the opponents carried the day and the Zionist movement would have decided in 1937 to reject the principle of partition and demand sovereignty over the entire Land of Israel. Although our ability to predict the reactions of others is limited, we can suggest some avenues of speculation. Let us take as given that British policy in the region was set according to its own global interests on the brink of World War II and not the desires of other parties.[61] There are two hypothetical cases. One, if the Palestinian movement would have also rejected the proposal, the 1939 White Paper policy would not have been significantly different. But then the Zionist movement after 1945 would have been in an inferior position internationally, particularly vis-à-vis Great Britain, in its demand to carry out the principle that it had previously rejected. And would the United Nations committee in 1947 (UNSCOP) have recommended partition—the option preferred by the Zionist movement—among the other alternatives it considered?[62]

The other possibility—that the Palestinians would have endorsed the royal commission—would certainly have made it easier for the British to carry out their veiled promise in 1939 to establish an Arab, and possibly a Palestinian, state separate from Transjordan. A situation could even be imagined in which the events of 1947–1948 would have taken place in 1937, but reversed: An Arab state would be established in Palestine, with or without autonomy for the Jews in their strongholds.

Beyond this speculation, the least that can be said is that the decision in 1937 did not in any way harm the Zionist endeavor and even scored an important victory in the face of Palestinian refusal. Internally, the 1937 decision prepared the ground for adoption of the partition plan in 1947, which contributed to attainment of Jewish sovereignty one year later. Externally, it should be said to the credit of the political vision of Weizmann and Ben-Gurion, that their prediction that the partition plan would return sooner or later did indeed come true. The fact that all this is known to us after the fact strengthens the claim of this book: that, when all is said and done, political developments are what determine the significance of territorial decisions.

11 Territorial Decisions in the Zionist Movement (1919–1949)

The great debate of 1937 and the decision taken then have receded into the background, because of both the turnaround in British policy on the eve of World War II and the more famous United Nations partition plan of 1947. The significance of the 1937 decision is not in its concrete consequences, but in its having been a crossroads into which other decisions led and from which they issued. This was the first time the Zionist movement felt incumbent upon it to make a decision about the territorial boundaries of the Jewish state; this was the first public debate about the subject since the earliest days of Herzlian Zionism; this was the first opportunity to view the range of internal opinions and put them to a test, translating attitudes to a binding democratic decision. To the credit of the 1937 debate, very few new thoughts have been added since then to the internal Jewish debate about a state, territory, and boundaries. Although over half a century has passed and despite the changed circumstances, almost no single argument is heard today in the debate in Israel about territories and boundaries that had not been sounded in those days. For example, the argument that Israel should not "offer a map," lest this become the minimal demands of the opposite side.

This chapter deviates from the material previously presented about the 1937 decision, because it deals with the general issue of territorial decisions in the Zionist movement. An attempt will be made to place the 1937 decision in the wider context of other central decisions of the Zionist movement leading up to the founding of the state of Israel.

1919

The 1917 Balfour Declaration in which Great Britain promised to "view with favor" the establishment in Palestine of a national home

273

for the Jews did not mention territories or boundaries. In 1919, the Zionist movement for the first time presented a map indicating its territorial aspirations for the boundaries of the Jewish national home (see Chapter Two). This map expressed political goals based on geographic principles, even relying, with some important exceptions, on the natural features of the region[1] (see Map 1.1). Thus it touched on the principles that sought objective justification for the geographical basis of the right of national self-determination (see Chapter One). We also saw how the willingness to make pragmatic compromises was already evident in the Zionist memorandum submitted to the Versailles Peace Conference: the understanding with Faisal that Zionist claims in the east would be moderated by Arab claims; consideration of France's ambitions in the Levant regarding claims in the north; willingness to make "concessions" to the British on the southern border; and the indication that the border between the Jewish national home and the Sinai would be agreed upon with the Egyptian government.

The territory requested by the Zionist movement in 1919 encompassed more than 45,000 km^2 and the ratio between the area and the length of its boundaries would have created a "compact" entity with relatively short and "natural" boundaries. The 1919 map presented the broadest territory ever officially demanded by the Zionist movement.[2] It was smaller, however, than the prevailing definition of the "Land of Israel in its natural boundaries," which encompassed approximately 59,000 km^2.[3] The Zionist claims in 1919 concerning Transjordan were also more limited than the territory of 90,000 km^2 that would become the future British mandate there. The 1919 map was based on a number of internal drafts and external political negotiations. Its preparation was not accompanied by a heated debate within the Zionist Organization about territory versus other considerations, and therefore it should not be viewed as a decision crossroads in the sense that we attribute to the 1937 decision. It can be regarded as a map of Zionist aspirations and a source of the various claims concerning the instrumental and expressive significance of territories that were gradually "removed" from the Jewish national home. Indeed, out of the 45,000 km^2 included in the original Zionist claim of 1919, only 27,000 km^2 remained for the "national home" in Palestine (E.I.) after the San Remo Conference (1920) and the establishment of Abdullah's emirate in Transjordan (1922).[4]

Even the separation of Transjordan was not accompanied by an internal debate that can be regarded as a decision crossroads.[5] The Zionist movement expressed its opposition, but was helpless in the face of British policy and the weight of the League of Nations mandate. Despite the continuous debate with the Revisionists, the status of Transjordan in the territorial claims of the Zionist movement was never formally determined. However, the debate within the Zionist movement principally concerned the territory of western Eretz Israel, with the few exceptions already noted.

1937

The territorial proposal of the royal commission would have left approximately 10 percent of the original 1919 claim in Jewish hands, totalling only 20 percent of the territory of western Eretz Israel (see Map 2.1). However, the proposal was the first opportunity for the Jews to have a state of their own, and this was the dilemma of "territory versus sovereignty" around which the great debate of 1937 revolved. The unprecedented nature of this debate is evident by comparison with all debates on this matter to this day.

The fact that the dilemma was not defined in "all or nothing" terms made possible a serious discussion of the issues. The actual influence of the Zionist movement at that time was rather limited and the weight of its decision was far from crucial. Moreover, the British proposal seemed to be so unattractive and so risky that the instinctive initial reaction of most Zionist leaders was negative (see Chapter Five). This is also why the undecided were the largest group until just before the decision was made at the congress. This in turn influenced the substance of the argument as well as the complexity of the decision-making process. In examining today the vast body of material remaining from the 1937 debate, one cannot but be impressed by the forcefulness and cogency of the arguments. Applying the 1937 debate to the post-1967 debate in Israel about territories and boundaries would enrich the latter, despite the profound changes that stem primarily from the establishment of the state. Many of the terms of discourse serving the current argument were first used in 1937. To note a few,

- In general: partition, historic rights, natural boundaries, secure borders, transfer, drawing maps.

- Among the opponents: not an inch (of land), Greater (undivided) Israel, the integrity of the land, both banks of the Jordan River, a state on both banks of the Yarkon River, the promised land, the land of our forefathers.

- Among the proponents: compromise, peace in exchange for . . . , a state now, the Massada complex, political boundaries, "Eretz Israel" as an aspiration only.

The 1937 debate was open and public, but the leadership took upon itself the task of defining the agenda for decision. Despite the complexity of the issue, the positions were divided into two main camps, colloquially termed *opponents* and *proponents*, and consequently into two identifiable options. This dichotomy created a public agenda of structured possibilities and of a choice between two real options. In Chapter Nine, we pointed out that the leadership avoided the option of "deciding not to decide" out of a belief that this would be a lost opportunity. It also did not avoid the necessity of presenting a map of specific territorial demands to the 1938 Woodhead commission. The 1937 decision was made under overbearing external constraints, and indeed shortly thereafter the British retracted their offer. Thus, the immediate impact of the Zionist movement's 1937 decision was relatively limited; its internal significance, however, was crucial.

The fact that a decision was taken, qualified but unprecedented, provided a response to all four conditions of the undecided camp, who had feared that the proposed state would (a) be too small, (b) not have a clear Jewish majority, (c) be opposed by the Arabs, and (d) have indefensible borders. These conditions also reflected the key issues that arose, despite the changed circumstances, in the following round: the United Nations proposal of 1947 and the de facto partition of 1948–1949. The response given in 1937 was that, despite these risks, the advantages of sovereignty and agreement in principle to partition exceed the disadvantages of territorial loss. We labeled the willingness to adopt this approach a victory of instrumentalism over expressivism in the Zionist movement. In retrospect, the 1937 decision created the basis for the policy of step-by-step realization of the Zionist goals of territorial sovereignty—a political application of the incremental approach, which was already being applied in matters of land acquisition and settlement.[6] It also paved the way for thirty years (1937–1967) of consensus among the great majority of the Jewish public on the territorial partition of western Eretz Israel.

1947

Can one speak of continuing trends in the Jewish world and the Zionist movement after the rupture of World War II and the destruction of European Jewry? A great deal had changed for the Jewish world and the Zionist movement after the Holocaust. In the two and a half event-filled years between the end of World War II and the United Nations decision in November 1947, it seemed as if everything was different. Indeed, far-reaching changes had taken place in the realm of international relations, in the context of which the Zionist movement adopted its second partition resolution in 1947. What had not fundamentally changed was the Arab-Jewish conflict in Palestine/Eretz Israel, the dominant involvement of out-side powers in the local conflict, and the continuing dilemma faced by the Zionist movement concerning the importance of territory versus other goals. Although the war was over, there was a need, now much more urgent, to find a solution to the suffering of the European Jewish refugees. The struggle to revoke the 1939 White Paper policies of the British government now dovetailed with the demand for Jewish self-government, or at least for control over immigration. In early 1941, Berl Katznelson wrote that from the day that the Peel commission uttered the "forbidden word"— a Jewish state—this became a practical possibility and the minimal demand of the Zionist movement.[7] Establishment of a Jewish state was now regarded by the Zionist leadership as the primary goal. A flyer published by the Jewish Agency executive on the day of the Allied victory declared: "The Jewish people must be awarded the status it deserves among the world community of free states. Let the Jewish state of Eretz Israel be one of the fruits of victory."[8]

But let us not run ahead. Although the royal commission par-tition proposal was officially interred in 1938, partition continued to serve as the basis for discussions between the British govern-ment, headed by Churchill, and Weizmann. Outwardly, the Zionist leadership started to demand the entire Land of Israel, although it remained willing to discuss partition even during the war.[9] One important stepping stone was the "Biltmore Declaration" in the May 1942 conference of American Zionists, ratified that November by the Jewish Agency executive. The Biltmore Declaration called for the establishment of "Eretz Israel as a Jewish commonwealth," integrated with the new democratic world order, and the opening up of the gates of the country to unlimited immigration under the supervision of the Jewish Agency. The Biltmore Declaration was regarded as a victory for the maximalists and criticized by those who believed in an incremental realization of Zionist goals, which did not depend on the immediate realization of a Jewish state.[10]

The declaration did not mention partition, territories, or bound-aries, but was perceived as a return to the original demand for

Jewish control of the entire Land of Israel. But partition was not ruled out by this declaration, which was essentially an internal compromise intended to rally around it all those who had supported the immediate creation of a Jewish state in the 1937 debate, both opponents and proponents. Its main purpose was to give legitimacy to a Jewish state and win support for the idea in the United States. There was no surrender of Weizmann or Ben-Gurion to the concept of "the integrity of the land," as Dothan argues, because the strong opponents too were upset that the declaration failed to take a clear stand against partition.[11] For example, this is how the opponents of "Faction B" (Ahdut Ha'Avoda) formulated their reservations about the Biltmore Declaration: "Missing from the decisions is an unrelenting demand for the entire Land of Israel, unpartitioned, entirely open to immigration and settlement, to concentration of the Jewish people, and to full political independence."[12]

The Biltmore Declaration was more extreme than the 1937 decision, because the Arabs of Palestine were not mentioned at all, and Eretz Israel was presented as the land of the Jews only. A. Shapira views this as "resignation to the existence of a national conflict between Jews and Arabs which cannot be resolved [and] secret acceptance that only the sword could unravel this Gordian knot."[13] But partition was not on the internal agenda during the period of the war, and thus the declaration was not a decision crossroads on this issue.

The period after the war was characterized by the twists and turns of British policy toward Palestine (E.I.) and increasing involvement of the United States and later of the United Nations. For our purposes, we will concentrate only on the key decisions in the Zionist movement concerning the issue of territory and borders in the crowded years of 1946–1947.

The first important decision was taken during the deliberations of the Anglo-American committee of enquiry set up in November 1945, which published its report in April 1946.[14] At the outset, there was a debate about whether the agency should appear before the commission, with those opposed viewing the committee as yet another British conspiracy and preferring instead to intensify the struggle against the British through the combined forces of all the Jewish underground military movements. In December 1945, the Zionist general council decided to have representatives from the Jewish Agency and other Jewish organizations appear before the committee, but this decision was publicized only in February 1946. The debate over which line the Zionists should take with the committee again touched on the old controversy: a maximalist demand to establish a Jewish state or a limited demand to allow entry to the European refugees and revocation of the 1939 White Paper? The question of partition hovered between these two positions in the internal discussions, and contributed to the fact that there was a gap between the formal position presented by the Jewish Agency to the Anglo-American committee and the unofficial position.[15] Officially, the Agency demanded the transformation of Eretz Israel into a Jewish commonwealth and the immigration of Jewish refugees from Europe under the supervision of the agency. In a thick tome presented by the agency to the committee, almost everything was said about the history of Zionism and its aspirations, but nothing about territory. The policy was "not to say a word in order to prevent dissension."[16] On the other hand, in meetings of the Zionist general council and the Jewish Agency executive in February–March 1946, Ben-Gurion prevented decisions against partition and made do with a general and noncommittal summation.[17] Ultimately, the Jewish Agency representatives had no choice but to present their real position, and they discreetly conveyed their support of partition to those committee members considered pro-Zionist.[18] Weizmann, Ben-Gurion, Shertok, and Goldmann were behind this ploy. According to unofficial testimony, they presented a map to the Anglo-American committee, showing the territories and borders of the proposed Jewish state. The territory of this proposed Jewish state greatly resembles the armistice lines of 1949, excluding the Gaza Strip.[19]

The report of the Anglo-American committee proposed the establishment of a trusteeship in Palestine—not a division between Arabs and Jews—and 100,000 immigration certificates to Jewish refugees from Europe.[20] This was the only international report that came close to the opinion of those Jews who supported a binational solution.[21] Concerning the territorial position, it should be emphasized that in the internal discussions, already in early 1946, the maximalist position did not carry the day, and the unofficial position of the Zionist leadership was to support partition. This was accomplished indirectly and covertly so as not to deviate from the Biltmore Declaration and, primarily, not to ignite prematurely the internal debate with the opponents of partition. Heller believes that the position taken by the central Zionist leaders in the affair of the Anglo-American committee of enquiry marks the "victory of the moderate forces of Zionism" following World War II.[22]

The second and more important decision about territory and boundaries was taken at the emergency meeting of the expanded Jewish Agency executive in August 1946 in Paris. Paragraph 2 notes: "The Executive is prepared to discuss the proposal to establish a viable Jewish state in an appropriate territory of the Land of Israel."[23]

Fifteen of the twenty-one participants voted in favor of this clause. This decision was taken in the wake of the conclusions of the Anglo-American committee and in reaction to the British "Provincial Autonomy Plan" publicized in July 1946.[24] According to this plan, known as the Morrison-Grady plan, Palestine would be divided into four areas: Jewish, Arab, an enclave of Jerusalem, and the Negev. The proposed Jewish territory would comprise the coast and the valleys, resembling the majority proposal in the 1938 Woodhead report. Governance would be conferred to a trusteeship, and the Jerusalem enclave and the Negev region would remain under British administration. This was the final unsuccessful British effort to return to the old canton plan to please the Jews and the Arabs and especially the United States. The executive decision in Paris was taken against the background of the events in Palestine: the intensified military struggle against the British of the Jewish underground movements; the tough British response in arresting most of the Jewish leaders on June 29, 1946; and the explosion in the King David Hotel by the I.Z.L. on July 22, 1946.

However the executive's decision goes beyond these events, because its goal was to destroy the logjam created by the deliberations around the Anglo-American committee report, and primarily, to convince the United States government that the desirable and viable solution is partition. Unlike the Biltmore Declaration, the Paris decision was intended to introduce a new dynamic into the political standstill concerning Eretz Israel in the summer of 1946. It was born of the belief that the Zionist movement must take a stand about its political goal and that this stand would influence the United States to adopt the preferred solution.

The grounds for the decision supporting partition had already been prepared during the deliberations about the testimony before the Anglo-American committee. At a meeting of the Jewish Agency executive in March 1946, Ben-Gurion presented a plan for the establishment of two independent states: one Jewish and the other under Abdulla. At the Paris conference, the opponents made a last ditch effort to prevent partition, but most participants felt that the events dictated another reality.[25] The executive's decisions were defined as "the basis for Dr. Goldmann's mission in America," and were all internal and secret. Despite the consensus at the conference, it is doubtful that it would have been possible at the time to pass an explicit decision in favor of partition in the official bodies of the Zionist movement.

As noted, the Paris decision harbored an attempt, and even a calculated risk, to take an initiative toward the United States by rejecting the "Morrison-Grady plan." In its place, a compromise (from the Zionist point of view) was offered of exchanging partition for the establishment of a Jewish state. Also note that the formulation *a viable state* indicated a criterion that is not necessarily territorial. Indeed, other clauses in the same resolution raised demands for full and immediate autonomy in government and the administration of the economy, as well as the right to supervise immigration, within the territory designated to become the Jewish state. In contrast, the term *appropriate territory* goes a step beyond the qualified support in the 1937 decision, which favored partition only on principle. Borders were not mentioned in the Paris decisions, but in the meeting of the Va'ad Le'ummi of August 1946, Ben-Zvi stated that under discussion was "Peel + the Negev," with a question mark about including the entire Galilee in the Jewish state.[26] The reaction of the opponents in 1946 again provides clear evidence of the meaning of the decision. As Rabbi Berlin responded to the Paris resolution in the name of the religious Mizrahi party:

> Instead of continuing the struggle and being prepared for suffering and distress until such time as the Lord will favor his people and his estate, they wrote and signed a deed of sale which relinquishes the largest portion of Eretz Israel ... all for the name of a state and a flag of sovereignty.... Is it permissible for the representatives of the people ... to transfer the land of our forefathers, to violate a heavenly command, and *to hand over willingly* to another people that which is not theirs, but ours?[27] [emphasis in the original]

Hence, the Paris decision was the first resolution of a Zionist institution in favor of partition. Internally, it solidified a majority of the leadership and prepared the ground for future decisions around the formulation: a Jewish state "in an appropriate territory of Eretz Israel." Outwardly, the dispatch of Goldmann to the United States did not bring immediate results, but although the entire matter was transfered in early 1947 to the United Nations, the seeds were planted for United States support of partition a short time afterward.

The third decision relevant to this discussion was adopted at the twenty-second congress, which convened in Basel in December 1946. No concrete partition proposal was under consideration at that time, and the subject was not raised explicitly on the agenda, even though it came up in the context of other discussions. The destruction of European Jewry, the plight of the refugees, and the anti-Zionist British policy united most of the Zionist streams in outright support for the immediate establishment of a Jewish state. However, the critical need for sovereignty under these conditions compelled most Zionist leaders to agree in principle to partition and considerably weakened the influence of the ardent opponents. Rabbi Fishman from Mizrahi, a former moderate opponent, noted: "I love the Land of Israel and the People of Israel, but the love for the People of Israel comes first, and if, heaven forbid, the People of Israel will be destroyed, we have no hope of living under any government, even the government of England. But if now we establish a state on part of Eretz Israel, I hope that the People of Israel will survive and will some day have all of Eretz Israel."[28]

Some former opponents also expressed remorse for their 1937 positions, questioning whether more resolute support for a partitioned state might have helped save some European Jews.[29] The relevant clause in the resolution of the twenty-second congress called for "the establishment of Eretz Israel as a Jewish state to be incorporated into the world democratic structure."[30] This general formulation conceals two important facts. First, that the congress was well aware of the executive's pro-partition resolution in Paris and did not repeal it. Second, that the Revisionists and Ahdut Ha'avoda presented countermotions at the congress demanding total opposition to partition. The Revisionists suggested that the resolution say, "a state in the original territory of the Mandate"; and Ahdut Ha'avoda suggested that it say "to establish the entire and indivisible Eretz Israel as the Jewish state."[31] These motions never attracted enough support to be put to a vote. Neither was there the same fervor in the opposition of the Mizrahi and Hashomer Hatzair delegates as in the 1937 debate. This tacit agreement was expressed by Silver, who continued to oppose partition publicly, but who did not reject the Paris resolution that, he believed, constituted "our absolute minimum, which cannot be further reduced."[32]

On the other hand, Weizmann spoke forcefully about the historic need to agree to partition and he scolded his colleagues from Mizrahi: "Why don't you trust the Almighty? He will keep his promise; he will give Eretz Israel to the Jews when the time comes, and don't you importune him."[33] Ben-Gurion, as usual sensitive to the change of mood, decided to reveal to the congress delegates his secret plan, which had been presented to the Jewish Agency executive in March 1946, for establishing a Jewish state and an Arab state in the mandate area.[34] In contrast with the twentieth congress in Zurich, which served not only as a forum for the debate on partition but in which the decision had been taken, the participants in the twenty-second congress knew that this crossroads was already behind them and that the center of gravity in decision making in the Zionist movement had been moved to smaller bodies.

The fourth decision is the various responses of the Zionist movement to the 1947 United Nations partition plan, from the establishment of UNSCOP (the United Nations Special Commission on Palestine) in May 1947, until the adoption of the General Assembly partition resolution on November 29, 1947 (see Map 11.1). In comparison with 1937, there were no dramatic decisions in this period nor bitter fights in the public or the Zionist institutions about the "big questions": the establishment of the state and how to go about it. The ideological positions of the various factions of the Zionist movement continued as before: Hashomer Hatzair in support of a binational solution; Ahdut Ha'avoda advocating to keep the Land of Israel whole and under international supervision; and the Revisionist movement calling for a Jewish state on both banks of the Jordan River. But the political sting seemed to have gone out of these positions, in the face of the common challenge of mobilizing support from the two great powers and the member countries of the United Nations to support the establishment of a Jewish state. At that moment, the only way to attain this goal was through partition. What was perceived as "a great sacrifice" in 1937 had greatly shrunk by 1947, even among the fervent opponents, especially because many had become convinced that the question of territory and the borders would be settled in a war.

As a result, the internal deliberations were focused on the question of whether to allow opposition representatives to appear before the United Nations commission to present positions that contradicted those of the Jewish Agency executive. Finally, it was agreed that only official representatives would testify before the commission, but that they would first present the maximalist demands—the Land of Israel as the Jewish state—according to the Biltmore Declaration. Only later would they express willingness to compromise—a viable state in part of that land—in accordance with the Paris resolution.[35]

When UNSCOP began its work, the Jewish Agency executive made a great effort to convince the commission to recommend the establishment of a sovereign Jewish state in a significant part of the territory of Eretz Israel, defined as the Peel commission proposal plus the Negev plus the Jewish parts of Jerusalem (and international supervision of the holy sites). The main anxiety was that the commission would recommend a new international trust-

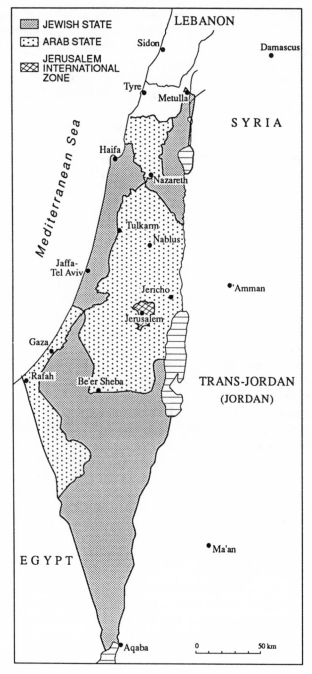

Map 11.1 The United Nations Partition Plan, 1947

eeship in Palestine or worse—that it would propose a canton solution that would cause the Zionist movement to fall between two
stools, a shrivelled territory and no sovereignty.[36] An additional
fear was that the commission would fail to formulate any recommendations whatsoever. For these reasons, and also because it correctly evaluated the inclinations of the majority of commission
members, the Jewish Agency resolved to present a clear position in
support of geographic partition along the lines just explained.[37]
This position was a return to the secret map presented to a number
of friends in the Anglo-American committee in 1946, and it can be
regarded as the third official map submitted by an authorized body
of the Zionist movement.[38] The territory of this proposed Jewish
state totaled approximately 18,000 km²—almost one-third of the
1919 map, and three times greater than the 1938 map submitted to
the Woodhead commission. In his testimony before the commission,
Weizmann was forthright: "I know that there is talk about a binational state, about a kind of federation, about what has been generally called the Morrison Plan. I do not believe that any of these
have the advantages of partition, which is final, clear-cut, and
well-formed."[39]

A completely opposing position was presented to UNSCOP by
Hashomer Hatzair and Magnes, in the name of the Ihud movement. Magnes repeated his proposal to establish a binational state
and he attacked the idea of partition, characterizing it as "placing
the Arabs in one ward of the insane asylum and the Jews in a
separate ward."[40] The UNSCOP report mentions the binational solution of Magnes but rejects it as artificial and impractical. Other
solutions proposed to the commission were also rejected: an Arab or
a Jewish state in all of Palestine and canton arrangements. The
commission focused on two possibilities: partition with economic
unity and an Arab-Jewish federation or confederation.

The majority proposal of UNSCOP was to terminate the British mandate, to establish two independent states in Palestine (E.I.)—
one Jewish, the other Arab, economically united—and to turn
Jerusalem into an international trusteeship under United Nations
supervision. The proposal divided Palestine into no less than seven
districts: three under the sovereignty of each state, with points of
confluence between them, and Jerusalem with a separate status.
The proposed territory of the Jewish state was approximately 16,000
km², some 62 percent of western Eretz Israel. At the time, more
than half a million Jews and approximately 380,000 Arabs (more
than 40 percent) lived in the territory designated for the Jewish
state. Some 700,000 Arabs and 10,000 Jews lived in the territory

intended for the Arab state. The main innovation in the UNSCOP plan compared to previous schemes was the proposal to establish a Palestinian Arab state independent of Transjordan.[41] The minority proposal of UNSCOP rejected the idea of partition and recommended a federative structure composed of an Arab and a Jewish province, with autonomy regarding internal matters. In this proposal, the territory intended for Jews was limited to the region of the valleys and to a large region in the heart of the Negev.

The Palestinian leadership, which had boycotted UNSCOP, rejected the majority plan as well as the commission's minority proposal, even though the latter was closer to their position. The Arab League rejected the recommendations of UNSCOP in October 1947 and decided to prepare for war if an independent Arab state was not established in Palestine.[42] The Zionist movement, on the other hand, regarded the majority proposal of UNSCOP as a great victory, despite the awkward territorial structure of the proposed Jewish state and the exclusion of most of the Galilee, Jerusalem, and thirty-nine Jewish settlements.[43] In a meeting of the enlarged Zionist general council in September 1947, the UNSCOP report was approved by a large majority.[44] But the official decisions had only secondary importance at that time. Ahdut Ha'avoda, ST, and the Revisionists continued to object to partition, but their opposition was weak because it was clear that the UNSCOP majority proposal was enthusiastically received by most of the Jewish public, and the Jewish Agency prepared to fight for its adoption by the United Nations General Assembly.[45]

In November 1947, more than two-thirds of the members of the United Nations assembly voted in favor of the partition plan. The assembly resolution reduced the territory of the Jewish state as proposed by UNSCOP from 16,000 km² to 14,000 km² (see Map 11.1). The territorial ratio between the Jewish and Arab states consequently changed to 55:45, respectively, the main difference being transfer of the western Negev to the Arab state. The dramatic vote in the United Nations was greeted with great excitement in the Jewish Yishuv and the Zionist movement. The Va'ad Le'ummi issued a statement the day after the vote, noting

> Our creation, our steadfastness, and the justice of our cause yesterday triumphed in the judgement of the nations. In opposition to a third, which included the six Arab states, the plan for the establishment of a Jewish state won a special majority of more than two-thirds—led by the two world giants, the

United States and the Soviet Union. This great deed, with all its three components—the majority conclusions in the Commission, the confirmation of this conclusion in the plenary of the Commission on Palestine, and the firm decision in the U.N. Assembly—all supporters will be proud in the future, while the opponents will be shamed by their opposition.[46]

Shertok defined the decision as a "Shofar blast" that heralded the redemption of the people;[47] and Ben-Gurion was carried away and called it "the greatest single achievement of the Jewish people in its history since it became a people" so much so that "a verse in the Bible should be revised: not 'from Dan to Beersheba' but 'from Dan to Eilat.'"[48] He even presented, again, a kind of double formula for the future borders of the state of Israel, in rejecting, on the one hand, the historical claim for the entire Eretz Israel, although, on the other hand, leaving the door open for territorial changes in the future:

> The borders of Eretz Israel under Jewish rule—from the time of the Judges until Bar-Kochba—changed incessantly, and there are few concepts as unclear and less specified as the concept 'historic borders.'
> Every schoolchild knows that history makes no final arrangements—not in regime and not in borders and not in international arrangements. . . . But arrangements and corrections are made in international life, and as long as they exist, they are to be respected and given loyalty, if at base they are desirable and lead to progress.[49]

The ill and infirm Weizmann, who had labored intensely for the success of the diplomatic struggle in the United States, did not conceal his excitement when he said that the assembly's decision was the greatest event since the Balfour Declaration precisely forty years earlier.[50] It was Coupland, the driving force behind the royal commission's recommendations, who regarded the 1947 partition plan as a direct continuation of the 1937 partition plan, adjusted to suit the times.[51]

Conclusions

The 1947 United Nations resolution provided international legitimacy for the Zionist goal of establishing a Jewish state in Palestine.

One may assume that without this, the Jewish unilateral declaration of the establishment of the state of Israel in 1948 would have been well nigh impossible. This was also the victory of the pragmatic policy of Weizmann and Ben-Gurion, who since 1937 had consistently striven to establish a sovereign state, even at the price of territorial partition. It should be mentioned that other possibilities were considered and rejected by the United Nations in November 1947: a binational federation; a new international trusteeship in place of the British mandate; and the temptation to delay the difficult decision on the fate of Palestine. Much more resolutely than in 1937, Zionist support for the partition proposal of 1947 was unequivocal. Ben-Gurion and Shertok were again the most outspoken leaders in emphasizing the importance and historic precedent of obtaining international recognition for a Jewish state that "was authorized in advance by the majority of humankind."[52]

The territory designated for the Jewish state in the 1947 general assembly resolution was almost three times greater than that in the 1937 royal commission's proposal. Moreover, there was no doubt that, this time, the resolution entailed full political independence under international auspices, in contrast to the justified doubts of British intentions in 1937. Nonetheless, the problems raised by the moderate opponents of partition and the doubts that had troubled the undecided camp in 1937 did not totally evaporate, as shown in Table 11.1.

Table 11.1 Conditions Raised in the 1937 Debate and the Response in the United Nations Plan of 1947

	YES	PARTLY	NO	REMARKS
Sufficient territory?		X		The Galilee was omitted from the Jewish state and most of the added territory was in the arid Negev
Defensible boundaries?			X	Approximately 1,400 km of winding boundaries.
Jewish majority?		X		Approximately 40 percent Arabs in the proposed Jewish state
Arab consent?			X	Absolute Arab opposition; slim chance for peace

The four conditions raised in the 1937 debate were fulfilled only partially or not at all. The expansion of the Jewish state as proposed in the 1947 partition plan did not add significantly to the arable land, which was then regarded as too little to absorb millions of Jews. The proposed borders did not provide a solution to the problem of security, which became critical when the events in 1947–48 made it clear that the Jewish state would not win the agreement of the Arabs from within or without. Finally, although the partition lines were drawn to ensure a Jewish majority in the Jewish state, it was only a 60 percent majority. The UNSCOP plan even specifically mentioned that the territory proposed for a Jewish state was intended to limit immigration, in an attempt to ease the fears of the Arabs from further Jewish territorial expansion.[53]

Willingness to ignore these shortcomings testifies that the Zionist decision to adopt partition was based on giving priority to sovereignty over other goals, including those we defined as expressive values. Politics, not geography, tipped the scale toward Zionist agreement to the partition plans of 1937 and 1947. In both cases, the instrumental pragmatic approach had the upper hand. Yet, we know that these proposals for territorial separation did not lead to a solution of the Jewish-Arab conflict in Eretz Israel/Palestine. Because of Arab opposition within and outside Palestine, the United Nations partition plan was not implemented. Consequently, de facto partition was implemented forcibly, as the result of war and the Armistice agreements of 1948–1949 (see Map 11.2). Under this partition, the boundaries of the state of Israel encompassed a territory of 20,600 km^2, approximately 75 percent of the territory of western Eretz Israel. As for the remaining territory, the West Bank was annexed to the kingdom of Jordan and the Gaza Strip remained under Egyptian administration between 1947 and 1967, and a Palestinian-Arab state has not been established. The partition that was carried out and held until 1967 was therefore not between the Jews and the Palestinian Arabs, but between the Jews and the Arab states.

The general conclusion from the 1937 Zionist decision, and in comparison with the other territorial decisions discussed here, is that territorial changes can be understood only within the broad context of political events. To illustrate this, we will present the shifting territory and boundaries of the Jewish entity (desired or realized, proposed or actual) over more than seventy years.

Table 11.2 Territories of Palestine/Eretz-Israel and the State of Israel Within Various Boundaries and Lines (approximate km² including lakes)

YEAR	TERRITORIAL DESCRIPTION	KM²	INDEX (1949=100)
	"Natural-historical" boundaries[a]	~59,000	281
1919	Zionist Organization proposal to the peace conference[b]	~45,000	214
1922–1948	British Mandate for Palestine (E.I.) after the separation of Transjordan	27,000	129
1937	The Jewish state according to the royal commission proposal	~5,000	24
1938	Jewish Agency proposal to the Woodhead Commission	~6,000	29
1946	Secret Jewish Agency proposal to the Anglo-American committee	~18,000	86
1947	The majority proposal of UNSCOP	~16,000	76
1947	The Jewish state according to the United Nations resolution	~14,000	67
1949	The state of Israel within the armistice lines	21,000	100
1956–1957	Under Israeli control after the Sinai campaign[c]	83,000	395
1967–1973	Cease-fire lines after the 1967 war[d]	90,000	429
1982	Under Israeli control, after the peace treaty with Egypt[e]	28,000	133

[a] According to the *Hebrew Encyclopedia*, the "natural-historical" boundaries are as follows: in the south, from Wadi El-Arish to the Gulf of Aqaba: in the east, a line running from Aqaba to Amman and from the Hijaz Railway to Dar'a; in the north, a line north of the sources of the Jordan River to the Mediterranean outlet of the Litani River (1957, vol. 6, p. 31).
[b] Including approximately 17,200 km² in Transjordan as far as the Hijaz Railway and additional territories in the north.
[c] The state of Israel within the armistice lines, plus the territories of the Gaza Strip (approximately 400 km²) and Sinai (approximately 62,000 km²).
[d] The state of Israel within the armistice lines, with the addition of the West Bank, the Gaza Strip, Sinai, and the Golan Heights (approximately 1,200 km²).
[e] As in d, excluding the territory of Sinai and a small territory in the Golan Heights; without territories in southern Lebanon under Israeli control in 1982–1985.

Table 11.2 and Figure 11.1 demonstrate that the question of territory and boundaries never left the agenda of the Zionist movement and the state of Israel from the time that the area of the "national home" was left undefined in the 1917 Balfour Declaration until today. We will now summarize the main territorial events in the history of the Zionist movement and the state of Israel, adding a few concluding remarks.

The First Map (1919) The close overlap between the 1919 map and the "natural boundaries" of Eretz Israel is due to the fact that the Zionist Organization's memorandum was initially guided by geographic-economic considerations. But this territorial proposal too was a political compromise reflecting the need to acknowledge the aspirations of Jews and Arabs in the region and the interests of Britain and France. The territorial conception of that map was never realized (see Map 1.1).

The Stable Boundaries (1922) The territory of the Jewish "national home" was restricted to western Eretz Israel due to British interests, disregarding Zionist claims and the desires of the Arab population on both sides of the Jordan River.[54] These mandatory boundaries established some facts that would remain unchanged for seventy years. The boundaries of Palestine with Lebanon in the north and with Egypt in the south have been the most stable despite the vicissitudes during the entire period.[55] They are political boundaries that completely disregard what could be considered a "natural boundary." In 1922, another political fact established the mandatory territory in western Palestine as the only territory relevant to the deliberations about the extent of the Jewish state. In reality, the debate has been mainly about this territory, and when the armistice agreements were signed in 1949, the state of Israel was one-third smaller than this territory of the mandate.

The First Partition Proposal (1937) The first attempt at a territorial separation between Arabs and Jews as a basis for political separation failed. The territory designated for the Jewish state by the royal commission was very small indeed, indicating to what extent the majority in the Zionist movement was willing to make do with a Jewish state of 6,000 km² or even less (see Map 9.1). Only 400,000 Jews then lived in Palestine, but the Zionist agreement to partition was intended to create a political framework for the absorption of more than 2 million Jews. That is, this decision implied a very high population density of more than 400

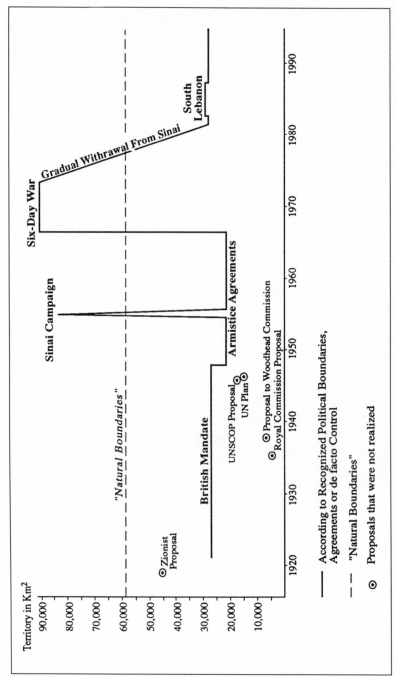

Figure 11.1 Palestine/Eretz-Israel and the State of Israel Within Various Boundaries and Lines

inhabitants per km² in a "finger state," dry and with rather limited arable land.

It is interesting, therefore, to examine the "economic viability" of this particular territory today. The same territory intended in 1937 to be the partitioned state of Israel currently affords a livelihood, more than fifty years later, for over 3 million residents, of whom 2.5 million are Jews.[56] The optimists of 1937 were correct, even though they never imagined that their calculations of economic viability based on population density would be refuted by the structural and economic changes of modern societies.

Implementation of Partition (1947–1949)   Palestinian-Arab support of the 1937 partition plan would have created a precedent for territorial division by consent. Palestinian and Arab support of the 1947 partition plan would have created a precedent for the establishment of two states for the two peoples in mandatory Palestine. It might also have limited the territory of the Jewish state to 14,000 km². No one knows what would have occurred if the two states had been established, but we should point out that the 1947 plan proposed no complete territorial separation. The seven proposed districts were intertwined, and there was to be economic unity between the two states. It was an attempt to establish two sovereign states, and at the same time, retain the territorial-economic unity of Palestine/Eretz Israel.

In any event, the map of the state of Israel was eventually determined on the battlefield (see Map 11.2). The territory of Israel according to the armistice agreements signed after the 1948–1949 war was approximately 7,000 km² greater than the territory of the United Nations partition plan and approximately 6,000 km² smaller than the territory of the British mandate for Palestine (E.I.).[57]

Three Withdrawals from Sinai   The greatest territorial changes took place after Israel conquered and controlled all or part of the Sinai peninsula on three different occasions: at the end of 1948, in 1956–1957, and in 1967–1982. The conquest of Sinai more than quadrupled the territory under Israel's control and dwarfed all the other territorial changes presented in Figure 11.1. This expansion was not launched mainly to attain "natural boundaries" (the Suez Canal and Gulf of Suez) or to conquer largely uninhabited territory but rather for political and military reasons. In all three cases, the parts conquered in Sinai were fully returned to Egypt. The treaty with Egypt in 1982 determined the only interna-

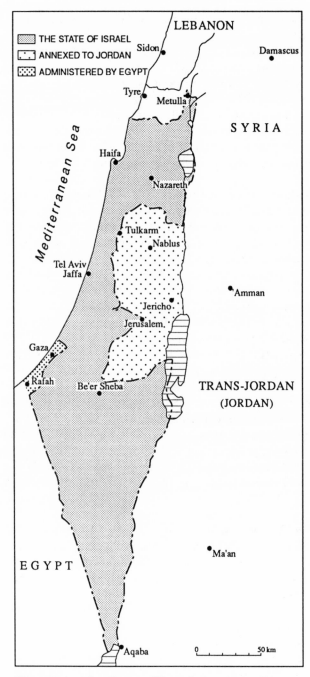

Map 11.2   The State of Israel, Armistice Lines of 1949

tional boundary of the state of Israel—a 209-km long line recognized and agreed upon by the two bordering states.

The Eastern Boundary Figure 11.2 demonstrates the contrast in the "historical record" of the two sides: the Arab perception of easterly territorial expansion of the Zionist movement and of Israel, and the Jewish perception of territorial reductions and Jewish willingness to make concessions. Many Arabs, especially among the Palestinians, interpret the events as continuous Jewish expansionism that over the course of years led to Jewish control over all of Palestine. They note the growth of the Jewish population from 70,000 in 1917 at the time of the Balfour Declaration to over 4 million in the early 1990s, and the diminution of the Arab population in Palestine from an absolute majority at the beginning of the period to 38 percent at its conclusion.[58] To those

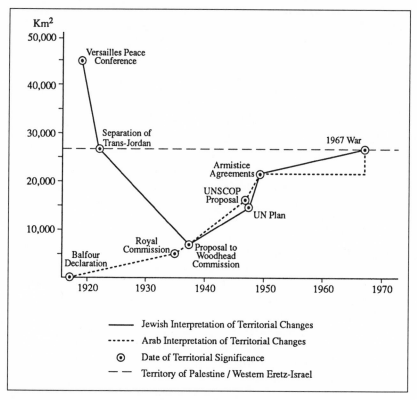

Figure 11.2 Territorial Reduction in the Jewish View and Jewish Territorial Expansion Eastward in the Arab View

who maintain that the Jews have no right to sovereignty over Palestine, these facts are evidence that the whole process is a Zionist-Western plot to dispossess the indigenous population from their homeland. According to this position, Arab opposition (the 1936 revolt, the war of 1947–1948) compelled the Jews and their Great Power patrons to accept partition as a temporary and tactical concession on their way to rule over the entire land. Zionism and Israel have never acknowledged the national rights of the Palestinians to sovereignty in Palestine, and thus the conquest of Palestine in 1967 revealed the true goals of Zionism. According to this approach, this is not a territorial conflict, because the Jews' original intention was to assume control over the entire country, and thus Arab consent to territorial partition at any stage of this process would have changed nothing.

By contrast, the interpretation of the Zionist movement and most Jews in Israel is of continued willingness for territorial compromise in the face of consistent Arab obstinacy, which, again, is not based on territorial motivations. In this view, Jewish rights stem from their continuous historic bond to Eretz Israel and the repeated international recognition of the Jewish right to return to their homeland and have their own state. Even though the Zionist movement was forced to concede Transjordan in 1922, it still expressed willingness to partition the rest of Eretz Israel in 1937 and again in 1947. Hence, the rejection by Arabs who continued to demand the entire country for themselves forced the Israeli territorial expansion in 1949 and 1967, in wars which Israel did not start. As to the charge of continuous expansionism, the Israeli position maintains that there have been several Israeli withdrawls from conquered territories: 1949, from eastern Sinai and Southern Lebanon; 1957, from all of Sinai and the Gaza Strip; 1974–1982, gradual withdrawal from all of Sinai and part of the Golan Heights; 1978, from southern Lebanon; 1985, from southern Lebanon; and 1988, from Taba in the Sinai. Moreover, although this list includes no withdrawal from territories on the east, Israel has not annexed the West Bank or the Gaza Strip after their conquest in 1967.

Figure 11.2 reflects the abyss between the two perceptions. It explains why no official direct negotiations took place between the Zionist movement and the Palestinian national movement in the period between the Weizmann–Faisal discussions in 1919 until the "Madrid Conference" in 1990. Nevertheless, the territory remaining under dispute since 1967 is relatively small (only some 8,000 km^2 in the West Bank, Gaza Strip, and the Golan Heights) by comparison with the changes that took place throughout the years.

From a strictly territorial point of view, the current dispute is over approximately 29 percent of the territory of Eretz Israel/Palestine. Hence, despite the major differences between the periods, the principle of the choice of 1937 as presented in this book—territory as an instrumental means or as an expressive end—typifies the dilemma confronting Israelis and Palestinians today.

Since 1937, the territorial question of Eretz Israel/Palestine has remained unresolved (with the exception of the border with Egypt), and this fact often serves to "prove" the existence of geographic determinism. Many Israelis and Palestinians claim the geographical unity of the land, seeking to prove that a small territory of 27,000 km² cannot meet the conflicting needs of two national movements. In addition, broad sectors of the two communities not only bear deep mutual suspicion, but also refuse to recognize the political legitimacy of each other. Some claim that this struggle, which has lasted for so many years ("a hundred years war"), is still being played out. This is the reason, they maintain, why the territory intended for the Jewish state underwent many changes during the mandate period and even more after 1948–1949 (see Table 11.2). Israel's boundaries of control (and to some extent its boundaries of sovereignty as well) have changed no fewer than ten times since the founding of the state as a result of wars, military operations, agreements, and unilateral withdrawals. This fact is sometimes brought as evidence of an "historical process" of shaping the national sovereign territory, not unlike the gradual, protracted and bloody delineation of the political map of western Europe.

The 1937 decision as presented in this book and Zionist agreement to the 1947 partition scheme contradict these conclusions. In both cases, the decisions of the Zionist movement indicate a willingness to define national interests as a choice between values that became contradictory in a particular political context. In that context, it is irrelevant whether the willingness to forego territory was merely tactical, as territorial concessions were viewed by the proponents as a very big risk and by the opponents as irreversible.

Comparison of the prestate decisions with those currently facing Israel does not ignore the very different circumstances that exist today. For example, since the establishment of the state of Israel, the issue of sovereignty has become secondary, as illustrated by transformation of the slogan "territories for sovereignty" into "territories for peace." Therefore, the comparison is not between the content of the decisions, but the very willingness to define choices in terms of conflicting values. This kind of choice exists in territorial decisions only when the territory itself is viewed instrumentally and its value is weighed against the probability of attaining other values: sovereignty, peace, and even economic objectives. The choice completely disappears when the whole territory is an expressive value, not negotiable under any conditions, even if the chances for peace are good.

Such a choice existed and formed the nucleus of the internal Israeli debate over the peace accords with Egypt following Sadat's 1977 visit to Jerusalem. The Israeli decision was to concede the entire Sinai Peninsula to Egypt in exchange for peace.[59] On the other hand, the ongoing internal debate in Israel over the future of the other territories captured in 1967 is fundamentally over the definition of the choice itself: Should it be instrumentally defined as a choice between conflicting values and thus put on the political agenda and tested?

As to the general question of the link between politics and geography, the 1937 decision indicates that the territorial component is central but not exclusive and not necessarily paramount in the process of achieving political aims. In retrospect, the words of Ben-Gurion before the 1937 decision still stand the test of time: "Before us is a decision, not a verdict."[60]

Notes

Introduction

1. Niccolo Machiavelli, *The Prince*, trans. George Bull (London: Penguin, 1975), p. 42.

2. For an explanation of the use of the terms Palestine and Eretz Israel, see Chapter Two, note 4.

3. Diskin and Galnoor, 1990.

4. The government decision to go to war (June 5, 1982) included a clause stating that the state of Israel continues to strive for the signing of a peace treaty with independent Lebanon while maintaining its territorial integrity. On May 16, 1983, the Knesset ratified a peace treaty between Israel and Lebanon that included a clause committing each of the two states to respect the territorial sovereignty of the other in accordance with the existing international boundary (clause 1). The treaty was never approved by Lebanon.

5. It is estimated that some 350 km^2 of the "northern Galilee," as it was included in the historic Land of Israel, is today located within the state of Lebanon. *The Hebrew Encyclopedia*, vol. VI, p. 35; also Tokachinsky, 1970. See Chapter Two regarding the Zionist Organization's demands in 1919.

6. The shorthand word used in Hebrew during the 1937 debate was *pulmus,* originally from the Greek *polemos*—an intensive warlike controversy. The Greek word is also the origin of the English polemics.

Chapter One. State, Territory, and Boundaries: A General Discussion

1. Sahlins, 1989, p. 7.

2. Maier, 1975, p. 18; Cranach et al., 1979, p. 109.

3. Jolly, 1972, p. 271.

4. The best known work in this field is the popular book by Ardrey, 1967. Ardrey claims that territorial aggression is instinctive in humans

and drives them just as it drives other territorial species. Accordingly, border disputes come to satisfy very basic human needs—identity, stimulation, and defense. See pp. 278 and 314.

5. Jolly, 1972, p. vii.

6. J.H. Hertz, 1968; Gottmann, 1973; Soja, 1971; Sack, 1983.

7. Gold, 1982, pp. 47–50.

8. Paddison, 1983, p. 21.

9. Spykman, 1938, p. 236.

10. Fichte maintained that nations have natural rights to the territories around them. His starting point is, nevertheless, national and not geographic. Translated by Kedourie, 1961, p. 70. See also Fichte, 1970, p. 138.

11. Sack, 1983, p. 62.

12. Knight, 1982, p. 117.

13. For example, "Territoriality is a strategy for the achievement of influence and control," Sack, 1983, p. 55.

14. Gottmann, 1973, pp. 14–16.

15. Ibid., p. ix.

16. Galnoor in Leibowitz et al., 1991, pp. 33–45.

17. MacIver, 1926, pp. 3–22, 426–454.

18. MacIver presents his reasons for preferring the conception of the state as an association, differentiated from other associations by its functions and not by its essence. He explains that kinship may turn a community into a society and the growth of nationalism helps society to create a state. Nationalism, however, is less than general civilization and more than a local loyalty. Ibid., p. 122.

19. F. Hertz, 1945, p. 151.

20. On language as a basis for self-determination, see Geertz, 1963, p. 105.

21. Sahlins documented in detail the formation of borders between France and Spain from the middle of the seventeenth century. The French monarchy defined sovereignty not in terms of territory, but of imposing jurisdiction on subjects. The 1789 revolution brought about "territorialization" of the homeland and clearly identified the *patrie* with the national territory: French territory became the property of the republic. The symbolic expression for this transition from the territorial state to the territorial nation-state was the final delineation of the border between France

NOTES TO CHAPTER ONE   301

and Spain in the Pyrenees, settled only in 1868. See Sahlins, 1989, pp. 191–192.

22. Murdock, 1967.

23. Taylor, 1985, p. 128.

24. Emerson, 1971, p. 463.

25. Kedourie, 1961, p. 133.

26. MacIver, 1926, p. 124.

27. Geertz, 1963, pp. 110–113.

28. Francis, 1976, pp. xvi, 75.

29. It is customary to list the following states as nearly monoethnic: Germany, Norway, Iceland, Denmark, Holland, Luxembourg, Ireland, Portugal, Lesotho, Nepal, Saudi Arabia, and Tibet.

30. Deutsch, 1963, p. 18.

31. Ibid., p. 178; see also Galnoor, 1982, pp. 18–20.

32. Deutsch, 1963, p. 205.

33. A materialistic version of this explanation can be found in Taylor, 1985, pp. 137–140.

34. Gellner, 1983, p. 93.

35. Duchacek, 1986, pp. 205–259.

36. Walzer, 1992, pp. 164–171.

37. Examples according to Knight, 1982, p. 521.

38. Montesquieu (1689–1755) in *L'Espirit des lois* (1748), was one of the first to examine the influence of the natural environment on human communal behavior and even on culture and human nature.

39. This school developed under the influence of Darwin (1809–1892), Spencer (1820–1903), and followers of scientific materialism, who sought to discover the natural laws that dictate developments in the world. See Bassin, 1987, p. 117.

40. Ratzel, 1903. The second edition of his book was the one more widely circulated. Ratzel's writings were not translated from the German and are cited in literature of political geography from secondary sources. His main book, *Anthropological Geography (Anthropogeographie)*, was published in two volumes between the years 1899 and 1912. His writings were acclaimed with the publication of Sempel's (1911) book in the United States, which contained an exhaustive and favorable description of Ratzel's theories.

41. Kjellén, 1917.

42. Van-Valkenburg, 1944, pp. 363–370.

43. Gyorgy, 1944, p. 179.

44. Bassin, 1987, p. 125.

45. Strauss-Hupe, 1942.

46. *Zeitschrift,* 17, no. 12, (December 1940). 590.

47. In his first writings, Haushofer divided the world into three regions: the Pan-American under U.S. hegemony; The East-Asiatic under Japanese hegemony; and the Euro-African under German hegemony. See Heske, 1987, p. 137.

48. Tal, 1979, p. 71.

49. Ibid., p. 72.

50. Bowman, 1942, p. 658.

51. This is the opinion of Fielding Eliot, who wrote the introduction to the 1942 edition of MacKinder's book. Despite its revisions, the book remains true to the original release in 1919.

52. Spykman, 1942.

53. Renner, 1942.

54. Spykman, 1942, p. 6.

55. Kristof, 1960, pp. 31–33.

56. Hartshorne, 1935, p. 795.

57. Hartshorne, 1950, pp. 119–120.

58. Jones, 1945; Wright, 1955; Burghardt, 1973. In a broader context, some researchers attempted to combine the study of political geography with global conceptions of political economy, most from a Marxist point of view. See Sack, 1983; Taylor, 1985; MacLaughlin, 1986.

59. Gottmann, 1951, p. 158.

60. Gottmann, 1952, p. 514.

61. Gray, 1988, pp. 1–2.

62. Jones, 1945, p. 16.

63. Prescott, 1987, p. 94.

64. Kristof, 1985, p. 1179.

65. Holdich, 1916a, p. 422.

66. Sahlins, 1989, p. 186.

67. Jones, 1945, p. vi. He was preceded by East, 1937; Hartshorne, 1936; and Boggs, 1940.

68. Tenner, 1944, p. 567.

69. Learmonth and Hamnett, 1971, pp. 28–32.

70. Muir, 1975, p. 129.

71. S. Cohen, 1973, p. xiii.

72. Douglas, 1966, pp. 4, 114–128.

73. Sempel, 1911, p. 4.

74. Ibid., p. 209.

75. Ibid., p. 215.

76. Cukwurah, 1967, p. 15.

77. Taylor, 1985, p. 110.

78. Boggs, 1940, p. 17.

79. Jones, 1945; Hartshorne, 1936; East, 1937, respectively.

80. Van Dyke, 1966; Emerson, 1971.

81. Charter of the United Nations, Chapter I, Article 2(4).

82. Fisher, 1949, p. 222.

83. Knight, 1982, p. 523.

84. Prescott, 1987, p. 110.

85. Turner, 1928, p. 3.

86. Kristof, 1959, pp. 271–272.

87. Boal and Livingstone, 1983, p. 139.

88. Kristof, 1959, p. 281.

89. Kimmerling, 1977; and in more detail, Kimmerling, 1983, pp. 19–26.

90. On the territories occupied by Israel in 1967 as frontiers and the degree of their connection to the state, see Kimmerling, 1989b, pp. 276–278. Incidentally, pre-World War II Germany is an exception to this point of view in Europe because even the term *frontier* (*staatgrenze*) was closely linked to the state.

91. Lattimore, 1962, p. 471, maintains that the "frontier spirit" is social and not geographical. Only when such a spirit exists can it later obtain a geographical configuration. Indeed, attempts are occasionally made to awaken and mold it into nongeographical terms, such as U.S. President Kennedy's "New Frontier" slogan, whose meaning was social and economic.

92. Taylor, 1985, p. 105.

93. Kimmerling, 1983, p. 7.

94. Muir, 1975, p. 54.

95. Based on East and Prescott, 1975, p. 57.

96. Sprout and Sprout, 1960, pp. 159–160; and supplementary discussion in Duchacek, 1986, pp. 205–255.

97. Gottmann, 1973, p. iii.

98. Ardrey, 1967, p. 317.

99. Brawer, 1988, p. 28.

100. Morgenthau, 1960, p. 27.

101. Boulding, 1962.

102. Wright, 1955, pp. 251–254.

103. Muir, 1975, p. 137.

104. Jones, 1945, p. 15.

105. Sprout and Sprout, 1960, p. 160.

106. On the post-1967 debate within Israel over "defensible borders" and the possibility of attaining them within the reality of the Arab-Israeli conflict, compare Allon (1980) with Shalev (1983).

107. Simon, 1957a, p. xxiv.

108. Brecher's analysis (1974, 1980) of the "internal environment" of Israeli foreign policy decisions is an outstanding and positive exception in this regard. However, our focus on internal decisions—while the "environment" is defined as an external constraint—limits the proper use of theories of policy making in foreign relations. See, for instance, Janis, 1982; Quandt, 1970; Allison, 1971.

109. Parsons, 1951, p. 97.

110. E. Cohen, 1976; Kimmerling, 1983.

111. Kimmerling, 1983, pp. 21–22.

112. Kristof, 1960, p. 19.

113. Deutsch, 1963, p. 129; Galnoor, 1982, pp. 24–25.

114. Lustick, 1990a, p. 40, broadens the meaning of *instrumentalism* beyond the collective boundaries discussed here and notes that territorial expansion or reduction has a direct influence on power positions of various groups within the society and state.

115. Prescott, 1987, p. 107.

116. Kimmerling, 1983, p. 216.

Chapter Two. The Background

1. Weizmann's testimony before the Royal Commission, December 18, 1936, p. 4, Weizmann Archives (hereafter, W. A.), Rehovot.

2. The prevailing term in British documents is *disturbances*, whereas the Jews call these the *events* of 1936–1939.

3. This policy was made official in the appendix to the White Paper of June 1922. Correspondence with the Palestine Arab Delegation and the Zionist Organization, London: Cmd. 1700, June 1922.

4. This book will use the official British term *Palestine* (E. I.) to designate the mandatory area west of the Jordan River; and the term *Land of Israel* (Eretz Israel) as the Zionist definition of the area, without Trans-Jordan. We will explicitly state when *Land of Israel* includes Trans-Jordan (that is, the entire British mandate zone). For the Arab definition, we will use *Palestine*. The question of the official name of the mandatory country arose many times. The Palestinian Arabs demanded to delete the E.I., while David Yellin, on behalf of the Jewish Yishuv, demanded to replace the term *Palestine* with *Land of Israel*. This matter also came up in the deliberations of the Royal Commission in 1937: see Memoranda by the Government of Palestine use of the Name 'Eretz-Israel': Palestine Royal Commission (Documents), no. 33, pp. 158–159.

5. H. M. Government, Statement of Policy, London: Cmd. 3692, October 1930.

6. Biger, 1983a, pp. 12–14; Brawer, 1988, pp. 51–53.

7. On the Sykes-Picot Agreement, see Temperly, 1924, pp. 13–17.

8. See correspondence between Sir Henry McMahon, H. M. high commissioner at Cairo, and the Sherif Hussein of Mecca, July 1915–March 1916, London: Cmd. 5957, 1939.

9. Frischwasser, 1955, pp. 112–141; Nevakivi, 1969, pp. 248–269; Rogel, 1988.

10. For the original memorandum, see PRO/FO/371/4170. Translation to Hebrew: Weizmann, (1968–1985), vol. 9, pp. 397–405. The reasoning also appears in Weizmann's letter to Lloyd George of December 29, 1919, ibid., pp. 277–279.

11. The memorandum does include historical arguments, but its main emphasis was on instrumental arguments: in the north, water sources; in the east, agricultural areas, the Dead Sea quarries, and railway access; in the south, an outlet to the Red Sea and arable lands in the northern Sinai. By contrast, in negotiations between the British and French on the northern border, both sides often quoted the Bible. The verse "from Dan to Beersheba" also appears frequently in British documents. Frischwasser, 1955, p. 87; Friesel, 1977, p. 197; Biger, 1983a, p. 33.

12. No map is attached to the memorandum itself, rather only a description of "the borders of Eretz-Israel."

13. The Zionist memorandum was influenced by the prevailing geopolitical literature of the period, especially documents prepared by geographers for the Paris Peace Conference. Background documents used by the British and French in negotiations on the northern border also strongly emphasized physical and geographic arguments. See, for example, *Syria and Palestine*, 1920, London: H. M. Stationary Office, p. 158; see also Holdich, 1916a.

14. According to Ben-Gurion and Ben-Zvi, the area of Eretz Israel is some 55,000 km^2, or about 60,000 km^2 if the southern border is adjusted from the Rafah-Aqaba line to El Arish-Aqaba. A new Hebrew edition of the book was published by Yad Yitzhak Ben-Zvi, 1980, pp. 46–50.

15. For comparison of earlier version submitted to the British Foreign Office in November 1918, see: PRO/F0371/3385/19182; and Friesel's discussion, 1977, p. 72

16. Ben-Gurion and Ben-Zvi, 1980, p. 46.

17. Under the Sykes-Picot Agreement, the northern border was intended to separate areas of French and British authority and ran from the Mediterranean Sea at Achziv to a point on the western coast of the Sea of Galilee, north of Tiberias.

18. See Brawer, 1988, pp. 103–124; Franco-British Convention of December 23, 1920, London: Cmd. 1195, 1921.

19. On the French position, see Nevakivi, 1969; Andrew and Kanyaa-Forstner, 1981.

20. See Klieman, 1970, pp. 205–207.

21. Agreement between the United Kingdom and Transjordan signed in Jerusalem, February 1928. London: Cmd. 3069, March 1928; see also Alsberg, 1974, p. 239.

22. On the Congress deliberations, see Friesel, 1977, pp. 277–280.

23. The Hebrew version, as it appeared in *Ha'Olam* (November 6, 1921).

24. Shertok: "A part of our body was amputated when Trans-Jordan was separated from Palestine." Interview to the *New York American* (November 5, 1936).

25. *Palestine Royal Commission Report*, (E. I.), London: Cmd. 5479, July 1937, p. 223. (Hereafter, Royal Commission Report).

26. Stein, 1984, pp. 192–199; Shaltiel, 1990, vol. B. pp. 395–418.

27. Biger, 1981b, pp. 132–135.

28. Letter from Weizmann to his wife Vera (December 9, 1933), W. A.

29. Friesel, 1977, p. 289; Feinberg, 1963, p. 433.

30. These documents do not directly concern the territorial question and deserve only brief mention: (A) Report of the Shaw Commission of Enquiry, appointed to investigate the reasons for the 1929 disturbances. See *Report of the Commission on the Palestine Disturbances of August 1929*, London: Cmd. 3530, March 1930. (B) Following the Shaw Commission report, Hope-Simpson was sent to Palestine to investigate the land and settlement problems. See *Report on Immigration, Land Settlement and Development* by Sir John Hope-Simpson. London: Cmd. 3686, May 1930. (C) The new British policy received official authorization in the White Paper of Secretary Fasfield. See London: Cmd. 3692, October 1930.

31. Hebrew version in Joseph, 1948, pp. 280–284.

32. Royal Commission Report, pp. 106–112.

33. Proposed New Constitution for Palestine, London: Cmd. 5119, 1953; see also Joseph, 1948, pp. 115–117.

34. Royal Commission Report, p. vi.

35. Summary of cantonization proposals. See Avniel, 1937; Nitzan, 1978.

36. The report quotes Cust's article, but reaches the conclusion that cantonization entails almost all of the disadvantages of partition, without the benefit of attaining peace, Royal Commission Report, pp. 377–379.

37. Eliash, 1971, p. 20; Katzburg, 1974, pp. 24–25; Dothan, 1981, pp. 123–129.

38. Weizmann's letter to Cust of June 9, 1936; Weizmann, 1968–1985, p. 262.

39. Ibid., p. 293.

40. Ibid., pp. 295–297.

41. This matter was mentioned in a meeting between the colonial secretary and Weizmann held immediately afterwards, on June 30, 1936. Ben-Gurion also participated in the meeting. Ibid., pp. 295–297.

42. PRO/Cab 24/263 CP 190(36).

43. From the introduction to Weizmann, 1968–1985, vol. 17, p. xviii.

44. Ibid.

45. The plan for a solution to the land problem (ibid., p. xix), which Weizmann prepared with Ruppin's assistance, shows that Weizmann then thought only in terms of "land reservations."

46. "Peel was a confidant of the Colonial Secretary, agreed with his views on Palestine and was therefore appointed to his position" (Dothan, 1981, p. 130).

47. Ben-Gurion, 1971–1988, vol. 3, p. 355.

48. Weizmann maintained that the subject of partitioning Eretz Israel was first discussed by the commission in a closed meeting on January 8, 1937, Weizmann, 1953, p. 375.

49. G. Cohen, 1974.

50. Sheffer, 1980, p. 382.

51. Ormsby-Gore to Wauchope, June 10, 1936, PRO/CO/733/318/75550.

52. Wauchope to Ormsby-Gore, June 24, 1936, PRO/CO/733/297/75156 Part III.

53. Ben-Gurion 1971–1982, vol. 3, p. 306; Dothan holds that Weizmann opposed this because he preferred a "plan for political partition," but there is no proof of this (1981, p. 123).

54. Parkinson to Wauchope, July 3, 1937. PRO/CO/733/302/75288.

55. Ben-Gurion, 1971–1982, vol. 3, p. 324.

56. See his speech in a meeting of the Mapai Central Committee on July 9, 1936, ibid., p. 327.

57. Ben-Gurion, 1967, pp. 57–69.

58. Katzburg, 1974, p. 25.

59. Sheffer, 1980, p. 397.

60. Hebrew version in *Ha'aretz* (May 23, 1936).

61. Text of the government announcement in Katzburg, 1974, pp. 113–116.

62. Parliamentary Debates (Commons) 5th session, 326, July 21, 1937, pp. 2247–2380.

63. Hebrew version in Merhavia, 1944, pp. 465, 469.

64. See Rendel's memorandum of March 12, 1938, which contains the Foreign Office primary arguments against the proposal, FO 371/21862/1439. On the debate within the British government see Klieman, 1979; Sheffer, 1988, p. 46.

65. Text in Katzburg, 1974, pp. 118–123.

66. Policy in Palestine, Dispatch from the Secretary of State for the Colonies to the High Commissioner for Palestine, London: Cmd. 5634, January 4, 1938.

67. See Colonial Secretary Ormsby-Gore's letter to the Royal Commission Chairman of March 22, 1938, PRO/FO/371/218621/1653. See also Ben-Gurion, *Diary*, vol. 5, p. 119.

68. PRO, FO/21870 E 1319.

69. *Palestine Partition Commission*, 1938 (hereafter, Partition Commission Report, 1938).

70. *Palestine Statement of Policy*, London: Cmd. 6019, May 1939.

71. *Palestine Land Transfers Regulations*, London: Cmd, 6180, February 1940.

Chapter Three. The Predecision Phase

1. See report of the Jewish Agency executive meeting and the Va'ad Le'ummi [National Council] announcement, *Ha'aretz* (May 23, 1936). Berl Katznelson and Yitzhak Tabenkin also proposed to boycott the royal commission. See A. Shapira, 1980, vol. 2, pp. 523–524.

2. See Katzburg, 1974, p. 23, and the comparison of the Jewish Agency proposal, with the commission's terms of reference, p. 107.

3. Protocol of Mapai Central Committee, June 23, 1936, Ben-Gurion Archive, Sde Boqer.

4. *Ha'aretz* (September 1, 1936).

5. *Ha'aretz* (September 3, 1936).

6. Shertok played a central, and at times decisive, role in this process, but not during the testimony before the Commission. Detailed in Sheffer, 1990, Ch. 2.

7. Testimonies: (A) First testimony, public, November 25, 1936. Published as a separate pamphlet in Hebrew, see Keren Hayesod, 1937. For closed hearings, I relied on the original protocols in the Weizmann Archives, Rehovot, as follows: (B) Second testimony, private, November 26, 1936. Palestine Royal Commission, *Notes and Evidence* taken on November 26, 1936, Ninth Meeting (Private). (C) Third testimony, private, December 18, 1936, ibid. (D) Fourth testimony, private, December 23, 1936, ibid. (E) Fifth testimony, private, January 8, 1937, ibid. These testimonies also appear in *The Letters and Papers of Chaim Weizmann, Series B,* vol. 18, 1984. (hereafter, Weizmann, *Letters*). He also sent a letter clarifying and amending his comments to the commission chairman on January 19, 1937. See Weizmann, *Letters*, pp. 22–23.

8. Shertok testified to this before the Jewish Agency Executive. See the protocol in Ben-Gurion, 1971–1982, vol. 4, p. 22. See also Chapter Two.

9. Weizmann referred to this testimony only in his report to the restricted Zionist General Council. See protocol of the meeting of January 13, 1937, p. 3.

10. Weizmann mentioned this no less than four times in his fourth testimony and again in the fifth.

11. This was also Weizmann's answer to Mussolini in their 1934 meeting, G. Cohen, 1974, p. 371.

12. See Lord Peel's comments, quoted at the beginning of this chapter, during Weizmann's fourth testimony, p. 249.

13. It should be noted that Weizmann reported on his testimony before the Peel Commission to a Jewish Agency executive meeting of December 25, 1936. But he did not tell the executive member that he had been asked about cantonization and partiton two days earlier, during his private testimony of December 23. See the protocol of this meeting in Ben-Gurion, 1971–1982, vol. 3, pp. 528–535.

14. Note the wording of the January 19, 1937 letter in Weizmann, *Letters*, p. 17. See also the protocol of the restricted Zionist General Council meeting in Jerusalem, February 13, 1937 (CZA).

15. Sharett, 1972–1979, vol. 2, pp. 13–15.

16. The source for what transpired at the Nahalal meeting is Weisgal and Carmichael, 1963, pp. 240–241. There are also discrepancies as to the date of the Nahalal meeting, see Rose, 1973, pp. 127, 147.

17. Sharett, 1972–1979, vol. 2, p. 16.

18. Sykes, 1967, p. 176.

19. Rose, 1973, p. 128. And in a private letter of January 22, 1937: "There may be a solution whose meaning could be a new beginning but I can speak of this only on a personal basis" (Weizmann, *Letters*, p. 23).

20. Dothan, 1981, p. 131.

21. On Wauchope's support, see the protocol of his meeting with Weizmann and Shertok on March 14, 1937 in which the high commissioner said that he now tended to agree with separation. Sharett, 1972–1979, vol. 2, p. 64.

22. In a conversation on March 14, 1937, with the high commissioner, Weizmann referred to "the entire coastal plain from the northern border to the Egyptian border and Eilat." Shertok quickly added the Galilee, the northern Jordan Valley, and a portion of Transjordan. Sharett, ibid.

23. In early February 1937, Weizmann met with Leon Blum and telegrammed Kaplan in New York: "Blum is prepared to support Coupland's partition plan." See Weizmann, *Letters*, p. 25.

24. Teveth, 1987, p. 196.

25. Ibid.

26. Ben-Gurion and Ben-Zvi, 1980, p. 44. Also Teveth, 1976, p. 356.

27. Ben-Gurion and Ben-Zvi, 1980, p. 43.

28. Ibid., p. 47.

29. The line between realism and prophecy was somewhat blurred—already in 1918—on the subject of the Negev: "Beersheva is not the most southerly point of the Land of Israel, but rather the Gulf of Aqaba, as in the days of King Solomon" (ibid., p. 45). Ben-Gurion's loyalty to the Negev remained consistent throughout his political shifts concerning the partition of Eretz Israel.

30. In a 1935 memorandum that he prepared in New York, Ben-Gurion surveyed the land shortage due to the inaccessibility of Transjordan under British policy, the unsuitability of the mountain ridge for extensive Jewish settlement, the dense population of the coastal region and high

price of land, and the small size of the Jordan Valley. Ben-Gurion concluded that the future of the national home depended on settlement of the Negev and seamanship to establish a fait accompli. D. Ben-Gurion, "The Land Problem with Special Regard to Negev and Araba," New York, June 4, 1935. CZA S25/9945. It is unclear why this memo was prepared and sent to Kaplan and Shertok.

31. "In their opinion and in their [the commission members'] proposals, there would be great and perhaps decisive value both in governmental circles and the wider circles of the British people." Stated during the Zionist General Council meeting of November 10, 1936. Ben-Gurion, 1971–1982, vol. 3, p. 482; on his ambivalence see ibid., pp. 518–526; and 1971–1982, vol. 4, pp. 1–2, Teveth, 1987, pp. 168, 185.

32. Text of the testimony in 1971–1982, vol. 4, 1937, pp. 8–18.

33. Ibid., pp. 5–6.

34. In the handwritten draft he apparently prepared prior to his testimony before the royal commission, he wrote: "A large Arab federation in Eretz Israel." The implication is unclear, because the matter did not arise. Ben-Gurion Archive, Sde Boqer, File 3340, p. 6.

35. Ben-Gurion, 1971–1982, vol. 4, pp. 22–23 and 26 in a letter to Stephen Wise.

36. Shabtai Teveth wrote about Ben-Gurion's position at this meeting: "This turning point was consciously one of the greatest political gambles of his lifetime." See "The Basis for the Double Formula in Ben-Gurion's Thought," address at the L. Davis Institute symposium, the Hebrew University of Jerusalem, June 10, 1987, p. 13.

37. Protocol of Mapai Central Committee meeting, February 5, 1937, Beit Berl Archive.

38. Ibid., pp. 3–4.

39. Ibid., p. 8.

40. In the Mapai Central Committee meeting of April 10, 1937, Berl Locker complained that Ben-Gurion's plan was not seriously considered. See protocol, p. 21.

41. Mapai Central Committee protocol, February 5, 1937, p. 13.

42. Mapai Central Committee meeting protocols, April 10 and 15, 1937, Beit Berl Archive.

43. For example, a *Ha'aretz* headline, "A Jewish State on the Coast and an Independent Arab State, the Commission's Proposal?" (April 4, 1937); headline in the *Daily Telegraph* (April 2, 1937); see Sharett's response, 1972–1979, vol. 2, p. 104.

44. This was still only a hypothetical possibility, and Ben-Gurion asked his colleagues not to "make final decisions." Mapai Central Committee protocol (April 10), p. 43.

45. Ben-Gurion, 1971–1982, vol. 4, p. 167; Sharett, 1972–1979, vol. 2, p. 178.

46. Protocol of the Mapai Central Committee, June 8, 1937; Ben-Gurion, 1971–1982, vol. 4, pp. 209–219; Teveth, 1987, pp. 210–211.

47. *Davar* (July 13, 1937). We will return to this resolution in Chapter Nine.

48. Ben-Gurion, 1971–1982, vol. 4, p. 249.

49. The quotations below are all from Jabotinsky, *Writings,* 1947–1959, unless otherwise indicated. Jabotinsky, "What Do the Revisionist Zionists Want?" *On the Road to Statehood,* vol. 11, p. 283.

50. *Speeches, 1927–1940,* vol. 5, p. 182. See also Jabotinsky's "Ten-Year Plan," which was approved by the same conference, Ibid., p. 180.

51. Jabotinsky, 1937. Excerpted here from the Hebrew version: Jabotinsky, 1946, pp. 76–112 (hereafter: Testimony Before the Royal Commission).

52. Ibid., p. 94.

53. Ibid., pp. 77, 80, 100.

54. Jabotinsky's "Environmental Principles" suggested that the "landscape of the homeland" determined the connection between the People of Israel and the Land of Israel. See Bilski Ben-Hur, 1988, p. 164.

55. Testimony Before the Royal Commission, p. 84.

56. Gorny, 1985, p. 341.

57. Royal Commission Report, pp. 142–143.

58. Royal Commission Report, p. 309. On the similarities between the positions of Weizmann and Jabotinsky in their testimony before the royal commission, see Heller, 1984.

59. On the internal events among the Palestinian Arabs and their positions toward the royal commission, see Porath, 1978; Arnon-Ohana, 1981.

60. Sheffer, 1988, p. 35.

61. Porath, 1985, p. 177.

62. See document of November 6, 1936 in Merhavia, 1944, pp. 433–484.

63. Ibid., p. 435.

64. Palestine Royal Commission, *Notes and Evidence*, 56th meeting, January 12, 1937, pp. 292–368 (hereafter, Royal Commission Protocol). Another interesting testimony was that of George Antonius. But, because he did not relate to the question of state and territory, we will not review it here. Ibid., Testimony of January 19, 1937, pp. 358–367.

65. Ibid., Articles 4561, 4611, 4617, pp. 293–295.

66. Ibid., Article 4637, p. 297. See also "Memorandum of the Arab Higher Committee as Submitted to the Royal Commission," Hebrew translation in Merhavia, 1944, p. 439.

67. Ibid., articles 4643, 4645, 4650, p. 298.

68. Royal Commission Report, pp. 107–110.

69. Ibid., pp. 130–136, 363.

70. This period saw quite intense contacts, recorded in Sharett, 1972–1979, vol. 2, pp. 23–90. It is worth mentioning Weizmann's meetings with Lord Samuel and Lloyd George preceding their appearance before the royal commission.

71. Weizmann met Blum in February 1937 and again in May, concerning the Galilee's inclusion in the Jewish state. On the scope of the diplomatic efforts, see Dothan, 1981, pp. 132–133.

72. Of the executive members, Shertok was in contact with the Arab leadership in Eretz Israel, primarily through Yehudah Magnes, his contact with Mussa El-Alami. See Sheffer, 1990, Chapter 12, pp. 4–6. On the contacts with Iraqi leader Nuri El-Said, see Porath, 1977, pp. 208–209. On Shertok's meeting with Arab leaders in Paris on March 16, 1937, see Sharett, 1972–1979, vol. 2, pp. 72–78; and with Arab leaders in Eretz Israel in May 1937, ibid., pp. 132–133. On Rutenberg's meetings with Emir Abdullah in May 1937, see Shaltiel, 1990, vol. 2, p. 477.

73. Correspondence between Shertok and Weizmann, June–July 1937, CZA 525/1716. See also Sharett, 1972–1979, vol. 2, p. 40.

74. Ben-Gurion, *Diary*, vol. 4, pp. 270, 291–296.

75. Rose, 1973, p. 130; Sharett, 1972–1979, vol. 2, p. 69. After meeting with Coupland (apparently on March 23), Neimer reported that Coupland believed he would be able to convince his colleagues to adopt the "broad plan," namely, partition and independence.

76. Weizmann, *Letters*, p. 82; Diary of Blanche (Baffy) Dugdale, April 27, 1937, as quoted in Rose, 1973, pp. 130–131. Ben-Gurion also notes having heard about the conversation from Weizmann, 1971–1982, vol. 4, p. 173.

77. Sharett, 1972–1979, vol. 2, p. 196; Dothan, 1981, p. 134.

78. Weizmann met Blum on May 29. See Rose, 1973, p. 131.

79. On the meeting in London (attended also by Katznelson), see Ben-Gurion, 1971–1982, vol. 4, pp. 196–198.

80. Ibid., p. 75. Shertok met with the colonial secretary on March 5, but the content of the royal commission deliberations were apparently not discussed. Sharett, 1972–1979, vol. 2, p. 51.

81. Ibid., p. 87.

82. Teveth, 1987, pp. 205–206, based mainly on Ben-Gurion, 1971–1982, vol. 4, pp. 219–221. Also Rose, 1973, pp. 131–133, based mainly on the Dugdale diary.

83. Ben-Gurion, ibid., p. 228.

84. Text in Weizmann, *Letters*, vol. 17, pp. 118–119.

85. Document in Katzburg, 1974, p. 109.

86. Sharett, 1972–1979, vol. 2, pp. 201–205; Teveth, 1987, p. 210.

87. Cab 29/270 in Katzburg, 1974, pp. 112–113.

88. Ibid., pp. 113–116.

89. Teveth, 1987, p. 199.

90. Rose, 1970, 1971, 6, p. 311.

91. Representatives of Agudat Israel and Poalei Agudat Israel testified before the commission on behalf of the "Opposition," Session 28, December 21, 1936, pp. 193–198; as did Jabotinsky, who said "We want a state." Testimony Before the Royal Commission, pp. 12–13.

92. Protocol in Ben-Gurion, 1971–1982, vol. 4, p. 75.

93. Ibid., p. 82.

94. See the earlier note 49.

95. *Ha'aretz* (April 6, 1937).

96. *Ha'aretz* (April 8 and 14, 1937).

97. A. Shapira, 1984, p. 24.

98. Protocol of the enlarged Zionist General Council meeting, April 1937, pp. 21–22 (CZA S/5/2141).

99. *Ha'aretz* (April 27, 1937).

100. Dothan, 1980, p. 52. It should be emphasized that this proposal was not explicitly accepted by the plenum of the Zionist General Council. Ben-Gurion made a statement on this matter in the Policy Committee and reported the committee's unanimous acceptance in the plenary. See Sharett, 1972–1979, vol. 2, p. 213.

101. Dothan, 1980, p. 53; see Ussishkin "The Question of Partitioning Eretz Israel," *Ha'aretz* (June 4, 1937).

102. See his comments in the Jewish Agency executive meeting, May 2, 1937, Sharett, 1972–1979, vol. 2, p. 116; Ben-Gurion, 1971–1982, vol. 4, p. 167.

103. Sharett, 1972–1979, vol. 2, pp. 202, 210.

104. Ibid., pp. 212–213.

105. Ibid., p. 249.

106. Letter to Shertok, July 3, 1937, 1971–1982, vol. 4, p. 278. At Ben-Gurion's request, the letter was read at a meeting of the Mapai council in early July.

107. Royal Commission Report, p. xi.

108. On British policy in the region from 1936–1939, see M. J. Cohen, 1988, pp. 78–98.

109. "Note of an Informal Discussion Between the Chiefs of Staff Sub-Committee and Members of the Royal Commission on Palestine" (March 1, 1937), PRO/CO/733/346/9/99093.

110. The air force chief also expressed concern that the Jewish state could turn Communist and anti-British. Lord Peel tried to allay his fears by saying that Jewish immigrants with Communist tendencies would change their views in a developed state.

111. Ibid, p. 13.

112. See, for example, Royal Commission Report, p. 373.

113. Ibid., p. 281. In private comments, Sir Horace Rumbold opposed the establishment of a strong Jewish army, which he felt the Jewish state could use for "aggressive purposes" beyond its borders and against Transjordan, Syria, and Saudi Arabia. PRO/CO/733/346/9.

114. Royal Commission Report, p. 363.

115. Ibid., p. 33.

116. Katzburg, 1974, pp. 34–35, 38–45.

117. Ben-Gurion, 1971–1982, vol. 4 (July 20, 1937), p. 296.

118. Royal Commission Report, pp. 280–281, 307, 308–309, 362.

119. Ibid., p. 379.

120. There are several theories about how the royal commission arrived at its recommended partition plan. Some credit this mainly to Coupland and point to the different style of Chapter 22, which deals with partition, in contrast to the remaining parts of the book. It can be noted, conversely, that commission member Hammond was a full partner to the recommendations. See the memorandum of R. C. (Reginald Coupland) written on June 8, 1937, after consulting Hammond: "Notes for Discussion of Partition," PRO/CO/733/346/9/99093.

Rumbold also supported partition. See his (undated) memorandum: "Some Considerations Connected with the Clean Cut," PRO/CO/733/346/9/99093. Moreover, as we saw previously, four Commission members—Peel, Rumbold, Morris, and Coupland—already presented the partition plan to the Chiefs of Staff on March 1, 1937. Professor Coupland was more involved than his colleagues in political contacts concerning the report. In addition to his direct contacts with Weizmann, he was in touch with the colonial secretary. See, for example, his letter to Ormsby-Gore from June 26, 1937: PRO/FO/371/20808 E 3630/22/31.

121. The map was attached to the *Royal Commission Report*. The recommendations appear on pp. 380–392.

122. Ibid., p. 389.

123. Ibid., pp. 266–268.

124. On the Jewish Agency deliberations preceding testimony before the Woodhead commission and the establishment of six subcommittees to prepare material on the subjects of boundaries, population, finance, security, Haifa, and Jerusalem, see the protocol of Jewish Agency executive meetings (May 1–10, 1938), CZA.

125. Reichman, 1979, p. 62.

Chapter Four. Choice Analysis

1. As explained in Chapter Two, the Zionist movement's first territorial decisions were made in the 1919–1922 period concerning the granting of the British mandate for Palestine (E.I.) and the territory included therein. Nevertheless, this was not a "decision crossroad," by our definition, because the Zionist movement did not actually confront real policy options among which it was possible to choose.

2. A. Shapira, 1989, p. 312.

3. The most convincing discussion of rational decision making is still Herbert Simon's. See the collection of his articles in Simon, 1957b, pp. 196–273.

4. The question of "Eastern Eretz Israel" (Transjordan) is a ramification of this position and requires a separate discussion.

5. The main tactical considerations were the following: the Jews must continue to demand continuation of the mandate; they cannot support partition publicly; they should not commit themselves to future boundaries; and the leadership should be given freedom to negotiate expansion of the proposed territory.

6. This position did not support the territorial proposal at any price but rather felt that this was the only practical opportunity for sovereignty and should therefore be seized immediately. It does not preclude the possibility that new situations could facilitate territorial changes in the future.

7. On arguments used in territorial demands of states, see Burghardt, 1973, pp. 226–238; on reasons for territorial identification, see Duchacek, 1986, pp. 6–28; and on the use of these arguments in the Israeli context, see S. Cohen, 1986, pp. 22–24.

8. Kimmerling, 1985, notes that primordial and civilian sentiments toward the "state of Israel," as opposed to the "Land of Israel," are not necessarily contradictory, p. 275.

9. On political and economic viability, see Hartshorne, 1960, pp. 62–64.

10. Brecher, 1972, pp. 11–13; 229–250.

11. Fromkin, 1989, p. 513.

12. Lustick (1987) distinguishes between two types of "thresholds" in the processes of territorial expansion or contraction. The first is related to the regime's interests whereas the second is psychological. The transition between them marks a shift from problems that can be tested in cost-benefit (instrumental) terms to problems that demand ideological hegemony. He applied this analysis to an examination of nineteenth century British policy toward Ireland (Lustick, 1990a). He feels that the current arguments on the future of the territories occupied by Israel in 1967 also straddle this type of threshold (Lustick, 1987, p. 171; and for the model, pp. 164–165).

Chapter Five. Predecision Positions

1. Dothan, 1980, p. 55.

2. Text in Merhavia, 1944, pp. 471–473.

3. Eliash, 1971, p. 42.

4. *Davar* (July 22, 1937).

5. This image appears in strong colors in the poems of poet Shaul Tchernikovsky, who believed in the territorial integrity of Eretz Israel on both sides of the Jordan and wrote three poems against the partition proposal. See Dothan, 1980, p. 118.

6. Beitar's leaflet was composed by Jabotinsky in London and published in *Hayarden* on July 16, 1937.

7. Shlaim, 1988, pp. 58–59. This was indirectly confirmed during Abdullah's meeting with Dov Hoz on May 15, 1937, in which Abdullah said that the British government had not even mentioned Palestine to him. See document from the Ben-Gurion Archives in Avizohar and Friedman, 1984, p. 215.

8. On the Iraqi reaction to the report, see Porath, 1977, p. 274.

9. Shlaim, 1988, pp. 59–62; Porath, 1977, p. 229; Porath, 1985, pp. 90–92; Caplan, 1986, pp. 63–65; Shaltiel, 1990, vol. 2, pp. 458–461; Ran, 1991, pp. 60–82.

10. Katzburg, 1974, p. 32. On a meeting between Eliyahu Sasson and Abdullah's representative in Jerusalem on August 5, 1937, see CZA S/125/3486. On the position of Abdullah, see Klieman, 1983, pp. 20–22.

11. Porath, 1977, pp. 230–232.

12. Based on the Hebrew text in Merhavia, 1944, pp. 477–478.

13. Arnon-Ohana, 1981, pp. 77–78.

14. Porath, 1978, p. 272; also see Hassassian, 1990, p. 125.

15. Abboushi, 1974, p. 40.

16. Heller, 1989, vol. 1, pp. 41–43.

17. Gorny, 1985, pp. 314–317.

18. Hashomer Hatzair belonged to the World Union of Poalei Zion and the Zionist Socialists, but remained organizationally and ideologically distinct.

19. Internal memorandum (No. 332) to Mapai branch committees, June 23, 1937, Beit Berl Archive.

20. Protocol of General Council discussions, Beit Berl Archive.

21. "Statement of Policy of the Mapai Party," *Davar* (July 13, 1937).

22. Teveth, 1987, p. 211.

23. Ben-Gurion, 1971–1982, vol. 4, (entry of July 17, 1937), p. 306; letter to Amos Ben-Gurion (July 27, 1937), p. 331.

24. Ibid., p. 333.

25. Shlomo Lavie of Ein Harod was the only central figure within this Kibbutz movement who supported partition; see his article in *Davar* (June 9, 1937).

26. *Ha'aretz* (July 14, 1937).

27. *Mibefnim* 4, no. 2, Kibbutz Hameuchad publications, Ein Harod, July 1937. These statements preceded the publication of the commission report.

28. M. Dorman, *Mibefnim* (May 1941), as quoted in Yishai, 1978, p. 42.

29. *Mibefnim* 4, no. 2: 8–9, 12, 16, 21.

30. Tsur maintains that the split was not caused by the opposition to partition, but notes that the disputes concerning this issue did have a substantial effect, Avizohar and Friedman, 1984, p. 168.

31. *Mibefnim* 4, no. 3 (August–September 1937): 8.

32. This presentation relies upon the seminar paper of Avner De-Shalit, 1986.

33. Text of the resolutions in *Hashomer Hatzair*, no. 14 (July 15, 1937).

34. Ibid., p. 2.

35. Statement of Hashomer Hatzair policy, July 1937, *The Book of Hashomer Hatzair*, vol. 1, 1956, p. 290.

36. Leibner, 1937. The booklet can be found at the ZA in New York.

37. *Davar* (July 25, 1937); Margalit, 1976, p. 277.

38. Resolutions of the Eighth National Congress of Poalei Zion, September 1937, as reprinted in Ben-Avram, 1978, p. 132.

39. Margalit, 1976, p. 279.

40. Dothan, 1991, pp. 235, 237.

41. Ibid, p. 274.

42. *Kol Ha'am* (August 2, 1937).

43. Eliash, 1971, p. 98; Dothan, 1980, pp. 215–219.

44. Ben-Avram, 1978, p. 147.

45. The "civic camp" was a loose conglomerate of parties and organizations whose common denominator was a laissez-faire economic orientation. See Galnoor, 1982, pp. 59–64; Horowitz and Lissak, 1977, pp. 100–102, 127–128.

46. On the "civic camp" in the preceding period, see Giladi, 1973.

47. *Ha'aretz*, (June 4, 1937). The article states: "We will not concede, not today, tomorrow or ever, one inch of our historic land" and "We have the power of absorption and they have the power of birth."

48. Dothan, 1980, p. 91. The editorials of *Haboker* (July 7–8, 1937) vehemently opposed the royal commission report and the partition proposal.

49. M. Smilansky, *Bustanai*, 14 (July 14, 1937), reprinted in Ben-Avram, 1978, p. 172.

50. Dothan, 1980, pp. 252–253.

51. *Ha'aretz* (August 1 and 11, 1937).

52. *Hayarden* 640 (August 6, 1937).

53. See text in Merhavia, 1944, p. 475.

54. *Hayarden* (July 9, 1937).

55. Akzin, in Avizohar and Friedman, 1984, p. 164. See also Heller, 1983, pp. 88–89; and 1987b, p. 302.

56. See Yosef Klauzner's article, *Haboker* (September 5, 1937).

57. *Hayarden* (July 16, 1937).

58. Sharett, 1972–1979, vol. 2, p. 231.

59. Akzin, in Avizohar and Friedman, 1984, pp. 162–165.

60. Eliash, 1971, p. 168; Dothan, 1980, p. 180, note 17.

61. Protocol of the Twentieth Zionist Congress, p. 93.

62. Detailed review of the "Grossman Affair" in Eliash, 1971, pp. 75–88; Dothan, 1980, pp. 110–112. He was convicted of revealing a secret document and damaging the interests of the Zionist movement.

63. S. Z. Shragai, *Netiva*, no. 30 (April 16, 1937).

64. Text in Dothan, 1980, p. 91.

65. Ibid., p. 172.

66. Text in Ostrovsky, 1944, p. 208 [also see Histadrut Hamizrahi, 1937.

67. Eliash, 1971, pp. 44–46.

68. Texts in ibid. pp. 191–192.

69. Royal Commission Testimony, December 21, 1936, p. 193.

70. Dothan, 1980, pp. 192–193.

71. Gretz, 1988, pp. 37–38.

72. Literally, *Brit Shalom* means "covenant of peace." It was founded in 1925 by a group of prominent intellectuals such as Martin Buber, Uriel Simon, Hans Cohen, and Hugo Bergmann. It was influenced by Yehuda Magnes's political positions.

Kedma Mizraha ("forward to the east") was founded in 1936, after the dissolution of Brit Shalom, specifically to bring Jews closer to the east and to form social and cultural ties with Arabs. The organization took on a more political, if not very influential, cast in 1937, when it supported the realization of Zionism through integration with the east, and felt that the best way to accomplish this would be within a binational framework as part of a wider regional federation. Veteran Jerusalem Oriental Jews, Sephardim, headed by Raphael Molcho and Menashe Elissar, were among the organization's activists. Hattis, 1970, pp. 138–144.

Ichud (union) started its operation in 1942 and was a direct continuation of Brit Shalom.

73. On the influence of Buber, see Tal, 1987, pp. 89–90; Keidar in Ben Zion and Keidar, 1978, p. 102.

74. From the Brit Shalom proposal to the Jewish Agency (1930) in Merhavia, 1950?, p. 485.

75. Ben-Avram, 1978, p. 204.

76. Herman, 1989, pp. 161–169.

77. The article was reprinted in *Ha'aretz* (July 19, 1937).

78. Protocol of the Fifth Jewish Agency Council, 1937, pp. 47–52.

79. Ben-Gurion, letter to Shertok and Kaplan of July 22, 1937, in 1971–1982, vol. 4, pp. 311–312.

80. Ibid., p. 309.

81. Dothan, 1980, pp. 223–228.

82. Such as Y. Leshchinsky, who said: "Even if the word 'state' would be ridiculed and scorned, in the ears of the Jewish people it rings like the bells of redemption." Protocol of the Fifth Jewish Agency Council, pp. 44–45.

83. Protocol of the Twentieth Zionist Congress, pp. 133, 204.

Chapter Six. The Opponents

1. Koifman, 1938, pp. 4, 6.

2. According to Nettl, 1968, the state is a collectivity that summates a set of functions and structures, a unit in international relations, an autonomous collectivity as well as a summating concept of high societal generality, a sociocultural phenomenon. On territory and sovereignty as part of the definition of the state, see Vincent, 1987, pp. 19–20.

3. On the "Uganda Affair," which also came up in the 1937 partition polemos, see Vital, 1982, pp. 350–360.

4. On universal ideologies among the Jews, see Talmon, 1982, vol. 1, pp. 231–235.

5. This caused intense arguments over non-Zionist representation on the enlarged executive before the convening of the Jewish Agency council in 1937. See Weizmann *Letters*, vol. 18, pp. 33–38, 147.

6. Karpf, 1938, pp. 7–8, 13–14.

7. Ibid., p. 22.

8. Protocol of the Fifth Jewish Agency Council, 1937, p. 29. Warburg was previously involved in Magnes's attempt to talk with the Arab leaders. See Porath, 1977, p. 21; Hattis, 1970, pp. 68–69.

9. Protocol of the Fifth Jewish Agency Council, 1937, p. 31.

10. *The Jewish Chronicle* (April 30, 1937).

11. See, for example, Friesel, 1984; Wasserstein, 1992, pp. 269–270.

12. Wasserstein, ibid., pp. 226, 237–239, 268–270.

13. House of Lords Debates, vol. 106, July 20, 1937, pp. 629–645.

14. Similar positions were presented by Hyamson, former head of the British government's Immigration Department in Palestine. He was later involved in Jewish-Arab contacts. See Hyamson, 1942, pp. 178–188.

15. His entire speech was published in *Ha'aretz* on July 28 and 29, 1937.

16. Samuel reiterated his ideas in an article in *Foreign Affairs:* Samuel, 1937, pp. 143–155. The article had an impact on Churchill in his opposition to the royal commission proposal. See Wasserstein, 1992, p. 386.

17. Protocol of the Fifth Jewish Agency Council, 1937, p. 27.

18. Ibid., pp. 45–46.

19. On the binational idea, see Hattis, 1970, pp. 136–208; Katzburg, 1977, pp. 77–82, 144–149; Mendes-Flohr, 1983, pp. 72–73, 82–91; and Herman, 1989, pp. 161–171.

20. Although he did not advocate a binational solution, Martin Buber can also be included in this group. His opposition to a Jewish state at that time stemmed from the fear of change in the Jewish spiritual world as a result of their becoming a nation like all other nations.

21. Cited in Hattis, 1970, pp. 51–52.

22. Protocol of the Fifth Jewish Agency Council, 1937, p. 48.

23. Ibid., pp. 49–50.

24. Weizmann, *Letters*, Series A, vol. 18 (September 24, 1937), p. 203.

25. Ruppin, a member of the Jewish Agency executive, would later support the partition plan because he saw no other option: "If in this way (partition) we will be able to attain peace with the Arabs and a large immigration into the Jewish part, the plan deserves consideration," Ruppin, 1971, p. 238.

26. Rutenberg was the founder of the Palestine Electric Company. See Shaltiel, 1990, vol. 2, pp. 471–489.

27. Talmon, 1982, vol. 1, p. 201.

28. Such as the Soviet Union's attempt to create an autonomous Jewish region in Siberian Birobijan.

29. Protocol of the Twentieth Zionist Congress, p. 201, 205.

30. M. Ben-Tov (Hashomer Hatzair) stated explicitly that the minority resolution at the congress "is the result of mutual concessions." Ibid., p. 210.

31. Protocol of the Fifth Jewish Agency Council, 1937, p. 69.

32. Ibid., p. 60.

33. Ibid., pp. 60–61. Weizmann then shot a sharper arrow at Warburg: "There are Jews who fear that upon the establishment of the Jewish State, all the Jews in the world will be sent to that state. Today they send the Jews to hell." Ibid., p. 64.

34. Protocol of the Twentieth Zionist Congress, p. 83.

35. Jabotinsky, 1937, pp. 11–12.

36. Protocol of the Zionist General Council meetings in London, summary of decisions [in English], March 1938, Archive of the Ben-Gurion Heritage Center, Sde Boqer.

37. Namely, the need to take a position on the "question of time and Zionism," as phrased by A. Shapira, 1989, p. 314.

38. Margalit, 1971, pp. 201–226.

39. Prai, 1972, pp. 20–21.

40. "Public Statement Against the Partition of the Land," *Hashomer Hatzair*, no. 13 (July 1, 1937).

41. Based mainly on De-Shalit, 1986.

42. *Hashomer Hatzair*, no. 9 (May 1, 1937).

43. Protocol of the Kibbutz Ha'artzi Council, No. 13, February 1937, Givat Haviva Archive, File (1)2.20.5.

44. *Hashomer Hatzair*, no. 14 (July 15, 1937).

45. *Hashomer Hatzair*, no. 1 (January 1, 1938).

46. The possibility of expanding the revolutionary boundaries to include Transjordan and Syria was not excluded, De–Shalit, 1986, p. 18.

47. Mordechai Oren, "Good Partition and Bad Partition," *Hashomer Hatzair*, no. 14 (July 15, 1937).

48. Protocol of the Twentieth Zionist Congress, p. 86.

49. Ibid., p. 142. See also Leibner, 1937, pp. 3–5.

50. Protocol of the Twentieth Zionist Congress, p. 210.

51. Ibid., pp. 219–220.

52. Protocol of the Mapai council, April 1937.

53. *Mibefnim* (December 1937), p. 9.

54. Keidar, 1984, p. 135.

55. Sharett, 1972–1979, vol. 2, p. 272.

56. Tabenkin's lecture in 1956 is quoted in Keidar, 1984, Vol. 2, p. 411 (n. 94).

57. Perhaps the most convincing proof is not to be found in the ideological arguments, but rather in the emotional images presented by members of this Kibbutz movement. See *Bibritech* ("in your covenant"), a pamphlet published by Hakibbutz Hameuchad youth movement in 1938. For these young people, love of the land came before ideology, and signing a covenant with Eretz Israel stood above the politics of establishing a state.

58. See Tabenkin speech, Protocol of the Twentieth Zionist Congress, p. 181.

59. Ibid., p. 132.

60. Ibid., pp. 151–152.

61. Grossman, of the State Party and an extreme opponent, did not rule out Ben-Gurion's approach: first to accept the "concept of a Jewish state" in the commission's report. Ibid., p. 93.

62. Ben-Aharon, Protocol of the Mapai central committee, April 15, 1937, Meeting II, p. 13.

63. On concepts and images of the "Holy Land" in other religions, see Ben Arieh in Kark, 1989b, pp. 37–53.

64. Dushinsky's evidence before the royal commission, December 21, 1936, p. 193.

65. Binyamin Mintz, quoted by Dothan, 1980, p. 193.

66. Protocol of the Twentieth Zionist Congress, pp. 50–52.

67. S. Z. Shragai, *Netiva* (July 5, 1937). On the Halachic aspects of the debate concerning the Royal Commission's partition proposal, see Dothan, 1980, pp. 176–184; Eliash, 1984, pp. 56–59.

68. See, for example, the comments of Z. Warhaftig, Protocol of the Zionist Congress, p. 214.

69. S. Z. Shragai, "National Home—Jewish State," *Netiva*, no. 30 (April 16, 1937).

70. Galnoor, 1982, pp. 88–93.

71. Kimmerling, 1985, pp. 264–269.

72. Ussishkin, 1943, pp. 9–10.

73. All the following references to Ussishkin are excerpted from the Protocol of the Twentieth Zionist Congress, pp. 36–38, 132, 187.

74. Protocol of the Mapai central committee, February 5–6, 1937, p. 2; April 15, 1937, p. 23.

75. Protocol of the Twentieth Zionist Congress, p. 100.

76. Ibid., pp. 33, 70.

77. Berlin, 1958, p. 38.

78. A. Shapira, 1989, p. 314.

79. Protocol of the Twentieth Zionist Congress, p. 56.

80. Jabotinsky, 1937.

81. Jabotinsky, 1947–1959a, "Confronting the Partition Plan–The Ten-Year Plan," in *Speeches, 1927–1940*, vol. 5, p. 293. Opposition to partition based on the need to settle millions of Jews is also emphasized in the NZO Declaration of July 1937; see Merhavia, 1944, p. 475.

82. Jabotinsky, 1986, p. 96.

83. Jabotinsky, 1947–1959a, "Majestic Zionism," vol. 5, p. 128.

84. *Hayarden* (August 13, 1937).

85. Jabotinsky, 1947–1959a, "Confronting the Partition Plan—The Ten-Year Plan," vol. 5, p. 294.

86. Ibid., "Transjordan and the Ten-Year Plan," vol. 6, p. 231.

87. *Hayarden* (August 13, 1937).

88. Ibid.

89. Jabotinsky, 1947–1959a, "On Partition," (Address before Members of the British Parliament, July 13, 1937), *Zionist Policy, Selected Writings*, vol. 3, p. 114; see also *Hayarden* (July 30, 1937).

90. Heller, 1983, p. 89.

91. Jabotinsky, 1986, p. 30.

92. Jabotinsky, 1947–1959a. Written in 1912, in "Self-Government of a National Minority," *Nation and Society* 9: 3–16. See also Bilsky Ben-Hur, 1988, p. 140; Adiv, 1978, pp. 116–118.

93. J. Shavit, 1986, p. 211.

94. Adiv, 1978, p. 118.

95. "The romanticism that is lacking in Jabotinsky's writings concerning the Land of Israel is found in his description of the ideal Jew," Bilsky Ben-Hur, 1988, p. 187.

96. Quoted in Bela, 1975, p. 102.

97. Heller, 1983, pp. 88–89; Bar-Nir, 1987, p. 133.

98. Ben-Gurion, 1971–1982, vol. 5, p. 7.

99. Protocol of the Twentieth Zionist Congress, pp. 93, 126.

100. Ibid., pp. 133–134.

101. Protocol of the Jewish Agency Executive, Jerusalem, July 17, 1937, p. 2, Ben-Gurion Archives, Sde Boqer.

102. Protocol of the Mapai central committee, April 10, 1937, Beit Berl Archive, p. 11.

103. Remarks of Kaplan and Meirov, ibid., p. 41.

104. Protocol of the Twentieth Zionist Congress, p. 92.

105. Ibid., p. 132.

106. Ibid., p. 67. Tabenkin charged that limiting the area would cause an urbanization of the Yishuv in Eretz Israel and a return to the nonproductive Jewish professions of the exile. See *Paths of Our Policy*, 1938, p. 187.

107. Sharett, 1972–1979, vol. 2, pp. 258–260.

108. The Haganah was the illegal military arm of the organized Jewish community in Palestine.

109. Protocol of the Mapai central committee, April 15, 1937, pp. 3–4.

110. Protocol of the Labor party council, July 9–11, 1937, pp. 64, 70.

111. Protocol of the Mapai central committee, April 10, 1937, p. 41.

112. Idelson, Protocol of the Mapai council, July 9, 1937, p. 52.

113. Protocol of the Mapai central committee, April 10, 1937, pp. 42–43.

Chapter Seven. The Undecided

1. Leshchinsky, in Protocol of the Fifth Jewish Agency Council, 1937, p. 44.

2. Protocol of the Mapai central committee, April 10, 1937, p. 12.

3. Protocol of the Twentieth Zionist Congress, pp. 31–32; Protocol of the Fifth Jewish Agency council, p. 17.

4. Ben-Gurion Diary: Conversation Held on June 14, 1937 in London, Ben-Gurion Archives, Sde Boqer. The meeting is mentioned generally in Ben-Gurion, 1971–1982, vol. 4, p. 233.

5. Jabotinsky, 1947–1959a, "Address Before British Members of Parliament," vol. 3, p. 114.

6. The lower estimate is that of the royal commission and the higher, of the Jewish Agency. See Report of the Royal Commission, p. 235.

7. Ibid., pp. 218–222.

8. Ibid., p. 226.

9. The royal commission did not cite specific numbers and the borders of the Jewish state referred to in the report are not identical to those that appear in its attached map (see Appendix II). An internal Jewish Agency memorandum estimated the area of the proposed Jewish state as 4,953 km². See "Comments on the Partition Proposal," July 19, 1937, presented in Reichman, 1979, pp. 242–245.

10. Ibid., p. 31. See a detailed discussion in Chapter Ten.

11. Weitz, 1947, p. 14.

12. Stein, 1984, p. 221.

13. Resolutions, Protocol of the Twentieth Zionist Congress, p. 202.

14. On Hakibbutz Hameuchad's position, see *Paths of Our Policy*, 1938, p. 118.

15. Protocol of the Mapai Central Committee meeting, February 5, 1937, pp. 4, 7–8.

16. Ben-Gurion, 1971–1982, vol. 4 (letter dated July 27, 1937), p. 331.

17. *Paths of Our Policy*, 1938, p. 76.

18. Protocol of the Mapai national council, July 9–11, 1937, pp. 13, 15.

19. Ibid., pp. 21–25.

20. Shertok's speech in Protocol of the 20th Zionist Congress, p. 174.

21. *Paths of Our Policy*, 1938, p. 88.

22. Other economists used similar data fixing the ceiling of Jewish population that can be sustained by agriculture at 2.5 million. See Protocol of the Twentieth Zionist Congress, pp. 89–90, and Mapai Council Protocol, July 1937, pp. 227, 233.

23. *Mapai Council Protocol*, p. 245.

24. Dothan, 1980, p. 127.

25. A. Shapira, 1980, vol. 2, p. 555.

26. Mapai Council Protocol, July 1937, pp. 180–186.

27. Ibid., p. 192.

28. *Paths of Our Policy*, 1938, pp. 171, 178, respectively.

29. Protocol of the Twentieth Zionist Congress, p. 76.

30. A. Shapira, 1980, vol. 2, p. 558.

31. Protocol of the Fifth Jewish Agency Council, p. 54.

32. M. Avner, in Protocol of the Twentieth Zionist Congress, p. 140.

33. Ibid., p. 152. Clearly, Brodetsky was referring only to the western Land of Israel, although he did say "all" the Land of Israel.

34. Protocol of the Mapai Central Committee, April 10, 1937, p. 21, also second session, p. 13.

35. "Note of an Informal Discussion Between the Chiefs of Staff Sub-Committee and Members of the Royal Commission on Palestine," March 1, 1937, PRO/CO/733/346/9/99093.

36. Royal Commission Report, pp. 110, 201, respectively.

37. Ibid., p. 376.

38. Jabotinsky, 1947–1959a, vol. 5, pp. 235, 243–244.

39. "Against the Partition Plan," ibid., p. 280.

40. "To Die or Conquer the Mountain" (July 1938), in ibid., p. 310.

41. Dothan, 1980, pp. 128–129.

42. *Paths of Our Policy*, 1938, p. 186; Protocol of the Twentieth Zionist Congress, p. 159, *Mibefnim* (August–September 1937): 5–6.

43. *Mibefnim*, no. 2 (July 1937): 9.

44. Mapai central committee Protocol, April 1937, second session, p. 17.

45. Mapai council Protocol, July 1937, p. 52.

46. Protocol of the Twentieth Zionist Congress, p. 67.

47. Ibid., p. 135.

48. *Paths of Our Policy*, 1938, p. 179.

49. Text of the letter in Heller, 1985, pp. 190–193. Ben-Gurion also valued the proximity of the boundaries with Lebanon, which "has a Christian minority with an interest in being at peace with us." Mapai central committee, February 1937, p. 2.

50. Mapai central committee, April 1937, 2nd session, pp. 192–194.

51. Ibid., pp. 66–70.

52. Ibid., p. 264.

53. *Paths of Our Policy*, 1938, p. 163.

54. Mapai central committee Protocol, April 1937, p. 47.

55. Protocol of the Twentieth Zionist Congress, p. 110; letter to Moshe Shertok, July 3, 1937, Ben-Gurion, 1971–1982, vol. 4, p. 277.

56. James MacDonald, a friend of the Zionist movement, was an exception in his belief that a strong independent Jewish state would contribute to British security goals. He felt that the military capabilities of the Jews would be an asset to the British empire in the Middle East and accordingly suggested a significant expansion of the Jewish state to include parts of Transjordan. He proposed an eastern border of surprising similarity to the 1949 armistice line with Jordan. See Malcolm, 1938. There is a possibility that Churchill was also of this opinion—according to Martin Gilbert, lecture at the Hebrew University on November 28, 1989. There is no substantiation of this in Churchill's testimony before the Royal Commission.

57. "Map Illustrating Jewish Proposals," Report of the Woodhead Commission, Map No. 7. See discussion of these demands on pp. 111–115. This map was based on the work of a "boundaries committee" set up by the Jewish Agency after the publication of the commission report. See protocol of committee deliberations in CZA S25/10109.

58. Royal Commission Report, p. 300.

59. The assessment of the Jewish institutions concerning natural increase among the Arabs was much higher: 32 per thousand per year. See *Paths of Our Policy*, 1938, p. 162.

60. Royal Commission Report, pp. 280–283.

61. Palestine Royal Commission, *Notes and Evidence*, 1936–1937, p. 91.

62. Ibid., p. 96.

63. Ibid., p. 308.

64. Palestine Royal Commission, "Memoranda Prepared by the Government of Palestine," in *Notes and Evidence*, 1936–1937, p. 2.

65. Royal Commission Report, p. 389.

66. Ibid., p. 391.

67. "Note for Discussion on Partition," by R. C., June 8, 1937, PRO/CO/733/346/9/99093, pp. 18–19.

68. Teveth, *Ha'aretz* (September 23 and 25, 1988).

69. This figure is higher than the commission's estimate of 225,000 Arabs who were intended to remain in the Jewish state, because it includes the Arab residents of the four cities proposed to remain under British protection for an intermediate period.

70. Protocol of the Fifth Jewish Agency Council, 1937, pp. 47–52.

71. Mendes-Flohr, 1983, p. 204.

72. Protocol of the Twentieth Zionist Congress, p. 278. Yet in a short paragraph that was deleted from his speech in the official protocol, Ruppin spoke about the possibility of voluntary transfer. CZA S5/1543.

73. Hazan in ibid., pp. 85–86.

74. Riftin in ibid., p. 142.

75. *Mibefnim* (August 1940), quoted by Keidar, 1984, vol. 1, p. 136.

76. Mapai Council Protocol, July 1937, p. 90.

77. *Paths of Our Policy*, 1938, p. 191.

78. Idelson, in Mapai Council Protocol, July 1937, p. 50.

79. Protocol of the Twentieth Zionist Congress, p. 51.

80. Ibid., p. 37.

81. Ibid., p. 189.

82. Jabotinsky, 1947–1959a, "The Iron Wall," vol. 11, p. 253.

83. Ibid., "Against the Partition Plan," vol. 5, p. 278.

84. Ibid., p. 297.

85. *Hayarden* (August 13, 1937).

86. Teveth, *Ha'aretz* (September 23, 1988).

87. Heller, *Ha'aretz* (January 29, 1982); Heller, 1983, p. 89.

88. Jabotinsky, 1947–1957a, "The War Front of the Jewish People," vol. 3, p. 249.

89. Ibid., p. 244.

90. Teveth, *Ha'aretz* (September 23, 1988).

91. *Hayarden* (August 13, 1937).

92. *Paths of Our Policy*, 1938, pp. 122–123.

93. Ibid., pp. 126, 128, 183, 196; on similar positions in Hakibbutz Hameuchad, see pp. 93–94, 107.

94. David Remez, Mapai leader, ibid., p. 168.

95. Ibid., pp. 162–163. The royal commission's estimates differed, forecasting that an annual immigration rate of 60,000 Jews would bring about numerical equality between Jews and Arabs within ten years. (See Table 7.1).

96. A. Shapira, 1980, vol. 2, p. 608.

97. *Paths of Our Policy*, 1938, pp. 179–180.

98. Mapai Council Protocol, July 1937, pp. 186, 193. He repeated these remarks at the Labor movement convention in Zurich and emphasized more strongly that there was no chance of realizing the idea. See *Paths of Our Policy*, 1938, p. 180.

99. Protocol of the Twentieth Zionist Congress, p. 79.

100. July 11, 1937, *Diary*, vol. 4, p. 297.

101. Ibid., July 12, 1937, p. 298.

102. All in ibid., pp. 298–299.

103. On Ben-Gurion's hesitation during this month, see Teveth, *Ha'aretz* (September 25, 1988).

104. See his letter to his son, in which he wrote that the giving of the Galilee to the Jews and the transfer proposal are "two great matters whose value cannot be overestimated." *Diary*, vol. 4, pp. 306, 320, 331, respectively.

105. *Paths of Our Policy*, 1938, p. 71.

106. Protocol of the Twentieth Zionist Congress, p. 106; for a paragraph that was deleted from the Protocol, see Morris, 1994 (AZM S5/1543).

107. Protocol of the "Population Transfer Committee," November 21, 1937, in Heller, 1985, pp. 224–228.

108. Katz, 1988, pp. 167–189.

109. Cmd. 5634, December 23, 1937.

110. Commission's Letter of Reference, PRO Cab 24/273 from December 23, 1937.

111. Partition Commission Report, p. 235.

112. Ibid., p. 52.

113. Teveth mentions other examples, but concludes that these were fleeting ideas which "lurked alone on the margins of Zionism," *Ha'aretz* (September 23, 1988).

114. Royal Commission Report, p. 375.

115. Protocol of the Twentieth Zionist Congress, p. 72.

116. This was Berl Katznelson's position. See *Paths of Our Policy*, 1938, pp. 174–175.

117. Jabotinsky, 1937.

118. Protocol of the Twentieth Zionist Congress, p. 72; *Paths of Our Policy*, 1938, pp. 90, 135, 167.

119. Mapai central committee Protocol, April 1937, 2nd session, p. 4.

120. *Paths of Our Policy*, 1938, p. 204.

121. Ben-Gurion, *Diary*, vol. 4, p. 307.

122. Mapai central committee Protocol, February 1937, p. 17.

123. Protocol of the Twentieth Zionist Congress, p. 130.

124. Ibid., pp. 75–76.

125. Kolatt, 1984, p. 50.

Chapter Eight. The Proponents

1. Lubyanker (Lavon), Mapai central committee, 2nd session, April 1937, p. 13.

2. A. Shapira, 1980, vol. 2, p. 543.

3. Weizmann, *Letters and Papers*, vol. 18, p. 118.

4. Ibid., p. 135.

5. Ibid., p. 180.

6. By Grossman of the State Party, who claimed that everyone, including the British, knew that the partition proposals originated with the Jews, Protocol of the Twentieth Zionist Congress, pp. 92–93. See document in Eliash, 1971, p. 185.

7. Review of the House debate in Klieman, 1983, pp. 45–48.

8. Golomb, *Mapai Council*, July 1937, p. 64.

9. Mapai Central Committee, April 10, 1937, p. 14.

10. Ibid., p. 25.

11. Ibid., pp. 23, 36, 50.

12. Protocol of the Zionist executive meeting, Zurich, August 1, 1937. Ben-Gurion Archive, Sde Boqer.

13. Protocol of the Twentieth Zionist Congress, p. 38.

14. Mapai Central Committee Protocol, October 27, 1937, p. 11.

15. Mapai Central Committee Protocol, February 1937, p. 9.

16. Ibid., p. 15.

17. Shertok's letter was read in the Mapai central committee meeting, April 1937, Protocol, p. 7.

18. Mapai Council Protocol, July 1937, pp. 25–28.

19. On the Arab reaction to the royal commission report, see Chapter Five.

20. This was also the language of the Balfour Declaration: "The establishment in Palestine of a national home for the Jewish people."

21. Teveth, "Basis of the Double Formula in the Political Thought of Ben-Gurion," address at a conference of the L. Davis Institute, The Hebrew University, June 10, 1987 (unpublished), p. 20; and Teveth, 1987, p. 216.

22. Teveth, "Basis of the Double Formula," ibid., pp. 14–15.

23. Mapai Central Committee Protocol, February 1937, p. 15.

24. For the initial formulation, see Mapai Central Committee Protocol, April 15, 1937, p. 2.

25. Hazan, Protocol of the Twentieth Zionist Congress, p. 87.

26. Lubyanker, Mapai central committee Protocol, April 1937, p. 14.

27. Remez, Protocol of the Twentieth Zionist Congress, p. 59.

28. League of Nations, *Mandate for Palestine*, Preamble (2).

29. Resolutions, Protocol of the Twentieth Zionist Congress, p. 201.

30. Ibid., p. 206.

31. Wasserstein, 1992, p. 386.

32. Kolatt, 1984, p. 53.

33. Jabotinsky, 1947–1959a, vol. 5, p. 279.

34. Akzin, in Avizohar and Friedman, 1984, p. 163.

35. Locker, Mapai central committee Protocol, April 1937, p. 20.

36. Sprinzak, ibid., second session, p. 15.

37. *Mibefnim* 4, no. 2 (July 1937): 7.

38. *Paths of Our Policy*, 1938, p. 178.

39. Mapai Central Committee Protocol, July 1937, p. 192.

40. Letter to the Mapai council (July 1937), 1971–1982, vol. 4, p. 268.

41. *Paths of Our Policy*, 1938, pp. 76–77.

42. Ben-Gurion and Ben-Zvi, 1980, pp. 44–47.

43. *Paths of Our Policy*, 1938, pp. 72–74.

44. Mapai Central Committee Protocol, April 1937, pp. 26–27.

45. On Weizmann's position see *Letters and Papers*, vol. 18, p. 136.

46. Kolatt maintains that Coupland, a member of the royal commission, shared this conception that the partition "will create a possibility for the Jews to occupy the entire area through peaceful means," 1984, p. 51.

47. Mapai Central Committee Protocol, August 29, 1937, p. 7.

48. Sharett, 1972–1979, 2, p. 210.

49. Shaltiel, 1990, vol. 2, p. 480.

50. Ben-Gurion, 1971–1982, vol. 4, pp. 206–207.

51. Sharett, 1972–1979, 2, pp. 258–259.

52. Ibid., pp. 106–107.

53. Protocol of the Twentieth Zionist Congress, pp. 128–130.

54. Protocol of the Restricted Zionist General Council Meeting, April 21, 1937.

55. Shaltiel, 1990, Vol. 2, pp. 449–458, 479–480.

56. Letter from Rutenberg to B. Katznelson, October 10, 1937, cited in ibid., p. 487.

57. Mapai Council Protocol, July 1937, pp. 259–260.

58. Ibid., pp. 263–266a.

59. Ibid., p. 13. He reiterated these comments in his speech at the Congress. See Protocol of the Twentieth Zionist Congress, p. 176.

60. Letter to Shertok (July 3, 1937), 1971–1982, vol 4, p. 278.

61. Letter to Amos Ben-Gurion (July 27, 1937), ibid., p. 331. See also the discussion in Chapter Seven.

62. Letter to Moshe Shertok (July 23, 1937), ibid., p. 320.

63. Protocol of the Twentieth Zionist Congress, p. 110.

64. Ibid., p. 71. Members of the royal commission were aware of Weizmann's position and his tactical considerations. In a memorandum to his colleagues before composition of the final report, commission member Horace Rumbold detailed the reasons why Weizmann would support the partition plan: "I feel that Dr. Weizmann is favourable to the clean cut scheme because he realizes that the present Mandate is impossible, because of the increasing pressure on the Jews in Germany and Poland, and because establishing a strong position in that part of Palestine to be assigned to the Jewish state, he relies on being able to penetrate into the neighbouring Arab countries." "Some Considerations Connected with the Clean Cut," PRO/CO 733/346/9/99093, (no date), p. 3.

65. Weizmann, *Letters,* letter of January 20, 1938, vol. 18, p. 296; and letters of December 1937, pp. 275, 277 and 281.

66. Letter of March 14, 1938, ibid., p. 339. See also his testimony before the Woodhead commission, which is marked by his opposition to any further reduced partition proposal. Ibid., p. 387.

67. Protocol of the Twentieth Zionist Congress, pp. 179–180.

68. Goldmann, 1969, p. 170.

69. *Paths of Our Policy,* 1938, p. 198. See also Shlomo Lavie, "Partition of the Land or Correction of the Boundaries," *Davar* (June 9, 1937).

70. *Paths of Our Policy,* 1938, pp. 124–125.

71. Royal Commission Report, p. 375; Klieman, 1980, p. 295.

72. Protocol of the Twentieth Zionist Congress, p. 72.

73. Ruppin, 1971, p. 283.

74. Protocol of the Twentieth Zionist Congress, p. 72.

75. Dothan, 1980, pp. 59–60.

Chapter Nine. The Decision

1. Ben-Gurion, *Diary,* vol. 5, p. 16.

2. Protocol of the Twentieth Zionist Congress, pp. 2–4.

3. Ibid., p. 34.

338 *NOTES TO CHAPTER NINE*

4. *Paths of Our Policy*, 1938, pp. 7–8.

5. Wise speech, Protocol of the Twentieth Zionist Congress, pp. 202–204.

6. See Shertok's explanation of this paragraph's inclusion, in Sharett, 1972–1979, Vol. 2, p. 286.

7. Karpf, 1938, p. 23.

8. See announcement of the New Zionist Organization, "Conclusions of the Zurich Congress," *B'maarechet* (September 10, 1937).

9. Y. Hazan, "The Twentieth Zionist Congress," *Hashomer Hatsair*, No. 18 (September 19, 1937), p. 4.

10. Ben-Gurion, 1971–1982, vol. 4, p. 420.

11. The argument is that no decision was made at the Zionist congress, principally because of the vague formulation and the paragraph concerning the need to present the matter to the newly elected congress. For example, Eliash claims that the congress resolution did not decide the question of partition one way or the other, and that a decision was actually rejected by giving the Zionist Organization limited authorization to conduct negotiations, 1971, p. 180. This interpretation does not stand the test of the political reality.

12. A. Shapira, 1980, vol. 2, p. 555. *Ha'aretz* (August 8, 1937).

13. *Ha'aretz* (August 11, 1937); Eliash, 1971, p. 73; Dothan, 1980, pp. 275–276.

14. Eliash, 1971, pp. 90, 168.

15. Protocol of the Twentieth Zionist Congress, pp. 244, 308, 328.

16. At a meeting of the Mapai central committee, October 27, 1937, 1971–1982, vol. 4, p. 405.

17. Weizmann at a meeting of the Jewish Agency executive, December 12, 1937, ibid., p. 470.

18. Eliash, 1971, p. 172.

19. See Weizmann's comments to Coupland at the end of September 1937; Sharett, 1972–1979, vol. 2, p. 344; as well as Goldmann's remarks to members of the League of Nations, Dothan, 1981, p. 293. On another occasion Ben-Gurion also maintained that the congress deliberations were based on the understanding that the *state* meant a state in a partitioned Land of Israel. Protocol of the Mapai central committee, July 13, 1938, Beit Berl Archive, File 2–3, 1938.

20. See Ussishkin's remarks at the meeting of the restricted Zionist general council, January 11, 1938, CZA S5/307.

21. This was Rabbi Berlin's position, see Eliash, 1971, p. 178.

22. Tabenkin, Protocol of the Mapai Central Committee, April 7, 1938, Beit Berl Archive, 27/28.

23. Hashomer Hatzair in *Ha'Olam*, no. 48 (April 4, 1938), p. 923.

24. *Diary*, vol. 4, p. 307; letter to Shertok (July 23, 1937), pp. 320–321.

25. Letter to Amos Ben-Gurion (July 28, 1937), ibid., p. 333.

26. *Diary* (July 30, 1937), ibid., p. 334.

27. Letter to Ben-Gurion (March 31, 1938), 1971–1982, vol. 5, p. 147.

28. Statement of the Mapai Party, *Davar* (July 13, 1937).

29. In a very emotional letter to Weizmann after the Jewish Agency council meeting, Ben-Gurion expressed his admiration and love for Weizmann calling him "the personal focal point" of the strength of the Jewish people. Letter of August 22, 1937, in 1971–1982, vol. 4, pp. 422–424.

30. Sharett, 1972–1979, vol. 2, p. 286.

31. Protocol of the Fifth Jewish Agency Council, 1937, p. 79.

32. Letter to Katznelson, March 16, 1938, in 1971–1982, vol. 5, p. 140.

33. Sharett, 1972–1979, vol. 2, p. 205.

34. Ibid., p. 203.

35. Protocol of the Fifth Jewish Agency Council, 1937, p. 61.

36. Eliash, 1971, p. 134.

37. On Zionism as an ideological movement, see Horowitz and Lisak, 1990, p. 9.

38. *Paths of Our Policy*, 1938, p. 201.

39. Kleinman, 1938, pp. 240–241.

40. Ibid., p. 249.

41. Koifman, 1938, p. 4. See the quotation from his article at the beginning of Chapter Six.

42. *Diary*, vol. 5, p. 389.

43. Gorny, 1985, pp. 315–316.

44. A. Shapira, 1989, p. 316.

45. Letter to Ben-Gurion (March 3, 1938), 1971–1982, vol. 5, p. 139.

46. *Haboker* (November 24, 1937); *Davar* (November 26, 1937).

47. *Haaretz* (December 10, 1937); *Ha'Olam* (January 6, 1938).

48. Ben-Gurion, *Diary*, vol. 4, p. 447.

49. Protocol of the Jewish Agency executive meeting (December 12, 1937).

50. Ben-Gurion despaired of the negative stance of Wise, president of the Zionist Organization of America, and unsuccessfully tried to convince Brandeis to support his own position. *Diary*, vol. 4, p. 430. When Berl Katznelson arrived in New York, opponents there regarded him as a traitor. A. Shapira, 1980, vol. 2, p. 566.

51. *Haboker* (September 20, 1938).

52. Dothan, 1980, p. 304.

53. The material is presented in its entirety in Ben-Gurion, 1971–1982, vol. 5, pp. 135–148.

54. Ibid., p. 139.

55. Ibid., pp. 192–201.

56. Testimony Before the Partition Commission, Ben-Gurion Archive, Sde Boqer.

57. Ben-Gurion at a meeting of the restricted Zionist general council, January 11, 1938, 1971–1982, vol. 5, p. 23.

58. Ibid., p. 140.

59. Sharett, 1972–1979, vol. 2, pp. 310 and 344, respectively.

60. On the deliberations of the mandate commission, see League of Nations, Permanent Mandates Commission, Minutes of the 32nd (extraordinary) session, Geneva, 1937.

61. Katzburg, 1974, p. 113; Hurewitz, 1951, p. 76.

62. See Chapter Two. Concerning the position of the Foreign Office in November 1937, see PRO/FO 37/20912; as well as Sheffer, 1980, p. 390.

63. Protocol of Zionist general council meeting in London, March 1938, Archive of the Ben-Gurion Center, Sde Boqer.

64. Ibid., Meeting 8, pp. 5–7.

65. Ben-Gurion (April 1938), 1971–1982, vol. 5, p. 179.

66. See the colorful description of the "acrobatics" (original usage) necessary to avoid submitting maps to the commission, ibid., p. 215.

67. "Partition Commission" file, Ben-Gurion Archive, Sde Boqer (undated), and CZA 525/10109. Another commission dealt with transfer (see Chapter Seven).

68. A summary of the territorial demands of the Jewish Agency was placed on a map appearing in the Woodhead report, Appendix III. A detailed map appears in Gilbert, 1974, p. 28.

69. The boundaries committee also prepared a "Third Proposal," which contained a minimal addition of only some 400 km², "limiting itself to essential matters only." See Protocol of the Boundaries Committee, Partition Commission file, Ben-Gurion Archive, Sde Boqer, p. 4.

70. Partition commission Report, p. 243.

71. Ibid., p. 243.

72. Ben-Gurion, 1971–1982, vol. 5, p. 233.

73. Letter to A. Katznelson, (September 8, 1938); *Diary*, September 15, 1938), ibid., pp. 240 and 249, respectively.

74. Ibid., pp. 263 and 291, respectively.

75. Statement by H. M. Government, Cmd. 5893, London: November 1938. The government's decision was based on the recommendations of the cabinet committee for Palestine affairs, which had been established a month earlier to discuss the Woodhead commission report. PRO FO/371/21865, document numbers 6379, 6471, 6487, 6824.

76. Ben-Gurion, 1971–1982, vol. 5, pp. 390–391.

77. Teveth, 1987, p. 257; Katzburg, 1974, p. 56.

78. Ben-Gurion, 1971–1982, vol. 5, p. 392.

79. Ibid., vol. 6, p. 534; Katzburg, 1974, p. 73; Rose, 1986, p. 352.

80. Statement of Policy, Cmd. 6019, London: May 1939, p. 6.

81. Sheffer, 1988, pp. 35–37.

82. Kimmerling and Migdal, 1993, pp. 122–123.

Chapter Ten. 1937 and Its Aftermath

1. Ben-Gurion, 1971–1982, vol. 5, p. 316.

2. See Map No. 2, "Lands Held by the Jews 1918, 1936, 1947," in Reichman, 1979, p. 48.

3. Oren, 1978, p. 14.

4. Stein, 1984, p. 206.

5. Known as *Homa u-Migdal* settlements. See Oren, 1978, pp. 29, 241.

6. Granovsky, 1938, pp. 33, 39.

7. Ibid., p. 59.

8. Stein, 1984, p. 207.

9. Granovsky, 1938, p. 62.

10. Weitz, 1947, pp. 193–196. An additional four settlements were established in June and July 1939, which explains the fifty-four settlements cited by Oren, 1978, p. 204.

11. See, for example, Ussishkin in H. Merhavia, *Kolot Kor-im L'Zion* [*Voices Calling out to Zion*]. (Jerusalem: Zalman Shazar Center, 1981), pp. 234–235.

12. Ruppin, 1968, vol. 3, p. 281.

13. The following discussion refers to Oren, 1978, pp. 207–211.

14. Arnon-Ohana in Avizohar and Friedman, 1984, p. 79; Hassassian, 1990, p. 125.

15. On the differences in political organizing between the Jewish and the Arab communities in Palestine (E.I.), see Horowitz and Lissak, 1977, pp. 20–21, 26–33.

16. Royal Commission Report, 1937, p. 379.

17. Porath, 1978, p. 270.

18. Memorandum of the Va'ad Le'ummi (National Council of the Jews in Eretz Israel) presented to the League of Nations Standing Committee on Mandate Affairs, June 1930, pp. 8–10.

19. The British used the term *riots* or *disturbances*. See A. Shapira, 1992, p. 307.

20. In a conference of graduates of the Mahanot Olim youth movement in December 1937. Quoted by A. Shapira, ibid., p. 363.

21. Ibid., p. 376. Porath cites the "riots of 1929" as an important turning point in the national movement of the Palestinian Arabs (1978, p. 349).

22. Royal Commission Report, 1937, p. 131.

23. For Lechi activities in this regard, see Heller, 1989, vol. 1, pp. 113–114, 125–135.

24. For the activities of these three individuals, see Protocol of the Jewish Agency executive meeting, November 21, 1937.

25. Ben-Gurion, 1971–1982, vol. 4, p. 438–445, 469.

26. Shlaim, 1988, pp. 59–62.

27. The British government was also cautious in this regard, and in his meeting with Jewish leaders in London on May 15, 1937, Abdullah said that the British government said not "even one word to him about the western Land of Israel." See document in Avizohar and Friedman, 1984, p. 216.

28. Sharett, 1972–1979, (October 19, 1937), vol. 2, pp. 387–388.

29. Ran, 1991, pp. 88–95.

30. Ibid., p. 103.

31. For a detailed study of the internal struggle within the Palestinian camp and its implications for the positions toward the royal commission, see Hassassian, 1990, pp. 123–128.

32. Abboushi, 1977, p. 40.

33. Hale, 1982, p. 130; Porath, 1978, p. 272.

34. Klieman, 1983, pp. 4–5.

35. Evidence before the royal commission, January 18, 1937, p. 358.

36. Abdullah greatly feared such a development and, in a memorandum to the royal commission, he emphasized his desire to be the spokesman for the Palestinians. Klieman, 1983, p. 21; Ran, 1991, p. 57.

37. Sheffer, 1974.

38. On the conflicting interests of Iraq, Saudi Arabia, and Transjordan concerning the Palestinian question, see Klieman, 1983, pp. 92–99.

39. Official version of the Higher Committee announcement of May 30, 1939, ibid., p. 117. The moderate Mu'arada, by contrast, welcomed the British policy. Hassassian, 1990, pp. 127–128.

40. Kedourie, 1978, p. 45.

41. Gellner, 1983, pp. 101–102; Hobsbawn, 1990, pp. 47–48.

42. Arendt, 1965, p. 35.

43. Porath, 1989, pp. 134, 155, 191, 339, 387. See also J. Shavit, 1984, pp. 53, 79–81.

44. Porath, 1989, p. 56.

45. This was apparently Shertok's formulation. See Horowitz, 1951, pp. 91–92; Elath, 1982, vol. 2, p. 101.

46. Tabenkin, who objected to the "premature birth" of the state and to partition, frequently used this argument—subjugating the state to the idolatry of "statism" and perceiving it as "the ideal of life." See Chapter Five.

47. Akzin, 1980, pp. 158–170.

48. In addition to several non-Zionists mentioned in Chapter Five, in 1937 the German-Jewish writer Leon Feuchtwanger (1844–1958) still supported the founding of a Jewish republic in Birobizhan.

49. Galnoor, 1982, pp. 82–84.

50. On the need to expand the study of nationalism beyond the territorial borders, see Marx, 1980, pp. 18–19.

51. Porath, 1989, p. 345.

52. Much later, Ze'ev B. Begin argued that in the debate about the future borders of the state of Israel, "even when a point of view is rooted in ideology—and is therefore axiomatic—it is not necessarily a mistaken view of reality nor one which makes untenable predictions." "Attitudes and reality in the natural sciences and politics," *State, Government, and International Relations*, no. 35 (1992): 17.

53. Blaut, 1987, p. 9.

54. Herb, 1989; Monmonier, 1991, p. 102.

55. G. Cohen, 1974.

56. Kimmerling and Migdal (1993, p. 121) believe that the Arab revolt in Palestine in 1936 was the most serious opposition to British imperialist rule other than Ghandi's opposition in India.

57. Prescott, 1987, p. 94.

58. Gottmann, 1952, p. 514.

59. For a fascinating discussion of the role of "place" in the Jewish-Israeli identity, see Gurevitch and Aran, 1991; and the response of Kimmerling, 1992.

60. Lustick suggests a different approach to the analysis of territorial expansion or contraction of states. His analysis of the separation of Ireland from Britain and Algeria from France emphasizes the internal struggle among the elites, but in a different context: What type of "disruption" accompanies the territorial change? He presents a continuum with

two thresholds. One is the "regime threshold" through which struggles for control change into struggles for the status of the regime. The other is the "ideological hegemony threshold" that implies a change in the agenda from questions of regime to questions of ideology. Lustick's analysis partially overlaps the distinction presented in this book between expressive and instrumental arguments. Lustick, 1990b.

For an attempt to apply these approaches to the study of Israeli positions toward the territories acquired in 1967, see Lustick, 1987.

61. Sheffer in Shavit, 1987, p. 84.

62. For a discussion of the UNSCOP report as "a remarkable Zionist achievement" in comparison with other alternatives, see Shertok in Heller, 1985, pp. 525–529; Horowitz, 1951, pp. 91–92.

Chapter Eleven. Territorial Decisions in the Zionist Movement (1919–1949)

1. Arnon Sofer, in Doron, 1988, pp. 8–9.

2. The territory under post-1967 Israeli control totaled approximately 90,000 km². Of this, approximately 61,000 km² were in Sinai and 1,000 km² in the Golan Heights.

3. This territory includes 27,000 km² of western Palestine; approximately 17,000 km² in Transjordan; 11,000 km² in Syria (the Golan Heights and Bashan); 1,000 km² in southern Lebanon (up to the Litani River), and 3,000 km² in Sinai. See A. Brauer, 1957, pp. 31–35.

4. For a new discussion of the separation of Transjordan, see Fromkin, 1989, pp. 504–506, 525–526.

5. See notes 23–25 in Chapter Two.

6. In contrast, we have noted the 1937 positions of the Palestinian leadershp, derived from their need to protect themselves from Zionist expansionism. They were suspicious of any precedent-setting agreements to territorial compromise in Palestine and took the position of "all or nothing," ending up with nothing.

7. Katznelson, 1946–1950, vol. 5, pp. 23–24.

8. Jewish Agency announcement, May 8, 1945, in Merhavia, 1950?, p. 403.

9. Heller, 1984, p. 144.

10. Protocol of the discussion in the restricted Zionist General Council, November 10, 1942, CZA, File S/25/293. See Bauer, 1966, pp. 201–210.

11. Dothan, 1981, p. 221.

12. Gallili on behalf of "Faction B" in Mapai in the Histadrut general council, April 13, 1944. In Avizohar and Friedman, 1984, p. 262. See also the resolutions of the second session of the Yishuv fourth elected assembly, December 2–6, 1944, CZA, File S25/1778.

13. A. Shapira, 1992, p. 385.

14. Rich material exists about the Anglo-American committee of enquiry. See, for example, Nachmani, 1987; M. J. Cohen, 1988; and Heller's comprehensive bibliography in 1987b.

15. Heller, 1987a, pp. 287–288.

16. The quote is from Horowitz, 1951, p. 77. See Jewish Agency for Palestine, *The Jewish Case Before the Anglo-American Committee on Palestine* (Jerusalem: Author, 1947).

17. Heller, 1987a, pp. 238–239; 1987b, 305.

18. Nachmani, 1987, p. 115; Dothan, 1981, pp. 312, 331–332.

19. Heller, 1987b, pp. 295, 312, and map at the end of the book. According to this map, the Jewish state would comprise 18,000 km^2 of western Eretz Israel, including the Negev, and excluding a triangle of approximately 8,000 km^2 in the hilly area in the center of the country, which would be given to the Arabs and the Jerusalem-Jericho corridor that would be placed in an international trusteeship.

20. *Report of the Anglo-American Committee of Enquiry Regarding the Problem of European Jewry and Palestine* (London: H. M. Stationery Office, Cmd. 6068, 1946).

21. Hattis, 1970, p. 298.

22. Heller, 1987b, p. 346.

23. Full text of the decision and voting distribution in Heller, 1985, p. 436.

24. Proposals for the Future of Palestine, July 1946–February 1947, London, Cmd. 7044.

25. Discussion of the Ben-Gurion plan and the deliberations of the Paris conference in Heller, 1987a, pp. 249, 255–264.

26. CZA File J1/7264.

27. *All of the Land*, 1947, pp. 91–92.

28. Heller, 1985, pp. 453–454.

29. The change was particularly evident in the position of former opponent Stephen Wise, who now voted in favor of the Paris resolution and spoke in support of partition at the Twenty-second congress. See Twenty-Second Zionist Congress, 1947, p. 331.

30. Ibid., clause 4(A), pp. 498–500.

31. Ibid., pp. 500–501. Congress participants also received a copy of *All of the Land* (1947) issued by the partition opponents.

32. Ibid., p. 50.

33. Ibid., p. 342.

34. Ben-Gurion, 1952, vol. 5, pp. 141–142.

35. Joint meeting of the Jewish Agency executive with representatives of the opposition parties, June 18, 1947; Heller, 1985, p. 97. See also Sheffer, 1990, Chapter 20, p. 20.

36. A large body of reliable archival material exists about UNSCOP. The Zionist positions can be found in "Reports about the Commission and the Testimonies Before It," CZA, Files S/5436, S/5440, S/5452.

37. Horowitz, 1951, pp. 221, 227, 237–238.

38. Heller, 1984, p. 145.

39. United Nations, *Evidence Before UNSCOP*, Vol. III, Annex A, New York, 1947.

40. Ibid., p. 171.

41. On Abdullah's position, see Ran, 1991, pp. 207–209.

42. Ibid., p. 210.

43. Shertok defined the majority proposal as "a tremendous achievement" in a letter to Golda Meyerson from September 7, 1947. See Heller, 1985, p. 528. See also a description of the sense of victory in Horowitz, 1951, p. 248.

44. Meeting of the enlarged Zionist general council, Zurich, September 1947, CZA, File S5/320.

45. Elath, 1982, vol. 2, pp. 197–199; Avizohar and Bareli, 1989, vol. 1, p. 174.

46. Attiash, 1963, p. 422.

47. Sharett, 1958, p. 152.

48. Meeting of the Histadrut general council (December 3, 1947), Ben-Gurion Archive, Sde Boqer.

49. Protocol of the Jewish Agency Executive meeting (November 30, 1947); Ben-Gurion, 1952, vol. 5, pp. 256, 266.

50. Elath, 1982, vol. 2, p. 468.

51. Horowitz, 1951, p. 255.

52. See note 49.

53. Report of the Special Commission on Palestine, 1947, p. 42.

54. Fromkin, 1989, pp. 515–526.

55. The boundary between the state of Israel and Egypt is the only international boundary recognized by the two bordering states in accordance with a bilateral treaty between them. The 1983 treaty between Israel and Lebanon stipulated that each country would respect the territorial integrity of the other and would not infringe upon the existing international border between them (paragraph 1). The treaty was ratified by the Knesset on May 16, 1983 (fifty-seven in favor, six against, and forty-five abstentions), but was never ratified by the government of Lebanon. Despite the existence since 1985 of an Israeli "security zone" in southern Lebanon, the state of Israel officially recognizes the Rosh Hanikra–Metulla line as the international border.

56. The approximate calculation was made according to the current official division of the state of Israel into districts and "natural regions" by the Central Bureau of Statistics. According to this calculation, the partition state of 1937 did not include the districts of Jerusalem, Haifa, Ramle, and Beersheva, nor the Beit Shean Valley and most of the Ashkelon district. See Israel Annual Statistical Abstract, no. 43, 1992, pp. 50–53.

57. On the design of the map of the State of Israel in 1948–1950, see Reichman, 1989, pp. 320–330.

58. Based on the following statistics for December 1991: 4.1 million Jews and 914,000 Arabs in the state of Israel, with another 1.7 million Arabs in the territories, for a total of 6.7 million residents. Israel Annual Statistical Abstract, no. 43, 1992, pp. 43, 51, 732.

59. Diskin and Galnoor, 1990.

60. *Paths of Our Policy*, 1938, p. 201.

Bibliography

[H] = in Hebrew

Abboushi, W. F. (1974). *The Angry Arabs*. Philadelphia: Westminster Press.

————. (1977). "The Road to Rebellion: Arabs in Palestine in the 1930s." *Journal of Palestine Studies* 7, no. 3: 23–47.

Adiv, Z. (1978). "The Zionist Ideology of Zeev Jabotinsky." In Y. Ben-Zion and A. Keidar (eds.), *Ideological and Political Zionism*. Jerusalem: Shazar Center. [H]

Akzin, B. (1980). *States and Nations*. Tel Aviv: Am Oved. [H]

————. (1989). *From Riga to Jerusalem: A Memoir*. Jerusalem: Zionist Organization. [H]

All the Land. (1947). A collection of articles concerning the partition of the land. Submitted to the Delegates of the 22nd Zionist Congress. Jerusalem: Opponents of Partition Publishers. [H]

Allison, G. T. (1971). *Essence of Decision*. Boston: Little Brown and Co.

Allon, Y. (1980). *Communicating Vessels*. Tel Aviv: Hakibbutz Hameuchad. [H]

Alsberg, A. (1974). "Setting the Eastern Boundary of Eretz-Israel." *Hatzionut* 3: 229–246. [H]

Andrew, C. M., and Kanya-Forstner, A. S. (1981). *France Overseas: The Great War and The Climax of French Imperial Expansion*. London: Thames and Hudson.

Ardrey, R. (1967). *The Territorial Imperative*. London: Anthony Blond.

Arendt, H. (1965). *Eichmann in Jerusalem*, rev. ed. New York: Viking Press.

Arnon-Ohana, Y. (1981). *The Internal Struggle Within the Palestinian National Movement 1929–1939*. Tel Aviv: Hadar and the Shiloah Institute. [H]

Atiash, M. (ed.). (1963). *Book of Documents of the Va'ad Le'ummi in Eretz-Israel, 1918–1948*. Jerusalem: Rafael Cohen Publishers. [H]

Avineri, S. (1980). *Varieties of Zionist Thought*. Tel Aviv: Am Oved. [H]

Avizohar, M., and Bareli, A. (eds.). (1989). *Now or Never: Mapai's Proceedings in the Closing Year of the British Mandate*, 2 vols. Beit Berl: Ainot. [H]

Avizohar, M., and Friedman, I. (eds.). (1984). *Studies in the Palestine Partition Plans, 1937–1947*. Sde Boqer: Ben-Gurion Research Center. [H]

Avniel, B. (1937). *The Problem of the Cantons*. Tel Aviv: publisher unknown. [H]

Bar-Nir, D. (1987). *The Conflict, Ben-Gurion and the Revisionists.* Tel Aviv: Am Oved. [H]

Bassin, M. (1987). "Race Contra Space: The Conflict Between German Geopolitik and National Socialism." *Political Geography Quarterly* 6, no. 2: 115–134.

Bat-Yehuda, G. (1979). *Rabbi Maimon in his Generations.* Jerusalem: Rav Kook Institute. [H]

Bauer, Y. (1966). *Diplomacy and Underground.* Tel Aviv: Sifriat Poalim. [H]

Bela, M. (ed.). (1975). *The World of Jabotinsky.* Tel Aviv: Defusim. [H]

Ben-Arieh, Y. (1989). "Perceptions and Images of the Holy Land." In R. Kark (ed.), *The Land That Became Israel: Studies in Historical Geography,* pp. 37–53. New Haven, Conn.: Yale University Press.

Ben Avi, I. (1930). *Yehuda Miadit.* Tel Aviv: Bnei Binyamin. [H]

Ben-Avram, B. (1978). *Political Parties and Organizations During the British Mandate for Palestine 1918–1948.* Jerusalem: Shazar Center. [H]

Ben Gurion, D. *Diary.* Sde Boqer: Ben-Gurion Archives. [H]

———. (1952). *The War,* 5 vols. Tel Aviv: Mapai Publishers. [H]

———. (1967). *Talks with Arab Leaders.* Tel Aviv: Am Oved. [H]

———. (1971–1982). *Memoirs,* 5 vols. Tel Aviv: Am Oved. [H]

——— and Ben-Zvi, I. (1980). *Eretz Israel in the Past and in the Present.* Jerusalem: Yad Ben-Zvi [H] [originally published in Yiddish in 1918].

Ben-Zion, Y., and Keidar, A. (eds.). (1978). *Ideological and Political Zionism.* Jerusalem: Shazar Center. [H]

Berkowicz, S. M. (1991). "Developing Perspectives upon the Areal Extent of Israel." *Geojournal.* 23, no. 3: 187–196.

Berlin, I. (1958). *Chaim Weizmann.* London: Weidenfeld and Nicolson.

Berry, B. J. L. (1969). "Geographical Reviews." *Geographical Review* 59: 449–459.

Biale, D. (1980). "Arendt in Jerusalem." *Response* 12, no. 3: 33–44.

Bibritech (1938). Summary of a youth movement camp held in Kibbutz Gvat, Summer 1937. Tel Aviv: Tnuat Hanoar Halomed B'Eretz Israel, Hamahanot Ha'olim. [H]

Biger, G. (1981a). "Setting the Eastern Border of Mandatory Palestine." *Katedra* 20: 203–206. [H]

———. (1981b). "The Problem of Setting the Southern Border of Eretz-Israel after the First World War." *Hamizrah Hehadash* 30: 124–137. [H]

———. (1983a). *Crown Colony or National Homeland.* Jerusalem: Yad Ben-Zvi. [H]

———. (1983b). "Political and Geographical Issues in the Process of Setting the Northern Border of Eretz Israel." In A. Shmueli et al. (eds.), *Artzot Hagalil,* vol. A, pp. 427–442. Haifa: University of Haifa. [H]

————. (1989). "The names and Boundaries of Eretz-Israel (Palestine) as Reflections of Stages in its History." In R. Kark (ed.), *The Land That Became Israel*, pp. 1–22. New Haven, Conn.: Yale University Press.

Bilski Ben-Hur, R. (1988). *Every Individual Is a King: The Social and Political Thought of Zeev Jabotinsky*. Tel Aviv: Dvir. [H]

Blaut, J. (1987). "A Theory of Nationalism." *Antipode* 18, no. 1: 5–10.

Boal, F. W., and Livingstone, D. N. (1983). "The International Frontier in Microcosm." In N. Kliot and S. Waterman (eds.), *Pluralism and Political Geography: People, Territory and State*, pp. 138–158. London: Croom Helm.

Boggs, S. W. (1940). *International Boundaries: A Study of Boundary Functions and Problems*. New York: Columbia University Press.

Boulding, K. E. (1959). "National Images and International Systems." *The Journal of Conflict Resolution* 3: 120–137.

————. (1962). *Conflict and Defense: A General Theory*. New York: Harper and Row.

Bowman, I. (1921). *The New World: Problems in Political Geography*. Chicago: Chicago University Press.

————. (1942). "Geography vs. Geopolitics." *Geographical Review* 32, no. 4: 646–658.

Brauer, M. (1957). "Boundaries [of Eretz Israel]." *Hebrew Encyclopedia*, vol. 6, pp. 28–40. Jerusalem: Encyclopedia Publishers. [H]

Brawer, M. (1988). *Israel's Boundaries: Past, Present and Future*. Tel Aviv: Yavneh. [H]

Brecher, M. (1972). *The Foreign Policy System of Israel*. London: Oxford University Press.

————. (1974). *Decisions in Israel's Foreign Policy*. London: Oxford University Press.

————. (1977). "Toward a Theory of International Crisis Behavior." *International Studies Quarterly* 21, no. 1: 39–74.

————. (1980). *Decisions in Crises*. Berkeley: University of California Press.

Brown, P. E., and Shue, H. (eds.). (1981). *Boundaries: National Autonomy and Its Limits*. Totowa, N. J.: Rowman and Littlefield.

Broyer, Y. (1937). *A Proposal for a Plan, Poalei Agudat Israel Organization*. Tel Aviv: publisher unknown. {H}

Buber, M. (1945). *Between People and Land: The Essence of the Idea*. Jerusalem: Schocken Books. [H]

————. (1988). *A Land of Two Peoples*. Jerusalem: Schocken Books. [H]

Burghardt, A. F. (1973). "The Bases of Territorial Claims." *Geographical Review* 63: 225–245.

Burke, P. (ed.). (1973). *A New Kind of History: From the Writings of Lucien Febre*. London: Routledge and Kegan Paul.

Burnett, A. D., and Taylor, P. J. (eds.). (1981). *Political Studies from Spacial Perspectives*. New York: John Wiley and Sons.

Caplan, N. (1986). *Futile Diplomacy: Arab-Zionist Negotiations and the End of the Mandate*. London: Frank Cass.

Cohen, E. (1976). "Environmental Orientations: A Multi-Dimensional Approach to Social Ecology." *Current Anthropology* 17, no. 1: 49–70.

Cohen E. (ed.). (1987). "The Price of Peace: The Removal of the Israeli Settlements in Sinai." *The Journal of Applied Behavioral Science* 23, no. 1.

Cohen G. (1974). "The Idea of Partition and a Jewish State: 1933–1935." In D. Karpin (ed.), *Zionism*, vol. 3, pp. 346–417. Tel Aviv: Hakibbutz Hameuchad. [H]

———. (1976) *The British Cabinet and the Question of Eretz-Israel (April–July 1943)*. Tel Aviv: Hakibbutz Hameuchad. [H]

———. (1985). "The United Nations as a Solution." In Y. Waloch (ed.), *As If We Were Dreaming*. Tel Aviv: Massada. [H]

Cohen, M. J. (1988). *Palestine to Israel*. London: Frank Cass.

Cohen, S. (1973). *Geography and Politics in a World Divided*, 2nd edition. New York: Oxford University Press.

———. (1986). *The Geopolitics of Israel's Border Question*. Boulder, Colo.: Westview Press.

Cranach, M., Poppa, K., Lepenies, W., and Ploog, D. (eds.). (1979). *Human Ethology*. Cambridge: Cambridge University Press.

Cukwurah, A. O. (1967). *The Settlement of Boundary Disputes*. Manchester: Manchester University Press.

Cust, L. A. (1936). "Cantonization—A Plan for Palestine." *Journal of the Royal Central Asian Society* 23: 194–220.

De-Shalit, A. (1986). "The Concept of Boundaries in the Radical Zionist-Socialist Ideology of Hashomer Hatsair." Seminar paper, Jerusalem: Political Science Department, Hebrew University. [H]

Deutsch, K. W. (1953). *Nationalism and Social Communication*. Boston: M.I.T. Press.

———. (1963). *The Nerves of Government*. New York: The Free Press.

Dickestein, P. (1930). "The Canton System." *Ha'Olam* 7: 121–123. [H]

Diskin, A., and Galnoor, I. (1990). "Political Distances Between Knesset Members and Coalition Behaviour: The Peace Agreements with Egypt." *Political Studies* 38: 710–717.

Doron, A. (ed.). (1988). *The State of Israel and the Land of Israel*. Beit Berl: Ainot. [H]

Dothan, S. (1980). *Partition of Eretz-Israel in the Mandatory Period*. Jerusalem: Yad Ben-Zvi. [H]

———. (1981). *The Struggle for Eretz-Israel*. Tel Aviv: Ministry of Defense Publications. [H]

———. (1991). *The Reds: The Communist Party in Eretz-Israel*. Tel Aviv: Shavna Hasofer. [H]

Douglas, M. (1966). *Purity and Danger: A Comparative Study of Concepts of Pollution and Taboo*. London: Routledge.

———. (1968). "Pollution." *International Encyclopedia of Social Sciences*, vol. 12, pp. 336–342.

Duchacek, I. D. (1986). *The Territorial Dimension of Politics*. Boulder, Colo.: Westview Press.

Duff, B. (1936). *Palestine Picture*. London: Hodes and Stonghton.

Dugdale, B. (1972). *The Diaries of Blanche Dugdale 1936–1947*, N. Rose. (ed.), London: Valentine Mitchell.

East, W. G. (1937). "The Nature of Political Geography." *Politika* 2: 259–286.

———. (1938a). *The Geography Behind History*. London: Thomas Nelson.

———. (1938b)."The Mediterranean Problem." *Geographical Review* 28: 83–101.

——— and Prescott, J. R. V. (1975). *Our Fragmented World: An Introduction to Political Geography*. New York: Macmillan.

Editorial Essay (1982). "Political Geography—Research Agendas for the Nineteen Eighties." *Political Geography Quarterly* 1, no. 1: 1–17.

Elath, E. (1982). *The Struggle for Statehood*, 3 vols. Tel Aviv: Am-Oved. [H]

Eliash, S. (1971). "The Jewish Community in Palestine and the Peel Report of 1937." Master's Thesis, Department of History, Bar-Ilan University. [H]

———. (1984). "The Religious Zionist and Anti-Zionist Attitudes Toward the Partition Plan." In M. Avizohar and I. Friedman (eds.), *Studies in the Palestine Partition Plans, 1937–1947*, pp. 55–75. Sde Boqer: Ben-Gurion Research Center. [H]

Emerson, R. (1971). "Self Determination." *American Journal of International Law* 65: 459–475.

Fébure, L. (1925). *A Geographical Introduction to History*. New York: Doubleday.

Feinberg, N. (1963). *Palestine Under the Mandate and the State of Israel*. Jerusalem: Magnes Press. [H]

Fichte, J. G. (1970). *The Science of Rights* (trans. A. E. Kroger). London: Routledge & Kegan Paul.

Fifth Council of the Jewish Agency. (1937). See Twentieth Zionist Congress.

Fisher, E. (1949). "On Boundaries." *World Politics* 1: 196–222.

Francis, E. K. (1976). *Interethnic Relations: An Essay on Sociological Theory*. Amsterdam: Elsevier.

Friesel, E. (1977). *Zionist Policy After the Balfour Declaration 1917–1922*. Tel Aviv: Hakibbutz Hameuchad and Tel Aviv University. [H]

———. (1984). "Herbert Samuel's Reassessment of Zionism in 1921." *Studies in Zionism* 5: 213–237.

Frischwasser, R. H. F. (1955). *The Frontiers of a Nation*. London: Batchworth Press.

Fromkin, D. (1989). *A Peace to End All Peace: Creating the Modern Middle East (1914–1922)*. London: Penguin Books.

Galnoor, I. (1982). *Steering the Polity*. Beverly Hills, Calif.: Sage Publications.

———. (1991). "The Meaning of the State." In Y. Leibowitz et al., *People, Land, State*, pp. 33–45. Jerusalem: Keter. [H]

—— and Diskin, A. (1981). [H]. See Diskin and Galnoor (1990).

Geertz, C. (1963). "The Integrative Revolution: Primordial Sentiments and Civil Politics in the New States." In C. Geertz (ed.), *Old Societies and New States*, pp. 105–157. New York: The Free Press.

Gellner, E. (1983). *Nations and Nationalism*. Oxford: Basil Blackwell.

Giladi, D. (1973). *The Yishuv During the Fourth Aliyah*. Tel Aviv: Am Oved. [H]

Gilbert, M. (1974). *The Arab-Israeli Conflict, Its History in Maps*. London: Weidenfeld and Nicolson.

Gold, J. R. (1982). "Territoriality and Human Spatial Behavior." *Progress in Human Geography* 6: 45–67.

Goldmann, N. (1969). *Memories*. London: Weidenfeld and Nicolson.

Gorny, Y. (1985). *The Arab Question and the Jewish Problem*. Tel Aviv: Am Oved. [H]

Gottmann, J. (1937). "The Pioneer Fringe in Palestine: Settlement Possibilities South and East of The Holy Land." *Geographical Review* 27: 550–565.

——. (1951). "Geography and International Relations." *World Politics* 3: 153–173.

——. (1952). "The Political Partitioning of our World." *World Politics* 4: 512–519.

——. (1973). *The Significance of Territory*. Charlottesville: University Press of Virginia.

Granovsky, A. (1938). *The Redemption of the Land*. Jerusalem: Keren Kayemet. [H]

Gray, C. S. (1988). *The Geopolitics of Super Power*. Lexington: University Press of Kentucky.

Gretz, N. (1988). *Literature and Ideology in Eretz Israel in the 1930s*. Tel Aviv: Open University. [H]

Gurevitch, Z., and Aran, G. (1991). "On Place (Israeli Anthropology)." *Alpaim* 4: 9–44. [H]

Gyorgy, A. (1944). *Geopolitics: The New German Science*. Berkeley: University of California Press.

Haim, Y. (1978). "Zionist Attitudes Toward Partition." *Jewish Social Studies* 40: 303.

Hale, G. A. (1982). "Diaspora versus Ghourba: The Territorial Restructuring of Palestine." In D. G. Bennet (ed.), *Tension Areas of the World*, pp. 130–153. Champaign, Ill.: Park Press.

Harkabi, Y. (1970). *Arab Positions Toward Israel*. Tel Aviv: Dvir. [H]

Hartshorne, R. (1935). "Recent Developments in Political Geography." *American Political Science Review* 29: 785–804, 943–966.

——. (1936). "Suggestions on the Terminology of Political Boundaries." *Annals of the Association of American Geographers* 26: 56–57.

——. (1950). "The Functional Approach in Political Geography." *Annals of the Association of American Geographers* 40: 95–130.

——. (1960). "Political Geography in the Modern World." *Journal of Conflict Resolution* 4, no. 1: 52–66.

Hassassian, M. S. (1990). *Palestine: Factionalism in the National Movement (1919–1939)*. Jerusalem: PASSIA.

Hattis, S. (1970). *The Bi-National Idea in Palestine During Mandatory Times*. Haifa: Shikmona.

Haushofer, K. (1927). *Grenzen, in Ihrer Geographischen und Politischen Bedeutung*. Berlin.

———— and Kjellén, R., et al. (1932). *Jenseits der Grossmachle*. Leipzig-Berlin: B. G. Teubner.

Heller, J. (1983). "Weizmann, Jabotinsky and the Arab Question—The Peel Commission Affair." *Zmanim* 11: 79–90. [H]

————. (1984). "Zionist Policy and the Partition Plans in the 1940s." In M. Avizohar and I. Friedman (eds.), *Studies in the Palestine Partition Plans, 1937–1947*, pp. 143–148. Sde Boqer: Ben-Gurion Research Center. [H]

————. (1985). *The Struggle for the Jewish State*. Jerusalem: Shazar Center. [H]

————. (1987a). "From Black Saturday to Partition: The Summer of 1946 as a Turning Point." In J. Shavit (ed.), *Struggle, Revolt, Resistance*, pp. 225–272. Jerusalem: Shazar Center. [H]

————. (1987b). "Zionist Policy in the International Arena after World War Two." In J. Shavit (ed.), *Struggle, Revolt, Resistance*, pp. 273–348. Jerusalem: Shazar Center. [H]

————. (1989). *Lehi: Ideology and Politics*, 2 vols. Jerusalem: Keter. [H]

Herb, G. H. (1989). "Persuasive Cartography in Geopolitik and National Socialism." *Political Geography Quarterly* 8, no. 3: 289–303.

Herman, T. (1989). "From Brit Shalom to Peace Now." Ph.D. thesis, University of Tel Aviv. [H]

Hertz, F. (1945). *Nationality in History and Politics: A Study of National Sentiment*. London: Kegan Paul.

Hertz, J. H. (1957). "Rise and Demise of the Territorial State." *World Politics* 9: 473–493.

————. (1968). "The Territorial State Revisited." *Polity*, no. 1: 12–34.

Heske, H. (1987). "Karl Haushofer: His Role in German Geopolitics and Nazi Politics." *Political Geography Quarterly* 6, no. 2: 135–144.

Hill, N. (1945). *Claims to Territory in International Law and Relations*. Oxford: Oxford University Press.

Histadrut Hamizrahi. (1937). *Report to the Fourteenth World Committee in Zurich*. Jerusalem: publisher unknown. [H]

Hobsbawn, E. J. (1990). *Nations and Nationalism Since 1780*. Cambridge: Cambridge University Press.

Holdich, T. H. (1916a). "Geographical Problems in Boundary Making." *Geographical Journal* 48: 421–439.

————. (1916b). *Political Frontiers and Boundary Making*. London: publisher unknown.

Horowitz, David (1951). *Mission for a State to be Born*. Tel Aviv: Schocken Books. [H]

Horowitz, Dan and Lissak, M. (1977). *The Origins of the Israeli Polity*. Tel Aviv: Am Oved. [H]

————— and Lissak, M. (1990). *Trouble in Utopia: The Overburdened Polity of Israel*. Tel Aviv: Am Oved. [H]

Hunter, J. M. (1983). *Perspective on Ratzel's Political Geography*. Lanham, Md.: University Press of America.

Hurewitz, J. C. (1951). *The Struggle for Palestine*. New York: Greenwood Press.

Hyamson, A. (1942). *Palestine: A Policy*. London: Methuen.

Jabotinksy, Z. (1937). *Evidence Submitted to the Palestine Royal Commission*. London: The New Zionist Organization [original text in Jabotinsky Institute Archive, Tel Aviv, File G6/1].

—————. (1946). *Selected Writings*, 3 vols. Jerusalem: Massada. [H]

—————. (1947–1959). *Writings*, 18 vols. Tel Aviv: A. Jabotinsky Publishers. [H]

—————. (1984). *The Road to Zionist Revisionism*. Tel Aviv: Jabotinsky Institute. [H]

—————. (1986). *Towards a Change in Zionist Revisionism*. Tel Aviv: Jabotinsky Institute. [H]

Janis, I. L. (1982). *Victims of Groupthink*, 2nd ed. Boston: Houghton Mifflin.

Jolly, A. (1972). *The Evolution of Primate Behavior*. New York: Macmillan.

Jones, E., and Eyels, J. (1977). *An Introduction to Social Geography*. Oxford: Oxford University Press.

Jones, S. B. (1945). *Boundary Making: A Handbook for Statesman, Treaty Editors and Boundary Commissions*. Washington, D. C.: Carnegie.

Joseph, B. (1948). *The British Government in Palestine: The Failure of a Regime*. Jerusalem: Bialik Institute. [H]

Kark, R. (1974). *The History of Settlement in the Negev Until 1948*. Tel Aviv: Hakibbutz Hameuchad. [H]

—————. (1989a). "Land and the Idea of Land Redemption." *Karka* 31: 22–35. [H]

————— (ed.). (1989b). *The Land That Became Israel: Studies in Historical Geography*. New Haven, Conn.: Yale University Press.

————— (ed.). (1990). *Land Redemption in Eretz-Israel*. Jerusalem: Yad Ben-Zvi. [H]

Karpf, M. J. (1938). *Partition of Palestine and its Consequences*. New York: American Jewish Commitee (ZA, New York 956.5K).

Katz, Y. (1988). "The Deliberations of the Jewish Agency Committee and Population Transfer: 1937–1938." *Zion* 53, no. 2: 167–189. [H]

Katzburg, N. (1974). *From Partition to the White Paper: British Policy in Palestine 1936–1940*. Jerusalem: Yad Ben-Zvi. [H]

—————. (1977). *Policy in Confusion*. Jerusalem: Yad Ben-Zvi. [H]

Katznelson, B. (1946–1950). *Writings*, 12 vols. Tel Aviv: Mapai Publishers. [H]

—————. (1961–1984). *Letters*. Tel Aviv: Mapai Publishers. [H]

Kedourie, E. (1961). *Nationalism*. London: Hutchinson, rev. ed.

—————. (1978). "How to (and How Not to) Seek Peace in the Middle East." *Encounter* 50, no. 5: 44–49.

Keidar, A. (1978). "The Viewpoints of Brit Shalom." In Y. Ben-Zion and A. Keidar (eds.), *Zionist Ideology and Policy*, pp. 97–114. Jerusalem: The Shazar Center. [H]

––––––. (1984). "The Political and Ideological Development of Hakibbutz Hameuchad 1933–1942." Ph.D. thesis, The Hebrew University. [H]

Keren Hayesod. (1937). *The People of Israel and the Land of Israel*. Jerusalem: Author. [H]

Kimmerling, B. (1977). "Sovereignty, Ownership and Presence in the Jewish-Arab Territorial Conflict." *Comparative Political Studies* 10: 155–175.

––––––. (1979). "A Conceptual Framework for the Analysis of Behavior in a Territorial Conflict: The Generalization of the Israeli Case." Jerusalem Papers on Peace Problems, Jerusalem: The L. Davis Institute.

––––––. (1983). *Zionism and Territory*. Berkeley: University of California, Institute of International Studies.

––––––. (1985). "Between the Primordial and the Civil Definitions of the Collective Identity: Eretz Israel or the State of Israel?" In E. Cohen, M. Lissak, and U. Almagor (eds.), *Comparative Social Dynamics*, pp. 262–283. Boulder, Colo.: Westview Press.

––––––. (1987). "Exchanging Territories for Peace: A Macrosociological Approach." *Journal of Applied Behavioral Science* 23, no. 1: 13–88.

––––––. (ed.). (1989a). *The Israeli State and Society: Boundaries and Frontiers*. Albany: State University of New York Press.

––––––. (1989b) "Boundaries and Frontiers of the Israeli Control System." In B. Kimmerling (ed.), *The Israeli State and Society*, pp. 265–284.

––––––. (1992). "On Place . . . " *Alpaim* 6: 57–68. [H]

–––––– and Migdal, J. S. (1993). *The Palestinians: The Making of a People*. New York: The Free Press.

Kjellén, R. (1917). *Der Staat als Lebensform*. Leipzig: S. Hirzel.

Kleinman, M. (1938). "On the Problems of Partition and the State." *Moznaim* 7: 240–250. [H]

Klieman, A. S. (1970). *Foundations of British Policy in the Arab World: The Cairo Conference of 1921*. Baltimore: John Hopkins University Press.

––––––. (1979). "The Divisiveness of Palestine: Foreign Ofice versus Colonial Office on the Issue of Partition, 1937." *Historical Journal* 22: 423–441.

––––––. (1980). "The Resolution of Conflicts Through Territorial Partition: The Palestine Experience." *Comparative Studies in Society and History* 22: 281–300.

––––––. (1983). *Divide or Rule: Britain, Partition and Palestine, 1936–1939*. Jerusalem: Yad Ben-Zvi. [H]

Kliot, N., and Waterman, S. (eds.). (1983). *Pluralism and Political Geography: People, Territory and State*. London: Croom Helm.

Knight, D. B. (1982). "Identity and Territory: Geographical Perspectives on Nationalism and Regionalism." *Annals of the Association of American Geographers* 72, no. 4: 514–531.

Kohn, H. (1946). *The Idea of Nationalism.* New York: Vintage Books.

Koifman, Y. (1938). "The National Movement at this Hour." *Moznaim* 7: 1–13. [H]

Kolatt, I. (1984). "The Debate on Partition Within the Labor Movement." In M. Avizohar and I. Friedman (eds.), *Studies in the Palestine Partition Plans, 1937–1947*, pp. 40–50. Sde Boqer: Ben-Gurion Research Center. [H]

Kristof, L. K. D. (1959). "The Nature of Frontiers and Boundaries." *Annals of the Association of American Geographers* 49: 269–282.

———. (1960). "The Origins of Evolution of Geopolitics." *Journal of Conflict Resolution* 4, no. 1: 15–51.

———. (1985). "Review Essay." *American Political Science Review* 79, no. 4: 1178–1179.

Laponce, J. A. (1980). "The City Center as Conflictual Space in a Bilingual City: The Case of Montreal." In J. Gottmann (ed.), *Center and Periphery*, pp. 149–162. Beverly Hills, Calif.: Sage.

———. (1986). "The Spatial Structure of Ideologies." Paper presented at the Ottawa round table on Crisis in Political Thought.

———. (1988). "Ethno-Linguistic Separatism: An Essay in Predictive Topography." In A. Gutter (ed.), *Languages and Their Territories.* Toronto: University of Toronto Press.

Lattimore, O. (1962). *Studies in Frontier History.* Oxford: Oxford University Press.

Learmonth, A. T. A., and Hamnett, C. (1971). *Approaches to Political Geography.* London: Bletchley.

Leibner, J. (1937). *The Case Against Partition.* New York: Hashomer Hatzair. [This publication is in the ZA, New York.]

Leibowitz, Y., et al. (1991). *People, Land, State.* Jerusalem: Keter. [H]

Levinson, C. (1980). *Vodka Cola.* Biblios: Horsham.

Louis, W. R., and Stookey, R. W. (eds.). (1986). *The End of the Palestine Mandate.* Austin: University of Texas Press.

Lustick, I. S. (1987). "Israeli State-Building in the West Bank and the Gaza Strip: Theory and Practice." *International Organization* 41, no. 1: 164–177.

———. (1990a). "Becoming Problematic: Breakdown of a Hegemonic Conception of Ireland in Nineteenth-Century Britain." *Politics and Society* 18, no. 1: 39–73.

———. (1990b). "Re-Scaling the Irish and Algerian Questions in Britain and France." Paper presented at the APSA Meeting.

MacIver, R. M. (1926). *The Modern State.* London: Oxford University Press.

Mackinder, H. J. (1904). "The Geographical Pivot of History." *Geographic Journal* 23, no. 4: 421–444.

———. (1919). *The Landsman's Point of View: Democratic Ideas and Reality*. New York: Holt.

MacLaughlin, J. (1986). "The Political Geography of Nation Building." *Political Geography Quarterly* 5, no. 4: 299–329.

MacPherson, C. B. (1977a). *The Life and Times of Liberal Democracy*. Oxford: Oxford University Press.

———. (1977b). "Do We Need a Theory of the State?" *Archives of European Sociology* 18: 223–244.

Maier, E. (1975). "Torah as a Movable Territory." *Annals of the Association of American Geographers* 65: 18–23.

Malcolm, J. A. (1938). *Partition of Palestine: Suggested Alterations and Proposed Frontiers*. London: Apollo Press.

Mallison, T. W., and Mallison, S. V. (1986). *The Palestine Problem in International Law and World Order*. Harlow: Longman.

Malmberg, T. (1980). *Human Territoriality*. New York: Mouton Publishers.

Margalit, E. (1971). *Hashomer Hatzair: 1913–1936*. Tel Aviv: Hakibbutz Hameuchad. [H]

———. (1976). *Anatomy of the Left: Poalei Zion-Smol in Eretz-Israel 1919–1946*. Jerusalem: Hebrew University. [H]

Marx, E. (ed.). (1980). *A Composite Portrait of Israel*. London: Academic Press.

Meinertzhagen, R. (1973). *Middle East Diary: 1917–1956*. Haifa: Shikmona. [H]

Mendes-Flohr, P. R. (ed.). (1983). *Martin Buber: A Land of Two Peoples*. Oxford: Oxford University Press.

Merhavia, H. (ed.). (1944). *Zionism: Collection of Political Documents*. Jerusalem: publisher unknown. [H]

——— (ed.). (1950?). *People and Homeland: A Collection of Documents*. Jerusalem: Halevi Publishers. [H]

Monmonier, M. (1991). *How to Lie with Maps*. Chicago: University of Chicago Press.

Morgenthau, H. J. (1960). *Politics Among Nations*, 3rd ed. New York: Alfred A. Knopf.

Morris, B. (1994). "The Zionist Documents Were Reconstructed," *Ha'aretz*, February 4, 1994. [H]

Muir, R. D. (1975). *Modern Political Geography*. London: Macmillan Press.

Murdock, G. P. (1967). *Ethnographic Atlas*. Pittsburgh: University of Pittsburgh Press.

Na'aman, N. (1986). *Borders and Districts in Biblical Historiography*. Tel Aviv: Biblical Studies, Simor.

Nachmani, A. (1987). *Great Power Discord in Palestine (The Anglo-American Committee of Inquiry)*. London: Frank Cass.

Nettl, J. P. (1968). "State as a Conceptual Variable." *World Politics* 20, no. 4: 559–592.

Nevakivi, Y. (1969). *Britain, France and the Arab Middle East, 1914–1920*. London: Athlone Press.

Nitzan, M. (1978). *Proposals for Federal Solutions, 1917–1977*. Jerusalem: Jerusalem Institute of Federal Studies. [H]

Oren, E. (1978). *Settlement Amid Struggles, 1936–1947*. Jerusalem: Yad Ben-Zvi. [H]

Ossenbrugge, J. (1989). "Territorial Ideologies in West Germany 1945–1985." *Political Geography Quarterly* 8, no. 4: 387–399.

Ostrovsky, M. (1944). *The History of Mizrahi in Eretz-Israel*. Jerusalem: The Zionist Organization Executive. [H]

Paddison, R. (1983). *The Fragmented State: The Political Geography of Power*. Oxford: Basil Blackwell.

Palestine Royal Commission. (1936–1937). *Notes and Evidence*. London: H. M. Stationery Office.

Palestine Partition Commission. (October 1938). *Report*. London: H. M. Stationery Office, Cmd. 5854.

Palestine Royal Commission. (July 1937). *Report*. London: H. M. Stationery Office, Cmd. 5479.

Parker, G. (1987). "French Geopolitical Thought in the Interwar Years and the Emergence of the European Idea," *Political Geography Quarterly*, 6, no. 2: 145–150.

Parsons, T. (1951). *The Social System*. New York: The Free Press.

Paterson, J. H. (1987). "German Geopolitics Reassessed." *Political Geography Quarterly* 6, no. 2: 107–114.

Paths of Our Policy. (1938). World Council of the Labor Movement, "Minutes" (Zurich, July 29–August 7, 1937). Tel Aviv: Labor Zionist Federation Publishers. [H]

Pearcy, G. E., and Fifield, R. H. (1948). *World Political Geography*. New York: T. Y. Crowell.

Pialkov, A. (1975). *Settlement and the Boundaries of Eretz-Israel* (in memory of I. Tabenkin). Efal: Hakibbutz Hameuchad and Yad Tabenkin. [H]

Porath, Y. (1977). *The Palestinian Arab National Movement, 1929–1939*. London: Frank Cass.

———. (1978). *From Riots to Rebellion: the Palestinian-Arab National Movement 1929–1939*. Tel Aviv: Am Oved. [H]

———. (1985). *The Test of Political Action: Palestine, Arab Unity and British Policy 1930–1954*. Jerusalem: Yad Ben-Zvi. [H]

———. (1989). *The Life of Uriel Shelah (Yonathan Ratosh)*. Tel Aviv: Zmora. [H]

Prai, E. (1972). *Selected Writings*. Merhavia: Sifriat Poalim. [H]

Prescott, J. R. V. (1987). *Political Frontiers and Boundaries*. London: Allen and Unwin.

"The Problem of Palestine: A Note on the Report of the Royal Commission." (1937). *Geographical Review* 27: 566–573.

Protocol of the Fifth Council of the Jewish Agency. (1937). See Twentieth Zionist Congress. [H]

Protocol of the Twentieth Zionist Congress. (1937). See Twentieth Zionist Congress. [H]

Quandt, W. B. (1970). *United States Policy in the Middle-East*. Santa Monica, Calif.: Rand Corporation.
———. (1971). *Palestinian Nationalism*. Santa Monica, Calif.: Rand Corporation.
Ran, Y. (1991). *The Roots of the Jordanian Option*. Tel Aviv: Citrin. [H]
Ratzel, F. (1903). *Politische Geographie*, 2nd ed. Munich and Berlin: R. Oldenbourgh.
Reichman, S. (1979). *From Foothold to Settled Territory, 1918–1948*. Jerusalem: Yad Ben-Zvi. [H]
———. (1989). "Partition and Transfer: Crystallization of the Settlement Map of Israel Following the War of Independence 1948–1950." In R. Kark (ed.), *The Land That Became Israel*, pp. 320–330. New Haven, Conn.: Yale University Press.
Renner, G. T. (1942). "Maps for a New World." *Collier's* 109, no. 25: 14–16.
Rogel, N. (1988). "The Territorial Goals of the Zionist Movement." *Kivunim* 33: 37–73. [H]
Rokkan, S., and Urwin, D. W. (1983). *Economy, Territory Identity: Politics of West European Peripheries*. Beverly Hills, Calif.: Sage.
Rose, N. (1970, 1971). "The Debate on Partition, 1937–38: The Anglo-Zionist Aspect." *Middle Eastern Studies* 6: 297–318; 7: 3–24.
———. (1973). *The Gentile Zionists*. London: Frank Cass.
———. (1986). *Chaim Weizmann: A Biography*. New York: Viking Books.
Roucek, J. S. (1942). "German Geopolitics." *Journal of Central European Affairs* 11: 180–189.
Rowley, G. (1989). "Developing Perspectives upon the Extent of Israel: An Outline Evaluation." *Geojournal* 19, no. 2: 99–111.
Ruppin, A. (1937). "Jewish Autonomy in Eretz-Israel—Thirty Years of Development." Memorandum to the Zionist Organization Executive Committee, Jerusalem. [H]
———. (1968). *My Life and Work (Autobiography)*, 3 vols. Tel Aviv: Am Oved. [H]
———. (1971). *Memoirs, Diaries, Letters*, A. Bein. (ed.). New York: Herzl Press.
Sack, R. D. (1976). "Magic and Space." *Annals of the Association of American Geographers* 66: 309–322.
———. (1981). "Territorial Bases of Power." In A. D. Burnett and P. J. Taylor (eds.), *Political Studies from Special Perspectives*, pp. 53–71. New York: John Wiley and Sons.
———. (1983). "Human Territoriality: A Theory." *Annals of the Association of American Geographers*, 73: 54–74.
———. (1986). *Human Territoriality: Its Theory and History*. Cambridge: Cambridge University Press.
Sahlins, P. (1989). *Boundaries: The Making of France and Spain in the Pyrenees*. Berkeley: University of California Press.
Samuel, H. (1937). "Alternatives to Partition." *Foreign Affairs* 16: 143–155.
Semple, E. C. (1911). *Influences of Geographic Environment on the Basis of Ratzel's System of Anthropogeography*. New York: Holt.

Shalev, A. (1983). *The West Bank: Line of Defense*. Tel Aviv: Hakibbutz Hameuchad. [H]

Shaltiel, E. (1979). "David Ben Gurion on Partition 1937." *Jerusalem Quarterly* 10: 38–59.

———. (1990. *Pinhas Rutenberg: 1879–1942*, 2 vols. Tel Aviv: Am Oved. [H]

Shapira, A. (1980). *Berl Katznelson: A Biography*, 2 vols. Tel Aviv: Am Oved. [H]

———. (1984). "Time Perception as a Factor in the Partition Controversy of 1937." In M. Avizohar and I. Friedman (eds.), *Studies in the Palestine Partition Plans, 1937–1947*, pp. 21–39. Sde Boqer: Ben-Gurion Research Center. [H]

———. (1989). *Visions in Conflict*. Tel Aviv: Am Oved. [H]

———. (1992). *Land and Power*. Tel Aviv: Am Oved. [H]

Shapira, Y. (1975). *The Organization of Power*. Tel Aviv: Am Oved. [H]

Sharett, M. (1958). *In the Gates of Nations*. Tel Aviv: Am Oved. [H]

———. (1972–1979). *Political Diaries*, 5 vols. Tel Aviv: Am Oved and the Zionist Library. [H]

Shavit, D. (1984). *Conversations with Ben-Aharon*. Tel Aviv: Hakibbutz Hameuchad. [H]

Shavit, J. (1984). *From Hebrew to Canaanite*. Jerusalem: Domino. [H]

———. (1986). *The Mythologies of the Right*. Tel Aviv: Emda. [H]

——— (ed.). (1987). *Struggle, Revolt, Resistance*. Jerusalem: Shazar Center. [H]

Sheffer, G. (1974). "The Involvement of the Arab States in the Palestine Conflict in British-Arab Relationship Before World War Two." *Asian and African Studies* 10, no. 1: 59–78.

———. (1980). "Appeasement and the Problem of Palestine." *International Journal of Middle East Studies* 2: 377–399.

———. (1987). "British Policy in Palestine in the Years 1939–1948." In Y. Shavit (ed.), *Struggle, Revolt, Resistance*. Jerusalem: Shazar Center, pp. 83–120. Jerusalem: Shazar Center. [H]

———. (1988). "The Arab Revolt and the Main Events in Palestine, 1936–1939." In A. Makover-Katlab and A. Shiran (eds.), *The Army of the State in the Making*, pp. 32–48. Tel Aviv: Ministry of Defense Publishers. [H]

———. (1990). *Moshe Sharett: A Political Biography*. Manuscript in press. [H]

Shlaim, A. (1988). *Collusion Across the Jordan*. New York: Columbia University Press.

Sieger, R. (1925). "Die Grenze der Politischen Geographie." *Zeitschrift fuer Geopolitik* 2, no. 9: 661–684.

Simon, H. A. (1957a). *Administrative Behavior*, 2nd ed. New York: The Free Press.

———. (1957b). *Models of Man: Social and Rational*. New York: John Wiley and Sons.

Soga, E. J. (1971). "The Political Organization of Space." *Commission on College Geography*, Resource Paper No. 9, pp. 1–54. Washington, D.C.: Association of American Geographers.

Sprout, H., and Sprout, M. (1960). "Geography and International Politics in an Era of Revolutionary Change." *Journal of Conflict Resolution* 4, no. 1: 145–161.

Spykman, N. J. (1938). "Geography and Foreign Policy." *American Political Science Review* 32: 28–50, 213–236.

———. (1942). *America's Strategy in World Politics: The United States and the Balance of Power.* New York: Harcourt, Brace and Co.

———. (1944). *The Geography of the Peace.* New York: Harcourt, Brace and Co.

Stein, K. W. (1984). *The Land Question in Palestine, 1917–1939.* Chapel Hill: University of North Carolina Press.

Strauss-Hupe, R. (1942). *Geopolitics: The Struggle for Space and Power.* New York: George Putnam's Sons.

Sykes, C. (1965). *Crossroads to Israel: Palestine from Balfour to Bevin.* Tel Aviv: Ma'arachot. [H]

Syria and Palestine (1920). London: H. M. Stationery Office

Tabenkin, I. (1972). *Writings.* Tel Aviv: Hakibbutz Hameuchad. [H]

Tal, A. (1979). "Territories and Space in Nazi Ideology." *Zmanim* 1: 68–75. [H]

———. (1987). *Myth and Reason in Contemporary Judaism.* Tel Aviv: Sifriat Poalim. [H]

Talmon, J. L. (1982). *The Myth of the Nation and Vision of Revolution,* 2 vols. Tel Aviv: Am Oved. [H]

Taylor, P. J. (1985). *Political Geography.* London: Longman.

Temperley, H. W. V. (1924). *A History of the Peace Conference of Paris,* vol. 6. London: Frowde, Hodder and Stoughton.

Tenner, G. T. (ed.). (1944). *Global Geography.* New York: Thomas Y. Crowell.

Teveth, S. *The Life of David Ben-Gurion.* Jerusalem: Schocken Books. [H] Vol. 1, (1976), *The Young Ben-Gurion.* Vol 2 (1980), *Years in the Histadrut.* Vol. 3 (1987), *The Burning Ground.*

———. (1985). *Ben-Gurion and the Palestinian Arabs.* Jerusalem: Schocken Books. [H]

———. (1988). "The Evolution of Transfer in Zionist Thought." *Ha'aretz* (September 23 and 25). [H]

Tokachinsky, N. A. (1970). *The Land and Its Boundaries—Pictures of Jerusalem.* Jerusalem: Solomon. [H]

Troll, C. (1949). "Geographic Science in Germany During the Period 1933–1945." *Annals of the Association of American Geographers* 39: 99–137.

Turner, F. J. (1928). *The Frontier in American History.* New York: Holt.

Twentieth Zionist Congress and the Fifth Council of the Jewish Agency. (1937). *Minutes.* Jerusalem: The Zionist Organization and the Jewish Agency. [H]

Twenty-First Zionist Congress. (1939). *Minutes.* Jerusalem: The Zionist Executive. [H]

Twenty-Second Zionist Congress. (1947). *Minutes*. Jerusalem: The Zionist Executive. [H]

Tzur, Z. (1984). "The Position of Hakibbutz Hameuchad Concerning the Partition Plans." In M. Avizohar and I. Friedman (eds.), *Studies in the Palestine Partition Plans, 1937–1947*, pp. 166–171. Sde Boqer: Ben Gurion Research Center. [H]

United Nations Special Commission of Palestine (UNSCOP). (1947). *Report*. Tel Aviv: Ha'aretz. [H]

Ussishkin, M. (1943). *The Voice of the Land*. Jerusalem: Keren Kayemet LeIsrael. [H]

Van Dyke, V. (1966). *International Politics*, 2nd ed. New York: Appleton-Century.

Van-Valkenburg, S. (1944). *Elements of Political Geography*. New York: Prentice-Hall.

———. (1946). *Whose Promised Lands? A Political Atlas of the Middle East and India*. New York: Foreign Policy Association.

Vincent, A. (1987). *Theories of the State*. Oxford: Basil Blackwell.

Vital, D. (1982). *Zionism: The Formative Years*. Oxford: Oxford University Press.

Walzer, M. (1992). "The New Tribalism." *Dissent*: 164–171.

Wasserstein, B. (1978). *The British in Palestine: The Mandatory Government and The Arab-Jewish Conflict 1917–1929*. London: Royal Historical Society.

———. (1992). *Herbert Samuel: A Political Life*. Oxford: Clarendon Press.

Waterman, S. (1987). "Partitioned States." *Political Geography Quarterly* 6, no. 2: 151–170.

Weinstein, B. (1979). "Language Strategies: Redefining Political Frontiers on the Basis of Linguistic Choices," *World Politics*, vol. 31, no. 3: 345–364.

Weisgal, M., and Carmichael, J. (1963). *Chaim Weizmann: A Biography by Several Hands*. New York: Methuen.

Weitz, Y. (1947). *Our Settlement in the Years of Struggle*. Merhavia: Hakibbutz Ha'artzi. [H]

Weizmann, C. (1953). *Trial and Error*. Tel Aviv: Schocken Books. [H]

———. (1968–1985). *The Letters and Papers of Chaim Weizmann, Series A*, S. Stein (ed.). 23 vols. London: Oxford University Press.

———. (1983). *The Letters and Papers of Chaim Weizmann, Series B*, B. Litvinoff (ed.). 2 vols. New Jersey: Transaction Books.

Williams, C. H. (1979). "Ethnic Resurgence in the Periphery." *Area*, no. 11: 279–283.

Wright, Q. (1955). *The Study of International Relations*. New York: Appleton-Century.

Yishai, Y. (1978). *Factionalism in the Labor Movement: Faction B in Mapai*. Tel Aviv: Am Oved. [H]

Archives

Beit Berl = The Archives of the Labor Party, Beit Berl
CZA = Central Zionist Archives, Jerusalem
Givat Haviva = The Archives of Hashomer Hatzair (ST), Givat Haviva
Jabotinsky Archives = The Archives of the Revisionist Movement, The
    Jabotinsky Institute, Tel Aviv
PRO = Public Record office, British Government Archives, London
Sde Boqer = Ben-Gurion Archives, the Center of Ben Gurion Heritage, Sde
    Boqer
State Archives = The State of Israel Archives, Jerusalem
W.A. = Weizmann Archives, Rehovot
ZA = Zionist Archives, New York

Name Index

Abdullah, Emir, 40, 41, 97, 98, 177, 246, 250, 251, 252, 253, 254, 274, 280
Akzin, Benyamin, 109, 110, 191
Alterman, Natan, 95, 96
Antonius, George, 51, 254
Arendt, Hannah, 256
Atlee, Clement, 72

Bart, Aharon, 148, 164
Ben-Aharon, Yitzhak, 198, 199
Ben-Avi, Itamar, 45, 46, 202
Ben-Gurion, David: alliance with Weizmann, 71, 72, 74, 203, 211, 226; Anglo-American Committee, 279, 280; Arabs, 181, 249; boundaries and size of E.I., 39, 157, 161, 192, 193, 194, 258; building coalition, 76, 77, 185, 221, 222, 223, 224; cantons, 49; 20th congress resolution, 214, 215, 216, 219, 221, 222, 227; 22nd congress, 282; his book (1917), 193; his partition plan, 75, 153; internal front, 233, 234, 235, 238, 240; and Jabotinsky, 146; and non-Zionists, 117; and opponents, 127, 128, 132, 141, 142, 147, 148, 150; position on partition, 60–65; predecision phase, 50, 56, 73, 74, 76, 77; a pragmatist, 61, 62, 102, 184, 185, 229, 230, 258, 262, 270, 278; and proponents, 184, 185; relations with British, 51, 101, 102; Royal Commission partition plan, 77, 199, 200, 298; "statism," 259; and Tabenkin, 165; tactics, 184, 186, 187, 188, 189, 190; territorial demands, 195, 197; and transfer, 176, 177, 178, 179; United Nations' partition plan, 287, 288
Ben-Zvi, Yitzhak, 39, 61, 281
Bentwitch, Norman, 127
Berlin, Meir, 112, 117, 128, 139, 172, 281
Bernstein, Peretz, 108, 131, 136, 148
Blum, Leon, 71
Bograshov, Chaim, 108
Bowman, Ishayahu, 19
Brandeis, Louis, 108, 147
Brodetsky, Zelig, 136, 160
Buber, Martin, 114, 171, 256

Carter, Morris, 52
Chamberlain, Neville, 53, 71, 236
Churchill, Winston, 40, 42, 72, 74, 79, 190, 226, 277
Coupland, Reginald, 45, 50, 51, 52, 57, 58, 59, 71, 72, 170, 185, 228, 236, 287
Cust, Archer, 45, 47, 49, 50, 51, 57, 58, 59

Deutsh, Karl, 14, 15, 22, 31
Dickenstein, Paltiel, 45, 46
Douglas, Marry, 22
Duff, Douglas, 45, 48
Dushinsky, Yosef, 113, 138

Eden, Anthony, 71
El-Alami, Mussa, 45, 47, 50
El-Husseini, Jamal, 99
El-Husseini, Amin (mufti of Jerusalem), 231, 240, 251, 252; response to Royal Commission report, 97, 98, 99; testimony

The index was prepared by Daniela Ashur.

Subject Index